In correspondence and conversation, James Joyce kept himself aloof from his age and denigrated recent art and thought at almost every opportunity. "In the last two hundred years," he declared, "we haven't had a great thinker." This book reveals that in spite of his denials, Joyce was profoundly influenced by one of the major figures of nineteenth-century European culture, the composer and dramatist Richard Wagner. Timothy Martin documents Joyce's exposure to Wagner's operas and defines a pervasive Wagnerian presence in Joyce's work, identifying scores of allusions for the first time. Wagner emerges as a significant figure in the development of literary modernism and assumes a place, with Flaubert and Ibsen, among Joyce's most important influences from the previous century. The revisionary impact of this empirical study in cultural history will be to present Joyce as much more a child of the nineteenth century than the iconoclastic Irish writer wished to acknowledge, much more than Joyce's students have heretofore recognized.

JOYCE AND WAGNER

JOYCE AND WAGNER

A study of influence

TIMOTHY MARTIN

Associate Professor of English
Rutgers University

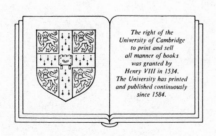

The right of the
University of Cambridge
to print and sell
all manner of books
was granted by
Henry VIII in 1534.
The University has printed
and published continuously
since 1584.

CAMBRIDGE UNIVERSITY PRESS

Cambridge
New York   Port Chester
Melbourne   Sydney

Published by the Press Syndicate of the University of Cambridge
The Pitt Building, Trumpington Street, Cambridge, CB2 IRP
40 West 20th Street, New York, NY 10011-4211, USA
10 Stamford Road, Oakleigh, Melbourne 3166, Australia

First published 1991

Printed in Great Britain at the University Press, Cambridge

British Library cataloguing in publication data
Martin, Timothy
Joyce and Wagner: a study of influence.
I. Title
823.912

Library of Congress cataloguing in publication data
Martin, Timothy Peter.
Joyce and Wagner: a study of influence / Timothy Martin.
p.   cm.
Includes bibliographical references.
ISBN 0 521 39487 2
1. Joyce, James, 1882–1941 – Knowledge – Music. 2. Wagner, Richard.
1813–1883 – Influence. 3. English fiction – German influences.
4. Modernism (literature) 5. Music and literature. I. Title.
PR6019.097268 1991
823'.912–dc20   90-21754   CIP
ISBN 0 521 39487 2 hardback

For my mother,
Rosemary Lyons Martin

in memory of my father,
Luke Francis Martin
(1920–1980)

Contents

Preface

The proposition that the mind and art of James Joyce were shaped by Richard Wagner should not surprise Joyce's students. The quickest of glances suggests, at the very least, a strong artistic kinship: both artists exploit the resources of myth, emphasize sexual themes, pursue "totality" of form and subject matter, and represent the "modern" or "revolutionary" in art. Joyce's knowledge of Wagner has long been evident to readers of his letters and critical writings, and Joyce's impressions of Wagner's music and stagecraft have been recorded by his associates. Indeed, as chapter i will show, Wagner's position in early twentieth-century culture made him virtually inescapable, and Joyce, himself a progressive artist and a sensitive musician, had his own reasons for taking the German composer into account.

Over the past twenty-five years, a number of published articles, together with occasional papers at scholarly conferences, have helped establish the importance of the subject and have begun to suggest what sort of form a thorough investigation might take. Among my predecessors in this territory I identify three scholars whose footprints are most distinct: David Hayman, whose work on Tristan and Isolde in *Exiles* and *Finnegans Wake* assesses the relative contribution of Joyce's several sources for the legend; William Blissett, whose pioneering articles on Wagner's presence in modern literature have suggested several useful lines of inquiry and directed my reading into many fruitful areas; and Matthew Hodgart, who has identified scores of subtle allusions in the *Wake*. Their work and that of the other scholars cited in the notes to chapter i help justify my own and establish its point of departure. Several factors make a comprehensive study of the relationship between Joyce and Wagner especially desirable: their proximity in cultural history; the number of works in question; the magnitude of these works, both individually and collectively; their deep cultural resonance. Only a full-length study can thoroughly assess the connection. Only a full-length study, in fact, can define its limits.

It should be emphasized that, as an exercise in literary history and criticism, *Joyce and Wagner* is intended, primarily, to advance our understanding of Joyce's work, its sources, and its cultural background. Some fresh insight about Nietzsche's "old Klingsor" may emerge when he is viewed from Joyce's coign of vantage or simply juxtaposed to the rare artist of comparable stature; but, as always with Joyce, his use of sources – witness Homer, Vico – tells us more about him than about his sources. Furthermore, because this study considers Wagner and his work from Joyce's historical perspective, the writings of contemporaries such as Shaw, D'Annunzio, and Nietzsche hold greater importance here than they do for today's student of Wagner; for it was to these early Wagnerites that Joyce was indebted for much of his understanding of the composer and his work. I acknowledge the limitations of these critics and attempt, especially in my notes, to qualify their readings with more current views of the composer. As an argument for a pervasive Wagnerian presence in Joyce's work, *Joyce and Wagner* may extend our awareness of Wagner's immense importance in the culture of his descendants and especially in the development of literary modernism; but the book's first aim is to illuminate the background of Joyce's writing, to deepen our understanding of his books, and to follow the transmission of material from a major influence through important conduits to its eventual manifestation in the art of James Joyce. The intent, moreover, is less to produce new "readings" or "interpretations" of Joyce's individual works than it is to situate Joyce's work more precisely in cultural history.

The relationship between Joyce and Wagner would be circumscribed by several factors: that opera and the novel generally accommodate different subject matter; that literature cannot in any absolute sense achieve what Pater had called "the condition of music" – as chapter 6 suggests, even the "musical" influence on Joyce's work is ineluctably "literary" (and, of course, if Wagner were not a great deal more than a musician this study could not have been undertaken); that Joyce and Wagner ultimately developed profoundly different attitudes toward experience, especially contemporary experience; and that "great" artists, the most powerful of those whom Harold Bloom would call "strong" poets, must finally make their own way even if they are at first inspired and guided by a powerful predecessor. Indeed, between alternative models of literary influence advanced by Bloom and by T. S. Eliot, one of struggle and appropriation and one of "continual surrender ... to something which is more valuable," the case of Joyce and Wagner more closely approximates that of Bloom.[1] It is not a contradiction to suggest, however, that as the maturing Joyce came more and more into "his own," as his tastes in art became less and less "Wagnerian," his own work became, in several important respects, more and more so: more extravagant, more ambitious, more, to borrow Fritz Senn's recent coinage, "provected."[2] In fact, much of what we regard as Joyce's originality may to a considerable extent consist in his application of the idea of being "Wagnerian" – of being, that is, the "total artist" that Wagner epitomized – to the forms and methods of fiction in the twentieth century. "[N]ot only the best," Eliot writes, "but the most individual parts of [the poet's] work may be those in which the dead poets, his ancestors, assert their immortality most vigorously."[3]

This book identifies several powerful themes and aesthetic questions current in nineteenth-century culture and central to Wagner's work, and it discusses their persistence in a writer generally thought to epitomize the modern period in literature. Taken up in the five interior chapters, they include the artist as revolutionary, the artist as exile, the redemptive woman, the mythic method, the idea of musical expression in literature. The principle is to focus, in these thematic chapters, on areas where Wagner's influence on Joyce runs especially deep and to assign to the appendix the task of documenting the breadth of the connection. If Thomas Mann was right in asserting that Wagner epitomized the nineteenth century,[4] then Joyce's engagement with Wagner is to some extent his dialectic with his immediate past; and his lifelong commitment to Wagner's art, however conditioned by his own artistic temperament and independence of spirit, signifies his ongoing attachment to many of the most important strands of nineteenth-century culture. Indeed, the fact that Joyce's knowledge of Wagner was conditioned by a large number of intermediaries not only demonstrates the pervasiveness of Wagner in nineteenth-century culture but also argues for Joyce's entanglement in it. In this sense *Joyce and Wagner* may be seen to correct or at least to qualify the impression that the Irish writer, in holding himself aloof from his age and in denigrating recent art and thought at nearly every opportunity, helped create: that his most important influences are to be found only among the arcane and the antique. Precisely because Wagner's impact on Joyce transcended the merely local use of allusion and extended into theme, structure, aesthetics, and scale, it becomes necessary to count the German composer among the most important of Joyce's more contemporary influences – with Flaubert, perhaps, and Ibsen.

Joyce and Wagner demonstrates Joyce's thorough exposure to Wagner, both direct, through his habituation of the library and the opera house, and indirect, through conduits like Shaw, Yeats, Moore, Symons, Nietzsche, and D'Annunzio. It defines Wagner's contribution to Joyce's texts by identifying allusions that, as they proliferate through Joyce's career, exert hundreds of local pressures and assert, collectively, a pervasive Wagnerian presence. It assesses Wagner's role as a shaping force in Joyce's life and art and shows Joyce's engagement with the culture of the nineteenth century that Wagner, in some sense, epitomizes. It suggests, finally, with necessary diffidence, that Joyce's work may represent a response to the challenge that one ''great'' artist issued another.

Acknowledgments

I wish to acknowledge those who have shown a particular interest in this study and whose advice has contributed to its substance and form. For comments on individual portions of the manuscript, I thank Richard Beckman, David Borodin, John Hannay, David Hayman, Geert Lernout, Ira Nadel, Margot Norris, and Bonnie Scott. I owe special thanks to those who have read the manuscript in its entirety: to Peter Conn and Alice Kelley, who examined the book in its earliest form; to David Austin; and above all to Donald Mull, who found a number of errors of fact in an intermediate draft.

I thank the staff of the Humanities Research Center at the University of Texas, and especially Erik Stocker, for help with Joyce's library; Helen Hayes, for unstinting assistance in locating reference materials and books; Laura Montagnaro Erwin, for help with the French; Christine Dougherty, for help with the German; Pauline Brown, for a musical illustration in chapter 2; Connie Brooks, Roberta Klein, and especially Megan Thomas, for help with the typing; and Phyllis Triestman, for general secretarial support over the past six years. At Cambridge University Press, I thank Josie Dixon, Trudi Tate, and, for sustained interest in the project and for many courtesies, Kevin Taylor. I thank Fritz Senn for permission to quote from an unpublished essay, and I thank the editors of *Comparative Literature*, *James Joyce Quarterly*, and *Journal of Modern Literature* for permission to use previously published portions of the manuscript. I acknowledge with gratitude the Rutgers University Research Council, which supported this study with three grants.

I also wish to acknowledge those whose contributions to the project have been less direct but no less significant. For inspiration, encouragement, and many favors, large and small, I thank Marie Cornelia, David DeLaura, Maurice Johnson, Morton Levitt, Robert Lucid, Fritz Senn, and especially Peter Conn; for fellowship and professional sustenance, I salute the Philadelphia Ideal Insomniacs, the group with which I have been reading *Finnegans Wake* over the past five years.

My greatest debt is to my dissertation director Robert Storey, whose suggestion that I consider *Joyce and Wagner* as the subject for a research project was only the first of many professional favors that I cannot hope to return. His critical acumen and good sense have shaped this book from the outset; his generosity and faith in the project have helped assure that it was carried out.

Abbreviations

Quotations from the following works are cited in the text, parenthetically:

JJ   Ellmann, Richard. *James Joyce.* Rev. edn. New York: Oxford University Press, 1982.

CP   Joyce, James. *Collected Poems.* New York: Viking, Compass, 1957.

CW   *The Critical Writings of James Joyce.* Ed. Ellsworth Mason and Richard Ellmann. New York: Viking, 1959.

D   *Dubliners.* New York: Viking, Compass, 1968.

E   *Exiles: A Play in Three Acts.* New York: Viking, Compass, 1961.

FW   *Finnegans Wake.* New York: Viking, 1958.

L   *The Letters of James Joyce.* 3 vols. Vol. 1, ed. Stuart Gilbert. Vols. 2 and 3, ed. Richard Ellmann. New York: Viking, 1966.

P   *A Portrait of the Artist as a Young Man.* New York: Viking, Compass, 1964.

U   *Ulysses: The Corrected Text.* Ed. Hans Walter Gabler with Wolfhard Steppe and Claus Melchior. New York: Random, 1986.

         Ulysses. New York: Random, 1961.

FD   Wagner, Richard. *The Flying Dutchman.* [Libretto, English and German, with commentaries.] Trans. David Pountney. English National Opera Guide no. 12. New York: Riverrun, 1982.

MS   *The Mastersingers of Nuremberg.* [Libretto, English and German, with commentaries.] Trans. Frederick

Jameson, rev. Norman Feasey and Gordon Kember. English National Opera Guide no. 19. New York: Riverrun, 1983.

Pars *Parsifal.* [Libretto, English and German, with commentaries.] Trans. Andrew Porter. English National Opera Guide no. 34. New York: Riverrun, 1986.

PW *Prose Works.* Trans. William Ashton Ellis. 8 vols. 1892–99. Rpt New York: Broude, 1966.

R *The Ring of the Nibelung.* [Libretto, English and German.] Trans. Andrew Porter. New York: Norton, 1977.

Tann *Tannhäuser.* [Libretto, English and German, with commentaries.] Trans. Rodney Blumer. English National Opera Guide no. 39. New York: Riverrun, 1988.

TI *Tristan and Isolde.* [Libretto, English and German, with commentaries.] Trans. Andrew Porter. English National Opera Guide no. 6. New York: Riverrun, 1981.

Italics in quotations are original, unless otherwise noted; likewise, original punctuation and capitalization are preserved without comment. In the text, Wagner's operas are identified by the familiar German titles, except for *The Flying Dutchman*; titles of his prose works are generally given in English. Where translations are not, for my purposes, sufficiently literal, I have attempted my own. These are identified in notes or parentheses. To save space, acts and scenes may be designated with Arabic numerals, as in "*Siegfried* 1.2."

Passages from *Ulysses* are identified in both editions. Where they differ, readings in the far superior 1986 edition are accepted without comment, except in one case, discussed in a note to chapter 6. Following the editor's suggestion, citations to the 1986 edition give the episode and line number. Those to the 1961 edition give the page number. Sections of *Finnegans Wake* are identified by book (Roman numeral) and chapter (Arabic), as in "I.6." Quotations from the *Wake* are identified by page and line numbers – "116.25–36" – except that marginalia and notes in II.2 are designated L, R, and F. Thus, "301.L2" is the second note in the left-hand column on page 301.

CHAPTER 1

Joyce and literary Wagnerism

> We shall always have to credit Wagner with the fact that
> in the second half of the nineteenth century he impressed
> art upon our memory as an important and magnificent
> thing.   Nietzsche, *Selected Aphorisms*

> I've always told him he should give up writing and take up
> singing. To think he was once on the same platform with
> John McCormack!   Nora Barnacle Joyce

Richard Wagner, who left us ten magnificent works for the
operatic stage, was the most important force in the development
of opera in the nineteenth century. The most determined of
"musical idealists" in the operatic realm, Wagner changed
forever the way audiences regarded opera and raised standards
in all aspects of production and performance. Analogous to
the various autonomous theories of art current in the nineteenth
century, musical idealism was a reaction against the prevalent
worship of the virtuoso at the expense of the work and against
the trivialization of the performance into a social occasion.
Much of what we have come to associate with Wagnerism –
musical idolatry, a quasi-religious musical experience, the
Wagnerian "hush" at performances, the idea of an elite community of musical artists – was anticipated by idealist trends
elsewhere in the musical culture of Wagner's time. Berlioz, for
example, had written of an imaginary city called "Euphonia,"
free from the social and commercial pressures of the day;
Schumann had criticized the behavior of concert audiences;
and festivals devoted to Handel's oratorios and Beethoven's
symphonies had been established well before the peak of

Wagner's influence. Wagner's challenge (and the source of his celebrity) was to have chosen an art form – grand opera – especially ripe for virtuosity and far more dependent than any other on fickle circumstance – the brittle ego of a tenor, the patronage of a king, the competence of a conductor, the co-operation of an unruly horse. The idea of Bayreuth, a community dedicated to producing opera under ideal conditions, was the logical extension of the concept of artistic autonomy applied to opera and the result of the apparent incompatibility between the contemporary theatre and opera taken seriously as "drama."[1]

Wagner felt that his mission was to elevate opera to the status of a serious art form – in particular, to that of Greek drama, the ideal his prose writings continually invoke – and his autocratic determination to do so accounts for most of his contributions to the genre. Wagner argued that the traditional opera, as a "bandbox" of more or less discrete musical "numbers" (*PW* 2:46), exalted the singer and his technique at the expense of dramatic illusion. As a lapidary passage in *Opera and Drama* puts it, "a Means of expression (Music) has been made the end, while the End of expression (the Drama) has been made a means" (*PW* 2:17). His approach, beginning with *The Flying Dutchman*, was composition by "scene" rather than by number, using what he called "infinite" or "endless" melody, an arioso that blurred the conventional distinction between aria and recitative and often, in fact, spilled from one scene into the next.[2] Wagner's audience would generally have to withhold its applause until the end of a full act. Wagner also recognized that, traditionally, in opera's aggregation of arts, the text had been sacrificed to the music. "What is too silly to be said," he wrote, borrowing from Voltaire, "one gets it sung" (*PW* 2:355). In his attempt to achieve a true marriage of poetry and music, Wagner declared independence from the professional librettist and wrote his own texts. The poet-musician's synthesis, "*Versmelodie*," would abandon conventional four-bar phrasing in favor of motivic "musical prose" that allowed greater rhythmic flexibility and sensitivity to the text.[3] According to George Bernard Shaw, "There is not a single bar of 'classical music' in *The Ring* – not a note in it that has any other point than the single direct point of giving musical expression to the drama."[4] Duets, ensembles, finales, and choruses all came under Wagnerian attack as artificial or "operatic"; singing in harmony was virtually out of the question in "music drama" (*PW* 2:303).[5]

Wagner's emphasis on dramatic illusion had many implications for his theatre and for operatic theatre after him. (Nietzsche, in fact, argued that Wagner's primary genius was theatrical rather than musical.[6]) In order to focus concentration on the stage, Wagner modeled his festival hall at Bayreuth after the Greek amphitheatre, eliminated blind spots and side boxes, placed his huge orchestra beneath the stage and out of view, and opened and closed his curtain from the center instead of raising and lowering it.[7] Wagner's exacting stage directions, especially for the *Ring*, drew many technical innovations from Bayreuth's engineers – steam curtains, sideways-moving scenery, and improved stage lighting. Wagner more than any other individual is responsible for the fact that lights are now turned out during performances, that audiences come to quiet attention when the music begins, and that doors are closed to latecomers.[8] The Wagnerian "Prelude" replaced the traditional overture, preparing the listener for a mystical experience instead of diverting him with a series of tunes. The intricate system of leitmotifs spread over works as long as five hours presented an intellectual challenge without operatic precedent. Indeed, Wagner felt that his work only came into being through the exertions of the audience, the "sole enablers of [the] artwork's Becoming" (*PW* 2:338). But the Wagnerian audience would require some cultivation, as a review of an 1875 production in London suggests:

the Teutonic element in the house had a marvellous effect in teaching the audience that "Lohengrin" was not to be judged by the ordinary standard; so when the usual round of applause was given for the favourite singers on their entrance and the boisterous marks of approbation burst forth after an effective *morceau*, a very decided "hush" convinced the astonished Opera habitués that the vocalists must be considered as secondary to the work they were interpreting, and that any congratulations to individual performers must be reserved for the fall of the curtain.[9]

Performances at Bayreuth elevated standards for stagecraft, conducting, singing, and acting everywhere, "even," Shaw wrote, "in apparently incorrigible centres of fashion and frivolity."[10]

Wagner's influence, however, spread far beyond the opera house and concert hall; indeed, more ink had been spilled over the composer by the time of his death than over any other historical figure but Christ or Napoleon – some ten thousand books and articles.[11] As Jacques Barzun has written, "A King had chosen an Artist as his master, a people had adopted a man's work as the expression of their spirit – both in the lifetime of the creator himself. A city had been dedicated to his uses, and his rare and difficult music made money."[12] By the end of the century, Wagner had been studied and borrowed by progressive artistic movements across Europe – by Parnassians, Symbolists, and Impressionists in France, by Pre-Raphaelites, theosophists, and "decadents" in England. The idea of a "*Gesamtkunstwerk*" inspired the symbolist drama of Maurice Maeterlinck and Arthur Symons and influenced the development of Diaghilev's Ballets russes. The example of Bayreuth encouraged movements for national theatres in England, Russia, Italy, and Ireland. *Bayreuther Blätter, Revue wagnérienne, Cronaca wagneriana*, and *The Meister* all devoted themselves to Wagner's music and aesthetic program. Cézanne, Fantin-Latour, Redon, and Jacques Emile Blanche produced paintings and lithographs on Wagnerian subjects; Renoir sought and received permission to paint Wagner's portrait.[13] Most major European cities created Wagner Societies to support the first Bayreuth festival; the group in Marseilles, in fact, numbered Cézanne and Zola among its members. Works as diverse and influential as Nietzsche's *Birth of Tragedy*, Huysmans' *A Rebours*, Villiers' *Axel*, and, later, Mann's *Magic Mountain* all bear the Wagnerian stamp. According to French man of letters Romain Rolland, toward the end of the century in France, "writers not only discussed musical subjects, but judged painting, literature, and philosophy, from a Wagnerian point of view ... [T]he whole universe was seen and judged by the thought of Bayreuth."[14] Even those Wagnerites who knew little about music were impressed by the representations of sexual feeling and of subconscious life in Wagner's scores.

For the serious artist at the end of the nineteenth century, Wagner was inescapable.

The German composer first attracted attention in literary circles in the 1850s, when Gérard de Nerval and Théophile Gautier, writing for French journals, reviewed productions of Wagner's operas in Germany. But literary Wagnerism really began in Paris in 1860 and 1861, when Wagner was making his second attempt, after the frustrations of 1839 to 1842, on the Parisian musical establishment.[15] In 1860 Wagner conducted several concerts of his music, issued a French translation of four librettos, and spent much of the year preparing a revised *Tannhäuser*, commanded by Louis Napoleon, for the Paris Opera. This catastrophic 1861 *Tannhäuser*, a test case for the cause of musical idealism in a setting where it was least welcome, would pass quickly into operatic lore. Its collapse, after just three performances, was inevitable. The Parisian press, which Wagner had not courted, had shown almost unanimous hostility, taking sides with Meyerbeer and Berlioz against this much-bruited "music of the future."[16] Moreover, Wagner's most active and important supporter in the emperor's court, the Austrian princess Pauline Metternich, was disliked by both republicans and legitimists, and much of the anti-Austrian sentiment directed at her found a convenient outlet in what Baudelaire, already a member of Wagner's Parisian circle, would call "the first passer-by" – *Tannhäuser*.[17] Whatever chance Wagner had to overcome these liabilities, if indeed he had any, was lost when he refused to sacrifice dramatic illusion – and artistic principle – by adapting his opera to conciliate an influential group of opera subscribers. According to Wagner's biographer Ernest Newman, the "Jockey Club" was a group of wealthy young aristocrats that "did not know much or care much about art, but... knew what it wanted after dinner and could be trusted to see that it got it."[18] Members of the club were not accustomed to arriving at the opera till it was half over, at which time they expected to see the grand ballet that, according to French tradition, was reserved for the second act. (Wagner's friend Malwida von Meysenbug explained the club's enthusiasm for dance when she remarked that "the ladies of the ballet had their wages increased by these gentlemen."[19])

Wagner would yield only so far as to allow a "Bacchanal" at the beginning of act I, where a chorus of dancers made some dramatic sense; but this concession was ineffective, for the musician of the future and protégé of the princess had become a *cause célèbre*. Despite the emperor's presence, the three performances were interrupted continually by catcalls and fistfights; street vendors sold "Wagner whistles" for use in the audience. The result of the Paris *Tannhäuser*, however, was not what Wagner's detractors might have wished. It was to make Wagner an object of sympathy and admiration, a virtual archetype of the uncompromising artist, and to attract supporters from all of Europe, including the literary figures who would become his most ardent spokesmen.[20]

James Joyce was uniquely qualified to appreciate Wagner's position in nineteenth-century culture, for he was a more serious and better-trained musician than nearly all the Wagnerites in the literary world.[21] Joyce was born into a musical family, and his knowledge of opera and other vocal music developed rapidly. His father's voice was once described as the finest tenor in all Ireland, and Joyce himself started piano lessons at the age of nine, had his own tenor trained intermittently, and resolved on several occasions in his twenties to make singing his profession. Joyce first sang publicly when he was six, performing in a concert with his parents, and by his early teens he was singing opera arias in company. Stanislaus Joyce reports that his brother was always well ahead of his schoolwork and able to devote his free time to reading opera scores.[22] In 1904 he placed third in the Feis Ceoil in Dublin, disqualifying himself for first place by stalking off the stage when asked to sight-sing, and later that year, in one of many concerts, he performed with the young John McCormack, eventually the most celebrated of Irish lyric tenors. The story of Joyce's reconciliation with his father after James had eloped with Nora Barnacle reveals the importance of music in the family life of the Joyces.[23] In 1909, in a concert program in Trieste, Joyce performed in the quintet from *Die Meistersinger*. Later in life Nora would express sentiments that were undoubtedly shared by much of Joyce's family: "I've always told him he should give up writing and take up singing. To think he was once on the same platform with John McCormack!" (*JJ* 561). Apparently Joyce himself often felt the same way: according to Sylvia Beach, "The Joyces were all singers, and Joyce never quite ceased to regret his choice of a writer's instead of a singer's career. 'Perhaps I would have done better,' he would say to me.''[24]

Joyce also dabbled in composition. He composed music for two of James Clarence Mangan's poems and for Yeats's lyric "Who Goes with Fergus" (*JJ* 94, 67); fragments of other compositions are among his papers at Cornell.[25] His son Giorgio pursued a singing career actively, and Joyce gave him detailed advice on a range of repertoire, including Irish folk songs, Russian opera, Handel, Verdi, and Wagner (*L* 3:332–49). In Zurich in 1919 Joyce played impresario, organizing a recital of Irish music by Irish baritone Augustus Milner, and in the 1920s he suggested to American composer George Antheil that the two collaborate on an opera. Antheil found Joyce's knowledge of music "encyclopedic": "He would have special knowledge, for instance, about many a rare music manuscript secreted away in some almost unknown museum of Paris, and I often took advantage of his knowledge."[26] Around 1930 Joyce met John Sullivan, the dramatic tenor he had first heard singing the title role in *Tannhäuser*, and, partly because he empathized with Sullivan's position as an Irishman in "exile," became one of the tenor's most active partisans. On one occasion, in the cataloguing spirit of "Ithaca," Joyce followed the score of Rossini's *William Tell*, "counting ecstatically the number of his friend's high notes. 'I have been through the score of *Guillaume Tell*,' he reported, 'and I discover that Sullivan sings 456 G's, 93 A-flats, 54 B-flats, 15 B's, 19 C's and 2 C-sharps. Nobody else can do it' " (*JJ* 620). In 1931 Joyce's tireless efforts in promoting Sullivan's career (and in assuaging, perhaps, his own frustrated ambition) brought him into contact with Ernest Newman, to whom Joyce spoke about publicizing Sullivan's performance of *William Tell* in London (*L* 3:223).[27]

Joyce's first encounters with Wagner were probably at second hand, in the writings of intermediary figures already under Wagner's influence.[28] Among the most ardent were the French writers whom Joyce studied and translated during his years at University College. After its beginnings in the turmoil of the 1861 *Tannhäuser* and in Baudelaire's famous review essay "Richard

Wagner et *Tannhäuser* à Paris,"[29] literary Wagnerism in France had peaked between 1885 and 1888, the lifetime of Edouard Dujardin's *Revue wagnérienne*. Dujardin's contributors, recruited from Mallarmé's "Mardis" in Paris, included Verlaine, Villiers de l'Isle-Adam, Swinburne, Catulle Mendès, Stuart Merrill, Huysmans (whose Wagnerian *A Rebours* had appeared in 1884), and Mallarmé himself. Most of these figures would turn up in Arthur Symons' influential *Symbolist Movement in Literature*, which Joyce read with keen interest soon after its appearance in 1899.[30] Among the *Revue*'s most important publications were Mallarmé's essay "Richard Wagner, rêverie d'un poète français," Swinburne's poem "La Mort de Richard Wagner," and sonnet sequences of eight and nine poems. Among these were Mallarmé's "Hommage" and Verlaine's "Parsifal," the last line of which would work its way famously into *The Waste Land*. Pervasive as Wagner was in French aesthetics late in the century, the Wagnerism that came to Joyce through these sources was decidedly more literary than musical. After the 1861 production of *Tannhäuser*, and excepting an 1869 production of the little-known *Rienzi*, there were no performances of Wagner's operas in France till *Lohengrin* was produced in 1887, *Die Walküre* in 1893, and a resuscitated *Tannhäuser* in 1895.[31] Unless they traveled to Germany, French Wagnerites had to make do with excerpts of Wagner's operas in concert form; many, in fact, knew the widely circulated prose works of 1849–51 better than they did his music. The less Wagner was heard, it turns out, the more he grew in the imaginations of his admirers.[32]

From the outpost of Dublin, the young Joyce made a specialty of Continental literature, and he met Wagner at almost every turn. His attachment to Ibsen led to his first publication, his review in 1900 of *When We Dead Awaken*, where Ibsen's allusion to *Lohengrin* is quoted (*CW* 58). Among the novels of Joyce's beloved Gabriele D'Annunzio, two, *Il fuoco* and *Trionfo della morte*, borrow Wagnerian imagery freely and enlarge on Wagnerian aesthetics.[33] (As a young man Joyce thought *Il fuoco*, where Wagner is virtually deified, "the highest achievement of the novel to date."[34]) Another important Continental source of Joyce's information about Wagner, a source that may have balanced the enthusiasm

of D'Annunzio and the Symbolists, was Nietzsche, sev‹
whose works, including *The Birth of Tragedy, The Case of W‹*
and *Nietzsche contra Wagner*, Joyce owned.[35] Indeed, the ca‹
Nietzsche illustrates the ubiquity of Wagner in Joyce's cultu
background. Lurking behind Stephen Dedalus' cynical remark in
"Eumaeus" that his father is "Irish ... all too Irish" (*U* 16.382 – 4;
623) is not only Nietzsche but also Wagner: Nietzsche's *Menschlich,
allzumenschliches* (*Human, All-too-Human*), begun during the first
Bayreuth festival, marks the philosopher's split with Wagner and
disillusionment with Wagnerian ideals. Finally, Joyce did not
make the personal acquaintance of Dujardin until shortly after
he came to Paris in 1920. But he had bought *Les Lauriers sont coupés*
at a railway kiosk in 1903, and, after *Ulysses* had made the "interior
monologue" famous, he was always careful to credit Dujardin's
book as its inspiration. Dujardin, it turns out, got the idea from
Wagner's "infinite melody."[36]

Joyce encountered more Wagnerites among English and Irish
writers. In England Wagner's operas had won gradual acceptance
both in artistic circles and with the musical public; English
Wagnerites, unlike their French counterparts, were not forced
to travel to Germany to see Wagner on stage.[37] Unimpeded by
the Franco-Prussian War or by the increasing Francophobia in
Wagner's prose writings, and despite the notoriety engendered
by the anti-Semitism and abuse of Mendelssohn in *Judaism in
Music*,[38] all the mature operas, excepting *Parsifal*, would be
staged in London by the early eighties.[39] Wagner's well-known
role in the Dresden uprising of 1849 and his status as a political
exile did not deter Queen Victoria, possibly at the instigation of
the more musical Prince Albert,[40] from several expressions of
enthusiasm: commanding a performance of the Overture to
Tannhäuser during the Old Philharmonic Society's concert series
in 1855; receiving Wagner afterward; and, during London's
Wagner Festival in 1877, renewing the acquaintance over lunch
at Windsor Castle.[41] Wagner's advent in literary and artistic
circles was assured in 1869, when Francis Hueffer, already a
Wagnerite and eventually the father of Ford Madox Ford,
emigrated to England.[42] Hueffer, soon to be author of several
books on Wagner, including the two-volume translation of

Wagner's correspondence with Franz Liszt, quickly became an
influential member of the group of painters and writers who
gathered in the home of Ford Madox Brown in the late sixties
and early seventies: the Rossettis, Holman Hunt, William Morris,
and Swinburne, among others.[43] Through Hueffer and Edward
Dannreuther, the founder of the Wagner Society in London,
many of England's leading cultural figures were presented to
Wagner during his stay in 1877: George Henry Lewes, Robert
Browning, D. G. Rossetti, Edward Burne-Jones, and George
Eliot, who is supposed to have wept profusely over music from
Die Walküre.[44] Eliot evidently knew *Judaism in Music*: "Your
husband," she said to Cosima with friendly candor, "does not
like Jews; my husband is a Jew."[45] One of the Wagner Society's
most distinguished members was Jessie Weston, author of the
first English translation of Wolfram's *Parzival* and eventually
the writer of the influential *From Ritual to Romance*. In 1896 Weston
would publish *Legends of the Wagner Drama*, a study of the sources
of Wagner's librettos in Scandinavian and Germanic sagas, eddas,
and legends.[46] From 1888 to 1895 the society published *The
Meister*, a quarterly modeled on the *Revue wagnérienne*. In this
journal appeared translations of Wagner's writings, essays on his
dramas and aesthetic theories, poetry on Wagnerian subjects,
and announcements of performances. The editor of *The Meister*,
William Ashton Ellis, had already published *Theosophy in the Works
of Richard Wagner* and would soon translate Wagner's complete
prose writings and Glasenapp's biography.

Outside this circle of aficionados were several important literary
figures who admired Wagner's music and studied his essays.
Oscar Wilde, who brought the composer into *The Importance of
Being Earnest, The Picture of Dorian Gray*, and "The Soul of Man
under Socialism," and Aubrey Beardsley, whose saucy *Under the
Hill* follows the plot of *Tannhäuser* closely, were at least occasional
Wagnerites. In 1909 Joyce considered translating "The Soul of
Man," where Wagner appears in an important passage, into
Italian (*JJ* 274), and in 1932 he gave Lucia a copy of Beardsley's
book, hoping its drawings, one of which was based on *Das Rhein-
gold*, would encourage her own artistic inclinations (*L* 1:328).[47]
But the first and best of these Wagnerites was Bernard Shaw,

who saw the Meister conduct on two occasions during the 1877 Festival and later made several trips to Bayreuth. Playwright and drama critic William Archer would find Shaw pursuing his two great passions at the British Museum: "Day after day for weeks he had before him two books, which he studied alternately, if not simultaneously, – Karl Marx's *Das Kapital* and an orchestral score of *Tristan and Isolde*."[48] Shaw's musical knowledge earned him positions from 1888 to 1894 as music critic for the *Star* and for the *World*, where, as "Corno di Bassetto," he argued, with characteristic independence of mind, that Wagner was not the "musician of the future" but a nineteenth-century composer in the tradition of Beethoven. (Years later W. H. Auden would describe Shaw as "probably the best music critic who ever lived."[49]) In addition to frequent commentary in his many volumes of music criticism, Shaw devoted two books to Wagner. *The Sanity of Art* (1908), originally an 1895 review of Max Nordau's notorious *Degeneration*, defended the composer against the charge of "decadence." More influential was *The Perfect Wagnerite*, the socialist interpretation of the *Ring* first published in 1898.[50] Joyce never met Shaw, but he knew his work; and he read *The Perfect Wagnerite* carefully: his own copy of the book, in fact, is heavily marked as if for use in the English lessons he periodically gave, with passages bracketed and difficult or unusual words underlined.[51] Joyce's eventual acquisition of *London Music in 1888 – 89*, a collection of reviews Shaw published in 1937, may reflect the rekindling of an early interest in Shaw's writings on music.[52]

Two other important Wagnerites were George Moore and Arthur Symons, both of whose enthusiasm for the composer originated in France. Symons first went to Paris around 1890, at which time he became a close friend of Verlaine and made the acquaintance of Huysmans and Mallarmé. His relationship with these writers led to the seminal *Symbolist Movement*, which helped establish him as the leading proponent of French aesthetics in English letters.[53] In this book Wagner was the consummate Symbolist: "Carry the theories of Mallarmé to a practical conclusion," wrote Symons, "multiply his powers in a direct ratio, and you have Wagner."[54] Elsewhere Symons would praise Wagnerian opera as "the most complete form of art yet realised."[55] During his career as a man of letters, Symons wrote performance reviews and essays on Wagnerian aesthetics, including "The Ideas of Richard Wagner," a 1905 essay that Yeats would find useful in his own work.[56] Symons also wrote poems on Wagnerian subjects, and his *Tristan and Iseult* (1917), inspired by a 1902 performance of *Tristan*, was his own attempt to write a symbolist drama in the tradition of earlier Wagnerites like Villiers (*Axel*) and Maeterlinck (*Pelléas et Mélisande*).[57] Swinburne's presentation copy of Baudelaire's "Richard Wagner et *Tannhäuser* à Paris" eventually came into Symons' possession. Joyce, who, as we have seen, studied *The Symbolist Movement* carefully, first met Symons, through Yeats, in 1902. Symons would eventually make good on a promise to help Joyce get *Chamber Music* published and would review the book favorably for the *Nation*.

Among the most devoted of Wagner's English and Irish admirers was George Moore, who tried perhaps more than any other writer in English to bring the composer into his work. Moore spent the years from 1873 to 1880 in Paris, where, as a student of painting at the Julian Academy, he made the acquaintance of Wagnerites like Villiers, Mallarmé, Mendès, and Dujardin, the last of whom would eventually read his fiction for musical howlers.[58] Moore's autobiographical *Hail and Farewell* gives a sixty-page account of his trip to Bayreuth with Irish playwright Edward Martyn in the early nineties, on which occasion Moore met Wagner's son Siegfried and Cosima. He returned, with Dujardin, in 1901. In *Confessions of a Young Man*, Moore wrote of his attempt to imitate Wagner's continuous melody in his writing – "I hear," said Wilde about one of Moore's books, "it has to be played on the piano"[59] – and in *Hail and Farewell* he wondered whether he might be an artist-smith like Siegfried, destined to wake Ireland from its centuries of cultural slumber.[60] The heroine of *Evelyn Innes* (1898), the most thoroughly Wagnerian of Moore's novels, finds her musical and sexual careers mirrored in a chronological succession of the operas, including *The Flying Dutchman, Tannhäuser, Lohengrin, Tristan,* and *Parsifal.*[61] *Sister Teresa* (1901) and *The Lake* (1905) borrow freely from Wagner as well.[62] Joyce and Moore met only once, in 1929, and Joyce gave his writing mixed reviews. But Joyce's library betrays a strong interest in his fellow Irishman. Among the fourteen volumes in the Trieste collection are the Wagnerian *Hail and Farewell, Memoirs of My Dead Life, Sister Teresa, The Lake*, and *Evelyn Innes*, the last of which is heavily marked.[63]

Wagner, in fact, exerted a particular fascination on the Irish literary imagination. On the musical culture of Ireland the composer's effect was slight, for, because of the complexity, scale, and moral audacity of the operas, very few staged productions were attempted in Ireland at this time.[64] But here, as elsewhere, Wagner's reputation preceded his operas, and his name crops up frequently, with Ibsen's, in connection with the movement for an Irish literary theatre.[65] Yeats's interest in Wagner dates from London in 1887, when he became acquainted with Ashton Ellis, soon to be editor of *The Meister*. Yeats also knew well Symons and Moore, and in 1905 he wrote Symons, praising "The Ideas of Richard Wagner," citing the essay's compatibility with his own thinking, and acknowledging its help in his revision of *The Shadowy Waters*.[66] Several early essays follow *The Symbolist Movement* in describing Wagner as the consummate "Symbolist," and "The Celtic Movement in Literature" credits Wagner for much of the current interest in myth as a source for contemporary art:

In our own time Scandinavian tradition, because of the imagination of Richard Wagner and of William Morris and of the earlier and, as I think, greater Henrik Ibsen, has created a new romance, and, through the imagination of Richard Wagner, become all but the most passionate element in the arts of the modern world.[67]

Yeats believed that a drama based on Irish myth could focus Irish political aspirations and develop national consciousness, much as Wagner's mythic drama and Bayreuth, in the context of German unification, had apparently done for Germany.[68] Joyce made Yeats's acquaintance in Dublin and, according to Stanislaus, he read "everything that Yeats had written in prose or verse."[69] His library included the essays collected in *Ideas of Good and Evil*, where "The Celtic Element in Literature," "William Blake and the Imagination," "Symbolism in Painting," and "The Symbolism of Poetry" assign Wagner a central role in modern art.

Two key figures in the national theatre movement, Edward Martyn, who helped found, in 1899, the Irish Literary Theatre,

and Annie Horniman, who established the Irish National Theatre
in the Abbey in 1904, were serious Wagnerites. Miss Horniman,
in fact, had helped Ellis with his eight-volume translation of the
Prose Works. Many of the early plays produced by the movement
show Wagner's imprint, including Martyn's *Heather Field*, Yeats
and Moore's *Diarmuid and Grania*, Yeats's *Shadowy Waters*, and
Synge's *Dierdre of the Sorrows*.[70] Yeats's 1902 letter to Irish actor
Frank Fay shows the poet's keen awareness of the precedent
provided by Wagner:

Now as to the future of the National Theatre Company. I read your
letters to a wealthy friend [probably Miss Horniman, according to
Yeats's editor], who said something like this[:] "Work on as best you
[i.e., Yeats] can for a year, let us say, [and] you should be able to
persuade people during that time that you are something of a dramatist
and Mr. Fay should be able to have got a little practice for his company.
At the year's end do what Wagner did and write a 'Letter to my Friends'
asking for the capital to carry out your idea."[71]

Wagner's widely read *Communication to My Friends* (1851) concludes
with an outline of a plan for "a specially-appointed Festival" of
"*three complete dramas*, preceded by a lengthy *Prelude*" and with
a broad hint that Wagner's "Friends ... alone can bring this thing
to pass" (*PW* 1:389 – 92). The "Festival," of course, would
become Bayreuth, the "dramas" and "Prelude," the *Ring*. In
the early days of the Irish literary theatre, before it became clear
that its repertoire would not include European drama, Joyce
made himself one of its most conspicuous supporters (*JJ* 66 – 7).

Entangled as Joyce was, then, in the progressive literary culture
of the late nineteenth century, it is not surprising that his earliest
Wagnerism was more literary than musical. Unlike those imperfect Wagnerites who preferred the composer's music, the
young Joyce swore allegiance to Wagner the poet, dramatist,
and mythmaker. In his first year at University College, Joyce
delighted his French professor when he coined an equivalent,
"*idée-mère*," for leitmotif (*JJ* 60), and in a portfolio that Joyce
put together in 1901 was a poem on Wagner's Valkyrie, written,
perhaps, in the tradition of the *Revue wagnérienne*, which had
published Verlaine's "Parsifal" and Mallarmé's "Hommage."
(Stanislaus called this poem one of the young Joyce's "longer

and more ambitious efforts."[72]) Joyce's early knowledge of
Wagner emerges most directly in his critical writings, where
references to *Tannhäuser, Lohengrin, Götterdämmerung, Parsifal*, and
Wagner himself appear. The most important of these essays was
"Drama and Life," the manifesto delivered before University
College's Literary and Historical Society in 1900. Identifying
Wagner with a new and superior school of "dramatic drama,"
Joyce invokes Valhalla and, by implication, Bayreuth: "Even
the least part of Wagner – his music – is beyond Bellini. Spite
of the outcry of these lovers of the past, the masons are building
for Drama, an ampler and loftier home, where there shall be light
for gloom, and wide porches for drawbridge and keep" (*CW*
40–1). In the same essay he praises *Lohengrin* as a "world drama"
(*CW* 45) and ascribes the artistic soundness of Wagnerian opera,
as Nietzsche (in *The Birth of Tragedy*) and proponents of the Irish
theatre did before him, to its use of myth:

I believe further that drama arises spontaneously out of life and is coeval
with it. Every race has made its own myths and it is in these that early
drama often finds an outlet. The author of Parsifal has recognized this
and hence his work is solid as a rock. (*CW* 43)

The author of *Opera and Drama* may even have inspired the title
of Joyce's essay. Just as, in 1900, Joyce would stick carefully to
Wagner's preferred term for his works – "dramas" – so in 1917
would he argue, tellingly, for the *literary* merit of *Tristan und Isolde*,
which, he claimed, portrays one of "hardly more than a dozen
original themes in world literature."[73] In his 1912 "Universal
Literary Influence of the Renaissance," which contrasts medieval
and modern art, Joyce, in selecting the composer as his prime
example of "a great modern artist," does not confine Wagner's
importance to the realm of music.[74]

Unlike many of the early literary Wagnerites, however, Joyce
would eventually have ample opportunity to experience the composer in actual performance. In Dublin whatever Wagner Joyce
heard was probably in excerpt form, since, as we have seen, little
Wagner had been staged in Ireland by the time he left in 1904.
But on the Continent the operas were widely performed after the
turn of the century, and the Joyces, who lived in cities with active

opera companies – Trieste, Zurich, Paris – would become in-
veterate opera-goers. According to George Antheil, not, evidently,
a Wagnerite himself, "Joyce's madness was opera, preferably
Purcell, but if no Purcell was available, just opera. On one
occasion he even managed to drag me to the Paris Opéra to see
'Siegfried.' "[75] We can be virtually certain that Joyce eventually
saw all Wagner's mature operas on stage. His letters and the
recollections of his friends mention particular performances of
Die Walküre, Siegfried, Götterdämmerung, and *Tannhäuser*; about
details of music from *Die Meistersinger, The Flying Dutchman, Das
Rheingold*, and *Tristan und Isolde*, we have Joyce's commentary;
the Grail scene from *Parsifal* is described in the *Wake* (43.21–44.9);
and the widely performed *Lohengrin* would have been hard for an
aficionado of opera to miss. Librettos or piano-vocal scores to at
least five of the operas – *The Flying Dutchman, Götterdämmerung,
Meistersinger, Rheingold*, and *Siegfried* – found their way into
Joyce's library in Trieste.[76] Joyce's first-hand knowledge of the
operas is reflected in the sensitivity to Wagner's orchestration that
emerges now and again in his writing. For example, when Robert
Hand "strums" "O du, mein holder Abendstern" in act 2 of
Exiles (57–8), he may be thinking more of the harp and pizzicato
strings that accompany the Minnesinger Wolfram in act 3 of
Tannhäuser than of the sound of his own percussive piano. And
when Joyce told John Sullivan that Rossini had saved Wagner
"the annoyance of finding flauts for his *Feuerzauber*" (*CW* 263),
he must have been thinking of the end of *Die Walküre* and the
prominent flutes at the top of the score. One does not find this
sort of detail in the essays of Yeats that make Wagner a "Symbolist," nor would Joyce require a Dujardin to check his writing
for musical accuracy.

Joyce's first opportunity to see one of Wagner's operas may
not have presented itself till 1903, when, during one of his brief
stays in Paris, he took advantage of a richer cultural milieu than
that of his native Dublin. On January 25 Joyce urgently wrote
to his mother, "Tell Stannie to send me *at once* (so that I may have
it by Thursday night) my copy of Wagner's operas" (*L* 2:25). (This
would be a book of librettos, since each piano-vocal score is a large
volume in itself.) Joyce evidently planned to attend a performance

and wanted, like a good Wagnerite, to follow the words closely. In Rome in 1906 Joyce heard a band play music from *Siegfried*, and he pronounced it "Very fine" (*L* 2:145). A 1907 performance of *Götterdämmerung* prompted a letter to Stanislaus:

I went to the *Dusk of the Gods* ... When Brunnhilde brought on the horse, the latter, being unable to sing, evacuated ... There were many spectators who followed the opera with scores and librettos. On the stairs coming away and in the street I heard many people hum correctly and incorrectly the nine notes of the funeral motive. Nothing in the opera moved me. I have heard the funeral march often before. Only when Siegfried dies I responded from the crown of my head to his cry "O sposa sacra." (*L* 2:214)[77]

This passage shows Joyce's familiarity with the opera, his keen ear for the music, and his awareness of the leitmotif.[78] His feeble response almost certainly results from a state of depression, which his letters document clearly, at a time when the weight of poverty and literary obscurity was especially heavy. A subsequent letter to Stanislaus speaks of a general "state of indifference" that "ought to indicate artistic inclination, but ... doesn't." Joyce's recent difficulty with *Dusk of the Gods*, he admits, "is more mine than Wagner's" (*L* 2:217–18). We can be sure, however, that the eventual author of *Ulysses* and *Finnegans Wake* took special pleasure in the juxtaposition of mythic opera and quotidian horse.

Joyce's recorded impressions of Wagner's music are contradictory, depending almost entirely upon the context in which they were elicited. In 1909, while rehearsing the *Meistersinger* quintet, he wrote to Irish composer G. Molyneux Palmer, "Do you understand the infatuation of people for this opera? I think it is pretentious stuff" (*L* 1:67). By 1919, however, Joyce had reversed himself: *Meistersinger* was "my favorite Wagnerian opera" (*JJ* 459). Ellmann reports that around 1914 and 1915, "Joyce had no patience with the current adulation of Wagner, objecting that '*Wagner puzza di sesso*' (stinks of sex); Bellini, he said, was far better" (*JJ* 382). A few years later Joyce complained during a performance of *Die Walküre* that Siegmund's love song in act 1 was in poor taste; he asked his friend Ottocaro Weiss ironically, "Can you imagine this old German hero offering his girl a box of chocolates?" Joyce's occasional impatience with Wagner, however, probably derives more from artistic rivalry than from distaste for the music. During the same conversation with Weiss, Joyce asked, ''Don't you find the musical effects of my *Sirens* better than Wagner's?'' When Weiss replied in the negative, ''Joyce turned on his heel and did not show up for the rest of the opera, as if he could not bear not being preferred'' (*JJ* 460). Inconsistently enough, however, Joyce would use Wagner as bait less than a year later in urging Frank Budgen to visit Trieste: ''Spring here is very pleasant. Opera continues also after Easter. *Sigfrido* with one of the greatest Italian tenors Bassi'' (*L* 1:140). In the 1930s Joyce, Léon-Paul Fargue, and Paul Valéry would gather at Louis Gillet's house in Paris to hear John Sullivan sing music from *Siegfried* and *Tannhäuser*,[79] and in 1935 Joyce hoped his son had enjoyed a performance of *Siegfried* with Lauritz Melchior (*L* 3: 344 – 5). Louis Gillet summarized Joyce's mature operatic tastes as follows:

He could not stand modern music and except for *Die Meistersinger* and some arias from *The Flying Dutchman* he had a dislike for Wagner; the Tetralogy irritated him. ''Operetta music,'' he used to say. On the other hand, he doted upon singing, adoring Rossini, Meyerbeer, Verdi ... He knew how many high-C's there were in all the scores.[80]

Though Joyce preferred *bel canto* opera to any other kind of music and though his highly developed musical tastes would soon exert a restraining influence on the literary side of his Wagnerism, his early interest in Wagner would be sustained by the composer's ubiquity in the opera houses of Europe and in books by Joyce's favorite writers.

The contents of Joyce's library, in fact, provide the best evidence, outside Joyce's own works, of an abiding interest in Wagner. Joyce began acquiring Wagnerian material as early as 1899, shortly before he wrote ''Royal Hibernian Academy 'Ecce Homo' '' and ''Drama and Life''; by 1920 his library included fifteen books by or about Wagner and many others in which Wagner figures importantly. Only Shakespeare occupied more space on Joyce's shelves. In addition to the five individual operas already mentioned, his collection included a book of librettos (now lost), volume 1 of Ellis' translation of the *Prose Works*, the notorious *Judaism in Music*, the widely read *Letters to August Roeckel*,

a two-volume edition of letters to Minna Wagner, and five studies
of Wagner or introductions to his work, including the afore-
mentioned *Perfect Wagnerite* and Nietzsche's *Case of Wagner* and
Nietzsche contra Wagner.[81] There is good evidence that Joyce
worked with several of these books. He probably drew material
for *Exiles* from May Byron's *Day with Richard Wagner*, a book in
a popular series on great writers, artists, and even saints, much
as he would borrow from the same author's *Day with William
Shakespeare*, for *Ulysses*, a short time later. Byron's book evidently
helped provide the setting for act 2 of *Exiles* and almost certainly
inspired Robert Hand's allusion to ''O du, mein holder Abendstern'' shortly after the act begins.[82] Joyce's copy of the *Letters
to Roeckel* shows stray pencil markings, and *The Perfect Wagnerite*,
as we have seen, more purposeful ones. As I argue in chapter 2,
these two books probably contributed to Joyce's understanding
of the relationship between Wotan and Siegfried, especially as
it is articulated in the published notes to *Exiles* (*E* 118–19).
Volume 1 of the *Prose Works*, which contains several of Wagner's
seminal essays of 1849–51, may have been the earliest of Joyce's
acquisitions. Wagner and his operas make seven direct appearances in essays and reviews Joyce had written by 1903, and
Wagnerian concepts, especially as Joyce would have encountered
them in the *Prose Works*, color this early criticism as well: the
rather un-Joycean but highly Wagnerian notions of ''Folk'' and
''Necessity'' (*CW* 42); the use of the expression ''world drama,''
possibly an echo of Wagner's ''universal Drama'' (*PW* 1:126),
to characterize both Munkácsy's painting ''Ecce Homo'' (*CW*
37) and *Lohengrin* (*CW* 45); the idea that all art – painting,
sculpture, or music – aspires to the condition of drama (*CW*
31–7, 38–46), not far conceptually from the exposition, in *The
Art-Work of the Future*, of how all the arts can be made to serve
drama; and the emphasis on drama as a ''communal art'' in
''an artloving and art-producing society'' (*CW* 42). All the major
essays in this volume, *Art and Revolution*, *The Art-Work of the Future*,
and *A Communication to My Friends*, are marked or otherwise
annotated in Joyce's copy. Traces of Joyce's early reading of
these essays linger in *Finnegans Wake*, where Shaun-Jaun is ''the
most purely human being that ever was called man'' (431.11).

The Wagnerian ideal of *das Reinmenschliche* is omnipresent in volume I of the *Prose Works*.[83]

Joyce's knowledge of Wagner extended well into the composer's career and personal life. *Finnegans Wake*, where Joyce's earliest interests often resurface, is littered with Wagner's friends and associates: for example, Wagner's first wife Minna appears, with a hint of *Meistersinger*, in "music minnestirring" (508.22), Cosima in "microbemost cosm" (151.1), Wagnerian conductors Hermann Levi and Hans von Bülow in "Professor Levi-Brullo" (151.11), and Wagner's patron Ludwig II in "ladwigs out of his lugwags" (243.17). Wagner's notorious affection for exotic perfume and rich fabric supports some reflections on women's underclothing: "Sure, what is it on the whole only holes tied together, the merest and transparent washingtones to make Languid Lola's lingery longer? Scenta Clauthes stiffstuffs your hose and heartsies full of temptiness" (434.21–4). This passage juxtaposes Senta, the chaste heroine of *The Flying Dutchman*, and Lola Montez, the Limerick-born mistress of Ludwig I, "limenick's disgrace" (434.21). (The wags of Munich, in recognition of Ludwig II's fascination for Wagner, nicknamed the composer "Lola Montez II."[84]) One of the densest Wagnerian passages in the *Wake* appears in II.1, where, immediately following a Wakean outline of *Ulysses*, a Shemish figure is identified with Wagner as both man and artist:

And ... writing with his quillbone ... a most moraculous jeeremyhead sindbook for all the peoples, under the presidency of the suchess of sceaunonsceau, a hadtobe heldin, thoroughly enjoyed by many so meny on block at Boyrut season and for their account ottorly admired by her husband in sole intimacy ... until he would accoster ... in teto-dous as a wagoner would his mudheeldy wheesindonk at their trist in Parisise after tourments of tosend years. (229.29–230.13)

Here the life and work of Wagner are inextricable. The "heldin" (German for "heroine") whose performance at "Boyrut" is so highly esteemed is probably Isolde; her love for Tristan ("trist in") is described as "tourments of tosend years." "Mudheeldy wheesindonk" is Wakean for "Mathilde Wesendonck," whose entanglement with "Wagoner" in the late 1850s was popularly thought to have inspired *Tristan und Isolde*. Mathilde's husband

Otto (in "ottorly admired by her husband") provided Wagner with financial support during the same period. (As Joyce knew, Wagner's life and work *were* inextricable.) The Wagnerian hush occurs at least four times in the *Wake* – "(Silent)" (14.6); "No applause, please!" (159.19); "(Silents)" (334.31); and "SILENCE" (501.7) – and Joyce's awareness of Wagner's appeal to the Nazis may be reflected in the goosestepping of "Fort! Fort! Bayroyt! March!" (500.24). Such detailed knowledge of Wagner's life and career is characteristic not of the common opera-goer but of a literary Wagnerite in the tradition of Dujardin, Moore, Symons, and the Symbolists. Sylvia Beach spoke with a good deal of justice when she described the Joyce of the 1920s as a "Wagnerian."[85]

The depth of Joyce's knowledge of Wagner is suggested by the ease with which allusions to the composer enter his letters and conversation. To Oscar Schwarz in Trieste he once "quoted the song of Brangäne in *Tristan und Isolde* as a perfect expression of Celtic envy" (*JJ* 382).[86] Some years later he wrote Stanislaus about the English lessons his brother was still giving in Trieste, "Surely to God it is not necessary for you to give barking lessons to fioi-de-cani [songs of dogs] from dawn till gutterdammerung!" (*L* 3:128). He played the wise fool Parsifal in a letter to George Antheil: "Possibly I am meddling in other men's matters ... but sometimes the words of a fool can be twisted into wisdom" (*L* 1:293). To Padraic and Mary Colum Joyce presented his theory that the legend of Tannhäuser was closely related to that of St. Patrick and his flowering staff,[87] and the famous Wakean letter to John Sullivan, published in 1932 as "From a Banned Writer to a Banned Singer," draws on *Die Walküre* and, even more extensively, on *Tannhäuser* (*CW* 258–68). In 1938, after Eugene Jolas had guessed the secret title of *Work in Progress*, Joyce wondered whether Brünnhilde's fate in *Die Walküre* would be appropriate for Jolas: "perhaps I should ask Loki to make a hedge of fire round [Jolas] until I have written the final full stop" (*L* 3:427). (Jolas would then be, as the *Wake* describes HCE, "Valkir lockt" [99.16].) The mythic and commonplace met, apparently, in Joyce's daily life, just as they do in *Ulysses* and *Finnegans Wake*.

The sources of Wagner's power in nineteenth and turn-of-the-

century literary circles were many, and Joyce, especially in the
initial encounters through intermediaries, doubtless felt many of
them. The operas, first of all, offered writers a rich store of
characters and situations on which they could draw for their own
work. The idea of a "total artwork," which Wagner's operas
seemed to embody, inspired attempts by many progressive artists
to mix artistic forms – in particular, attempts to bring the
techniques and expressive power of music to language. Wagner's
use of myth encouraged the widespread borrowing of mythic
material for literature. But most significant, though less tangible,
was the importance attached to Wagner himself. To many,
Wagner was a high priest of art, removed from the gross, material
world, indifferent to critical praise or blame, and uncompromising
in his dedication to art alone. Francis Hueffer spoke for nearly
all the Wagnerites when he wrote that "the principle of *l'art pour
l'art* has never found a more perfect earthly embodiment than it
did in Wagner." [88] The facts of Wagner's career – the years of
poverty, the long exile after his part in the Dresden uprising,
and the harsh treatment in Paris – did nothing to dispel the
image of a supremely principled and cruelly persecuted artist.
The ultimate vindication was Bayreuth, which seemed to make
tangible the Romantic idea of genius and to show that a high
priest of art might renounce the world and still become a cultural
Messiah. [89]

As Wagner's stature grew, he became more and more a can-
didate for adoption. Writing to the composer in 1860, Baudelaire
began a tradition by staking a personal claim on *Tannhäuser*:
"it seemed to me," he wrote, "that the music was *mine*"; and
in his 1861 review the poet associated Wagner's synthesis of arts
with his own theory of "correspondences." [90] Likewise, Wilde's
Dorian Gray saw in the Overture to "that great work of art"
Tannhäuser "a presentation of the tragedy of his own soul." [91]
The difficulty of Wagner's prose style and the relative scarcity
of actual performance before the last decades of the century
enabled Wagnerites to make of him what they would. "Lui,"
they discovered only too readily, "c'est moi." The battle over
the Paris *Tannhäuser*, as we have seen, was more about French
politics than about Wagner's music, and a similar uproar in 1873

over a performance of *Lohengrin* at La Scala was really over the preeminence of rivals Milan and Bologna as opera centers.[92] Dujardin's *Revue wagnérienne*, instituted to promote Wagner and his art, eventually lost its financial backing when it became apparent that its staff was using the guise of Wagnerism to pursue the Symbolist agenda. Yeats and Symons had not hesitated to number Wagner, all too inclusively, among Symbolists. The extreme case of self-interested identification with Wagner was that of the German National Socialists, who made the composer their musical standard bearer in the 1920s.

For many writers Wagner's art expressed a growing disillusionment with positivist social thought, bourgeois liberalism, organized religion, and the common values of the age.[93] Yeats, for example, regarded Symbolism as a reaction against the rationalism and materialism that had characterized the previous two centuries, and Symbolism, according to Yeats, had reached "perfection" in Wagner.[94] Critics of Wagnerism identified and deplored an escapist element in the alienation from ordinary experience and societal values among Wagner's followers. In *Degeneration* Max Nordau attacked the Christology of *Parsifal*, which, he alleged, purported to offer a substitute for genuine religious experience: "Listening to the music of *Parsifal* has become the religious act of all those who wish to receive the Communion in musical form."[95] A sense of the other-worldly in Wagner's music accounts, perhaps, for the frequency with which his admirers spoke of him in religious terms. "Only in Wagner," wrote Symons, "does God speak to men in his own language."[96]

With their religious symbolism and sexual themes, Wagner's operas represented a challenge to public standards of taste and morality, creating a division that only increased the enthusiasm of his admirers. George Moore found Wagner's position in the minds of average citizens analogous to that of Ibsen: "Both were regarded with oblique looks, and few were quite sure that the new music and the new drama were not an immorality, which it was perhaps the duty of the state to stamp out."[97] Many critics found *Parsifal*, the work that Wagner had called a "Bühnen-weihfestspiel," or "Festival of Consecration in a Theatre," blasphemous. In 1882 an Anglican rector, evidently Fricka's champion, called the love scene of *Die Walküre* "the most infamous scene ever put upon any stage in heathen or in Christian times. It consists of a glorification of incest, mingled with adultery, and the betrayal of the commonest rites of hospitality." Indeed, Siegmund and Sieglinde's scene at the end of act 1, when Siegmund seizes his sister "in a frenzy of passion" and vows to propagate the race of Volsungs, earned Wagner considerable notoriety. According to the composer's stage directions, "the curtain falls quickly"; and nineteenth-century audiences, both Shaw and Nordau testify, believed that it did not fall a moment too soon.[98] The same Anglican rector described *Tristan und Isolde* as "a scarcely less horrible glorification of an adulterous connexion."[99] Nordau, whose *Degeneration* constitutes one of the most articulate, if hysterical, Philistine attacks on "decadent" nineteenth-century art, described Wagner's characters as "tom-cats gone mad" and diagnosed Wagner himself as suffering from "erotic madness." Wagner, according to Nordau, is guilty of "a greater abundance of degeneration than all the [other] degenerates put together."[100] In *Legends of the Wagner Drama*, Jessie Weston apparently felt obliged to apologize for the twins of *Die Walküre*, explaining, with exquisite subtlety, that the world of myth, if not Victorian England, accommodated their precipitous behavior quite comfortably.[101]

Certainly the pleasures of exclusivity and romantic alienation stoked the enthusiasm of many early Wagnerites. In the aftermath of the Paris *Tannhäuser*, the sense of detachment from Philistine culture was not difficult to maintain. Judith Gautier, her husband Catulle Mendès, and Villiers helped form the circle around Wagner at Tribschen, the composer's home on Lake Lucerne. "What this wonderful genius meant to us," Gautier wrote, "it would have been difficult to make clear to those who were not of us, at that time when only a little group of disciples stood by the Master upholding him against the jeers of the masses who failed to comprehend him."[102] However, where Wagner's music was better received, it became necessary for the Wagnerites to "protect" him from the common herd and to insist, contrary to the composer's stated intentions, that Wagner was not for everyone.

In England, where a "Wagner Crusade," "Bayreuth Extension Lectures," and "Conversations" about the operas attest to Wagner's increasing popularity in the musical public,[103] the connoisseurs began to insist on a higher standard of appreciation, emphasizing the importance of his artistic and social theories. Wagner's dramas are "operas," according to *The Perfect Wagnerite*, only to the uninitiated, and though the *Ring* has become the current fashion, "It is generally understood ... that there is an inner ring of superior persons to whom the whole work has a most urgent and searching philosophic and social significance."[104] Fortunately, several distinguished critics were available to supply a respectable opposition. J. W. Davison of the *Times* found that, anxious to place his poetry and his music on equal footing, Wagner had undermined the power of both,[105] while Ernest Newman considered the ideas behind the *Ring* childish and Wagner's social theories "outside the pale of serious discussion."[106] Wilde's characterization of Lady Henry in *The Picture of Dorian Gray* predicted the composer's fate in the hands of an admiring public: "Yes ... dear 'Lohengrin.' I like Wagner's music better than anybody's. It is so loud that one can talk the whole time without other people hearing what one says. That is a great advantage: don't you think so, Mr. Gray?"[107] Years before, Baudelaire's essay had defined the same sort of opposition in its counterattack against bourgeois audiences that play cards, gossip, and eat sherbets during intermission.[108]

Perhaps the single unifying factor among the various strains of Wagnerism was the association of the composer's name and "music of the future" with movements for change, artistic and otherwise. Wagnerism became a way of doing cultural battle, and Wagner himself, as Baudelaire had shown when he called Manet the "Painter of the Future,"[109] could be invoked in the name of progressive causes – social, moral, musical – against conservatism and prudery.[110] To the young Joyce who invoked the Meister in his critical writings, this connection to a cultural avant-garde evidently constituted the most important source of Wagner's appeal. In "Drama and Life," for example, Joyce names Wagner and Ibsen (citing *Lohengrin* and *Ghosts*) as new dramatists who are "building for Drama, an ampler and loftier home" (*CW* 40–1).

The evidence provided by the mature writings suggests that Joyce would always associate Wagner with the idea of progress. In *Ulysses* Bloom's thoughts turn now and again to various civic-minded schemes, and in "Circe" his hallucinatory reign as Lord Mayor of Dublin seems to offer him the chance to realize one of them: "better run a tramline, I say, from the cattlemarket to the river. That's the music of the future. That's my programme" (*U* 15.1367–9; 478). Several passages in the *Wake* acknowledge Wagner's progressive harmonies and orchestration. In III.3 the Four Annalists or Masters of Ireland, with their donkey sidekick, are "mastersinging always with that consecutive fifth of theirs" (513.34–5), and among the musicians listed in II.3 are "you wheckfoolthenairyans with all your badchthumpered peanas" (360.8–9). All students of harmony know that parallel fifths are *verboten*, and Wagner's "badchthumpered peanas" contrast nicely with Bach's more traditional and more sonorous "Well-tempered Clavier."[III] The following passage, with its references to *Götterdämmerung* (here the Victorian *Godsgloaming*), *Die Walküre*, and Wotan, is evidently intended to evoke Wagner's crowded orchestra pit: "It is often quite guttergloomering in our duol and gives wankyrious thoughts to the head but the banders of the penta-politan poleetsfurcers bassoons into it on windy woodensdays their wellbooming wolvertones" (565.2–5). Joyce's association of Wagner with Ibsen, first revealed in "Drama and Life," persists in the *Wake*, in "dudder wagoners, pullars off societies" (540.24–5). Joyce's 1901 letter to Ibsen had praised the playwright as an artist who "in your absolute indifference to public canons of art, friends and shibboleths ... walked in the light of your inward heroism" (*L* 1:52). He might well have said the same of Wagner.[112]

A description of the cultural context in which Joyce presented "Drama and Life" helps illuminate his attitude toward Wagner at that time. In 1899 the *Daily Express* of Dublin had run a series of articles in which Yeats, John Eglinton, and others debated the merits of myth as a subject for national drama. In "A Note on National Drama," Yeats writes,

And I have given the example of Ibsen, whose "Peer Gynt" founded on "these subjects," is not only "national literature" ... but the chief glory of "the national literature" of its country, and the example of

Wagner, whose dramas, also founded upon "these subjects," are becoming to Germany what the Greek Tragedies were to Greece.

In his reply, Eglinton takes issue with Yeats and a tradition of literary Wagnerism, arguing that "Wagner's music, or fragments of it, will go down to posterity without the words. His weakness as a dramatist is perhaps proportional to the passionateness of his music." Yeats's rejoinder discusses the influence that Wagner has had upon "the best intellects of our day" (he mentions the Symbolist poets), to which Eglinton responds with a general attack on art "which only interests itself in life and humanity for the sake of art." Finally, an essay by William Larminie takes Eglinton's position on the subject of Wagner: "the most important part of his effort being in music, consummate success in that sphere would prove nothing as regards literature."[113] Joyce's "Drama and Life," delivered at University College soon (in January of 1900) after this public exchange, may be seen as a deliberate posturing in Yeats's favor and a defense, using Wagner as ammunition, of progressive art.[114] Joyce's insistence that "the least part of Wagner" is "his music" (*CW* 40) and his careful use of the term "drama" instead of "opera" identifies him as an aficionado and distances him from the views of Eglinton and Larminie: as Shaw had suggested in *The Perfect Wagnerite*, Wagner's dramas are "operas" only to the uninitiated.[115] Eglinton would be treated with a good deal of irony years later in "Scylla and Charybdis."

Wagner's association with progressive artistic tastes may have held a special appeal for a young writer trying to cut a literary figure and establish an artistic identity in a country where contemporary Continental artists were scarcely known outside intellectual circles and generally regarded with suspicion. Joyce's literary heroes in his late teens and early twenties – Ibsen, D'Annunzio, Hauptmann, Maeterlinck – together formed a cultural avant-garde, and Yeats and others had frequently linked Wagner with these writers. One cannot help but suspect the young Joyce of indulging on occasion in literary name-dropping. His contention at University College that "the least part of Wagner" was "his music" (*CW* 40) could only have set him apart from his audience, since, as we have seen, "old jogalong Dublin" (*D* 78) would have encountered the composer only through excerpts played in concerts. (At this time, maintaining an air of the esoteric was more easily managed by an Irish Wagnerite than an English one.) A sense of Wagner's remoteness from the common man emerges in Joyce's account of the 1907 performance of *Götter-dämmerung* in Rome: "Beside me in the gallery was an elderly man who smelt of garlic ... Every time the horn motive sounded my garlicy friend twisted to me and said confidently: Adesso viene Sigfrido. He yawned much during the third act and went away before the last scene" (*L* 2:214). In a subsequent letter to Stanislaus, Joyce "cannot help wondering what relation music like this can possibly have to the gentlemen I was with in the gallery" (*L* 2:218), and he may have remembered his garlicky friend in describing Bloom's game attempt to appreciate the Meister's uncompromising harmony and orchestration. "Wagnerian music," Joyce's common man observes to Stephen in "Eumaeus," "though confessedly grand in its way, was a bit too heavy ... and hard to follow at the first go-off" (*U* 16.1735 – 7; 661).[116]

Though reluctant to admit it, Joyce, like even the least musical of Wagnerites, was attuned to the sensuality of Wagner's music, especially that of *Tristan und Isolde*. Bernard Shaw, though he would minimize the sexual element in the *Ring*, conceded that "to enjoy Tristan it is only necessary to have had one serious love affair ... The truth is that all the merely romantic love scenes ever turned into music are pallid beside the second act of Tristan."[117] In "The Universal Literary Influence of the Renaissance," Joyce makes his awareness of the sensuality of *Tristan* plain: "A great modern artist wishing to put the sentiment of love to music reproduces ... each pulsation, each trembling, the lightest shivering, the lightest sigh; the harmonies intertwine and oppose each other secretly."[118] Old-fashioned and gentlemanly in company, Joyce would object to Oscar Schwarz in Trieste that Wagner "stinks of sex" (*JJ* 382), but we may be sure that the social – not the literary – Joyce was speaking. In fact, we have Joyce's own testimony that he did for literature what Wagner had done for music:

for though you criticize *Ulysses*, yet the one thing you must admit that I have done is to liberate literature from its age-old shackles ... Previously, writers were interested in externals and, like Pushkin and Tolstoy even, they thought only on one plane; but the modern theme is the subterranean forces, those hidden tides which govern everything and run humanity counter to the apparent flood: those poisonous subtleties which envelop the soul, the ascending fumes of sex."[119]

In 1922, when Joyce took exception to Nora's affection for Wagner, her rejoinder was a knowing "O, there are many obscenities in your book too!"[120]

It is certain, finally, that Joyce empathized with a man whose career paralleled his own so closely. Like Wagner, Joyce set out for Paris in his youth on the slimmest of prospects, in part, at least, to establish himself as an artist; like Wagner, he met indifference and grinding poverty. Both artists would spend much of their lives in exile from their homelands, supported by loyal women whose endurance would be put to the most severe of tests. During his residence in Zurich Joyce must have been aware of the mark Wagner had left on that city during his own exile two generations before. Recognition eluded both artists for many years. In his copy of *A Communication to My Friends*, Joyce found a first-hand account, attractively romanticized, of Wagner's miserable years in Paris from 1839 to 1842, and in letters to the imprisoned August Roeckel, Wagner's unlucky comrade in the 1849 revolt in Dresden, Joyce must have read passages like the following with a good deal of empathy: "With my whole nature, both as man and artist, in absolute opposition to my work and my position, the only hope of deliverance was in a complete severance of my bonds."[121] The sentiments, if not the diction, of a man beginning thirteen years' exile from his native Saxony would be worthy of chapter 5 of *A Portrait*. In May Byron's *Day with Richard Wagner*, Joyce read of the vicissitudes Wagner suffered before his eventual redemption: "many of his greatest works have been composed ... in poverty, discomfort, exile, and obloquy ... By long and stormy ways in the pursuit of an incalculable ideal, he has come to his own at last."[122] This romantic portrait of artistic alienation and eventual recognition describes Joyce's alter ego in *Exiles* perfectly. In act 1 Richard Rowan tells Beatrice Justice, "I lived years in exile and poverty too, or near it" (*E* 23). That Joyce may have identified Richard with Wagner is suggested not only by the allusion to the composer at the beginning of act 2

but also by one of the bits of dialogue, now among his papers at
Cornell, that Joyce wrote while composing *Exiles*. In that fragment
Richard tells Robert, "Sometimes I turn to look at her in our
room ... She is lying on the bed reading some book I have given
her – Wagner's Letters or a novel of Jacobsen."[123] Among
Joyce's books in Trieste, as we have seen, were not only the *Letters
to Roeckel* but, perhaps more appropriately in this context, both
volumes of his letters to the self-sacrificing Minna.

Joyce's Wagnerism, however uncritical in his Dublin youth,
would soon be restrained and conditioned by his pride, iconoclasm, and ironic temperament. As his own artistic powers
developed, he could not remain a disciple like Moore, Symons,
or Dujardin, nor could he accept the influence of a coterie. He
once told Padraic Colum, "I distrust all enthusiasms."[124] In his
youth, as we have seen, Joyce aligned himself with European
artists, including Wagner, who were relatively unknown in Ireland; and when he later lived in European cities where Wagner
was better known and much admired, he was less inclined to admit
an interest in the composer who had become "voguener" (*FW*
577.13). This would explain Sylvia Beach's penetrating comment,
about Paul Valéry and Joyce, respectively: "Strange to say, he
was a Wagnerian and, unlike Joyce, owned up to it."[125] Significantly, nearly all the criticisms Joyce directed at Wagner – the
remarks to Oscar Schwarz and to Nora about the sensuality of
his music, the comment to G. Molyneux Palmer about *Meistersinger*'s "pretentiousness" – were reactions to expressions of
enthusiasm by someone else. (When a companion in Paris praised
Flaubert with what apparently struck Joyce as excessive zeal, the
Irishman pointed out errors in Flaubert's grammar and diction
[*JJ* 492].) As he grew older, Joyce's ironic temperament prevented
absolute devotion to an artist whose approach to myth was as
serious as was Wagner's. It may be, in fact, that Joyce's detachment from his early, uncritical, and predominantly *literary*
Wagnerism began with his experience of the Wagnerian spectacle
on stage. Certainly the Joyce who took special delight in the
moment during the 1907 performance of *Götterdämmerung* when
Brünnhilde's horse, "being unable to sing, evacuated" (*L* 2:
214), and who imagined Siegmund "offering his girl a box of

chocolates'' (*JJ* 460) could not remain under the composer's spell. Joyce's ironic treatment of Wagner here and elsewhere certainly does not argue against the composer's importance to his work; in fact, it puts Wagner in the excellent company of such influences as Homer, Shakespeare, and Swift, who get the same treatment in *Ulysses* and the *Wake*. Joyce's mixture of the mythic and everyday ultimately levels all ranks.

Some critics regard the enigmatic *Exiles* as Joyce's effort to exorcise the *fin-de-siècle* enthusiasms of his youth, and it is tempting to include Wagner among them.[126] After all, Robert Hand's attempt to rationalize his treachery in the trite language of heroic self-expression makes him an easy mark for irony; and it is Robert who, as act 2 opens, self-consciously plays ''O du, mein holder Abendstern'' on the piano, drops Wagner's name in conversation with Richard, and speaks what Richard wearily calls ''the language of my youth'' (*E* 71). Indeed, Joyce's use of the phrase ''Boyrut season'' in the *Wake* (229.34) might support the idea that an attachment to Wagner reflects youthful ardor more than it does intellectual conviction. Joyce's introduction to one of the most fervent of Wagnerites went, according to Stanislaus, as follows:

During this meeting ... Symons told stories of the poets and artists he had known, of Verlaine and Dowson, of Lionel Johnson and Beardsley, and, hearing that my brother was interested in music, he sat down at the piano and played the Good Friday music from *Parsifal*.
—When I play Wagner, he murmured, closing the piano and standing up, I am in another world.[127]

Joyce was reportedly amused by Şymons' gesture, thinking it ''ninetyish'' (*JJ* 112), and he must have thought of Symons when he set the scene for act 2 of *Exiles*. But Joyce's amusement was directed at the disciple in Symons, not at Wagner, and Joyce felt the same irony toward his earlier, more impressionable self. About George Moore's Wagnerian *The Lake*, Joyce wrote Stanislaus in 1906, ''I bought and read *The Lake* ... The *Times* calls it a prose poem. You know the plot. She writes long letters to Father Oliver Gogarty about Wagner and the Ring and Bayreuth (memories of my youth!)'' (*L* 2:154). In a play that shows the mark of as many as five of Wagner's operas, Joyce may be writing off the enthusiasms of his youth, but he is not, in Wagner's case at least, writing off the object of the enthusiasm. In throwing out the bathwater of Wagnerism, decadence, and other excesses represented by Robert Hand, Joyce is careful to preserve Wagner's status as exile and artist-hero, as well as the composer's first name, for Richard Rowan. Joyce would never again be the ninetyish Wagnerite of turn-of-the-century Dublin, but he would remain keenly interested in the sensuality of Wagner's music, in the idea of a synthesis of arts, in Wagner's mythic characters, and in the artist whose career was so like his own.

Once Joyce had rejected the excesses of literary Wagnerism, the German composer took his place – a crucial place – among the artists who influenced this Irish writer and musician. Indeed, as a poet, theorist, and composer, Wagner the "total artist" was positioned to exert a far more pervasive influence than composers like Bellini, Bizet, and Verdi, each of whose work Joyce may have preferred as "opera." Joyce's early disentanglement from this enthusiasm of his university days left him with both the knowledge and the distance he required to bring the Meister productively into his own art. Joyce would draw most heavily on the *Ring, Tristan*, and *The Flying Dutchman*, but as the appendix shows, all Wagner's mature operas appear in his work at some point. Wagner's influence on Joyce, however, was much more than a mere matter of allusion. First, the heroic vitalist Siegfried, a revolutionary artist figure to many nineteenth-century Wagner-ites, contributed to the character and aesthetic principles of Joyce's own artist-hero in both *A Portrait* and *Ulysses*. Second, Wagner's Wandering Jew in *The Flying Dutchman* served as a model not only for Leopold Bloom but for Joyce's portraits of cultural and sexual alienation in *Exiles* and *Finnegans Wake* as well. Third, Wagner's contribution to the nineteenth century's romantic mythology of women helped Joyce portray his notion of *weibliche* redemption in all his work. Fourth, the "comic rhythm" of Wagner's mythic art, especially in the *Ring*, would underlie the mythic structures of both *Ulysses* and the *Wake*.[128] Finally, the Wagnerian synthesis of arts, filtered through Dujardin, Moore, and the Symbolists, helped inspire and form the "endless melody" of Joyce's interior monologue. The following chapters pursue these subjects in turn.

CHAPTER 2

The artist-hero

[Art] lives ... and has ever lived in the individual conscience, as the one, fair, indivisible Art. Thus the only difference is this: with the Greeks it lived in the public conscience, whereas to-day it lives alone in the conscience of private persons, the public *un*-conscience recking nothing of it. Therefore in its flowering time the Grecian Art was *conservative*, because it was a worthy and adequate expression of the public conscience: with us, true Art is *revolutionary*, because its very existence is opposed to the ruling spirit of the community.   Wagner, *Art and Revolution*

Welcome, O life! I go to encounter for the millionth time the reality of experience and to forge in the smithy of my soul the uncreated conscience of my race.
                                          Joyce, *A Portrait*

By the time of the publication of *A Portrait of the Artist as a Young Man*, the novel of the young artist, or *Künstlerroman*, was well established in European literature. As art began more and more to define its own values rather than simply to reflect the values of its culture, to give a subjective impression of life rather than pretend to "objectivity," the artist as a character in fiction and art itself as a literary theme became increasingly important. Whether the artist creates out of an abundance of life experience – whether, that is, he lives more fully than does the common person – or whether he withdraws from life to practice a religion of art, writers from Goethe in *The Sorrows of the Young Werther* and *Wilhelm Meister* and Flaubert in *Sentimental Education* to Dickens in *David Copperfield*, James in "The Lesson of the Master," and Lawrence in *Sons and Lovers* found the artist-adolescent a compelling subject for fiction.[1]

The figure of the artist, however, was not restricted to prose fiction. In fact, he makes several notable appearances in Wagner's operas. *Die Meistersinger*, with its guild of singers, its "sacred German art" (*MS* 125), and its discussions of musical principles, is certainly the most self-conscious of Wagner's works. But Hans Sachs and the artist-apprentice Walther von Stolzing are preceded in Wagner's canon by the Minnesinger Tannhäuser, and the vocal competition in Nuremberg is anticipated by the Wartburg's Tournament of Song. *Lohengrin*, according to *A Communication to My Friends*, depicts the tragedy of the modern artist, unable to express himself in the language of feeling (*PW* 1:344). Wagner's admirers and critics, identifying these artist-heroes with Wagner's own artistic heroism, found the composer himself in the operas. To D'Annunzio, for example, the Flying Dutchman was the young Wagner, wandering in search of artistic recognition; to recovered Wagnerite Nietzsche, the outcast Grail knight of *Parsifal* was Wagner the illusionist, "this old magician, mightiest of Klingsors."[2]

Among Wagner's artist-heroes certainly the most resonant in late nineteenth-century culture, perhaps contrary to Wagner's intentions, was Siegfried.[3] Admittedly, when, in *Siegfried* 2.2, the naive hero of the *Ring* attempts to fashion a reed pipe and imitate the voice of the Woodbird, he makes a poor performer compared to Tannhäuser or Walther; and Siegfried is clearly not the same figure of romantic alienation that Wagner's audiences had come to know in the Dutchman, Tannhäuser, and Lohengrin. But his exuberant forging of his sword, which represents the advent of a new humanistic era, and his destruction of Wotan's spear, which portends the extinction of the authoritarian gods, appealed to the imaginations of many artist-revolutionaries in Wagner's audience.[4] Early in the composition of the *Ring*, Wagner wrote to August Roeckel, "I have sought in Siegfried to represent my ideal of the perfect human being, whose highest consciousness manifests itself in the acknowledgment that all consciousness must find expression in present life and action."[5] To the extent that he is an artist, therefore, the hero of the *Ring* creates out of a surfeit of life energy and a heightened sense of self, out of his "heroic vitality."[6]

The idea that Siegfried served Joyce as a prototype for Stephen Dedalus has been widely acknowledged, but the implications of the parallel and its cultural importance have not been fully explored.[7] Both *A Portrait* and *Ulysses* draw upon a tradition that was firmly established by the early years of the twentieth century. In identifying Stephen with Siegfried and in linking him with this culturally defined artistic heroism, Joyce was not only asserting the heroic nature of the artist. He was also invoking Wagner's theories of art as they came to him directly from Wagner as well as through many intermediary sources. The penultimate entry in the journal at the end of *A Portrait* constitutes a declaration of Stephen's intentions as an artist: "Welcome, O life! I go to encounter for the millionth time the reality of experience and to forge in the smithy of my soul the uncreated conscience of my race" (252 – 3). In this passage the metaphors of forge and smithy and the bold spirit of confrontation are appropriate to Siegfried, while the theory of art that Stephen's resolution embodies – the embracing of idealized "life" as the material of art, the emphasis on the artist's individual "soul," the notion of a "public cons-cience," and the communal function of art – is, as we shall see, thoroughly Wagnerian.

The association between Siegfried and the artist-hero begins in Nietzsche's *Birth of Tragedy*, written when *Siegfried* and *Götter-dämmerung* were still unperformed. Wagner and *Tristan* were to the young Nietzsche what Beethoven and the Ninth Symphony had been to Wagner. Nietzsche had first met the composer in 1868, when he was an impressionable twenty-four, and he dedicated his 1872 study of Greek tragedy to Wagner, his "sublime protagonist" in the progress of art, "the highest task and the properly meta-physical activity of this life." Nietzsche thought he saw in Wagner's work a successful fusion of Dionysian music and Apollonian mythic drama heretofore unique to the Greek stage. He predicted that the reborn music drama would revitalize German culture:

Let no one believe that the German spirit has for ever lost its mythical home when it still understands so obviously the voices of the birds which tell of that home. Some day it will find itself awake in all the morning freshness of a deep sleep: then it will slay the dragons, destroy the

malignant dwarfs, and waken Brünnhilde – and Wotan's spear itself
will be unable to obstruct its course!

This passage, in which Wagner himself embodies this invigorated
spirit, provides a catalogue of Siegfried's heroic achievements
following *Siegfried* 2.2, where the young hero, having tasted the
blood of the slain dragon, comes to understand the Woodbird's
song. At another point, *The Birth of Tragedy* links Wagner's hero
with culture-heroes Kant and Schopenhauer, whose philosophy
offers a healthful pessimism and tragic wisdom:

Let us imagine a rising generation with this undauntedness of vision,
with this heroic desire for the prodigious, let us imagine the bold step
of these dragon-slayers, the proud and daring spirit with which they
turn their backs on all the effeminate doctrines of optimism in order
"to live resolutely" in the Whole and in the Full.[8]

Though Nietzsche later felt that what he had heard in Wagner
had more to do with his own younger self than with Wagner, and
though he came to regret whatever accreditation his youthful
enthusiasm had given Wagner's ascendancy, he would never
shake himself completely free of the composer's influence.

As a *Künstlerroman* D'Annunzio's 1900 *Il fuoco* was an excellent
source for *A Portrait*. Unlike Joyce's hero, however, and, indeed,
the heroes of most novels about young artists, the poet Stelio
Effrena is well known and securely established. His artistic
development consists in his eventual acceptance of Wagner and
Bayreuth as models for his own attempt to touch the soul of his
people and create a truly national art. The novel's time span,
from September of 1882 to February of the next year, coincides
exactly with the period of Wagner's actual residence in Venice
until shortly after his death on February 13. Indeed, Wagner and
his deteriorating health maintain an insistent presence in the
novel's Venetian setting. Early in the book Stelio and his artistic
friends take note of Wagner's recent arrival; later they assist the
unconscious composer from a gondola after a cardiac episode;
and eventually they receive Cosima's permission to serve as
pall-bearers in the journey to the railway station, which occupies
the last chapter. Stelio, we realize, having overcome his doubts
about the significance of "the barbaric creator" and his aesthetics

for Italian art, is to take up the Wagnerian mantle. The centrality of Wagner to *Il fuoco* is sealed by the book's last page, which D'Annunzio has dated "February 13, 1900." During the course of the book, Stelio and his entourage discuss Bayreuth and the fashionable idea of *Gesamtkunstwerk* and compare Wagner's work to that of the great Italian composers. *Lohengrin* and *Tristan* make brief appearances, and there are extended discussions, with quotations, of *Parsifal, The Flying Dutchman*, and the *Ring*. In one passage Stelio superimposes Kundry, "a wandering, implacable temptress," on to his lover "La Foscarina," a tragic actress modeled after D'Annunzio's own lover Eleonora Duse; at another point, Wagner himself, victim of age and exile, is the Flying Dutchman.[9]

D'Annunzio borrows Siegfried for his artist-hero at many points. For example, La Foscarina, conscious of her role as the young poet's inspiration, feels "drawn into [his] atmosphere, as fiery as the glow surrounding a lighted forge." Elsewhere the poet is a swordsman and "the word of the poet" is "comparable to the deed of a hero." Finally, at a point roughly analogous to the scene in chapter 4 of *A Portrait* that confirms Stephen's artistic calling, Stelio discovers Siegfried's heroic vitality in the aged, enervated Wagner. Then he absorbs it himself:

And suddenly the image of the barbaric creator seemed to Stelio to approach him; the lines of his face became visible, the blue eyes gleamed under the wide brow, the lips closed tight above the powerful chin, armed with sensuousness, pride, and disdain. The slight body, bent with the weight of age and glory, straightened itself, appeared almost as gigantic as his work, took on the aspect of a god. The blood coursed like a swift mountain torrent, its breath sighed like a forest breeze. Suddenly the youth of Siegfried filled the figure and permeated it, radiant as the dawn shining through a cloud. "To follow the impulse of my heart, to obey my instinct, to listen to the voice of Nature within myself – that is my supreme law!" The heroic, resounding words, springing from the depths, expressed the young and healthy will that had triumphed over all obstacles and all evil, always in accord with the law of the Universe ...

Ah, what heights and what depths had he not touched, that formidable Master of human souls! What effort could ever equal his? What eagle could ever hope to soar higher? His gigantic work was there, finished, amidst men ...

The young man saw his pathway blazed before him by victory –
the long art, the short life. "Forward, still forward! Higher, ever
higher!"[10]

"To live, to err, to fall, to triumph, to recreate life out of life!"
cries the Daedalian artist in chapter 4 of *A Portrait*. "On and on
and on and on!" (172).

In Shaw's influential *Perfect Wagnerite*, Wagner is as much a
political figure and social theorist as an artist and musician.
The *Ring*, according to Shaw, was the result of the "political
convulsion" of 1849 in which Wagner took part when he was
Dresden's Kapellmeister. After the revolt was suppressed,
Wagner was forced into his long exile, and two of his associates,
August Roeckel and the anarchist Michael Bakunin, were dealt
long prison terms. *The Perfect Wagnerite* quotes the *Letters to
Roeckel* freely, and Shaw writes that if Bakunin was Siegfried's
prototype, then Nietzsche's "overman" was his descendant.
In this book Siegfried, like Wagner himself, is as much a political
figure as an artist. Shaw identifies him with a spirit of vitality,
Protestantism, free-thinking, and anarchy – in general, with
assertion of self and resistance to authority. The young hero's
independence of spirit is nowhere more apparent than in his
penetration of the magic circle of fire that, for Shaw, represents
hellfire and, therefore, religious intimidation. Siegfried's artistic
nature is evident in Shaw's account of *Siegfried* 1.3, where, in
melting down the fragments of his father's sword and forging
it anew, the young hero "sets to at the bellows with the shouting
exultation of the anarchist who destroys only to clear the ground
for creation."[11]

Siegfried and Wagner's aesthetic theories also appear in the
writings of Yeats and other Irishmen, who, as we saw in chapter
1, were inspired by Wagnerian myth and Bayreuth in their efforts
to rejuvenate Irish culture and heighten Irish national consciousness. Herbert Howarth has shown, in fact, that the Irish sought
a counterpart to Siegfried in Celtic myth and found him in
Cuchulain.[12] It was appropriate, therefore, that, in "Poetry and
Tradition," Yeats should invoke Wagner's hero in a retrospective
discussion of the aims of the Irish literary revival:

A new belief seemed coming that could be so simple and demonstrable, and above all so mixed into the common scenery of the world, that it would set the whole man on fire and liberate him from a thousand obediences and complexities. We were to forge in Ireland a new sword on our old traditional anvil for that great battle that must in the end re-establish the old, confident, joyous world.

Here and elsewhere in these early essays,[13] Yeats's use of the image of the sword and his evocation of the Germanic *Götter-dämmerung* testify to the power of an apocalyptic vision among Irish nationalists who anticipated a "dusk of the nations" that would set Ireland free.[14]

The messianic strain among Irish writers was evident in Edward Martyn and George Moore, who, like many Wagnerites before them, represented their artistic ambitions with the help of Siegfried. Early in his autobiographical *Hail and Farewell*, Moore writes that Martyn "believes himself to be the Messiah – he who will give Ireland literature and her political freedom." When, later in the book, Martyn comes to Moore's door and whistles the Siegfried motive from the *Ring* (it is printed in the text), Moore responds, "Come in, Siegfried, though you were off the key." That Moore imagined himself in Siegfried's role as artist-revolutionary is borne out by a grandiose passage that evokes the memorable sounding of the sword motive, the prophecy of Siegfried's coming, at the end of *Das Rheingold*:

to heighten my inspiration I looked toward the old apple-tree, remembering that many had striven to draw forth the sword that Wotan had struck into the tree about which Hunding had built his hut. Parnell, like Sigmund, had drawn it forth, but Wotan had allowed Hunding to strike him with his spear. And the allegory becoming clearer I asked myself if I were Siegfried, son of Sigmund slain by Hunding, and if it were my fate to reforge the sword that lay broken in halves in Mimi's cave.

It seemed to me that the garden filled with tremendous music, out of which came a phrase glittering like a sword suddenly drawn from its sheath and raised defiantly to the sun.

[15]

In "Scylla and Charybdis" Stephen listens quietly as George Russell, Eglinton, and Mr. Best discuss the same general subject: "Our national epic has yet to be written, Dr Sigerson says. Moore is the man for it" (*U* 9.309–10; 192).

By the end of the nineteenth century, then, Siegfried had achieved wide currency as a certain kind of artist: a "Wagnerian" artist of heroic vitality who shatters the authoritarian traditions of art and society. This artist is a hero not only because he creates art, but also because, as a cultural messiah, he "redeems" his nation's art and, in some cases, its people. This idea of the artist was of special importance in Ireland, where the Irish writer came to be regarded as a "forerunner," like John the Baptist, or as an evangelist who, in a Sacred Book, would prophesy the nation's liberation. Indeed, the Irish writer often wondered whether the revolution might be accomplished through art alone – whether, in fact, as Moore's case implies, the spirits of Parnell and Siegfried might be incarnated in a single artist-hero.[16] "Faithful to the oldest instincts of his race," wrote D'Annunzio in *Il fuoco*, "Richard Wagner had foreseen, and had fostered by his own efforts, the aspiration of the German States to the heroic grandeur of the Empire ... Like the hero, the poet had accomplished an act of deliverance."[17] With the example of Bayreuth before them, it was only logical that these Wagnerites, Irish and otherwise, should appropriate Wagner's liberating hero to represent their artistic ideals and, in so doing, to acknowledge the extent to which Wagner had shaped their own ideas about art.

That Joyce was well acquainted with the *Ring* and with Siegfried in particular is beyond question. As we have seen, he almost certainly saw all four operas performed, and, as his comments about the Roman performance of *Götterdämmerung* suggest, he knew the music well (*L* 2:214). Furthermore, Joyce's library before 1920 included many books, published before or during the composition of *A Portrait*, about Siegfried and his place in nineteenth-century culture: among Wagner's works, the collection of librettos, the separate librettos for *Siegfried* and *Götterdämmerung*, volume 1 of the *Prose Works*, and the *Letters to Roeckel*; among intermediary sources, the essays of Yeats and the books by Nietzsche, Shaw, D'Annunzio, and Moore discussed earlier in this chapter. Two of these require special comment. *Il fuoco*, which Joyce in his University College days held in such high regard,[18] may have provided the idea for the Siegfried parallel in the first place. *The Perfect Wagnerite* certainly contributed to Joyce's understanding of the *Ring*, as a passage in the published notes to *Exiles* reveals (118–19, discussed below), and references in Shaw's book may have encouraged Joyce's acquisition of the *Letters to Roeckel*, which includes what is perhaps Wagner's best-known discussion of the *Ring*, and Bakunin's *God and the State*.[19] This group of books would have constituted for Joyce a kind of aesthetic association, since they all draw on or evoke Wagner, his operas, and his theories of art. They provided a rich source of material to which Joyce could refer and upon which he could reflect as he wrote *A Portrait* and *Ulysses*.[20]

The image of the artist-smith and his forge appears three times in *A Portrait*, all of them late in the book, as Stephen's destiny is revealed to him and to us. In a passage that might have come straight out of *Il fuoco*, Stephen finds in a vision of "the fabulous artificer" "a prophecy of the end he had been born to serve and had been following through the mists of childhood and boyhood, a symbol of the artist forging anew in his workshop ... a new soaring impalpable imperishable being" (169). The notion that Stephen was "born to serve" a particular "end" recalls Wotan's plan to breed a race of heroes that will deliver him from Alberich's curse. Early in chapter 5 Stephen thinks of himself as "striving to forge out an esthetic philosophy" (180), and the famous reference in the novel's conclusion (quoted above) to forging "in the smithy of my soul" invokes Siegfried's bold vitality: "Welcome, O life!" (252–3). Joyce, we are told, borrowed the image of the forge in discussing his work privately: "In *Ulysses*," he once told Arthur Power, "I have tried to forge literature out of my own experience, and not out of a conceived idea, or a temporary emotion."[21] In *A Portrait*, the many references to swords and spears, to the "art in lighting a fire" (185), and to the heroic "encounter" support the Wagnerian parallel.[22]

A direct allusion to the *Ring*, possibly inspired by the printing of leitmotifs in Moore's *Hail and Farewell*, appears in chapter 5, as Stephen and Cranly cross the University College quadrangle:

"The birdcall from *Siegfried* whistled softly followed them from the steps of the porch" (237). In act 2.2 the young hero is lounging under a tree when he hears the Woodbird's pentatonic tune and attempts, in artistic fashion, to imitate it on a crude reed pipe. His piping wakes the dragon Fafner, whom Siegfried promptly challenges and joyfully kills with his newly forged sword in his first heroic act. During the battle Siegfried inadvertently smears his hand with the dragon's hot blood, and when he licks his fingers, he suddenly understands the bird. (That is, a soprano voice adds text to the melody.) The bird warns Siegfried of his foster-parent Mime's plans to kill him and points the way to further exploits by informing him of Brünnhilde's captivity and of the powers of the ring and *Tarnhelm*.[23] In chapter 5 of *A Portrait*, Stephen is in Siegfried's position when he cannot yet understand the bird, the position of an apprentice hero who has slain no dragons and pierced no rings of fire but of whom a good deal is expected; and because Stephen is not prepared for the heroic "calling" that the birdcall represents, Dixon whistles rather than sings (with words) the motive. Wagner's Woodbird is one of many birds in *A Portrait*, the Holy Spirit foremost, that evoke the ideal realm in which the artist's "vocation" is determined. One example is the girl of chapter 4, the "envoy from the fair courts of life" who "seemed like one whom magic had changed into the likeness of a strange and beautiful seabird" (171–2), another the flock of birds in chapter 5 that might be "an augury of good or evil" (224). The appearance of the Woodbird's motive may also hint at treachery by one or more of Stephen's companions.[24]

A pattern of Wagnerian references that is oblique in *A Portrait* – to the ashplant Stephen picks up in chapter 5 – becomes more explicit in *Ulysses*. In *Die Walküre* Wotan has provided a sword for Siegmund – *Nothung* – by thrusting or "planting" it with such force into the ash tree around which Hunding's hut is built that only Siegmund will be able to draw it from the trunk. After Wotan takes Hunding's part against Siegmund and the sword shatters on Wotan's spear, Siegfried will be obliged to reforge it. Joyce may have had a Wakean pun in mind when he linked Stephen's walking stick with the "ashplanted" sword of the Volsungs. In *A Portrait* the ashplant, appropriately, does not appear till Stephen has put aside a career as a priest and accepted one as an artist, and Joyce does not make much of it when Stephen carries it in chapter 5. It is almost as if he were simply anticipating its more explicit and extensive use in *Ulysses*, where it appears more than two dozen times.[25] In "Proteus" Stephen refers to the ashplant as his "augur's rod of ash" (3.410–11; 48). He calls it a "sword" on two occasions (9.296, 9.947; 192, 210) and, more explicitly, his "ash sword" (3.16; 37) on another. For Stephen, as for Siegfried, the ashplant symbolizes both masculine creative power and independence from authority. *Ulysses* charts Stephen's gradual erection of the ashplant, from his "trailing" it (1.627; 20), "resting" it (3.284; 44), and "dallying" with it (3.489; 50); to his "swaying" (10.348; 228) and "flourishing" it (15.73, 15.99; 431, 432); and finally to his assault on Bella Cohen's light fixture in "Circe" when he shouts the Wagnerian name – "*Nothung!*"[26] In this climactic scene Stephen is asserting his independence from the hallucinatory image of his mother and all the weight of authority that she represents: "No! No! No! Break my spirit, all of you, if you can! I'll bring you all to heel!" Even his manner of brandishing the ashplant imitates Siegfried's destruction of Mime's anvil in the memorable forging scene of *Siegfried*: "He lifts his ashplant high with both hands and smashes the chandelier" (15.4235–44; 582–3).

If, in *A Portrait*, the Siegfried parallel emphasizes artistic promise and helps define Stephen's heroic aspirations, in *Ulysses* it emphasizes disillusionment and measures his inadequacy. *A Portrait* leaves Stephen apparently on the threshold of artistic distinction; *Ulysses* finds him mired once again in Dublin. Appropriately, Joyce's allusions to the *Ring* in *Ulysses* reflect the darker events of the cycle – drawing more on the brooding *Götterdämmerung* than on the relatively cheerful *Siegfried*[27] – and emphasize Stephen's distance from the ideal that Siegfried represents. In "Circe" Stephen abandons his ashplant as soon as he has used it, and Bloom has to carry it for him until he can get along on his own; the chandelier that Stephen appeared to have "smashed" turns out, upon Bloom's inspection, to have sustained only a broken chimney, "not sixpenceworth of damage" (15.4290–1; 584).

The passage in "Circe" in which the prostitute Zoe reads
Stephen's palm is densely Wagnerian. At the beginning of the
reading, Stephen "extends his hand to her smiling and chants
to the air of the bloodoath in *The Dusk of the Gods*." The German
text that follows matches exactly the meter of Wagner's music
in *Götterdämmerung* 1.2, where Siegfried and Gunther swear
oaths of blood brotherhood:

> Hangende Hunger,
> Fragende Frau,
> Macht uns alle kaputt. (15.3651–3; 560)[28]

The allusion is a dark one, for Hagen will eventually accuse
Siegfried of betraying Gunther, stab him in the back, and report
that Siegfried has been killed by a wild boar.[29] In this scene, Zoe,
ironically, is linked to the sympathetic Sieglinde, for "fragende
Frau" is Siegmund's name for his solicitous sister in *Die Walküre*
1.2 (*R* 84).[30] When Zoe finds "courage" in Stephen's palm, she
prompts a remark from Lynch: "Sheet lightning courage. The
youth who could not shiver and shake" (15.3660; 561). In *Siegfried*
much is made of the naive hero's ignorance of fear. When the
Wanderer advises Mime that he will forfeit his head to a hero
who does not know fear, the dwarf brings Siegfried to Fafner in
a useless attempt to make the boy fearful. In "Circe" Lynch must
be speaking sarcastically, since Stephen is afraid of dogs, thunder,
and even water. In fact, he broods on his timidity throughout the
book, comparing himself unfavorably with Mulligan: "You saved
men from drowning. I'm not a hero, however" (1.62; 4); "He
saved men from drowning and you shake at a cur's yelping"
(3.317–18; 45). In the same discussion with Lynch and Stephen,
Zoe claims that she can identify Stephen's character by something
she sees in his eye. Her speech recalls not only the accusation of
idling Father Dolan directs at Stephen in *A Portrait*, but also the
fact that the Volsungs – including Siegfried and his parents –
can be identified by the image of a snake or dragon in their
eyes.[31] As treacherous friends, Lynch (who in "Circe" will
desert Stephen) and Buck Mulligan (who in *Ulysses* as a whole
has violated the spirit of his brotherhood with Stephen) are in the
position of the feckless Gunther and the evil Hagen.

The parallel between Stephen and Siegfried is supported by other references in *Ulysses*. Among the dignitaries witnessing Robert Emmet's execution in 1803, according to "Cyclops," was the Wakean coincidence of contraries "Kriegfried Ueberall-gemein" (12.569; 307). Later in "Cyclops" the Citizen drinks to "the undoing of his foes, a race of mighty valorous heroes" (12.1212–13; 325). This speech, given the recent play on Siegfried's name, recalls Wotan's plan to breed, in Shaw's words, "a race of heroes [that is, the Volsungs] to deliver the world and himself from his limited powers and disgraceful bargains."[32] Wagner's giants Fafner and Fasolt, as Joyce admitted to Frank Budgen,[33] contributed to the passage in "Proteus" that describes the "sands and stones" of Sandymount Strand:

And these, the stoneheaps of dead builders ... Hide gold there ... I'm the bloody well gigant rolls all them bloody well boulders, bones for my steppingstones. Feefawfum. I zmellz de bloodz odz an Iridzman. (3.289–93; 44–5)

Thus the reference to the "horde of jerkined dwarfs" (3.304–5; 45) that appears two paragraphs later evokes, almost inevitably, the giants' subterranean counterparts, the Nibelungs. Finally, as we shall see in chapter 5, "Sirens" develops a pattern of references to *Das Rheingold* that links Bloom to the sexually frustrated Alberich and the Misses Douce and Kennedy to the Rhinedaughters of the *Ring*. These allusions aside, however, the general effect of the Siegfried parallel in *Ulysses* is opposite to that of *A Portrait*. In the earlier work Siegfried represents the ideal toward which Stephen is striving; in *Ulysses* Siegfried helps measure the distance between Stephen's aspirations and his accomplishments to date. The comparison inflates him in *A Portrait* and deflates him in *Ulysses*.

In addition to the many allusions to the *Ring* in *A Portrait* and *Ulysses*, there are important thematic parallels. The idea of betrayal, invoked by the references to the bloodoath in "Circe," is important not only in Stephen's personal sphere but also in relation to Parnell's betrayal by the Irish people. Tim Healy was to Parnell what Lynch and Mulligan are to Stephen. Both Stephen and Siegfried are members of a chosen but sternly tested race. *Ulysses*, especially in "Aeolus," compares the English subjugation of the Irish to the Egyptian bondage of the Jews, in both cases according to the apparent will of God. Wotan's severe treatment of his chosen Volsungs is reflected in the first question he asks Mime in the riddling episode of *Siegfried* 1.2: "What is the name of the race that Wotan treated harshly and yet holds most dear in his heart?" (*R* 174). Siegfried and Stephen are literal or figurative orphans, fretting over their parentage and over the mystery of parentage in general.[34] Finally, personal freedom is of crucial thematic importance to both Joyce and Wagner. *A Portrait* and *Ulysses* are the story of Stephen's attempt to free himself from the demands of God, country, and family in order to follow his artistic destiny; Siegfried's freedom from his divine progenitor is essential to his ordained purpose – the dissolution of Alberich's curse. The redemption of the world, the *Ring* insists, depends upon a man free from the influence of divine authority.

In providing Siegfried as a parallel for Stephen, Joyce was not only asserting the heroic nature of the artist; he was also invoking Wagner's theories on such issues as the relation between art and culture, the ideal of artistic freedom, the process of creation, and the function of art. Much of the theory of art implied in Joyce's early work is consistent with Wagner's own ideas, especially as articulated in the writings that Joyce encountered in his volume of the *Prose Works* and as interpreted by the many intermediaries discussed earlier in this chapter. Much of Stephen's aesthetic vocabulary, in fact, almost certainly derives from Wagner.

Wagner believed that, ideally, a work of art is the expression of its culture and the artist a spokesman for communal values. Because, however, it had lost touch with the "purely human" in nature and in "Life," modern industrial society, he felt, was inimical to true art:

If we consider the relation of modern art – so far as it is truly *Art* – to public life, we shall recognise at once its complete inability to affect this public life in the sense of its own noblest endeavour. The reason hereof is, that our modern art is a mere product of Culture and has not sprung from Life itself. (*PW* 1:182)

he true artist worked, by necessity, in isolation. *The Birth of* *gedy*, written when the composer's influence on Nietzsche was at its peak, echoes Wagner's sentiments about modern art and culture: "Never has there been another art-period in which so-called culture and true art have been so estranged and opposed, as is so obviously the case at present."[35] That Stephen Dedalus saw modern Irish culture in the same light in which Wagner saw modern culture generally is borne out by both *A Portrait* and *Ulysses*. In *A Portrait* Stephen feels he must leave Ireland altogether if he is to become an artist, and in "Telemachus" he borrows Wilde to describe Irish art as the "cracked lookingglass of a servant" (1.146; 6).

The drama of the Greeks, for Wagner and his followers, was the antithesis of modern art and the "Standard" for the "Art-Work of the Future."[36] Greek art seemed to represent a pinnacle of human creativity because it combined several art forms, because it was based on mythic subjects, and, most important, because it expressed the values and ideals of an entire community.[37] "Before what phenomenon," Wagner asks in *The Art-Work of the Future*, "do we stand with more humiliating sense of the impotence of our frivolous culture, than before the art of the *Hellenes*?" (*PW* 1:89). Nietzsche anticipated not only a rebirth of Greek tragedy, but even "a new form of existence" based on "Hellenic analogies."[38] The widespread admiration of Greek culture in the nineteenth century is reflected in Wilde's "The Soul of Man under Socialism," which calls for a "new Hellenism." Significantly, Mulligan's response to Stephen's indictment of Irish culture in "Telemachus" is "God, Kinch, if you and I could only work together we might do something for the island. Hellenise it" (1.157–8; 7). We might dismiss Mulligan's idea as mere talk, did Homer, Aristotle, and Daedalus not figure so importantly in *Ulysses*.

Though Wagner believed that modern society exercised a debilitating influence on the artist, he did allow for the creation of "true" art by a "richly-gifted individual" – an artist-hero – who could resist cultural pressure – as Siegfried had resisted Wotan – and, in effect, actualize *himself* in his art. *Art and Revolution*, an essay among those Joyce owned, claims, "Yet Art remains in its essence what it ever was; we have only to say, that it is not present in our modern public system. It lives, however, and has ever lived in the individual conscience, as the one, fair, indivisible Art" (*PW* 1:51). Wagner describes the process by which Beethoven had composed his Ninth Symphony:

it was *by no means a mutual cooperation between art-hood and publicity* ... but *simply a richly-gifted individual*, who took up into his solitary self the spirit of community that was absent from our public life ... [and] from the fulness of his being ... evolved within himself this spirit of community which his artist soul had been the first to yearn for. (*PW* 1:127)

Of particular importance here is the integrity of the artist or, as both Wagner and Joyce would have it, of that of his "soul." Even after his split with Wagner, Nietzsche had to admit that he admired the composer "wherever he sets *himself* to music," [39] and Wilde described Wagner as "Christlike ... when he realised his soul in music." [40] In *A Portrait* Stephen, creating in the Wagnerian "smithy of my soul" (253), certainly regards himself as one of these richly gifted individuals. The spirit that comes to him during the night before the villanelle's composition is announced by Gabriel, a seraph from "the fair courts of life" (*P* 172). In the creative intercourse between idealized Life – not, apparently, that of turn-of-the-century Dublin – and the imagination, the artist's purity is preserved: "In the virgin womb of the imagination the word was made flesh" (*P* 217).

For Wagner, as for Joyce, artistic freedom was achieved only through active resistance to political and cultural forces that inhibit the artist's individuality and prevent his self-actualization in art. True art, according to *Art and Revolution*, "is highest freedom, and only the highest freedom can bring her forth ... [N]o commandment, no ordinance ... no aim apart from Art, can call her to arise" (*PW* 1:35 – 6). Christianity in particular was inimical to art because it cut man off from his real nature and taught him to forgo life's pleasures, which for Wagner were essential to artistic creativity: "The Art of Christian Europe could never proclaim itself, like that of ancient Greece, as the expression of a world attuned to harmony; for reason that its inmost being was incurably and irreconcilably split up between the force of conscience and the instinct of life" (*PW* 1:39). [41] It is crucial to the argument of the *Ring* that Siegfried, unimpressed by divinity, represents a higher ethical status than Wotan and his generation of gods.[42] In attempting to mend the sword that Wotan once provided for Siegmund, Siegfried is successful only when he melts down the fragments (instead of trying to weld them together) and forges the sword *anew*, thus severing, symbolically, the link to Wotan – God and the State in one – that proved to be Siegmund's downfall. Wagner's notion of artistic freedom must have been especially attractive to Joyce, for Stephen's ambition in *A Portrait* is to "to express myself in some mode of life or art as freely as I can and as wholly as I can" (247). Resistance to authority, in fact, pervades *A Portrait* and *Ulysses*. Stephen tells his patriotic friend Davin, "When the soul of a man is born in this country there are nets flung at it to hold it back from flight. You talk to me of nationality, language, religion. I shall try to fly by those nets" (*P* 203). In *Ulysses* Stephen, tapping his forehead, emphasizes the psychological side of his rebellion: "But in here it is I must kill the priest and the king" (15.4436–7; 589). Joyce would have found Wagner's brand of artistic freedom reflected in *The Birth of Tragedy, The Perfect Wagnerite*, "The Soul of Man under Socialism," and Yeats's "Poetry and Tradition," among other sources.

The assertion of artistic freedom, however, does not imply a rejection of the cultural role of art. In fact, the artist's mission is to regenerate his culture by expressing his heightened sense of life and freedom in his work, so that art can become an expression of its culture, as it was for the Greeks:

[Art] lives, however, and has ever lived in the individual conscience, as the one, fair, indivisible Art. Thus the only difference is this: with the Greeks it lived in the public conscience, whereas to-day it lives alone in the conscience of private persons, the public *un*-conscience recking nothing of it. Therefore in its flowering time the Grecian Art was *conservative*, because it was a worthy and adequate expression of the public conscience: with us, true Art is *revolutionary*, because its very existence is opposed to the ruling spirit of the community. (*PW* 1:51–2)

Ellis' Victorian translation of *Bewusstsein* ("consciousness" in the contemporary sense) as "conscience" here and elsewhere in the prose writings, the very notion of a "public conscience," and Wagner's idea that art ought to nurture it constitute an important source for the conclusion of *A Portrait*, when Stephen resolves "to forge in the smithy of my soul the uncreated conscience of my race" (253). In Joyce's copy of the *Prose Works*, volume 1, this crucial passage from *Art and Revolution* is clearly marked in pencil.[43]

Joyce's idea of a public or collective "conscience" dates from at least as early as 1912, when he wrote Nora from Dublin, "The *Abbey Theatre* will be open and they will give plays of Yeats and Synge. You have a right to be there because you are my bride: and I am one of the writers of this generation who are perhaps creating at last a conscience in the soul of this wretched race" (*L* 2:311). The word appears many times in *A Portrait*. Interestingly, in the first three chapters "conscience" is always used in the more common sense, in relation to sin and guilt; in chapter 5, as Stephen's artistic ambitions become established, it is more collective and ethical – more like "consciousness" – than individual and religious, as in the following example: "How could he hit their conscience or how cast his shadow over the imaginations of their daughters ... that they might breed a race less ignoble than their own?" (*P* 238). The concept of "race" here and in the conclusion to *A Portrait* and the idea of breeding a new kind of race echo the *Ring* as well. In *Il fuoco*, one of Joyce's most important intermediary sources for the composer's aesthetic theories, a long section on Wagner interprets the role of the artist-hero as follows:

There was, then, in the multitude a secret beauty, in which *only the poet and the hero* could kindle a spark. Whenever that beauty revealed itself by the sudden outburst from a theater, a public square, or an entrenchment, a torrent of joy must swell the heart of him who had known how to inspire it by his verse, his harangue, *or a signal from his sword*. Thus, the word of the poet, when communicated to the people, was *an act comparable to the deed of a hero* – an act that brought to birth in *the great composite soul of the multitude* a sudden comprehension of beauty, as a master sculptor, from the mere touch of his plastic thumb upon a mass of clay, creates a divine statue.[44] (my emphasis)

The Wagnerian artist-hero, passing through the writings of Nietzsche, Shaw, D'Annunzio, Yeats, and Moore to Joyce, was complete: he was a cultural messiah.

Siegfried and Stephen differ in at least one important respect. Shaw describes Wagner's hero "as a type of the healthy man raised to perfect confidence in his own impulses by an intense and joyous vitality which is above fear, sickliness of conscience, malice, and the makeshifts and moral crutches of law and order which accompany them."[45] The notion of "manly health," which Wagner claimed was essential to the artist's creativity, is certainly remote from Joyce's artist-hero. In direct contrast to Siegfried, Stephen, as "Circe" makes clear, is fearful, brooding, and plagued by "agenbite of inwit"; he is more, in fact, like the gloomy Siegmund, who in *Die Walküre* is insufficiently "free" to carry out Wotan's plan for the redemption of the world. Indeed, Stephen's artistic impotence in *Ulysses* may stem partly from his failure to "live" according to the standard he established, with the help of a D'Annunzian Siegfried, in *A Portrait*: "On and on and on and on he strode, far out over the sands, singing wildly to the sea, crying to greet the advent of the life that had cried to him" (172). Stephen's sullen temperament in *Ulysses* and his rejection of the life around him may be as much a cause of his artistic torpor as an effect of it.

The identification of Siegfried with the Joycean artist is reinforced by a passage in the published notes for *Exiles*, which compares Wagner's hero to Richard Rowan:

If Robert really prepares the way for Richard's advance and hopes for it while he tries at the same time secretly to combat this advance by destroying at a blow Richard's confidence in himself the position is like that of Wotan who in willing the birth and growth of Siegfried longs for his own destruction. Every step advanced by humanity through Richard is a step backwards by the type which Robert stands for. (*E* 118–19)

This understanding of the relationship between Wotan and Siegfried may derive from Joyce's direct experience of the *Ring* or from interpretations in the *Letters to Roeckel* and *The Perfect Wagnerite*. In a much-quoted letter of 1854, Wagner tells Roeckel that in act 3 of *Siegfried*, "Wotan rises to the tragic height of *willing* his own destruction. This is the lesson that we have to learn from the history of mankind: *to will what necessity imposes*, and ourselves to bring it about."[46] In writing of Robert's attempt to "destroy at a blow Richard's confidence in himself," Joyce is almost certainly thinking of *Siegfried* 3.2, when Wotan, as the Wanderer, encounters the supremely confident young hero, and, though recognizing the necessity of Siegfried's advance and his own decline, attempts nonetheless to defeat him in combat. As Shaw puts Wotan's equivocal position in a passage Joyce encountered in *The Perfect Wagnerite*, "Now it is an excellent thing to triumph in the victory of the new order and the passing away of the old; but if you happen to be part of the old order yourself, you must none the less fight for your life."[47]

In *Exiles* the Siegfried – Wotan parallel operates more in sociological than in artistic terms. In his superficially chivalrous relationships with other people, Robert – Wotan is of an old, "backwards" order. One of his main functions in the play is to encourage Richard to acknowledge the dictates of authority and repudiate his unseemly past so that he can acquire a university position. Richard – Siegfried seeks unconventional relationships that are honest to the point of brutality, and he would destroy the "type" that Robert represents. Robert underscores the parallel between Richard and Siegfried and emphasizes his own Wotan-like admiration for his adversary when he says, "You do not know what moral fear is" (*E* 68). The presence of the theme of betrayal in both *Exiles* and the *Ring* reinforces the connection between Richard and Siegfried: Robert plays Gunther's part in his attempt, successful or not, to seduce Bertha, a violation of the "brotherhood" (69) in which Richard and Robert were once united.[48]

The value of the parallel between Stephen Dedalus and Siegfried is that it helps us see more clearly what sort of artist-hero Stephen aspires to be. The artist is a hero not only because he forges his art in defiance of cultural impediments like "Prince, Pope, and People," to borrow Wilde's formulation,[49] but also because he is potentially able, as Nietzsche, Shaw, D'Annunzio, Moore, Yeats, and Wagner himself believed, to redeem his nation's culture and people. The parallel suggests therefore that the artistic ideals of the young Joyce, at least, were closer to those of the Irish literary revival than he would ever, in his iconoclastic way, acknowledge publicly, though he did admit the kinship to

Nora (*L* 2:311, quoted above). As Joyce grew older, however, unmixed heroes like Siegfried began to interest him less, while more passive and equivocal ones – Tristan, Parsifal, and the Flying Dutchman, among Wagner's – began to interest him more. In *A Portrait* itself, Joyce is careful to distance himself from the "young man" whom he has identified with Siegfried; *Ulysses* retreats from the Wagnerian spirit of heroic encounter and abandons the aesthetic vocabulary of "forging," "conscience," and "race" altogether. Indeed, "Circe" makes Bloom more of a messiah than it does Stephen. Having tried on Siegfried's role, Joyce eventually found it unsuitable when he realized that the German "myther rector" (*FW* 126.10) and critic of contemporary culture could not remain an ideal for a novelist who would so thoroughly commit himself, in *Ulysses* and *Finnegans Wake*, to the modern world. In the *Wake*, where Joyce wrote less self-consciously about art and the artist, his distance from Siegfried and his earlier artistic self increases. In this book, where "all rogues lean to rhyme" (96.3), the artist is a "low sham" (170.25) and a forger not like Siegfried but like Macpherson, who uttered "an epical forged cheque on the public for his own private profit" (181.16–17).[50] Elsewhere in the *Wake* he practices legerdemain, carrying "nothung up my sleeve" (295.18). Though the *Ring* generally was an important source for the *Wake*, as we shall see in chapter 5, Siegfried, evoked in a handful of allusions, quietly joins the myriad gods, heroes, and historical figures who constitute HCE's powerful sons. As a youth, however, Joyce saw himself quite seriously in the role that the literary Wagnerites had sketched out for Siegfried and for themselves, a fact that George Russell might have perceived: for after his first encounter with Joyce, AE wrote to Lady Gregory that Yeats, like Wotan, "had succeeded in evoking the first of a new race and [again like Wotan] might live to regret it."[51]

CHAPTER 3

The Wandering Jew

Frisch weht der Wind
der Heimat zu:
mein irisch Kind,
wo weilest du?

Wagner, *Tristan und Isolde*

Joyce's creative imagination remained in Ireland long after he left in 1904, and the problem of exile, of separation from home and family, was never absent from his writing. In Joyce's earlier works, particularly *A Portrait* and *Exiles*, separation is the result of artistic alienation and a necessary condition of artistic independence. We know that Stephen will defend his integrity with "silence, exile, and cunning" and that Richard Rowan will head for the Continent in his wake. In "Scylla and Charybdis" we learn that Shakespeare's major tragedies were written in absence from Stratford and in estrangement from his wife. Indeed, the case of Shakespeare illustrates the way in which the Joycean theme of exile begins to focus less exclusively on artistic alienation and to include a more general idea of separation – marital, social, political. "Proteus," for example, devotes considerable attention not only to Stephen's recent sojourn in Paris but also to the political exile of the contemporary wild goose Kevin Egan: "They have forgotten Kevin Egan, not he them. Remembering thee, O Sion" (*U* 3.263–4; 44). Two figures in particular helped Joyce represent the cost of separation and the pain of estrangement: the wandering sailor – D. B. Murphy in "Eumaeus," Odysseus throughout *Ulysses*, the Norwegian Captain in the *Wake*, to cite just a few examples – and the Wandering Jew. Both are embodied in Joyce's most celebrated character, Leopold Bloom.

54

In seeking literary precedents for his exiles and outcasts, however, Joyce was not compelled to search as far back as the *Odyssey* or medieval legends of the Wandering Jew. In Wagner's canon he discovered a rich variety of characters that presents the problem of exile in its full complexity: Tannhäuser, twice exiled from the Wartburg and its circle of Minnesingers; Wotan, appearing as the "Wanderer" in *Siegfried*; Parsifal, searching for the Holy Grail; Kundry, representing a female version of the Wandering Jew; and Tristan, fleeing Cornwall after his disloyalty to Mark is discovered. Certainly the opening lines of *Tristan und Isolde*, in which the young sailor laments his separation from his Irish sweetheart, must have made a strong impression on the Irish expatriate. Reflecting on the title of his only published play, Joyce wrote, "Exiles – also because at the end either Robert or Richard must go into exile ... Robert will go. But her thoughts will they follow him into exile as those of her sister-in-love Isolde follow Tristan?" (*E* 123). None of Wagner's exiles, however, spoke so eloquently to Joyce as did the figure Wagner had called his "Wandering Jew of the Ocean," the Flying Dutchman.[1]

Wagner wrote *The Flying Dutchman* during his own exile around 1840 in Paris. In 1839 he and Minna had fled their many creditors in the Baltic city of Riga, where Wagner had held a conductor's post, and sailed for Paris, "the centre of the world," the composer believed in his youthful idealism, "where the arts of every nation stream together to one focus; where the artists of each race find recognition" (*PW* 7:47). When violent storms drove their boat off course, the Wagners took refuge in the Norwegian fjords, where, we learn in *A Communication to My Friends*, Wagner's plight seemed to resemble that of the legendary Dutchman, whose story he already knew well. In Paris, Wagner's career foundered. He and Minna would spend two and a half destitute years, subsisting only through the kindness of friends and the hack work Wagner was able to get as a writer and arranger of music. Wagnerian tradition has it that the composer was at one point jailed as a debtor.[2] Among the highly autobiographical works, in addition to the *Dutchman*, written during the deep alienation and frustration of these years was a transparent story of a consumptive musician, ominously titled "An End in Paris." In *A Communication* Wagner writes retrospectively,

To the handful of true friends ... who gathered cheerily around me of an evening in the triste retirement of my home, I had herewith passed the word that I had completely broken with every wish and every expectation of success in Paris, and that the young man who had come there with such wishes and expectations in his head was virtually dead and buried. (*PW* 1:304)

The Dutchman legend tells of a phantom ship and its blasphemous captain, condemned to wander the seas until Judgment Day. Among the several versions of the legend that he knew, Wagner followed Heinrich Heine's in *Aus den Memoiren des Herren von Schnabelewopski*, which included a sentimental and thoroughly romantic twist to the original tale: every seven years, the captain is permitted a brief respite ashore; if he can find a woman who will commit herself to him forever, his curse will be revoked. The foolish devil, Heine wrote, had no faith in women.[3] In the nineteenth century the Dutchman legend was commonly regarded as a nautical version of the tale of Ahasuerus, the Wandering Jew, who treated Christ rudely on the day of the Crucifixion.[4] In *A Communication* Wagner puts his "Ahasuerus of the seas" (*PW* 1:17) in a context that must have been especially attractive to the eventual author of *Ulysses*:

The figure of the "Flying Dutchman" is a mythical creation of the Folk: a primal trait of human nature speaks out from it with heart-enthralling force. This trait ... is the longing after rest from amid the storms of life. In the blithe world of Greece we meet with it in the wanderings of Ulysses and his longing after home, house, hearth and – wife ... The Christian, without a home on earth, embodied this trait in the figure of the "Wandering Jew": for that wanderer ... there bloomed no earthly ransom; death was the sole remaining goal of all his strivings ... Here [in the Dutchman legend] we light upon a remarkable mixture, a blend ... of the character of Ulysses with that of the Wandering Jew. (*PW* 1:307–8)[5]

Implicit in the Dutchman's longing for "home" and *weibliche* redemption is the desire for the artistic recognition that escaped Wagner during his first sojourn in Paris. For Wagner, artistic and sexual fulfillment were closely linked. Writing of Liszt's generosity during these miserable years, Wagner reiterates his sense of himself as Flying Dutchman and Wandering Jew: "Whilst

I was banned to wandering afar, the great world-wanderer had cast his anchor on a little spot of earth, to turn it into Home for me'' (*PW* 1:388).

In comparing himself to the Wandering Jew and his nautical cousin, Wagner was expressing a Romantic notion of the artist as ''cursed'' with superior sensitivity and ''exiled'' by his refusal to conform to artistic and moral standards. ''[T]he artist and ... the genius,'' wrote Nietzsche in connection with the *Dutchman*; ''these are of course the 'eternal Jews.' ''[6] On one occasion during his long political exile in Switzerland, Wagner wrote to August Roeckel, ''I am very lonely; I miss sympathetic surroundings, and more than ever I am painfully conscious that what in me is exceptional and peculiar acts like a curse, separating me from my kind, and cutting me off from the ordinary enjoyment of life.''[7] Wagner's admirers characterized the Meister in the same way. In an early review, Shaw discusses Wagner's refusal to compromise in his battles with musical and theatrical conservatism: ''He fought with the wild beasts all his life ... he had an air of having his life in his hand ... and of wandering in search of his right place and his own people, if any such there might be.''[8] And in Joyce's beloved *Il fuoco*, D'Annunzio cribs from *A Communication to My Friends* and from Senta's Ballad in act 2 as he develops an extended comparison between Wagner and the Dutchman:

Again his imagination conjured up the figure of Richard Wagner in youth; he saw once more the lonely one wandering in the living horror of Paris, poor yet undaunted, devoured by the fever of genius, his eyes fixed on his star, and his mind resolved to force the world to recognize it. In the myth of the shadowy captain, the exiled one had seen the image of his own breathless race, his furious struggle, his supreme hope. ''But some day the pale hero may be delivered, should he meet on earth a woman that will be faithful to him until death.''[9]

It is not surprising that Wagner saw other artists, especially those whose work he admired, as Dutchmen in their own right. According to *The Art-Work of the Future*, Beethoven, as a composer of orchestral music, had ''explored the broad and seeming shoreless sea of absolute Music unto its very bounds.'' This ''sea-weary mariner,'' dissatisfied with music alone and ''suffering beneath

the weight of longing of his artist soul,'' ''sought for a surer
haven wherein to anchor from the blissful storms of passionate
tumult.'' Beethoven, the passage concludes, achieved his redemption with the union of poetry and music in the Ninth Symphony, a ''universal Drama'' (*PW* 1:115 – 26). As we have seen,
the artistically and socially successful Liszt had found his ''little
spot of earth'' and broken, in effect, the Dutchman's curse.
Wagner's ancient mariner, it appears, was widely attached not
only to Wagner himself but to the more general figure of the
alienated artist as well.[10] In the Romantic period the Dutchman
was no longer the protagonist in a cautionary tale of sin and
punishment; he was a figure of sympathy.[11]

Wagner's comparison of the Flying Dutchman to the Wandering Jew and his use of both these figures to depict the artist are
especially ironic in light of his well-known anti-Semitism. In 1850,
motivated by frustration and professional jealousy, Wagner
published the infamous *Judaism* (sometimes *Jewry*) *in Music*, in
which he avers that ''the Jews have never had an Art of their
own'' and attacks the work of several Jewish contemporaries.
He argues that because ''without friends or sympathy the Jew
stands alone in the midst of a Society which he does not understand,'' he cannot participate in the communal spirit upon which,
according to theories here and elsewhere in Wagner's writings,
the creation of ''true'' art depends. The case of Mendelssohn,
Wagner writes, illustrates his point by the principle of *a fortiori*:

> By him we have been shown that a Jew may be gifted with the ripest
> specific talent, he may have acquired the finest and most varied educa-
> tion, he may possess the highest and most finely-tempered sense of
> honour – and yet … he may remain unable … to bring forth that deep
> effect upon our hearts and souls which we expect from Art… whenever
> a hero of our craft has designed … to open his mouth to speak to us.[12]

Wagner's anti-Semitism may have reached its peak – or nadir –
when he declared near the end of his life that the ascription of
Jewish blood to Christ was ''one of the most terrible derangements
of world history.''[13] The irony is that the very qualities as an
outcast that handicap the Jewish artist in *Judaism in Music* are
those that help identify the Dutchman and the Wandering Jew
as artist figures in *The Flying Dutchman* and *A Communication to*

My Friends. Wagner was perfectly capable of making an invidious distinction between the idea of the artist as Jew, to which he was attracted, and the actual Jewish artist, whom he maligned.[14]

Joyce encountered the *Dutchman* at many turns. As we have seen, it was one of the two Wagnerian operas produced in Ireland before Joyce's departure in 1904, and as a devoted opera-goer Joyce almost certainly saw this popular work frequently on the Continent. According to Louis Gillet, in fact, some of Joyce's favorite Wagnerian music was in the *Dutchman*.[15] Joyce would have found details of the opera in his copy of the libretto and in *Il fuoco*, and discussions of its sources and plot were available in Wolfgang Golther's *Richard Wagner as Poet* and John Runcimann's *Wagner*, both of which found their way into his Trieste library.[16] A substantial introduction in Joyce's libretto establishes the connection between the Dutchman and the Wandering Jew, identifies Heine's *Memoiren des Herren von Schnabelewopski* as Wagner's most immediate source, and quotes extensively from *A Communication to My Friends* and from Heine.[17] Joyce's library also included *Judaism in Music* and Eugène Sue's *Le Juif errant*. *A Communication*, part of the volume of Wagner's *Prose Works* that Joyce owned and annotated, may have been the Irish writer's most important source of information about the opera. Here he would have read of Wagner's identification of the Dutchman with the Wandering Jew, of the relationship of both figures to Odysseus, and of the circumstances surrounding the opera's composition, which would have invited his empathy.[18]

Like Wagner, Joyce made his own youthful attempt on Paris in a fruitless effort to establish himself as an artist. Joyce, too, would spend a good deal of his life in "exile" from his native land, much of it disappointingly unsuccessful. Joyce would not only have felt these biographical affinities; he would also have been attracted to the Wagnerian themes: the idea of a curse following a sin of blasphemy; "exile," geographic, artistic, and sexual; *weibliche* redemption; the transfiguring power of death. In two early essays on James Clarence Mangan, Joyce linked his Irish predecessor with the archetype of the Wandering Jew:

Mangan has been a stranger in his native land, a rare and bizarre figure in the streets, where he is seen going sadly and alone, like one who does penance for some ancient sin. Surely life... is a heavy penance for Mangan... an inheritance so much the more sorrowful, too, because of the delicate artist in him who reads so well the lines of brutality and of weakness in the faces of men that look at him with hate and scorn. (*CW* 180)[19]

In general, *The Flying Dutchman* became increasingly useful to Joyce as his career progressed. In the earlier works, there are many parallel motifs and themes, if few direct references. However, as Joyce recognized the significance of the *Dutchman* for his own work, he began to bring it into *Ulysses* and *Finnegans Wake*. Wagner's Wandering Jew helped Joyce express not only his romantic notion of the sensitive artist, cursed and set apart, but more important, especially as his career developed, his perception of the ordinary modern man, wandering through "the incertitude of the void" (*U* 17.1014–15; 697).

Among the stories in *Dubliners*, the *Dutchman* made several contributions to "Eveline," which offers the first of many Joycean pairings of sailors and home-bound women. In this case the story is told from the woman's point of view, as in the Spinning Song of act 2. Eveline's lover is a sailor and world traveler who promises to save her from the suffocating role of housemaid, cook, mother, and daughter. Her pensive demeanor as she gazes out the window and awaits her appointment with Frank recalls Senta's position in act 2, shortly before the Dutchman appears. The photograph of the mysterious priest hanging in Eveline's house asserts the same gloomy presence as does the portrait of the legendary Dutchman under which Senta broods in her own house. In several ways, however, Joyce may be deliberately playing against his Wagnerian source. In the opera Senta redeems the Dutchman, not the reverse, as would be the case here. Frank, who sings of "the lass that loves a sailor" (*D* 39), is less the baleful Dutchman than he is the Steersman of act 1, a conventional lover who sings a ballad and promises his sweetheart a wedding band. Eveline's ambivalence about forsaking her home and domestic responsibilities contrasts sharply with Senta's instinctive devotion to a man whom she has never met. The opera's conclusion works in perfect counterpoint to that of the story. Against the pleading of her spurned lover Erik, who warns her that she is giving herself to destruction, Senta follows the Dutchman to his ship, and seals her vow of fidelity by throwing herself into the sea. Eveline, on the other hand, reneges on her commitment to Frank at the very point of departure because she fears the destruction that Senta has courted: "All the seas of the world tumbled about her heart. He was drawing her into them: he would drown her" (*D* 41). "Eveline" is the story of one woman's inability to be Senta – that is, to make a huge leap of faith and commit herself to a doubtful man and an uncertain future. (This was a commitment that Nora Barnacle made with little apparent hesitation.) If Joyce was thinking of the parallel provided by *The Flying Dutchman*, he was using it as a contrast, to emphasize the paralysis in Eveline and in Irish life generally.

Wandering and exile are important themes in *A Portrait*, and, as in the *Dutchman*, they are closely connected with the idea of the artist. In chapter 4 we learn that Stephen's "destiny was to be elusive of social or religious orders ... He was destined to learn his own wisdom apart from others or to learn the wisdom of others himself wandering among the snares of the world" (*P* 162). (The isolation of the Wandering Jew endows him, according to tradition, with special insight and knowledge.[20]) In *A Portrait* one of Stephen's three artistic tools is "exile" (247), and his restlessness is strongest in chapter 4, when he discovers his artistic calling:

There was a lust of wandering in his feet that burned to set out for the ends of the earth. On! On! his heart seemed to cry. Evening would deepen above the sea, night fall upon the plains, dawn glimmer before the wanderer and show him strange fields and hills and faces. Where? (170)

As in the Dutchman legend, "wandering" has moral implications in *A Portrait*. In chapter 2 a dissolute Stephen wanders "into a maze of narrow and dirty streets" (100), and he imagines his state of sin in nautical terms: "He had known neither the pleasure of companionship with others nor the vigour of rude male health ... and he was drifting amid life like the barren shell of the moon" (96).

Wagner's Dutchman has formed an idealized vision of the angelic woman who will lift his curse. Senta, in their first encounter, represents for him the embodiment of that vision: "wie ich's geträumt seit langen Ewigkeiten, / vor meinen Augen seh' ich's hier" (*FD* 67).[21] Stephen, inspired by Romantic fiction, has created a similar ideal: "The vastness and strangeness of the life suggested to him ... sent him wandering in the evening from garden to garden in search of Mercedes" (*P* 66). From this adolescent vision of perfection, Joyce's artist-hero seeks his own sort of redemption:

> He wanted to meet in the real world the unsubstantial image which his soul so constantly beheld ... They would be alone, surrounded by darkness and silence: and in that moment of supreme tenderness he would be transfigured. He would fade into something impalpable under her eyes and then in a moment, he would be transfigured. (65)

There is an important distinction, however, between the isolation of Stephen Dedalus and that of the Flying Dutchman. Stephen relishes the role of outcast, because he regards it, romantically, as essential to his artistic integrity. He acknowledges on one occasion "the joy of his loneliness" (68) and on another "the pride of his spirit which had always made him conceive himself as a being apart in every order" (161). On the other hand, exile is imposed on Wagner's hero, and he passes his existence trying to find a place instead of trying to leave one. In *A Portrait* we are dealing with Stephen before he has left for Paris and returned, with the artist-hero who has not yet been disillusioned.

As its title suggests, Joyce's only published play has much in common with *The Flying Dutchman*. Indeed, the *Dutchman* becomes steadily more important in Joyce's work as exile and its implications assumed wider significance to Joyce. The protagonist of Joyce's play has been an exile geographically, socially, and artistically, and his return to Ireland as the curtain opens has a structural parallel in the expiration, as the opera begins, of the Dutchman's seven-year term. Bertha and Senta are closely linked, for, like Nora Barnacle (and, in 1839, Minna Wagner), Bertha was willing to abandon her home life and commit herself to a man of uncertain prospects: "I gave you myself – all. I gave up all for you'' (*E* III). Richard emphasizes the connection between Senta and Bertha when he admits, ''You were my bride in exile'' (III).[22] Indeed, it is in the nature of Richard and Bertha's relationship that the *Dutchman* parallel is most significant. Senta and the Dutchman are true soul-mates whose bond is instantaneous, almost metaphysical. Their attachment stands in sharp contrast to the bourgeois ideal of love typified by the choruses of sailors and spinsters, who sing of wealth, marriage, and domestic security. The counterpoint between a metaphysical bond based on empathy and bourgeois love following the rituals of courtship provides the *Dutchman* with much of its thematic energy. Richard and Bertha, whose unconventional union impedes Richard's professional development and financial well-being, are exiles in their detachment from Irish culture and values as well as in their actual absence from Ireland. Indeed, it is Bertha's ultimate commitment, despite occasional wavering, to Richard's societal values that seals her association with Senta. As in the *Dutchman*, the artist-outcast of *Exiles* is drawn to a woman who is at first more closely aligned to society and its values than he is. In taking him on his own terms and embracing his way of life, she grants him a victory over society and affirms his artistic nature.[23]

Bertha's Erik is Robert Hand, who attempted to prevent Richard and Bertha's elopement nine years before (Erik makes a parallel attempt in act 3) and who, however adulterously, speaks Erik's conventional language of romantic love – telling Bertha, for example, that she is a ''wild flower blowing in a hedge.'' Bertha counters Robert's trite lovemaking by telling him that she believes ''men speak like that to all women whom they like or admire,'' and she affirms her bond with Richard by reminding Robert that Richard is ''different,'' in this respect and others, from other men (*E* 32–3). Joyce's notes for the play consider what Bertha might have been like as ''Mrs. Robert Hand (because he intended to do it decently) ordering carpets in Grafton Street'' (*E* 116). The following exchange between Robert and Bertha in act 1 draws the *Dutchman* directly into *Exiles*:

ROBERT, *sighs*: My life is finished – over.
BERTHA: O, don't speak like that now, Robert.
ROBERT: Over, over. I want to end it and have done with it.

BERTHA, *concerned but lightly:* You silly fellow!
ROBERT, *presses her to him:* To end it all – death. To fall from a great
    high cliff, down, right down into the sea.
BERTHA: Please, Robert ...
ROBERT: Listening to music and in the arms of the woman I love –
    the sea, music and death. (35)[24]

In this variation on the opera's conclusion, Robert creates a literal
melodrama of love and death and tries, as Erik does, to blackmail
the object of his love with his own unhappiness. His posturing
suggests that he is thinking more of the conclusion to an opera
(perhaps the *Dutchman* itself) than of real life: tellingly, he is both
"listening to" his melodrama and performing in it. But Robert's
fancy talk is lost on the sensible and unselfconscious Bertha, who
has committed herself to the drama's real Dutchman and shared
the privations of his exile. Throughout the opera the desire for
woman and the longing for death are equivalent to the Dutchman,
since both represent the release of his curse, and with this maudlin
death-wish, Robert is putting himself in the Dutchman's place.
We would expect, however, that, as an artist figure and exile,
the Dutchman would be linked more consistently to Richard.
It seems that, in self-consciously evoking the *Dutchman* and in
attempting to seduce Bertha, Robert is trying to supplant the
man whom he envies in so many ways.

    In *Ulysses* the Dutchman appears in many guises, all of which
show Joyce's facility with details of the opera in elaborating his
own work. In "Proteus" Stephen encounters a cocklepicker and
imagines Death approaching her, administering the proverbial
kiss: "He comes, pale vampire, through storm his eyes, his bat
sails bloodying the sea, mouth to her mouth's kiss" (3.397–8;
48). Stephen will eventually revise these musings and arrange
them in the quatrain that appears in "Aeolus." Stephen's poem
is by now well known as an adaptation of a stanza from the Irish
"My Grief on the Sea." Robert Martin Adams has characterized
Stephen's addition to Douglas Hyde's translation as "a bit of
somber tempestry, and the demonology implied in the words 'pale
vampire.' "[25] In fact, as a hint from Stuart Gilbert would
suggest,[26] in both the proto-poem and the quatrain, the raw
material provided by "My Grief on the Sea" is spliced with

elements of the Dutchman legend, particularly as Joyce encountered it in Wagner's opera. Gilbert may have learned of the connection through Joyce's collaboration in *James Joyce's* Ulysses, or he may simply have drawn his own inference from the nautical description of this figure of Death. Gilbert was probably unaware, however, of the extent to which the departures from Hyde's version – nearly all the changes, in fact, that seem to be "originally" Stephen's – can be traced to Wagner's libretto. Striking corroboration of this contention is available in *Scribbledehobble*, Joyce's first notebook for *Finnegans Wake*. The entry of the words "Flying Dutchman" on the "Proteus" page of *Scribbledehobble* indicates not only that Joyce used the legend in "Proteus" but also that he planned to use it in the *Wake*.[27]

The key stanza from Hyde's "My Grief on the Sea," itself (like the *Odyssey* and the *Dutchman*) a version of the wandering sailor and home-bound woman motif, is as follows:

> And my love came behind me –
> He came from the South;
> His breast to my bosom,
> His mouth to my mouth.[28]

The "somber tempestry" and "demonology" in "Proteus" are evident in three changes and additions: the portrait of the lover as a "pale vampire," reinforced by the "bat sails"; the reference to a "storm"; and the description of the sails "bloodying the sea." In nearly all discussions about the opera and in the opera itself, the Dutchman's ship is described as having "blood-red sails and black masts" (*FD* 51, 60). Here the image of the "bat sails bloodying the sea" not only draws upon the Dutchman legend but also evokes the "winedark sea" of Homer and thus establishes the important connection between the Dutchman and Odysseus, a connection that, as we have seen, Wagner develops in *A Communication to My Friends*. Furthermore, Wagner's opera begins in the wake of a violent storm, after which the Dutchman meets Senta, whom the woman in this passage from *Ulysses* parallels. Finally, the opera continually emphasizes the Dutchman's "pale" or "spectral" appearance; the phrase "bleicher Mann" ("pale man") is almost formulaic. Though the opera does not characterize the Dutchman as a vampire, Joyce's use of him as the harbinger (or perhaps the agent) of the cocklepicker's death is appropriate, since he does bring about Senta's death. Wagner's *Dutchman*, however, is supposed to have been partially inspired by a production of Heinrich August Marschner's 1827 opera *Der Vampyr*, in which Wagner participated in 1833 and 1834.[29]

"Aeolus" presents a revision of Stephen's earlier musings in stanzaic form:

> On swift sail flaming
> From storm and south
> He comes, pale vampire,
> Mouth to my mouth. (7.522 – 5; 132)

This poem retains the "pale vampire" and "storm" motifs, with the Dutchman's blood-red sails now "flaming." The synecdoche implied in "swift sail" may have been inspired by the notorious speed of the Dutchman's ship, mentioned at the end of act 1 (*FD* 56). In the quatrain, with the restoration of Hyde's point of view in "mouth to my mouth," another parallel between Senta and the cocklepicker emerges. Senta has never met the Dutchman, but her morbid fascination with him and with his fate, indicated by her preoccupation with the portrait in act 2, alarms her circle of acquaintance (Erik in particular), which recognizes Senta's *idée fixe* for what it is. The speaker of Stephen's quatrain reveals the same preoccupation with death.

Nearly all the added details in the proto-poem and the quatrain can be found in Senta's Ballad, the "thematic germ," according to Wagner, of the opera's music (*PW* 1:370). The Ballad is heard near the beginning of act 2 and rehearses, for the audience, the legend of the Flying Dutchman:

Behold the ship with blood-red sail
unfurled against her blackened mast.
There stands her master, gaunt and pale,
who knows how long his watch must last? ...
Hui! Like an arrow he flies, without rest, without aim, without hope!
One chance remains to gain this poor man his peace and salvation,
only a woman true unto death can bring him redemption! (*FD* 60)

According to the legend, the Dutchman is condemned to eternal mortal life. In pledging a love that releases this curse, therefore, Senta is committing herself at once to both love and death. The *Liebestod* theme that emerges in Stephen's revision of "My Grief on the Sea" is the crux of *The Flying Dutchman*.

Two other notable songs in the opera probably contributed to Joyce's modification of Hyde's poem. First, the Steerman's Song, which appears at the beginning and end of act I, depicts the same situation that "My Grief on the Sea" depicts, though the point of view is the sailor's rather than the home-bound woman's:

> In the teeth of the storm across the seas –
> my darling, I am near!
> Over towering waves the Southern breeze –
> my darling, brought me here!
> My darling, when the wind is North,
> how lonely we both must be:
> O gentle South wind, blow once more!
> My darling is calling me. (*FD* 51)

The "tempestry" and repeated emphasis on the south wind in this song may have led directly to Joyce's conjunction of "storm and south" in the quatrain. Finally, the Spinning Song, sung by the "Chorus of Girls" at the beginning of act 2, acts as a counterpart to the Steerman's Song and repeats several of its elements: the mention of an absent lover on "southern" seas, the invocation of the wind as a means of uniting the couple (*FD* 58).[30]

The Dutchman also appears as D. B. Murphy, the sailor of "Eumaeus" whose ship, the *Rosevean*, Stephen spotted at the end of "Proteus." Murphy drinks "good old Hollands" gin (16.376–7; 623) and boasts of having "doubled the cape a few odd times" (16.902; 637). (The Dutchman, according to Senta's Ballad, acquired his curse trying to do exactly the same.) Like the many mariners who appear in *Ulysses*, Murphy has long been "exiled" from the love of woman. In "Eumaeus" he tells Stephen of his home in Carrigaloe: "My little woman's down there. She's waiting for me, I know... She's my own true wife I haven't seen for many years now, sailing about. Mr Bloom could easily picture his advent on this scene ... Across the world for a wife"

(16.419–24; 624). Here Murphy is midway between the Dutchman and his nautical cousin Odysseus: the prior existence of a wife from whom he has been absent for many years parallels the *Odyssey*, and, as Senta's Ballad tells us, the seven-year period matches the Dutchman's term at sea before he can come ashore to seek a woman. (Joyce once described the time he spent writing *Ulysses* as his "seven years' sentence" [*L* 1:173].) "Eumaeus" takes place in a cabman's shelter, which, as we learned in "Lotus Eaters," provides respite for "drifting cabbies" (5.223; 77). The connection between Murphy and Wagner's hero is most explicit in the following passage:

However reverting to friend Sinbad and his horrifying adventures (who reminded him a bit of Ludwig, *alias* Ledwidge, when he occupied the boards of the Gaiety when Michael Gunn was identified with the management in the *Flying Dutchman*, a stupendous success, and his host of admirers came in large numbers, everyone simply flocking to hear him though ships of any sort, phantom or the reverse, on the stage usually fell a bit flat as also did trains) ... (16.858–64; 636)[31]

Traditionally, the Dutchman's vessel is a "phantom ship." (In French, the opera's standard title is *Le Vaisseau fantôme*.) The same ship appears in Bloom's ruminations in "Nausicaa": "Were those nightclouds there all the time? Looks like a phantom ship" (13.1077–8; 376).

In "Circe" the Dutchman assumes still another guise – that of the American financier Cornelius Vanderbilt. Inspired by the Dutch name (the hero of the legend is "Vanderdecken" in many versions) and Vanderbilt's unofficial title "Commodore," Bloom compares his own entrepreneurial spirit to that of the eminently successful Vanderbilt: "better run a tramline, I say, from the cattlemarket to the river. That's the music of the future. That's my programme ... But our bucaneering Vanderdeckens in their phantom ship of finance" (15.1367–70; 478). As we have seen, Wagner's music was known as "the music of the future" even before the Paris *Tannhäuser*, and "programme music" is a term applied to much nineteenth-century music. Bloom continues this train of thought and attacks the robber barons as a class: "These flying Dutchmen or lying Dutchmen as they recline in their upholstered poop, casting dice, what reck they? Machines is their cry, their chimera, their panacea'' (15.1390–2; 479). In imagining the wealthy Vanderbilt's ''upholstered poop,'' Bloom, who, as ''Eumaeus'' suggests, may have seen the opera at the Gaiety Theatre, might be thinking of the fortune in jewels with which the Dutchman impresses Daland in act 1.

In *Ulysses* as a whole the story of the Dutchman matches the pattern of the sea-weary mariner established not only by Homer's hero but also by Coleridge's Ancient Mariner, another avatar of the Wandering Jew on which Joyce draws. Of course, the character in *Ulysses* to whom the Wandering Jew in his various forms corresponds most closely is Bloom, as Mulligan makes clear in ''Scylla and Charybdis,'' when Stephen and Bloom have one of their many encounters: ''The wandering jew, Buck Mulligan whispered with clown's awe. Did you see his eye? He looked upon you to lust after you. I fear thee, ancient mariner. O, Kinch, thou art in peril'' (9.1209–11; 217). The Citizen, in his racist tirade, will call Bloom ''Ahasuerus ... cursed by God'' (12.1667; 338). In comparing Bloom to the Dutchman, Joyce may have remembered Wagner's discussion in *A Communication to My Friends* of the relationship between Odysseus, Bloom's most important ancestor, and the Flying Dutchman (*PW* 1:307–8 [quoted above], 334). Like all these mariners, the Bloom who wanders the streets of Dublin is an exile: his Jewish background, as ''Hades,'' ''Cyclops,'' and ''Oxen of the Sun'' make clear, isolates or exiles him socially; and because he and Molly have not had ''complete'' (*U* 17.2278; 736) sexual intercourse for over ten years, he is a kind of sexual exile as well, like Odysseus and the celibate Dutchman. In this context Wagner's depiction of exile in *A Communication* must have been especially attractive to Joyce:

It was the feeling of utter homelessness in Paris, that aroused my yearning for the German home-land ... It was the longing of my Flying Dutchman for ''*das Weib*,'' – not, as I have said before, for the wife who waited for Ulysses, but for the redeeming Woman ... who hovered before my vision as the element of Womanhood in its widest sense. This element here found expression in the idea: one's *Native Home*, i.e. the encirclement by a wide community of kindred and familiar souls. (*PW* 1:310)

In Joyce's copy of the *Prose Works*, this passage shows a clear vertical pencil-marking in the left-hand margin.[32] All these exiles, in their wanderings and their search for the woman who represents home and stability, evoke the Jews in the diaspora: "The oldest people. Wandered far away over all the earth, captivity to captivity, multiplying, dying, being born everywhere" (*U* 4.225–6; 61).

Finally, for Joyce, as for Wagner, the Wandering Jew represented the artist-exile. Just as Bloom has "a touch of the artist" about him (*U* 10.582; 235), so is Stephen Dedalus a wanderer and, in figurative terms, a Jew. In "Scylla and Charybdis" Mulligan describes Stephen as a "drunken jewjesuit" (9.1159; 216), and Stephen's departure from 7 Eccles St. in "Ithaca" is an "exodus from the house of bondage to the wilderness of inhabitation" (17.1021–2; 697). Indeed, Stephen's wanderings in *Ulysses* are perhaps more aimless than Bloom's, and his ill-considered assault on Paris during the previous year, recollected in "Proteus," is reminiscent of Wagner's own position when he composed *The Flying Dutchman*. Joyce, who did not share Wagner's anti-Semitism, was always interested in the relationship between the Jewish people and the arts. His belief in Victor Bérard's theories about the Semitic origins of the *Odyssey* is well-known,[33] and in "Scylla and Charybdis" Stephen suggests that Shakespeare was Jewish. Joyce must have read with great interest the translator's note in his edition of *Judaism in Music*, which discusses widespread speculation that Wagner himself may have been of Jewish extraction.[34] Joyce's use of the *Dutchman* in *Ulysses* also supports the theme of a regenerative death by water, which is present in the many allusions to *The Tempest* and to "Lycidas." Finally, since Joyce's Wandering Jew is a kind of "everyman" in this novel, we may see Bloom's situation and that of the Dutchman as representing the condition of modern man generally – rootless, isolated, and in search of home.

In *Finnegans Wake* the use of *The Flying Dutchman* is pervasive and detailed, especially in II.3, the scene in Earwicker's pub, where Joyce maintains a continuous parallel between the Dutchman's story and the tale of a Norwegian sea captain popularly known in Ireland.[35] Richard Ellmann has paraphrased this

comic story "of a hunchbacked Norwegian captain who ordered
a suit from a Dublin tailor, J. H. Kerse of 34 Upper Sackville
Street. The finished suit did not fit him, and the captain berated
the tailor for being unable to sew, whereupon the irate tailor
denounced him for being impossible to fit" (*JJ* 23). Joyce first
revealed his interest in this story in "Calypso," when Bloom
reflects on a slight acquaintance: "Chap you know just to salute
bit of a bore. His back is like that Norwegian captain's" (4.214–15;
61). In II.3 of the *Wake*, Joyce's captain is parallel to the Dutchman, and both are avatars of the hunchbacked HCE. Joyce
embellishes the story of the Norwegian, as Wagner, following
Heine, embellished that of the Flying Dutchman, by providing
the tailor with a daughter whom the captain will eventually marry
and who therefore corresponds to Senta, to ALP in her girlhood,
and to Issy. The marriage of the Norwegian captain to the tailor's
daughter is thus both a reenactment of HCE's courtship of ALP
and an indication of HCE's attraction to his daughter. According
to this scheme, the tailor and Daland would be analogous, but
Joyce does not pursue the parallel. A possible source of confusion
is that Daland is himself a Norwegian captain, but Joyce is clear
in linking his hunchbacked Norwegian to the Flying Dutchman.
The name of Joyce's tailor – "Kersse" – is, for obvious reasons,
perfectly suited to the Dutchman legend.

The "Norwegian Captain" section of II.3 begins at 311.5:
"It was long after once there was a lealand in the luffing."
Here "lealand" may be an oblique reference to Daland, but as
Roland McHugh points out, Charles Leland was the author of
a poem about the Dutchman legend,[36] and Joyce's reference to
him at the beginning of his tale makes good, if obscure, sense.
Early in the story, the captain asks the ship's husband, "Hwere
can a ketch or hook alive a suit and sowterkins?" (311.22–3),
and the ship's husband presents him to the tailor. Throughout
this narrative, "suit" denotes both suit of clothes and suit of
marriage; the captain's need for a suit parallels his desire for a
woman. The scene toward the end of act 1 where Daland and
the Dutchman arrange the latter's marriage to Senta was almost
certainly one of Joyce's chief inspirations as he wrote the
"Norwegian Captain." After the tailor furnishes the ill-fitting

suit of clothes, the captain flees, apparently without paying his
bill: "And aweigh he yankered on the Norgean run so that seven
sailend sonnenrounders was he breastbare to the brinabath, where
bottoms out has fatthoms full, fram Franz José Land til Cabo
Thormendoso, evenstarde and risingsoon" (312.5–8). Here
"seven sailend sonnenrounders" matches the seven-year term
that the Dutchman is obliged to spend at sea (the case with D. B.
Murphy in "Eumaeus"), and the rest of the passage sketches the
wanderer's miserable condition at the mercy of the elements.
(In keeping with his frequent practice in the *Wake*, Joyce is combining allusions to Wagner: "evenstarde" is almost certainly a
reference to Wolfram's well-known aria in *Tannhäuser*, "O du,
mein holder Abendstern," often translated as "O Evening Star.")
The scene of the Dutchman's fateful crime, traditionally the Cape
of Good Hope, is evoked later on the same page in "Cape of
Good Howthe" (312.19–20). An interruption in the story follows,
during which the brief absence of the "dutchuncler" (314.22)
Earwicker from his pub is made to coincide with the captain's
departure on his first voyage. The patrons complain that the love
interest has not yet appeared in the story: "That's all murtagh
purtagh but whad ababs his dopter?" (314.30). Among the guests
at the pub is one who "swore his eric" (316.8), thereby drawing
the Dutchman's rival into the discussion.

The tale resumes at 315.9 with the return of the inn-keeper-
captain (now "Burniface") from his voyage: "hiberniating after
seven oak ages, fearsome where they were he had gone dump in
the doomering this tide where the peixies would pickle him down
to the button of his seat … with the help of Divy and Jorum's
locquor" (316.15–19). "Seven oak ages" reformulates the Dutchman's period of wandering, and the rest of the passage foreshadows the Dutchman's fate, which, it turns out, Joyce's captain
will not share. Here again Joyce is splicing Wagner's operas
together: "doomering" is a version of the German for "twilight,"
as in *Götterdämmerung*, which concludes as the Rhinedaughters
("peixies") drag Hagen into the river. The captain's invocation
of "Finnegan's Wake" at 317.3–4 ("when I'm soured to the tipple
you can sink me lead") suggests that his return is analogous
to Finnegan's "resurrection" at his celebrated wake. "Locquor,"

we recall, was Finnegan's downfall. After the captain restores himself with a quick meal, the bargainers are reconciled, and they now direct their attention to a "suit" of marriage between the captain and the tailor's daughter, as the mercantile Daland and the Dutchman do in act I of the opera. The significance of marriage to the captain is described as follows: "Take thee live will save thee wive? ... Her youngfree yoke stilling his wandercursus ... Him her first lap, her his fast pal, for ditcher for plower, till deltas twoport ... O wanderness be wondernest and now!" (318.3 – 17). The first quoted phrase, if "wive" and "live" are reversed, states the condition for the release of the Dutchman's curse, and, taking "youngfree" as a variant of the German for "virgin," the second phrase can be glossed as "his marriage to a virgin releasing his curse of wandering." The third group of phrases constitutes a marriage vow, with ALP evoked in both "lap" and "pal," and the fourth reflects the Dutchman's desire to exchange his itinerant celibacy ("wanderness") for marriage ("wondernest"). The Norwegian – Dutchman's advanced age relative to the youthful Senta-tailor's daughter is suggested in his characterization as "Ampsterdampster that had rheumaniscences in his netherlumbs" (319.16 – 17). The "gentlemeants agreement" (318.26 – 7) for the daughter's hand having been concluded, the ship's husband inopportunely asks the captain about the suit of clothes. The question enrages the captain, who reports that he has burned them behind the oasthouse. After cursing the tailor's incompetence, he sets off on another voyage, reneging, presumably, on the "gentlemeants agreement" and failing to pay the bill for his meal.

After another interruption, the story continues when the tailor returns the departed captain's compliments by cursing him for being "impossible to fit":

—And so culp me goose, he sazd ... the bugganeering wanderducken, he sazd ... the bloedaxe bloodooth baltxebec ... donconfounder him, voyaging after maidens, belly jonah hunting the polly joans, and the hurss of all portnoysers befaddle him ... One can smell off his wetsments how he is coming from a beach of promisck. Where is that old muttiny, shall I ask? ... [T]here is never a teilwrmans in the feof fife of Iseland ... could milk a colt in thrushes foran furrow follower width that a hole in his tale and that hell of a hull of a hill of a camelump bakk. (322.35 – 323.23)[37]

"Bugganeering wanderducken" here recalls the "bucaneering Vanderdeckens" of "Circe" (*U* 15.1369; 478), a phrase that, as we have seen, Bloom uses in reference to Commodore Vanderbilt; the alteration in the *Wake* emphasizes Vanderdecken's relationship to Earwicker ("bug-in-ear"). The tailor's curse ("the hurss of all portnoysers") makes him the counterpart of the devil, who is supposed to have imposed the Dutchman's curse, and the phrases "voyaging after maidens" and "belly jonah hunting the polly joans" describe the Dutchman's situation perfectly. The "muttiny" for which the tailor calls does not figure in Wagner's opera, but it does in some versions of the Dutchman legend, including Walter Scott's *Rokeby*.[38] During another break in the story, the guests at the pub, acknowledging the reappearance of their innkeeper-captain, invoke Coleridge's Wandering Jew: "They hailed him cheeringly, their encient, their murrainer, and wallruse, the merman, ye seal that lubs you lassers" (324.8–9). The last phrase recalls Joyce's allusion in "Eveline," where he first borrowed the *Dutchman*, to "The Lass That Loves a Sailor." A weather forecast – "the outlook for tomarry … beamed brider" (324.33–4) – and a news summary – "Birdflights confirm abbroaching nubtials" (324.36–325.1) – announce the imminent marriage of "the nowedding captain, the rude hunnerable Humphrey" (325.27–8); and the ship's husband exhorts the tailor and captain to remember their earlier *Götterdämmerisch* vow: "Brothers Boathes … ye have swallen blooders' oathes" (325.25–6). The tailor's daughter finally appears, satisfying the largely male audience in the pub, "titting out through her droemer window for the flyend of a touchman over the wishtas of English Strand … where our dollimonde sees the phantom shape of Mr Fortunatus Wright" (327.22–6). Joyce owes this description of the tailor's daughter to the opening of act 2, when Senta cannot join the singing of her friends because, absorbed in the portrait that hangs in her house, she thinks of nothing but the "flyend of a touchman" (her Mr. "Wright") and hopes for the arrival of his "phantom shape." Like the tailor's daughter, Senta will not be disappointed, for her father has already arranged the match.

The Flying Dutchman is most resonant in II.3, but the opera appears throughout the *Wake*. Among the witnesses called by the Phoenix Park inquisition in III.3 is Sigerson, who appears in the *Wake* both as the Earwickers' hired man and as the constable who observed HCE's crime: "Roof Seckesign van der Deckel and get her story from him! ... Seckersen, magnon of Errick" (530.20–1). The first quoted phrase is rough German for a bailiff's cry in court and might be rendered as "Call Seckesign from the roof"; the last phrase alludes to the Dutchman's rival. Near the end of the *Wake*, as she urges her sleeping husband to rise, ALP is reminded of the sexual vigor of HCE in his youth: "You make me think of a wonderdecker I once. Or somebalt thet sailder, the man megallant, with the bangled ears" (620.6–8). As McHugh points out, "decken" is "to copulate" in vernacular German.[39] The juxtaposition here of Vanderdecken and his nautical cousin Sinbad recalls the frequent allusions to Sinbad in *Ulysses*, including a similar juxtaposition to the Dutchman in "Eumaeus" (*U* 16.858–64; 636, quoted above). In I.8 the washerwomen are uncertain about the identity of ALP's first lover: "Doubt arises like Nieman from Nirgends found the Nihil" (202.19). This passage echoes the Dutchman's despairing cry in his aria from act 1, "Die Frist ist um": "Nirgends ein Grab! Niemals der Tod!" (*FD* 52).[40] "[H]ullender's epulence" (126.16) may be a reference to the wealth that, in act 1, the Dutchman promises Daland for Senta's hand, and in II.1 the narrator compares Glugg-Shem, an outcast like his father, to the Dutchman: "He's a pigtail tarr and if he hadn't got it toothick he'd a telltale tall of his pitcher on a wall" (232.36–233.2). The "pitcher on a wall" of a "pigtail tarr" recalls the portrait that fascinates Senta in act 2 (cf. *FW* 327.22–6, quoted above). Finally, in II.3 the three children of HCE and ALP are "keen and able and a spindlesong" (336.13–14). (The "Spinning Song" that opens act 2 contributes, as we have seen, to Stephen's vampire poem in "Proteus" and "Aeolus.") The analogy here is between Senta and Issy, and Senta appears in two more contexts in the *Wake* (268.3 and 434.23) that are discussed in chapter 4. Incidentally, the Dutchman is not the only Wandering Jew from Wagner's operas in the *Wake*. The witch Kundry from *Parsifal*, another avatar of Ahasuerus (*Pars* 114),[41] appears in I.6, among

several other references to that opera, in "watches cunldron
apan the oven" (151.13 – 14).[42]

The Flying Dutchman is perfectly suited for *Finnegans Wake*, since
it supports many of the book's major themes. As in Joyce's
previous work, the outcast is of central importance in the *Wake*,
and Joyce consistently associates Wagner's Wandering Jew with
HCE, who is ostracized because of his indecent, if obscure,
behavior in Phoenix Park. The oath for which the Dutchman
received his eternal punishment when he tried to round the Cape
of Good Hope parallels HCE's crime in the park and the all-
important Wakean notion of original sin. As the invading stranger
who takes a woman from her lover and from her home, the
Dutchman corresponds to the *Wake*'s many invaders – Tristan,
Patrick, HCE in his youth, and Scandinavians generally – who
steal in some literal or figurative way the women of Ireland.
The presence of the *Dutchman* in the *Wake* emphasizes the Joycean
theme of a death that transfigures, as does that of Senta and the
Dutchman in the opera's conclusion. Joyce's interest in the
regenerative implications of death is most apparent in book IV,
in which ALP is reunited with her father, the sea. Finally, Joyce's
use of *The Flying Dutchman* underscores his belief in the redemptive
character of woman, especially as wife and mother and as
embodied in ALP. Chapter 4 pursues this last subject more
fully.

After the *Ring* and *Tristan*, *The Flying Dutchman* was probably
next in importance, among Wagner's operas, to Joyce's creative
imagination. In the Dutchman Joyce found an excellent counterpart to another Wagnerian figure of the artist, Siegfried, whose
presence in Joyce's canon culminates in Stephen's assault on
Bella Cohen's chandelier with the cry of *"Nothung"* (*U* 15.4242;
583). But as Siegfried fades from Joyce's work, the Dutchman
looms larger and larger. The change reflects not only Joyce's
increasing commitment to passive and equivocal heroes like
Bloom, HCE, and the deflated Stephen of *Ulysses*, but also his
declining interest in unmixed heroes like Siegfried. It also suggests
that Joyce's idea of the artist changed as he grew older: in his
proud and ambitious youth he was more inclined to see the
revolutionary and vital Siegfried as representing his artistic ideal;

in the various frustrations of his mature years he felt more empathy with the outcast and sea-weary Dutchman. In Joyce's work, in fact, the Dutchman eventually loses his association with artists like Stephen and Richard Rowan and attaches himself to common men like Bloom and HCE. Indeed, it is a mark of Joyce's artistic maturity that the artist as a Romantic figure separate from others begins to lose his interest: ''We all, for whole men is lepers, have been nobbut wonterers in that chill childerness which is our true name after the allfaulters'' (*FW* 355.33 – 5). The case of *The Flying Dutchman* shows the extent to which Joyce outgrew the Romantic archetype to which, in his youth, he was so attached. The condition of alienation that Joyce had considered to be peculiar to the artist he eventually came to feel was the curse of all humankind.

CHAPTER 4

Redemption

Das Ewig-Weibliche
Zieht uns hinan. Goethe, *Faust*, Part II

A hundred cares, a tithe of troubles and is there one who
understands me? Joyce, *Finnegans Wake*

The Flying Dutchman, as we saw in chapter 3, elevates a longing
for "home, house, hearth and – wife" (*PW* 1:307) to the realm of
metaphysics and begins to define the theme that, in one variation
or another, would occupy Wagner's entire career: redemption.
"Wagner," wrote Nietzsche in *The Case of Wagner*, "pondered
over nothing so deeply as over salvation: his opera is the opera
of salvation."[1] Tannhäuser, a sinner and outcast like the Dutchman, ends his long exile in the Venusberg, reenters the temporal
world, and attempts reconciliation with his chaste beloved and
with the fellowship of Minnesingers. The quasi-divine Lohengrin
forsakes the chilly perfection of Monsalvat and seeks redemption
in the unquestioning love of a mortal woman. Tristan attaches
a longing for death and redemption to his passion for Isolde. In
Wagner's last two works the theme expands beyond the personal
realm and the players change. A flawed king, in both the *Ring*
and *Parsifal*, presides over a fallen world and awaits deliverance
by a naive hero, a messiah. Perhaps Joyce remembered Nietzsche
when, in 1917, he identified a figure in Wagner's operatic carpet:

There are indeed hardly more than a dozen original themes in world
LITERATURE ... *Tristan und Isolde* is an example of an original theme.
Richard Wagner kept on modifying it, often unconsciously, in *Lohengrin*,
in *Tannhäuser*; and he thought he was treating something entirely new
when he wrote *Parsifal*.[2]

78

In nearly every case, Wagner's plots are motivated by restoration of lost love, recovery of a state of grace or fullness, or reconciliation with elements of the past. "Redemption," with its theological overtones, generally conveys in Wagner its literal sense of "a buying back." Usually the task is accomplished through personal sacrifice: often, in fact, it is "bought" by a woman.

To yearn for redemption in this "regressive" sense and to identify redemption with a woman's love is to make what Mark Shechner has called the "sentimental journey." In *Joyce in Nighttown*, his provocative psychoanalytic reading of *Ulysses*, Shechner identifies "the exile's return" as one of the most "primitive and universal" of literary themes:

In *Ulysses*, as in the *Odyssey*, the grand dramatic movement ... is an archetypal oral theme. The hero's situation is the same in each: he is an isolated, separated, incomplete man ... Both epics are an expression of a universal, *individual* struggle – the struggle of the lost son to get back to the infinitely distant mother.

For Shechner this "dramatic movement" is "a calculated expedition to the buried past," a past that is "associated with one's first and most passionate love affair, the affair with the mother." The sentimental journey offers "psychic ... renewal or rebirth or ... renourishment through recollected love";[3] thus, as the protagonist regains this lost sense of completion, he is "transfigured" as well as "restored." The notion of *weibliche* redemption is not simply a borrowing from theology. In fact, the psychological longing for reunion with the mother may reflect the same impulse as the spiritual desire for reconciliation – or "atonement" (from "at one") – with God: the search for one's origin, the yearning for paradise lost. Only God and Mother love unconditionally. "Whatever else is unsure in this stinking dunghill of a world," Cranly tells Stephen in *A Portrait*, "a mother's love is not" (241–2).

The presence of this redemptive woman in nineteenth-century culture was of course not exclusively Wagnerian. In *Beyond the Tragic Vision* Morse Peckham identifies "redemption through woman and woman's love" as "one of the great themes of transcendentalism," and counterparts to Senta and Elisabeth may be found in figures like Leonore in *Fidelio*, Gretchen in *Faust*, and Solveig in *Peer Gynt*.[4] The tendency of the age, in fact, was to pursue problems of identity, particularly masculine identity, in the sexual relationship and to invest love (or to burden it) with the power of transfiguration. In "woman" the artist could create a self-sacrificing, Christ-like figure whose unconditional love and supreme faith in the errant male might arrange "deliverance." "Redemption," through woman, meant "consummation" of selfhood, "fulfillment" of individual potential, or "release" from insufficiency. It might also suggest a "completion" of personality, in a symbolic sexual union, when artists found opportunities to incarnate in "woman" personal qualities they desired for themselves. Whenever male protagonists pursue the "ewig" in romantic love, a confusion of sexual and spiritual yearning is inevitably present. Whenever they seek affirmation through a woman's love, they play, simultaneously, the roles of son and lover.

The desire for "redemption," attached sentimentally to woman and to maternal figures in particular, pervades the work of Joyce. When the lover in *Chamber Music* writes, "I would in that sweet bosom be" (*CP* 14), he expresses the aim of all Joyce's main characters and adumbrates Joyce's entire career. In *A Portrait* Stephen defines his personality with the help of a series of maternal figures – Emma, Mary, the prostitute of chapter 2, even Holy Mother Church and Mother Ireland.[5] In *Ulysses* Stephen speculates, belatedly accepting Cranly's teaching, that "*Amor matris* ... may be the only true thing in life" (*U* 9.842–3; 207). When the curtain opens on *Exiles*, Richard Rowan, one of Ireland's "most favoured children," has returned to the maternal bosom of "her whom in loneliness and exile [he has] at last learned to love" (*E* 99). (As an Irish exile in Rome, therefore, he was more "exmatriate" than expatriate.) Indeed, Gabriel Conroy, Stephen, and Richard are all haunted by irreconciliation with their actual, never mind symbolic, mothers. The "grand dramatic movement" of *Ulysses*, "the exile's return," is consummated as Bloom, "the childman weary, the manchild in the womb" (17.2317–18; 737), rearrives in Molly's bed, assumes the fetal position, and drifts into the state of unconsciousness that will become the main subject of the *Wake*. The aims and methods of Joyce's last book, finally, suggest that Joyce's career may itself be regarded as a sentimental journey toward the redemptive "foetal sleep" (*FW* 563.10) on which the book so regressively lingers. As he played the variations on Wagner's great and "original" theme, Joyce created his own expressions of metaphysical and psychosexual yearning, of "longing after rest from amid the storms of life" (*PW* 1:307).[6]

Senta, the first of Wagner's *weibliche* redeemers, must have been especially attractive to Joyce. In choosing Heine's version of the Dutchman story as the basis for his opera, Wagner had linked the legend of the Wandering Jew with the myth of Odysseus and made the self-sacrificing Senta, Penelope's counterpart, a central figure. The Dutchman is not an exile in the same sense that Odysseus is, but he nonetheless identifies his search for redemption with his search for his home: "I have neither wife nor child," he tells Daland in act 1, "and I shall never find my home" (*FD* 54). As the object of this sentimental journey, Senta is a richly ambiguous figure. In dissolving the curse of endless mortal life with her vow of fidelity and her willingness to share the Dutchman's fate, she is, paradoxically, his redeemer in one sense – she ends the curse – and his destroyer in another – she ends his life. The search for home, for the place of one's origins, is in the *Dutchman* the desire for death as well as for redemption. The sexual element in this quest is made plain in the duet from act 2, when the Dutchman sees Senta for the first time:

> Die düst're Glut, die hier ich fühle brennen,
> sollt' ich, Unseliger, sie Liebe nennen?
> Ach nein! Die Sehnsucht ist es nach dem Heil:
> würd' es durch solchen Engel mir zu Teil! (*FD* 67)[7]

Senta expresses the same confusion of sexual and metaphysical yearning in her part of the duet. The climax of the *Dutchman*, in which the sea engulfs the lovers before they rise, embracing and "transfigured" (*FD* 77), gives the opera's fusion of *eros, thanatos*, and *amor matris* dramatic form. *The Flying Dutchman*, linking love, death, and redemption, represents Wagner's early working with the *Liebestod* theme that would reach its full development in *Tristan*.[8]

As we saw in chapter 3, Senta informs "Eveline" by way of contrast, but in *Exiles* she provides a strong parallel for Bertha, Richard's "bride in exile" (*E* III). Just as, in act 2, Senta dismisses Erik's heartache as insignificant when compared to the Dutchman's eternal suffering (*FD* 64), so does Bertha decline to take Robert's unhappiness seriously. For Bertha herself, as for Senta, a higher standard of sacrifice than might have been expected of "Mrs. Robert Hand" (*E* 116) is required: "I gave everything for him," she proudly tells Beatrice in act 3, "religion, family, my own peace." ("With him," Senta tells Erik in act 2, "I must go to destruction!" [*FD* 65, my translation].) But in sharing her lover's exile, she alone among the women in Richard's life has changed, even "transfigured," him: "What have they ever done for him? I made him a man" (100). (Countless women, the Dutchman reminds Senta in the opera's finale, have failed him in the past [*FD* 76].) At the end of the play, Bertha renews her pledge of eternal fidelity: "Wherever you go, I will follow you" (III). The *Dutchman* ends on the same note. "Here stand I," Senta vows, "faithful to you until death" (*FD* 77, my translation). In the *Dutchman* and in *Exiles*, a woman's fidelity implies much more than a sexual commitment; it means an unswerving devotion to a man's essential nature and a willingness to share his fate.[9]

An important source of Senta's fascination is that her love is, in a sense, both destructive and redemptive. In his talk with Bertha in act I, Robert inserts himself in the conclusion to the *Dutchman*, as we saw in chapter 3, and unites sex and dissolution in the image of the sea:

ROBERT, *presses her to him:* To end it all – death. To fall from a great high cliff, down, right down into the sea.
BERTHA: Please, Robert …
ROBERT: Listening to music and in the arms of the woman I love – the sea, music and death. (35)

In a closely related passage in the play's notes, the desire for the maternal embrace implicit in Robert's medley of love and death is a good deal more explicit:

In the convent they called her the man-killer …
    She is the earth, dark, formless, mother … Shelley whom she has held in her womb or grave rises: the part of Richard which neither

love nor life can do away with ... She weeps ... over him whom her love has killed, the dark boy whom, as the earth, she embraces in death and disintegration. He is her buried life, her past. His symbols are music and the sea, liquid formless earth, in which are buried the drowned soul and body. (118)

This fantasy on Bertha's character draws on the image of a resurrected Shelley, buried in the place of Richard and Bertha's exile, and on that of the dead Michael Bodkin, Nora Barnacle's adolescent friend and the prototype for Michael Furey. Joyce's symbols for sex and dissolution, "music" and "the sea," appear in both passages. Bertha is both "mother" and "man-killer"; so too are "womb" and "grave" equated. But the identification of the risen Shelley "whom she has held in her womb" with "the part of Richard which neither love nor life can do away with" hints at the redemptive power in Bertha's love for the Richard who is, here, both her son and her lover. The sentimental journey, as the *Dutchman* and *Exiles* suggest, is attended by a good deal of ambivalence. Whenever male protagonists imagine transformation through a woman's love into something rich and strange, fear and desire intermingle: for "transfiguration" into a new self requires the "dissolution" of an old one; "redemption" and "perdition" are coincident contraries.

Senta, drawn subtly into *Ulysses* through the contribution of the *Dutchman* to Stephen's vampire poem, figures most immediately as a parallel for the patient wife of the *Rosevean*'s sailor, D. B. Murphy, but ultimately she stands, with Penelope, behind Molly. In "Eumaeus" Murphy tells Stephen and Bloom of his home in Carrigaloe: "My little woman's down there. She's waiting for me, I know ... She's my own true wife I haven't seen for seven years now, sailing about" (*U* 16.419–21; 624). As we saw in chapter 3, the seven-year period matches the time during which the Dutchman must remain at sea between attempts to find his redeemer; the reference later in "Eumaeus" to a production of the opera at the Gaiety Theatre (*U* 16.860; 636) reinforces the connection between Murphy's wife and Senta.

Senta's presence in *Ulysses* would clearly support a redemptive role for Molly with regard to Bloom, but in what sense is Molly her husband's redeemer? Joyce once described "Penelope," obscurely, as "the indispensable countersign to Bloom's passport to eternity" (*L* 1:160), and the complex use of Bloom's potato talisman in "Circe" to correspond to the protective "moly" of Odysseus certainly hints at Molly's redemptive powers. The parallel may suggest that Molly will "make a man" of Bloom in the same sense in which Bertha made a man of Richard in *Exiles* (100, quoted above) and in which Stephen imagines his "Mercedes" will make a man of him in chapter 2 of *A Portrait*: "He would fade into something impalpable under her eyes and then in a moment, he would be transfigured" (65). This idea that sexual union affirms manhood seems especially significant in Bloom's case when we consider that his ten-year abstinence from "complete" (*U* 17.2278; 736) intercourse with Molly has its parallel in the Dutchman's (and D.B. Murphy's) seven-year estrangement from women. It is also possible that Molly will "redeem" Bloom in a reproductive sense, by giving him a son, a prospect that Bloom considers in "Sirens" (*U* 11.1066–7; 285). Both readings are compatible with Joyce's most famous statement about the final chapter of *Ulysses*:

Penelope is the clou of the book ... It begins and ends with the female word *yes* ... Though probably more obscene than any preceding episode it seems to me to be perfectly sane full amoral fertilisable untrustworthy engaging shrewd limited prudent indifferent *Weib. Ich bin das Fleisch das stets bejaht.* (*L* 1:170)[10]

In this allusion to *Faust*, Joyce is playing against Mephistopheles, "der Geist der stets verneint" ("the spirit that always denies"), and he is invoking, with a Joycean twist, the affirming spirit of the *Ewig-Weibliche* with which Goethe's drama concludes. As the "flesh" that "affirms," Molly may salvage her storm-tossed husband. It may be, finally, that, like Senta, Penelope, and other objects of the sentimental journey, Molly is a redeemer by virtue of the motherly qualities on which the structure and symbolism of *Ulysses* insists, and that the love both Bloom and Stephen seek in woman is "amor matris." After his encounters with his mother and with Private Carr in "Circe," the unconscious Stephen assumes a fetal position (*U* 15.4934–44; 608–9), and when Bloom joins Molly in bed at the end of his long day's journey, he does the same:

In what posture?

... Narrator: reclined laterally, left, with right and left legs flexed, the indexfinger and thumb of the right hand resting on the bridge of the nose ... the childman weary, the manchild in the womb. Womb? Weary?

He rests. He has travelled. (17.2311–20; 737)

Significantly, Bloom's protective "moly" was a gift from his mother.

Chapter 3 traced the presence of the *Dutchman* in *Finnegans Wake*, with emphasis on the "Norwegian Captain" section of II.3. In this story the Irish tailor's daughter, like Eveline, is the image of a self-sacrificing young woman awaiting her future husband's approach from sea, and Joyce supports this characterization with several direct references to Senta. At one point, as at the beginning of act 2, the tailor's daughter is "titting out through her droemer window for the flyend of a touchman over the wishtas of English Strand ... where our dollimonde sees the phantom shape of Mr Fortunatus Wright" (327.22–6). The tailor's daughter's redemptive qualities have been made apparent in a reference – inspired, possibly, by the expository material in Senta's Ballad – to the Dutchman's curse: "Take thee live will save thee wive? ... Her youngfree yoke stilling his wandercursus" (318.3–10). Here woman's redemptive power is tied directly to the mysterious power of virginity – *Jungfrau* is "virgin" – that so fascinated Wagner in *A Communication to My Friends* (*PW* 1:322–3). Elsewhere Senta stands for the pure woman generally, though, as the hint of "demimonde" at 327.25 reveals, the *Wake* cannot resist undermining any clearly established categories. "Night Lessons" (II.2) identifies the contradictory qualities that Kev and Dolph find in their sister: "the chimes of sex appealing as conchitas with sentas stray" (268.2–3). ("Conchita," Roland McHugh points out, is a "temptress" figure in Pierre Louÿs' *La Femme et le pantin*.[11]) Jaun's sermon on chastity in III.2 links a figure from Wagner's Munich days with the heroine of the *Dutchman*: "Sure, what is it on the whole only holes tied together, the merest and transparent washingtones to make Languid Lola's lingery longer? Scenta Clauthes stiffstuffs your hose and heartsies full of temptiness"

(434.21–4). "Languid Lola" Montez, the Irish-born mistress of Ludwig I, is mentioned explicitly at 525.14 as well. As the references to lingerie and scented clothes ("Scenta Clauthes") suggest, this last passage, like the others in which Senta appears, adulterates Wagner's heroine with the old typology of virgin and temptress, which is also imposed on Emma in *A Portrait*, on Gerty MacDowell, and on Issy, Senta's clearest parallel in the *Wake*. Joyce maintained some distance from Wagner's "Senta-sentimentality," to borrow Nietzsche's epithet, even as he indulged in it.[12]

As a redemptive woman Elisabeth is a worthy successor to Senta. Wagner's adaptation of his several sources for *Tannhäuser*, as in the *Dutchman*, was consistent with his thematic preoccupation: it was to create, in Elisabeth, an ethical center for the work and to confer upon the German Minnesinger the redemption that was not forthcoming in Wagner's sources. In *Tannhäuser* Elisabeth assumes the role of Christ, shielding her lover from the wrath of the pious Minnesingers in act 2, upbraiding them for presuming to act as judges, and, through her direct appeal to God, overruling the Pope, who finds the hero beyond forgiveness. Indeed, Tannhäuser is finally redeemed not because he conquers sexual desire or repents his sins – he does not fully accomplish either – but simply because Elisabeth gives her life for him, as Senta does for the Dutchman. Elisabeth differs from Senta in her close association with Mary, a powerful presence in the at least superficially Christian *Tannhäuser*. Mary's importance is established when, as the Venusberg section closes, Tannhäuser asserts that his salvation lies elsewhere: "Mein Heil liegt in Maria!" (*Tann* 67); and it is reinforced in the Elder Pilgrims' song in act 1, in Elisabeth's prayer at the beginning of act 3, and in the shrine that graces the stage in acts 1 and 3.

Tannhäuser himself, as an exile driven toward redemption and death, follows the pattern established by the Dutchman. The return to mortal life and pursuit of redemption through Mary and Elisabeth is for Tannhäuser a continuation of his sentimental journey after a false start in the timeless sensuality of the Venusberg – "Under the Hill," Beardsley had styled it. When he encounters his erstwhile companions in act 1.3, he explains his exile, either evasively or forgetfully, as that of a wanderer pursuing "rest": "I travelled far, through distant lands, but never found the peace or rest I sought" (*Tann* 71). Through Mary and Elisabeth, Tannhäuser now seeks the maternal comfort that he apparently did not find in what Venus, describing her realm as seductively as she can, tellingly calls "der Erde wärmenden Schoss" (the earth's warming womb) (*Tann* 65, my translation). As in the *Dutchman*, the hero confuses sexual desire with the longing for redemption, and it is not surprising that Elisabeth should become the object of both. But Elisabeth stands apart from all the other characters in the Wartburg in her empathy for Tannhäuser and in her acknowledgment, made in the prayer to the Virgin in act 3, of his capacity to awaken sexual feeling in her. In this sense, their relationship, again, is like that of Senta and the Dutchman, whose sensibilities function on a different plane from those of the other participants in the drama. Elisabeth, like Senta, is the "one who understands" the outcast sinner. Finally, in rejecting the lulling sensuality of the Venusberg and entering the realm of temporal experience, Tannhäuser understands that he is pursuing his own mortality: "it is death I am seeking, and death that draws me on" (*Tann* 67). When, ultimately, Elisabeth's self-sacrifice and death make his own salvation and death possible, a second Wagnerian *Liebestod* is achieved.[13]

Joyce's earliest direct reference to *Tannhäuser* occurs in poem 25 of *Chamber Music*, "Lightly come or lightly go," where the unusual "evenstar" translates literally the "Abendstern" in Wolfram's "O du, mein holder Abendstern" of act 3 (*CP* 33). Poem 25, appearing after the love affair chronicled in *Chamber Music* has apparently been consummated, cannot make much of the chaste and courtly Wolfram's position as Elisabeth's unrequited lover; but poem 4, "When the shy star goes forth in heaven" (*CP* 12), appears to make a good deal of it. In act 3.2 Wolfram comes upon Elisabeth at sunset. She is kneeling in prayer. In poem 4, "When the shy star goes forth...at eventide" (an echo of "Abendstern"), the lover finds his beloved "ben[t]... in revery." Wolfram, the Minnesinger, addresses his aria to the evening star that represents Elisabeth in all her purity and inaccessibility. Joyce's lover, likewise, is a "singer" who offers a

"lover's chant," and though Joyce's poem is addressed directly
to the beloved rather than to the star, his "shy ... maidenly"
evening star takes on attributes of the beloved – the same qualities
Wolfram's aria gives Elisabeth – in the early, courtly phase of
the love affair in *Chamber Music*. The irony in Wolfram's
associating Elisabeth with an "evening star," the name often
given to the planet Venus, rather than with, perhaps, the
"morning star" that Catholicism associates with Mary would
not have been lost on Joyce. (In "Nausicaa" another Wolfram
will come upon his own Elisabeth in the same setting, with an
evening star in attendance: "A star I see. Venus? Can't tell
yet" [U 13.1076; 376].[4]) For both Joyce and Wagner, spiritual
and sensual love were closely intertwined.

In *A Portrait* Stephen is a perfect Tannhäuser, visiting prosti-
tutes and performing his duties as prefect "in the college of the
sodality of the Blessed Virgin" (104) in turn. In his adolescent
pursuit of maturity and affirmation, he desires "to meet in the
real world the unsubstantial image which his soul so constantly
beheld," and he eagerly anticipates "that moment of supreme
tenderness [in which] he would be transfigured" (65). Here
Stephen closely resembles, in what amounts to a confusion
between two sources of redemption, the figure that, years later,
Joyce would describe to John Sullivan: "What sort of a fellow
is this Tannhäuser who, when he is with Saint Elizabeth, longs
for the bordello of Venusberg, and when he is at the bordello
longs to be with Saint Elizabeth?" (*JJ* 619). Tannhäuser's confusion between sensual and spiritual love may derive from the
fact that Venus appears to offer what he most desires: peace, rest,
and comfort, which are ultimately to be found only in the chaste
and genuinely redemptive love of Elisabeth. Stephen, too, at first
imagines that in sexual love he will find his redemption.

Stephen associates his childhood and adolescent sweethearts
with Mary, as Tannhäuser does Elisabeth. Eileen Vance is discussed in connection with the Litany of Our Lady of Loreto
(42–3), and Emma, in Stephen's mind, intercedes for him with
Mary, as Elisabeth does for Tannhäuser: "But he imagined that
he stood near Emma in a wide land and, humbly and in tears,
bent and kissed the elbow of her sleeve" (116). Mary's position

as refuge of sinners of the flesh, the "one who understands," is
apparent in the advice of Stephen's confessor: "Pray to our mother
Mary to help you. She will help you, my child. Pray to Our Blessed
Lady when that sin comes into your mind" (145). Mary occupied
an important position in Joyce's imagination not only because
of his Catholic upbringing but also because, as virgin *and* mother,
she was doubly uplifting. In the opera, Tannhäuser's offense is
less in his having lingered in the Venusberg than in his imposing
sexual desire upon (and, possibly, in awakening sexual desire in)
Elisabeth.[15] Wagner's hero comes to this understanding at a
crucial point in act 2:

> To save a sinner from damnation,
> an angel came to guard my days,
> but I, I saw her, and desired her,
> soiled her with sly and lustful gaze. (*Tann* 82)

Stephen himself, as he acknowledges in the depths of his own
remorse, cannot confine his lust to the brothel: "The image of
Emma appeared before him ... If she knew to what his mind had
subjected her or how his brutelike lust had torn and trampled
upon her innocence! Was that boyish love? Was that poetry?"
(115). In Joyce's Wakean letter to Sullivan, "From a Banned
Writer to a Banned Singer," which parodies the opera's first two
scenes, Wagner's hero is "fickar" Tannhäuser (*CW* 264) – both
"ficker" (German *ficken*) and "vicar." Many of Joyce's women
share Elisabeth's close attachment to the Virgin. In "Nausicaa,"
for example, Joyce links Bloom's onanistic adoration of his virgin
on the rocks with the more orthodox worship of the litanists in
a nearby church: "there streamed forth at times upon the still-
ness the voice of prayer to her who is in her pure radiance a beacon
ever to the stormtossed heart of man, Mary, star of the sea" (*U*
13.6 – 8; 346). It may be, in fact, that, as refuge of sinners, Mary
inspired sexual as well as religious feeling. "Bluerobed, white
under, come to me," Bloom reflects as he passes the shop of a
statue maker. "That brings those rakes of fellows in: her white"
(*U* 11.151 – 5; 259 – 60).[16]

At the beginning of act 2 of *Exiles*, Robert Hand has perfumed
himself and his Ranelagh cottage, and he nervously awaits the

arrival of Bertha, whom he hopes to seduce. The stage directions
mention ''an open piece of music'' on the piano and then describe
Robert's playing ''softly in the bass the first bars of Wolfram's
song in the last act of 'Tannhäuser.' '' The allusion is reinforced
a few lines later when, in an awkward speech, a surprised Robert
tells Richard, ''I was just strumming out Wagner when you
came'' (57–8).[7] Robert, the studied sensualist, is certainly
nothing like the chaste Wolfram, nor does Robert show Wolfram's
unswerving loyalty to a faltering friend. But there is an important
structural parallel in Robert's devotion to a woman whose spirit,
at least, is distant and inaccessible. *Tannhäuser*, especially in
Wolfram's aria, depicts Elisabeth in celestial imagery, and Robert,
borrowing the language of the chivalrous Minnesinger without
its freshness and naiveté, describes Bertha in the same way.
During their discussion in act 1, Robert tells her, ''You were like
the moon,'' and then, in a speech that exactly describes Wolfram's
position with respect to Elisabeth, he says, ''I think of you always
– as something beautiful and distant – the moon or some deep
music'' (31–2). In *Exiles* Robert's experience is to discover, as
Wolfram does, that the bond between a man and a woman who
speak honestly to each other cannot easily be broken.

If Robert is the unchaste Wolfram of *Exiles*, then Richard is
its Tannhäuser, returning to his homeland after an exile begun
in disaffection and ''Hochmut'' or ''arrogance'' (*Tann* 70).
Tannhäuser, in abruptly leaving Thuringia, forsook Elisabeth,
whereas Richard abandoned two women: Beatrice, literally, in
leaving Ireland with Bertha, and Bertha, figuratively, through
infidelities that he admits to Robert in act 2. In having confessed
his adultery to Bertha and insisting that ''she must know me as
I am,'' Richard comes to feel that he has ''killed her,'' that he
has destroyed the ''virginity of her soul'' (66–8). Tannhäuser's
revelation that he has enjoyed the delights of the Venusberg
wounds Elisabeth in the same way, and the Minnesingers' assertion that, as a result, he has caused her death – ''Du gabst ihr
Tod'' (*Tann* 82) – is borne out by the opera's conclusion. Bertha,
however, like Elisabeth, accepts her lover in spite of his moral
failings. Tannhäuser's honesty about the power and importance
of sexual love finds its parallel in Richard's plain speaking,

especially in contrast to Robert's flowery palaver. "A kiss," says Robert in act 1, "is an act of homage." "It is an act of union," Richard replies, "between man and woman" (*E* 41). The crucial distinction between the two works is in their resolutions. At the end of the opera, Tannhäuser achieves salvation through Elisabeth's prayers, and the two are united in their quasi-Christian *Liebestod*; with the curtain of *Exiles*, however, Richard and Bertha remain incompletely reconciled. The play concludes with Bertha's plea: "O, my strange wild lover, come back to me again!" (112). *Exiles* is in this respect a "disappointed" *Tannhäuser*.

Wagner's opera owes a good deal of its thematic energy to its binary opposition of pagan and Christian, Venusberg and Wartburg, Venus and Elisabeth or Mary. In her analysis of the Tannhäuser legend, Jessie Weston ascribes the mixture of these elements to the intercourse between Christianity and the early mythology of Northern Europe:

It was no easy task which the apostles of Christianity set themselves when they undertook to dethrone the deities so securely enshrined in the outer life and inner being of their worshippers. Christianity triumphed, but the old gods, though defeated, were not destroyed, and even in their fall they were powerful enough to leave an indelible impression on the faith which took their place.[18]

In the *Wake* the conquest of one culture by another is a preoccupation. Patrick's conversion of Druidic Ireland may be the best Wakean parallel for the conflict Weston identifies here, but others are available in the many Scandinavian attempts on Ireland and in the victory of the Anglo-Normans over Roderick O'Conor. The Wartburg, where the pious Minnesingers hold their Tournament of Song, turns up late in the *Wake* in a list of churches with chiming bells, one of which is "Bride-and-Audeons-behind-Wardborg" (569.11). In this passage Joyce may be thinking of the bells that, in act 1.2, awaken the dreaming Tannhäuser and, in 1.3, welcome him as he leaves the Venusberg for the earth. *Tannhäuser*'s bells, as they intrude in the "realm of non-being,"[19] in Wagner's words, that anticipates the *Liebesnacht* of *Tristan*, symbolize the "daytime" or temporal experience from which Tannhäuser has escaped. It is especially appropriate that bells should sound as the *Wake* approaches its conclusion and as the dreamer, like a Tannhäuser leaving the arms of Venus to confront time and mortality, stirs in his sleep. The Venusberg appears in an account of the adolescent ALP's seduction of Father Michael Arklow: ''and one venersderg in junojuly, oso sweet and so cool and so limber she looked ... the kindling curves you simply can't stop feeling'' (203.19–23). Here ''venersderg'' is both ''Venusberg'' and ''Friday,'' the day traditionally assigned to the goddess of love. The chaste counterpart of Venus appears in I.6, where the Mookse and Gripes assume the roles of Pope Adrian IV and an unbeliever:

—Us shall be chosen as the first of the last ... obselved the Mookse nobily
...
    —Wee, comfused the Gripes limply, shall not even be the last of the first ... Mee are relying entirely, see the fortethurd of Elissabed, on the weightiness of mear's breath. (156.24–34)

In I.6 the Gripes's humble plea to the Mookse evokes Tannhäuser's petition to another Pope (Urban IV, according to the legend) for forgiveness; in both cases sanctimonious clergymen turn the penitents away. The reference here to Elisabeth is a reminder that Tannhäuser's redemption depends not on the Church but on the direct intercession of a devoted woman, ''the weightiness of mear's breath.'' (Neither Joyce nor Wagner felt much affection for ecclesiastics.) The Elizabeth of church history and the Venus of mythology, neither exclusively Wagnerian, of course, appear in many contexts throughout the *Wake*.

In *Tristan und Isolde* the Wagnerian idea of *Liebestod* reaches its apex. The association between erotic and metaphysical longing evident in the earlier operas is intensified in *Tristan* to the point of inextricability, and the desire for death implicit in the *Dutchman* and *Tannhäuser* is explicit. *Tristan*, in fact, makes clear what the earlier operas imply: that life itself is a painful exile from a peaceful place of origin, from an ''Ur-Vergessen'' (*TI* 81) accessible only in dissolution. The opposition between painful life and redemptive death is represented throughout the opera in imagery of light and dark, day and night. In daylight, which ''blinds'' rather than illuminates (*TI* 71), are falsehood, envy, and deceit; in night are peace, maternal comfort, and truth. ''In day's resplendent shine,'' Tristan asks in act 2, ''how could Isold' be mine?''

(68). In death, according to the celebrated *Liebesnacht* of act 2, Tristan will not only find oblivion but reenter the womb as well:

> O sink' hernieder
> Nacht der Liebe,
> gieb Vergessen,
> dass ich lebe;
> nimm mich auf
> in deinem Schoss,
> löse von
> der Welt mich los! (71)[20]

The "grand dramatic movement" of *Tristan*, to return to Shechner's theme, is "the exile's return" to "das dunkel / nächt'ge Land, / daraus die Mutter / mich entsandt'" (77), that is, "the dark land of night from which my mother sent me" (my translation). Birth, in *Tristan*, is thus a kind of "fatal slip," to borrow a Joycean formulation, into human existence, and death presents the opportunity to regain the lost paradise, to escape temporality, rationality, and the burdens of identity. The intense sensuality of *Tristan* and its music has always impressed its listeners, but the desire for sexual gratification only begins to express the sort of longing that is the opera's real subject.

In the *Dutchman* Senta's vow of fidelity acts as a "balm" that heals the metaphorical "wounds" of exile and alienation (*FD* 68). In *Tristan* Isolde, schooled in her mother's apothecary arts, heals the actual wound Tristan suffered at the hands of Morold, and, as Tristan's consort in *Liebestod*, she heals the metaphorical wound of mortal life. The sort of redemption pursued in *Tristan*, therefore, is that implied in the German "Heil," or "salvation": it is a "healing" or "making whole." In act 3 Tristan awakes or, as he puts it, returns from beyond "the door of death" (*TI* 81, my translation) so that, with Isolde, he may complete his sentimental journey:

> She who can close
> My wound forever,
> She comes like a queen,
> She comes here to heal.
> Dissolve O world,
> As I hasten to her. (88)

As with the lovers in the *Dutchman* and *Tannhäuser*, the love of Tristan and Isolde sharply divides them from others, especially in its repudiation of worldly values, including the ultimate worldly value, life itself. Even their closest companions scarcely understand them: Brangäne, in act I, wonders why the exalted position as Mark's queen means little to Isolde; Kurvenal, in act 3, attempts to restore his master to the life he does not desire. The opera concludes with the same triumphal death that we have encountered in the *Dutchman* and *Tannhäuser*.[21]

That Joyce thought highly of *Tristan und Isolde* is certain, though he studied other versions of the legend, including, most notably, the turn-of-the-century reconstruction by French medievalist and literary historian Joseph Bédier. Evidence of Joyce's knowledge of the opera dates from 1912, when, in two essays, he drew on *Tristan* for rhetorical purposes. "The Universal Literary Influence of the Renaissance" cites *Tristan* as its prime example of modern art, and *Daniel Defoe* contrasts the concrete realism of the English novelist with the "magical beguilements of music" in *Tristan*.[22] In 1922, as the *Wake* was taking shape in his imagination, Joyce described himself as "meditatively whistling bits of *Tristan and Isolde*" while he posed for a newspaper drawing (*L* 1:183). He was not speaking idly: the "Tristan and Isolde" sketch of *Work in Progress*, which is based on act I of the opera and now forms part of book II.4, was one of the first Joyce wrote. The Tristan legend, in fact, would occupy Joyce's attention during the entire composition of the *Wake*.[23] In 1925, by way of explaining Giordano Bruno's importance to his new book, Joyce found an illustration in *Tristan*: Bruno's "philosophy is a kind of dualism – every power in nature must evolve an opposite in order to realise itself and opposition brings reunion etc etc. Tristan on his first visit to Ireland turned his name inside out" (*L* 1:226).[24] Isolde's account of this first trip to Ireland is given, as part of the opera's exposition, in act 1.3.

Joyce's attachment to the opera and legend was deep and many-faceted. Certainly the Celtic roots of the tale, which the libretto's first few lines evoke, made a strong impression on him. Brangäne's "Einsam wachend," apparently one of his favorite bits of Wagnerian music,[25] confirmed, as we saw in chapter 1, his opinion that the "deadly sin" of the Celts was envy (*JJ* 382), and two of the "Irish heroes and heroines of antiquity" catalogued in "Cyclops" with claims to legitimacy are "Tristan and Isolde" (*U* 12.176 – 92; 296 – 7). Furthermore, because in its version of the Wagnerian synthesis of arts the music predominates, *Tristan* was not especially popular among literary Wagnerites;[26] but it may have appealed to the musically sensitive Joyce for precisely this reason. Joyce was also interested, like many Wagnerites before him, in the romance surrounding the opera's composition, as the passage in the *Wake* on "wagoner" and "his mudheeldy wheesindonk at their trist in ["Tristan"] Parisise" reveals (230.12 – 13). Discussions of Wagner's attachment to Mathilde Wesendonck were readily available in Joyce's copies of Moore's *Hail and Farewell* and *Memoirs of My Dead Life*. ("Dear me," wrote Moore, "when one thinks of it, one must admit that art owes a good deal to adultery."[27]) Joyce found in the opera many of his thematic preoccupations: betrayal, exile, adultery, cuckoldry, incest.[28] The opera's sensuality was not lost on him either. "A great modern artist," he wrote in 1912, "wishing to put the sentiment of love to music reproduces ... each pulsation, each trembling, the lightest shivering, the lightest sigh; the harmonies intertwine and oppose each other secretly."[29] Wagner, in fact, Joyce told Oscar Schwarz, "stinks of sex" (*JJ* 382). Joyce would have seen rich possibilities in the Isolde whom his *Daniel Defoe* takes as an embodiment of "the eternal feminine": a priestess and healer, a bride in an unconsummated marriage, and the forbidden wife of a trusted friend.[30] Finally, Joyce was attracted to the matrix of ideas surrounding the *Liebestod* – the idea of a love that is at once destructive and redemptive, the idea of redemption in death, the notion that the grave is a "womb" – all depicted in the language of night.

Tristan makes its Joycean debut in *Exiles*, where the consequences of an adulterous love – the betrayal of Mark by his nephew and vassal, the exile of Tristan from Cornwall, and the death of the lovers – found fertile ground.[31] In Joyce's notes for the play, a discussion of the title underscores the importance of the Wagnerian source: "Exiles – also because at the end either Robert or Richard must go into exile ... Robert will go. But her thoughts will they follow him into exile as those of her sister-in-love Isolde follow Tristan?'' (*E* 123). As the betrayer of a close friend, Robert is in Tristan's position with respect to Mark, though his character may be indebted to Melot as well.[32] (The libretto, in fact, hints that Melot betrays Tristan to Mark out of jealous love for Isolde [*TI* 78].) Like Tristan, Robert goes into ''exile'' when his adulterous love is exposed, and throughout the play he encourages Bertha to assume Isolde's role of unfaithful wife. A direct allusion to the *Liebesnacht* appears in act 3, when Robert asks Bertha, ''Were you mine in that sacred night of love?'' (*E* 106).[33] Robert's cultivation and deployment of Wagnerian vocabulary – this the third example in this chapter – shows his attempt to project himself into Richard's position as intellectual and artist-outcast. An outburst in act 2 may represent Robert's rough approximation of the general thrust of *Tristan*: ''The blinding instant of passion alone ... – that is the only gate by which we can escape from the misery of what slaves call life'' (*E* 71). Wagner's act 2 was of special importance to *Exiles*, especially in the characterization of Robert. David Hayman's analysis of Joyce's notes under *Exiles* in *Scribbledehobble* shows that act 2 of the opera, in fact, served as a working model for act 2 of the play.[34] Both acts are nocturnal and framed by acts set in daylight. In each a tryst takes place, and in each the betrayed husband arrives on the scene and reproaches his erstwhile friend for his treachery (though Richard's entrance anticipates rather than interrupts the lovemaking). With its uncertainties, comic misunderstandings, and reversals of expectations, act 2 of *Exiles* is a *Liebesnacht* manqué.

Though he is not the protagonist of *Tristan*, Mark is a highly sympathetic character, and he provides a close parallel for Richard in the role of aggrieved husband. For Joyce the cuckold was a source of personal interest as early as 1909 (*JJ* 278–91). The play's notes discuss the changing treatment of this figure in recent literary history: ''Since the publication of the lost pages of *Madame Bovary* the centre of sympathy appears to have been esthetically shifted from the lover or fancyman to the husband or cuckold'' (*E* 115). Indeed, Richard's complicity in the rapprochement of Robert and Bertha advances Mark's tolerant understanding and eventual release of Isolde to Tristan by just a few degrees. But in Joyce's fluid manipulation of the parallel, Richard, who, like Tristan, has deliberately sought the wound from which he claims he cannot recover, becomes Tristan as the play closes. Bertha's vow of fidelity evokes Isolde's as well as Senta's: "Wherever you go, I will follow you ... If I died this moment, I am yours." ("Where Tristan's home may be," Wagner's heroine promises at the end of act 2, "there goes Isold' with thee" [*TI* 78].) Richard is "wounded" and weak, and Bertha "closes her eyes" (*E* III – 12). The estranged lovers struggle toward, but fail to achieve, their symbolic *Liebestod*.[35]

In the *Wake* the role of *Tristan* is analogous to that of the *Odyssey* or *Hamlet* in *Ulysses*, providing one of the strongest and most intricate parallels to the book's main argument.[36] Generally, HCE is Mark; his marriage to the younger ALP and his attraction to Issy, who takes her name from the Wagnerian source, are analogous to Mark's marriage to Isolde and to Joyce's many pairings of older men and younger women – Lewis Carroll and Alice Liddell, Daddy Browning and Peaches, and so forth.[37] Shem and Shaun together are Tristan, though the highly sexed Shem is perhaps more so, and their assault on authority in the person of their father parallels Tristan's betrayal of his uncle. Both Wagner's opera and Bédier's *Romance* figure importantly in the *Wake*; indeed, they are so closely intertwined that it is difficult, and, ultimately, perhaps, unnecessary to distinguish precisely the influence of one from that of the other.[38] The inextricability of these sources is especially evident in book II.4, which Joyce composed in 1938 by splicing the 1923 piece based on Wagner (called "Tristan and Isolde") with a slightly later one based on Bédier (called "Mamalujo").[39] From Bédier, Joyce drew two important structural principles – embodied in Bédier's two Isoldes and four barons – as well as many episodes that Wagner had eliminated, for dramatic economy's sake, in his condensation of Gottfried's tale: to cite a few examples, Isolde's banishment to a leper colony (145.1 – 2); the spying of the barons on the trysting lovers (235.21 – 8); Tristan's use of wood shavings as a signal to Isolde (444.27 – 9 and 460.19 – 27); and Tristan's use, on two occasions, of disguise to gain access to his beloved

(527.24–5). From the opera, however, he drew the compelling Wagnerian themes of exile, renunciation, and betrayal, and he borrowed the setting of act 1, stage business from act 2, and, as will be seen, many details from the opera's libretto. Having just, in 1922, completed his book of the day, Joyce, "meditatively whistling bits of *Tristan*," was developing the most important structural features of his prospective "Nightletter" (*FW* 308.16). Wagner's opera of the night was ideally suited to help Joyce represent his thoroughly Wagnerian search for redemptive oblivion, for the "foetal sleep" (563.10) that is *Finnegans Wake*.

Tristan and Isolde are most prominent in II.4, the eventual home of Joyce's early sketches and the chapter from which much of Joyce's work with the legend grew. Book II.4 can be read in many ways: as HCE's dream of the lovers' voyage from Ireland to Cornwall, as a burlesque of the passion of Wagner's lovers, as the four annalists' sentimental view of young love, and as an anticipation of the lovemaking of the Porters in III.4. Joyce's "Tristan and Isolde" draws its setting – a ship at sea – from Wagner's act 1,[40] and it begins with a song of seagulls, who witness "the big kuss of Trustan with Usolde" (383.18):

> —Three quarks for Muster Mark!
> Sure he hasn't got much of a bark
> And sure any he has it's all beside the mark ...
> Fowls, up! Tristy's the spry young spark
> That'll tread her and wed her and bed her and red her
> Without ever winking the tail of a feather. (383.1–13)

The king whom Isolde, in act 1, calls "Cornwall's weary ruler" (*TI* 53) "hasn't got much of a bark"; in fact, Mark and Isolde's marriage, act 2.3 makes clear, has not been consummated (*TI* 77). Later in II.4 the love triangle provides an important example of the book's struggle between generations, in which fathers are supplanted by sons who, as is the case here, represent a new Arthurian regime:

Runtable's Reincorporated. The new world presses. Where the old conk cruised now croons the yunk. Exeunc throw a darras Kram of Llawnroc, ye gink guy, kirked into yord. Enterest attawonder Wehpen, luftcat revol, fairescapading in his natsirt. Tuesy tumbles. And mild aunt Liza is as loose as her neese ... Ne hath this thrysting. Fin. (387.36–388.6)

The "old conk" is Mark, who exits through an arras, while the "yunk" is Tristan, who, in comic tradition, enters through a window and "tumbles" Isolde. "Kram of Llawnroc," "Tuesy," "natsirt," and "Wehpen" are reverse spellings, inspired by Tristan's own alteration of his name (*TI* 52), of the three participants in this mock drama, the last constituting a reminder that Tristan, as Mark points out in his Lament in act 2, is Mark's nephew. The serendipitous "Weh" (German "woe") indicates Tristan's prevailing humor. "Thrysting" is both "Tristan" and "thrusting," a tribute to the hero's sexual prowess (compare "heroticisms" at 614.35), and "mild aunt Liza," derived from the first words of Isolde's *Liebestod* aria ("Mild und leise" [*TI* 91]), describes her legal relation to Tristan.[41] The lovemaking resembles a rugby match as the chapter nears its conclusion:

For it was then a pretty thing happened of pure diversion ... when ... the vivid girl, deaf with love ... one of romance's fadeless wonder-women ... with a queeleetlecree of joysis crisis she renulited their disunited ... and ... Armoricas Champius, with one aragan throust, druve the massive of virilvigtoury flshpst the both lines of forwards ... rightjingbangshot into the goal of her gullet. (395.26 – 396.2)

"Deaf with love" is a Wakean diminution of the *Liebestod* that Wagner's "vivid girl" sings after the "disunited" lovers have been "renulited" at Tristan's castle. "Armoricas Champius" evokes Tristan's Wakean cousin Armoricus Tristram, first Earl of Howth. The spying annalists attribute the adultery of the "modern old ancient Irish prisscess" (396.7 – 8) to Mark's loss of vigor: "What would Ewe do? With that so tiresome old milk-less a ram" (396.14 – 15). Isolde's canny mother, we learn in act 1.3, anticipating just such a problem with the aging Mark – "love potients for Leos, the next beast king," we read in the *Wake* (466.6) – has furnished Brangäne with the love potion that Tristan and Isolde will eventually consume. As the episode concludes, the voyeurs feel they have witnessed "death and the love embrace" (398.10). In the sustained use of the Tristan and Isolde legend in II.4, the burlesque is much more intense than it is elsewhere in the *Wake*, where Joyce has blended it with other material.[42]

Tristan himself is omnipresent in the *Wake*, as the quintessential lover and the foreigner – with Parnell, Patrick, and the English generally – who conquers Ireland or her women. More important for my purposes in this chapter, he is the union of opposites embodied in the contradictory natures of Shem and Shaun – "that siamixed twoatalk ... twist stern" (66.20–1) – especially in their orientation toward women. For Tristan, like Tannhäuser before him and Amfortas to come, is a divided man, caught between longing and renouncing, between desire for Isolde and respect for his uncle and king. The division is reflected in the two names, that, for Joyce, illustrated the "dualism" of Bruno. As "Tantris" (his "tristurned initials" [100.28–9]), he sought the Isolde of legendary healing powers, "the daughter of the queen of the Emperour of Irelande" (157.35–6). As "Tristan" he woos Isolde for Mark and betrays the love that, against her will, Isolde had begun to reveal. Tristan's ambivalent love for Isolde is evident from the outset of the opera, when he leaves the helm of the ship for her cabin only with extreme reluctance. In "Night Lessons" Shem's inconsistent behavior is a source of confusion to Issy. "Isolade," we learn, "gave him ... that vantage of a Blinkensope's cuddlebath at her proper mitts ... but ... she could never have forefelt ... such a coolcold douche as him ... doubling back ... under ... a vartryproof name" (289.28–290.19). In act 1.3, as Isolde rehearses this background to the opera, she still feels the effects of the "cold douche" she received when Tristan, "doubling back," returned to "Dublin" under a "waterproof" name. Isolde feels she has been led "to the halter" and "sold [that is, betrayed] in her heyday" (434.17). The same frustration with male inconstancy informs the "Mookes and Gripes" episode, where Nuvoletta "tried all the winsome wonsome ways her four winds had taught her" and "sighed after herself as were she born to bride with Tristis Tristior Tristissimus" (157.31–158.1). References to Tristan's melancholy – "my tristy minstrel" (521.22), "an always sadfaced man" (533.9), and "sad one of Ziod" (571.12); the reversal of his name – "tramtrees" (5.31), "tantrums" (189.5), and "tan tress" (480.4); and his dual nature – "twist stern" (66.21), "Treestone" (113.19), and "Tricks stunts" (282.L1): all are dispersed, like leitmotifs, throughout the *Wake*.

Joyce's Isolde is Issy, sometimes "Izod," "Isobel," even,

following the beginning of the *Liebestod*, "Mildew Lisa" (40.17). In one of her manifestations, Issy "divides" into the two girls who occasion the indiscretion in Phoenix Park that leads to HCE's undoing. Joyce found a parallel for these "two roses" (94.36) in Bédier's two Isoldes – Isolde the Fair of Ireland (Wagner's heroine) and Isolde of the White Hands of Brittany. Several extended "mirror-image" passages in the *Wake*, based on letters the young patient in Morton Prince's *Dissociation of a Personality* is supposed to have written to her "other self,"[43] are suffused with material from the Tristan legend. In one such passage, addressed, alternately, to her rival Isolde of Brittany and to her lover Tristan, Issy boasts that her "Irish accent," or (read with the German *eilen* in mind) her "quick assent," has entranced the foreigner Tristan: "My Eilish assent he seed makes his admiracion" (144.10–11). Another mirror-image passage, in III.3, with its use of the Litany of Our Lady of Loreto, links Issy to earlier Joycean figures like Eileen Vance (*P* 42–3) and Gerty MacDowell (*U* 13.281ff.; 354ff.):

Chic hands ... Winning in a way, only my arms are whiter, dear. Blanchemain, idler. Fairhair, frail one ... Mirror do justice, taper of ivory, heart of the conavent, hoops of gold! My veil will save it undyeing from his ethernal fire! (527.17–24)

Here and elsewhere in the *Wake*, Joyce draws on the celebrated veil with which Isolde signals Tristan at the beginning of Wagner's act 2, the veil which, because it promises consummation of love, acquires strong symbolic importance in *Tristan*. In a brief section of III.4, Issy's life passes in miniature before our eyes, from infancy, when "night by silentsailing night ... infantina Isobel ... took the veil," to maturity, when "Madame Isa Veuve La Belle ... [wore an] orange blossoming weeper's veil" (556.1–11). In his book on *Ulysses*, Stuart Gilbert had linked Isolde's veil with Calypso's veil in the *Odyssey*, identifying it as "the instrument of desire."[44]

If as the "two roses" Issy's appeal is primarily erotic and her influence is in some sense destructive, as a younger version of ALP she is a future mother, a prospective healer, and an apprentice redeemer. In the "Mime" Joyce compares Glugg-

Shem's wounded pride to the wound that Tristan suffered when
he met the Irish Morold's challenge to Mark and Cornwall. The
legend tells us that Tristan first sought Isolde after his injury
failed to heal: "how slight becomes a hidden wound? Soldwoter
he wash him all time bigfeller bruisy lace blong him" (247.22–4).
Here "*Sold*woter" is the balm with which Isolde, the student of
her mother's magic, healed the "bruisy place" of the stranger
"Tantris." In "Night Lessons" Issy's apprenticeship to the
redemptive ALP is reinforced in numerous allusions to Wagner's
Isolde. As we have seen, "Isolade" gives Shem "that vantage of
a Blinkensope's cuddlebath at her proper mitts" (289.28–290.13),
and elsewhere in the chapter Issy alludes to Tristan's exile in a
note that she has apparently written to Kev-Shem: "Dear old
Erosmas. Very glad you are going to Penmark" (301.F5). (The
cliff at "Penmarks," in some versions of the legend, is the site
of Tristan's castle in Brittany, where the opera concludes.) In
studying the alphabet and in writing this schoolgirl's letter to
"Erosmas," Issy – like Isolde an apprentice to her mother –
prepares for the role that ALP, the book's woman of letters,
currently fills. Indeed, it is through ALP's letter that the wounded
HCE is exculpated of the accusations against him and restored
to social and psychological health. In III.4 Issy demonstrates that
the work of her "schoolmistress" has achieved some success:

Do you can their tantrist spellings? I can lese, skillmistress aiding.
Elm, bay, this way, cull dare, take a message, tawny runes ilex sallow,
meet me at the pine. Yes, they shall have brought us to the water
trysting ... then here in another place is their chapelofeases, sold for
song ... Yes, sad one of Ziod? ... I, pipette, I must also quicklingly
to tryst myself softly into this littleeasechapel. (571.6–18)

Inspired by Bédier's account of a "tryst" arranged by secret
communication, the phrase beginning "take a message" is an
acrostic for "tamtris."[45]

The concept of *Liebestod*, the contribution of *Tristan* to the
"original theme" Joyce discussed with Georges Borach, is
especially important to *Finnegans Wake*. Redemption is implicit
in the book's cycles of death and resurrection, and the Wagnerian
search for an escape from the temporal process, for redemptive
oblivion, is reflected in Joyce's portrait of sleep and dream.

The opening phrase of Isolde's celebrated aria appears in many forms and in many contexts: "Mildew Lisa" (40.17), a variant of Issy's name, and "Mildbut likesome!" (424.28), a characterization of Jameson whiskey, to cite just two. Wakean translations of "*Liebestod*" itself appear with the same ubiquity: the "Grace-hoper" Shem is lost in "a jungle of love and debts" and "a jumble of life in doubts" (416.8–9); Isolde in her lovemaking with Tristan is "deaf with love" (395.29); and a passage in "Night Lessons" may represent Isolde's aria being conducted: "And his countinghands rose. Formalisa. Loves deathhow simple!" (304.1–3).[46] The *Wake* puts the potion or "love philter" of act I, in which the inextricability of love and death is symbolized, to the same protean uses: "love potients for Leos, the next beast king" (466.6); "a philtred love, trysting by tantrums, small peace in ppenmark" (189.5–6); and, in an evocation of Isolde's gesture at the end of act I, "Lethals lurk heimlocked in logans ... Dash the gaudy deathcup!" (450.30–2). Near the beginning of the *Wake*, a description of the Hill of Howth links the *Liebestod* to the book's central themes:

Mutt.—Fiatfuit! Hereinunder lyethey ... alp on earwig, drukn on ild, likeas equal to anequal in this sound seemetery which iz leebez luv.
Jute.—'Zmorde!
Mutt.—Meldundleize! By the fearse wave behoughted ... And thanacestross mound have swollup them all. This ourth of years is not save brickdust and being humus the same roturns. (17.32–18.5)

Here the departed lovers, "alp" and "earwig," are peacefully interred in "leebez luv," a sentimental variant of "*Liebestod.*" "Meldundleize," again, approximates the aria's beginning, and the passage concludes with a statement of the cyclical theory of history so integral to the structure of the *Wake*. These almost countless evocations of Isolde's *Liebestod* in the minutiae of *Finnegans Wake* express the centrality of Wagner's opera to the book's aims, methods, and themes.

For Joyce *Tristan* provided perhaps the most powerful artistic expression of the regressive longing for unconsciousness and escape from temporality that the *Wake* embodies. If, in fact, as John Bishop has recently argued, Joyce's main intention in the

Wake was to represent the world of darkness and of sleep, then
Tristan must be counted as the book's most important operatic
influence, notwithstanding the affection in Joyce the opera-goer
for the more singable Rossini, Bellini, and Bizet. In imagery of
light and darkness *Tristan* and the *Wake* assert that there is an alternative or even a higher reality in unconsciousness: in day are deceit
and pain, in night truth and comfort. *Tristan* opens just as dawn
breaks, and it is therefore appropriate that Tristan himself should
join Adam and Eve on the first page of the *Wake* and that his first
words in the opera should be evoked within a few paragraphs:
"But was iz? Iseut?" (*FW* 4.14; *TI* 50). The highly symbolic
torchlight that, near the beginning of the nocturnal second act,
Isolde extinguishes as a signal to Tristan is prominent in several
passages in the *Wake*. In I.4, to cite just one example, one of
Ireland's four annalists, here a judge at HCE's trial, claims to
have preceded HCE in the young Anna Livia's affections: "My
perfume of the pampas, says she (meaning me) putting out her
netherlights" (95.23–4). The extinguishing of the torchlight in
act 2 foreshadows Tristan's death in the opera's penultimate scene,
when he cries, "The torch now is out. To her! To her!" (*TI* 88).
Thus the conclusion to *Tristan* appears at several points in the
Wake, as in the following passage in the "Mime":

Woefear gleam she so glooming, the pooripathete I solde? Her
beauman's gone of a cool … If he's at anywhere she's therefor to join
him. If it's to nowhere she's going to too … And among the shades that
Eve's now wearing she'll meet anew fiancy, tryst and trow. (226.6–14)

As Isolde sinks upon the body of Tristan, already "gone of a cool,"
she joins her "beauman" in redemptive oblivion: it's "nowhere
she's going to too." Book III, near its end, offers the following
intimation of the conclusion of the *Wake*: "Ah, my sorrowful …
how it is triste to death, all his dark ivytod! Where cold in dearth"
(571.13–15). Here again Joyce, shortly after the lovemaking of Mr.
and Mrs. Porter in III.4, represents Isolde's point of view as
she sings her "ivytod" over the corpse of her "triste" lover.
In contrast to *Tannhäuser*, where the *weibliche* figure leads the hero
to his redemption, in *Tristan* the reverse is the case, and Isolde
gets the final word. Indeed, the rhapsodic description of ALP's

death in the book's climax owes a good deal, in both substance and tone, to Isolde's final scene: "If I seen him bearing down on me now under whitespread wings like he'd come from Arkangels, I sink I'd die down over his feet, humbly dumbly, only to washup" (628.9–11).[47] If, as Hodgart has suggested,[48] these lines also recall the "O sink' hernieder" from the *Liebesnacht* (*TI* 71), then Joyce has placed them perfectly: for the break of dawn will interrupt the *Liebesnachts* of both *Tristan*, when Mark enters, and the *Wake*, when the book "ends." The power of the *Liebestod* theme in Joyce's imagination is suggested by its appearance in the denouements of both *Exiles* and the *Wake*. For all the importance of this theme to the *Wake*, however, no material is exempt from Joycean irony, and in I.6 Issy pokes fun at the Robert Hand in her own Tristan: "to adore me there and then cease to be? Whatever for, blossoms?" (145.36–146.1).

As a descent into oblivion, the *Wake* represents the most complete expression of an irrationalist desire evident throughout Joyce's canon. As "The Dead" and *Dubliners* come to a close, Gabriel Conroy, beginning to reconcile himself to his mother country and to his own origins, feels his "soul swoon[ing] slowly" and "his own identity...fading out into a grey impalpable world" (*D* 223–4). *Exiles*, we have seen, closes with its attenuated *Liebestod*, and Bloom's day of wandering concludes as his consciousness collapses into the black dot of "Ithaca" that becomes the *Wake*'s main subject. The denouement of *A Portrait* does not match this pattern, but Stephen's loss of virginity in the arms of a suspiciously maternal prostitute at the end of chapter 2 is a "swoon of sin": "He closed his eyes, surrendering himself to her, body and mind, conscious of nothing in the world but the dark pressure of her softly parting lips" (*P* 101). I suggested at the outset of this chapter that this regressive yearning for unconsciousness represents, in Mark Shechner's words, "the struggle of the lost son to get back to the infinitely distant mother." In this context the end of the *Wake* can be seen to present the converse of this struggle. Just as a fetal Bloom, dropping off to sleep, is united with a woman who is both his wife and his mother, ALP, in her own *Verklärung*, is reconciled with a man who is both her lover and her father: "it's sad and weary I go back to you, my cold

father ... and I rush, my only, into your arms" (627.36–628.4).
The hint of the German "Tod" in "Carry me along, taddy"
(628.8) reinforces the dying ALP's relationship to Isolde in her
rhapsodic *Liebestod*. A sentimental journey, the *Wake* asserts, is
undertaken by woman as well as by man.

In *Parsifal* Wagner uttered his last word on the theme of
redemption, picking up many threads from earlier works. The
central motif of an unhealing wound, which is literal in *Tristan*
and metaphorical in both *Tristan* and the *Dutchman*, reappears,
and the salvation of a fallen or in some sense insufficient man,
as in the *Dutchman* and *Tannhäuser*, requires, once again, a
redeemer's intervention. In the earliest stages of planning
Parsifal, Wagner wrote to Mathilde Wesendonck that Amfortas,
suffering "the inability to die," was "my Tristan in the third
act, but inconceivably intensified."[49] But *Parsifal* is as notable
for modifying established Wagnerian patterns as for following
them. The salvation of Amfortas does not require or coincide
with his death, as it does in the case of his predecessors, and
the redemptive figure is not a woman but a "pure fool" who
develops into a worthy redeemer through compassion: "Durch
Mitleid wissend, / der reine Tor" (*Pars* 91). Parsifal, in fact, is
a composite of the earlier, *weibliche* redeemers in Wagner's canon:
his chastity is worthy of Elisabeth, his capacity for empathy worthy
of Senta, his power to heal worthy of Isolde.[50] In *Parsifal* the
important female figure is Kundry, whose character shows the
same reversal of established Wagnerian sex roles evident in
Parsifal himself. For Kundry, who mocked Christ at the time of
His Crucifixion, is, like the Flying Dutchman, a Wandering Jew
suffering an implacable curse (*Pars* 114). And like Tannhäuser,
she misguidedly pursues redemption in sexual love before finding
it in quasi-Christian renunciation and expiring. In suggesting that
Wagner "*thought* he was treating something entirely new when
he wrote *Parsifal*" (my emphasis), Joyce acknowledged the
development in Wagner's treatment of his theme even as he
emphasized its continuity.

Joyce's knowledge of *Parsifal* and its libretto dates from his
University College days. The 1900 "Drama and Life" asserts that
the use of myth makes the work of the "author of Parsifal ...

solid as a rock" (*CW* 43), and two years later an essay on James Clarence Mangan cites a detail from act I: "That was a strange question which the innocent Parsifal asked – 'Who is good?'" (*CW* 75–6).[5] Joyce first borrowed *Parsifal* for his creative work in the conclusion of *Exiles*, when Richard tells Bertha of his uncertainty about her fidelity:

> I have a deep, deep wound of doubt in my soul … I have wounded my soul for you – a deep wound of doubt which can never be healed. I can never know, never in this world … And now I am tired for a while, Bertha. My wound tires me. (112)

If *Tristan* provides the conclusion to *Exiles* with a close parallel, *Parsifal* gives it a direct allusion – to the gash that Gurnemanz, in act I, calls "the wound … that will never heal itself" (*Pars* 90, my translation). For Amfortas, as the Grail King of fertility myth, the cause of his unhealing wound, generally thought to be in the groin or genitals, is sexual desire, and its effect is physical debilitation; for Richard, the cause of the wound is lost faith in Bertha, and its effect, the parallel hints, is sexual dysfunction. In suggesting that Bertha has undermined his masculinity and made him vulnerable, Richard may be said to have reached the nadir of his faith in a woman who, actually, is far more closely allied to Senta or Isolde than she is to Kundry, the seducer of Amfortas. For it must be remembered that Richard courts this doubt and that his relationship with the self-sacrificing Bertha is debilitating only insofar as he desires it to be. In the conclusion of *Exiles*, Richard remains an unredeemed Amfortas, enduring the metaphorical wound that resonates throughout Wagner's canon. The strength of Richard's association with Amfortas is suggested by the fact that, among the five Wagnerian operas informing *Exiles*, *Parsifal* is the only one in which Robert is not given a role. An incomplete *Parsifal*, *Exiles* ends on a strong note of inertia and irreconciliation.

For *Ulysses* and the "Circe" episode, Joyce drew on act 2 of *Parsifal* and in particular the scene in Klingsor's Magic Garden. Joyce's Nighttown has much in common with the Magic Garden of *Parsifal* as, indeed, it has with the Garden's Wagnerian precursor, the Venusberg of *Tannhäuser*: all three are realms of fantasy and sensual imagination, and a powerful woman rules each. "The Kisses" that emerge in the phantasmagoria of Dublin's Nighttown owe a good deal to the gaily clad women who, "appearing like flowers themselves" (*Pars* 107), charm Parsifal but fail to seduce him:

([Bloom] *stands before a lighted house, listening. The kisses, winging from their bowers fly about him, twittering, warbling, cooing.*)

THE KISSES

(*warbling*) Leo! (*twittering*) Icky licky micky sticky for Leo! (*cooing*) ...
(*They rustle, flutter upon his garments, alight, bright giddy flecks, silvery sequins.*) (15.1268 – 76; 474 – 5)[52]

Bloom's resistance in this chapter to the magic of Circe and her minions puts him in Parsifal's position with respect to the Flowermaidens. Here, as in act 2 of the opera, the hero's impulses are ruled more by compassion for his erring fellow man – in Bloom's case, for Stephen – than by sexual desire.[53] Just as the Flowermaidens anticipate the entrance of the far more imposing Kundry, these "Kisses" prepare Bloom for his far more serious encounter with the leading lady – Bella Cohen, the whore-mistress. At Bella's hands Bloom endures, as Parsifal did before him, a merciless probing of his subconscious desires and exposure of his weaknesses before he emerges relatively intact and in some sense victorious. In linking the sensitive, empathetic, and above all *weibliche* Bloom, "a finished example of the new womanly man" (*U* 15.1798 – 9; 493) to Parsifal, Joyce may have been hinting at the possibility of Stephen's "redemption" as Amfortas.

In the *Wake* Kundry herself is almost indistinct, but her surrogates are virtually everywhere. Throughout the book, but especially in II.1, "The Mime of Mick, Nick and the Maggies," Joyce borrows the floral imagery associated with Wagner's Flower-maidens to represent all young women as avatars of Eve, respon-sible for man's demise. The "two roses" (94.36) who apparently inspired HCE's crime in Phoenix Park appear, multiplied, as the Maggies of II.1. In the Mime's cast of characters, they are "THE FLORAS ... a month's bunch of pretty maidens who ... form with valkyrienne licence the guard for IZOD" (220.3 – 7). The "bunch" of "Floras" comes straight from *Parsifal*, and the simultaneous presence of the similarly multiple Valkyries deepens the Wagnerian connection. The Maggies, both innocent and provocative, are descendants of earlier figures like Gerty MacDowell and the Misses Douce and Kennedy: "They war loving, they love laughing, they laugh weeping ... they think feeling, they feel tempting, they tempt daring, they dare waiting, they wait taking...to live and wive by wile and rile by rule of ruse 'reathed rose" (142.31–6). Their relation to the Flowermaidens is emphasized in a passage that recalls "Circe's" "Kisses":

Aminxt that nombre of evelings, but how pierceful in their sojestiveness were those first girly stirs, with zitterings of flight released and twinglings of twitchbells in rondel after, with waverings that made shimmershake rather naightily all the duskcended airs and shylit beaconings from shehind hims back. (222.32–6)

This passage describes the Maggies' power over Shem ("shimmer"). "Pierceful" emphasizes the link between Joyce's maidens and those in *Parsifal*, and "evelings" draws a connection between the Maggies and the original *femme fatale*. Elsewhere in the "Mime," the Maggies are a "florileague" (224.23), "fleurettes of novembrance" (226.32–3), "florals" (227.15), and "a floral's school" (250.33). Kundry, whose apothecary skills make her a witch figure, may herself be obscurely present in "the wordchary ... atvoiced ringsoundinly by their toots ensembled" (225.2–3) and in "whitchly whether to weep or laugh" (226.1–2), a phrase that evokes Kundry's peculiar curse – to laugh for all eternity (*Pars* 114). In III.1 the "wieds of pansiful heathvens" (426.21) are probably the flowery costumes of the "heathen" Flowermaidens (who live on the "heath" that Klingsor has transformed into a luxuriant garden), and Jaun's sermon in III.2 – "loveliest pansiful thoughts" (446.3) – exposes the sermonizer as another man divided between chaste and sensual love: "pansiful" evokes both the chastity of "Parsifal" and the sensuality of the "pansies," or Flowermaidens. Generally in the *Wake* Parsifal, a renouncer of the flesh, is closer to Shaun than to Shem; Tristan, a desirous lover, is, as I have suggested, closer to Shem.[54] Like Tannhäuser and the Stephen of *A Portrait*, the composite son of the *Wake* is both "vicar" and "ficker" (*CW* 263–4).

Joyce's use of female characters from *Parsifal* raises new questions and draws another archetypal female figure, the apparent antithesis of the redemptive woman, into the discussion: the "eternal temptress" or *femme fatale*. At the beginning of act 2, Klingsor identifies Kundry with this type when, calling her from sleep, he cites her earlier incarnations as the "Rose of Hades," "Herodias," and "Gundryggia" (*Pars* 101). With her Flowermaidens and Magic Garden, Kundry is a direct descendant of the Venus of *Tannhäuser*, with her Chorus of Sirens and Venusberg. Throughout this chapter I have noted the strong maternal qualities in the redemptive figure who, as the object of the sentimental journey, heals, affirms, or restores the hero. It may at first appear ironic or contradictory that the two great *femmes fatales* in Wagner's canon, in attempting a sexual conquest that will mean spiritual death, deploy the language of maternal love, offering comfort, rest, and peace. "Go to the frigid world of men," an enraged Venus tells Tannhäuser in act 1, "from whose pretentious, flaccid dreams we gods of pleasure long have fled, here in the earth's warm sheltering womb" (*Tann* 65). Kundry, too, when her attempt to seduce Parsifal begins to fail, famously plays what she regards as her trump card, Parsifal's recently deceased mother Herzeleide: "love sends you now a mother's blessing, greets a son with love's first kiss!" (*Pars* 113). If woman can redeem or "buy" man "back," evidently she can "sell" him as well. Joyce's "Oxen of the Sun" expresses these twin powers of redemption and destruction through the pillars of Catholic womanhood:

our mighty mother and mother most venerable ... hath ... an almight-iness of petition because she is the second Eve and she won us ... whereas that other, our grandam, which we are linked up with by successive anastomosis of navelcords sold us all, seed, breed and generation, for a penny pippin. (*U* 14.296–301; 391)

The temptress figures that linger in Joyce and Wagner, embody-ing a fear of seduction and of "surrender" to sexual feeling, testify to the ambivalence that attends the sentimental journey. On the one hand is the regressive, irrationalist desire for submersion, oblivion, and extinction of personality in sexual love – "redemp-tion"; on the other is the rationalist fear of absorption in sexual

feeling, of loss of reason and of individual identity achieved with
such difficulty – "perdition." Sirens, "Eumaeus" reminds us,
are "enemies of man's *reason*" (*U* 16.1890; 665, emphasis mine).
The *femme fatale* is thus not simply a pitfall on the sentimental
journey toward redemption: she is a projection of doubt that the
journey into sexuality may be safely undertaken at all.

In his discussion of women in Freud's work, Philip Rieff
writes of a pervasive "romantic mythology of women" in the
nineteenth century, and he identifies two strains of misogyny on
which this mythology rests, a "Victorian" form, "which idealized
women as natively innocent and above sex," and a newer form to
which Freud himself subscribed, "in which women are conceived
(by both women and men) as naturally more sensual":

The second misogynistic attitude is based on the *intellectual* deficiency
of women: the child-bearing female represents the natural heritage of
humanity, while the male carries on in spite of her enticements the
burden of government and rational thought.[55]

In adopting this increasingly conventional distribution of reason
to man and emotion or heightened sexuality to woman, Joyce
did not also adopt, as Freud did, the rationalist idea that "men
must come to terms with the sexual and overcome it."[56] On the
contrary, like Wagner's before him, Joyce's art expresses the
need for man, and particularly for the artist, to complete his
otherwise "sterile" personality by submitting to the emotional,
irrational, and unconscious impulses – the side of life convention
and the reality principle taught him to repress – that "woman,"
according to this newer formulation, could be made to represent.
In Joyce and Wagner, the far greater strength of the redemptive
woman, compared with a merely vestigial *femme fatale*, reflects
the importance of the regressive, irrationalist longing expressed
in the sentimental journey.

CHAPTER 5

The comic rhythm

> Every race has made its own myths and it is in these that
> early drama often finds an outlet. The author of Parsifal
> has recognized this and hence his work is solid as a rock.
>
> Joyce, "Drama and Life"

> In using the myth, in manipulating a continuous parallel
> between contemporaneity and antiquity, Mr Joyce is pur-
> suing a method which others must pursue after him ... It
> is simply a way of controlling, of ordering, of giving a shape
> and a significance to the immense panorama of futility and
> anarchy which is contemporary history.
>
> Eliot, "*Ulysses*, Order, and Myth"

The last three chapters have dealt with Joyce's use of mythic
material from nearly all Wagner's mature operas, *The Flying
Dutchman* to *Parsifal*. But the mythic quality of Joyce's work is
more than a question of allusion and thematic parallel. It is also
a question of mythic shape. Thomas Mann, in a retrospective
article on his Joseph novels, wrote of a change in his interests
as his career progressed:

The various stages of life have different inclinations, claims, tendencies
of taste ... It is probably a rule that in certain years the taste for all
purely individual and particular phenomena, for the individual case...
fades out gradually. Instead the typical, the eternally human, eternally
recurring, timeless – in short, the mythical – steps into the foreground
of interest.[1]

The mythopoeic imagination, as this passage implies, characteristically arranges experience in patterns that parallel the natural
cycles of the day and year. For all their importance as individuals,
mythic characters are ultimately participants in a recurring

elemental situation; they reveal "history repeating itself with a difference" (*U* 16.1525–6; 655). Joyce's canon developed along the lines sketched by Mann, from the highly specified *Dubliners* to the fully mythic *Finnegans Wake*, where "the Vico road goes round and round to meet where terms begin" (452.21–2). And whether or not Joyce's interest in "the individual case" diminished, his attraction to the "typical" and "eternally recurring" certainly increased. The cycles of the *Wake* are anticipated, even as early as "Proteus," in "Bridebed, childbed, bed of death, ghostcandled" (*U* 3.396; 47–8) and in Stephen's meditation on a drowned man: "God becomes man becomes fish becomes barnacle goose becomes featherbed mountain" (3.477–9; 50). The mythic shape of the *Wake* is most apparent in its four-part Vichian structure, in "their weatherings and their marryings and their buryings and their natural selections" (117.27–8), and in the book's title, which acknowledges death but promises resurrection.

The structure of the *Wake* has many sources in myth and mythology, and Wagner must take his place among them. Joyce's interest in classical myth, most apparent in the Homeric underpinning of *Ulysses*, is beyond dispute. Joyce was certainly influenced, despite the many disclaimers, by the Irish literary revival, though, as "The Day of the Rabblement" implies, the main effect of this movement was to turn him to the Continent (and to Wagner, among others). John B. Vickery has traced the presence of *The Golden Bough* in Joyce's work, and Atherton numbers The Book of the Dead and the Scandinavian *Eddas* among the most important mythic sources for the *Wake*.[2] Vico's *New Science* is justifiably credited with inspiring the four-part structure on which the *Wake* rests, though, as Hart points out, Blake's "The Mental Traveller" and Blavatsky's *Isis Unveiled* made important contributions as well.[3] Among works contemporary to the *Wake*, *A Vision* and *The Waste Land* may have reinforced the influence of Joyce's predecessors.[4]

Wagnerian myth had an important shaping influence on Joyce's work as well. The early critical writings frequently cite the importance of Wagner and his "world drama" (*CW* 45), and Joyce's praise for the Meister's *Parsifal* in the 1900 "Drama and Life" suggests that the Irish writer found the same "solidity" in Wagner's mythic art that Eliot, in 1923, would find in Joyce's (*CW* 43, quoted above). The mythic shape of the *Ring* in particular would hold Joyce's interest for his entire life. As early as 1902, in an essay on James Clarence Mangan, Joyce's use of the Germanic *Götterdämmerung* – inspired, apparently, by Ibsen[5] – links the mythic promise of daybreak and springtime to a resurrection of Irish literature:

With Mangan a narrow and hysterical nationality receives a last justification, for when this feeble-bodied figure departs dusk begins to veil the train of the gods, and he who listens may hear their footsteps leaving the world. But the ancient gods ... die and come to life many times, and, though there is dusk about their feet and darkness in their indifferent eyes, the miracle of light is renewed eternally in the imaginative soul. (*CW* 82–3)

Though, as we shall see, Wagner's gods will almost certainly *not* "come to life many times," the Wagnerian imprint on this passage – in the gods' resignation to their fate and in the repeated "dusk" (*Dusk of the Gods*, cited in "Circe," was a common turn-of-the-century translation of Wagner's title) – is unmistakable. Years later, Joyce would make a hybrid of Vico and Wagner in one of many evocations of the structure of his last book: "a good clap, a fore marriage, a bad wake, tell hell's well" (*FW* 117.5–6). *Das Rheingold*, concluding with Donner and Froh's construction of the rainbow bridge and with a thunderclap; *Die Walküre*, focusing on Hunding and Sieglinde's "poor marriage"; *Siegfried*, ending in Brünnhilde's awakening from her long sleep; and *Götterdämmerung*, culminating in the burning of Valhalla ("hell's well"), constitute a four-part structure that provides one of the strongest and most accessible precedents for Joyce's efforts in the *Wake*. What would give the *Wake* such a firm underpinning was not only the structure of the *Ring*, but also the ethical significance that Wagner had attached to it. The famous sentence from Edgar Quinet's *Introduction à la philosophie de l'histoire de l'humanité* that Joyce borrowed for his book applies equally to the *Ring* and the *Wake*:

Today, as in the time of Pliny and Columella, the hyacinth disports in Wales, the periwinkle in Illyria, the daisy on the ruins of Numantia; and while around them the cities have changed masters and names, while some have ceased to exist, while the civilisations have collided with one another and smashed, their peaceful generations have passed through the ages and have come up to us, fresh and laughing as on the days of battles.[6]

The work of man is self-destructive, sterile, fleeting; the work of maternal nature is resilient, self-sustaining, eternal.

The conceptual structure of the *Ring* inheres in its plot, which Wagner spliced together from a number of mythic sources, in particular, three closely related legends – the German *Nibelungenlied* and the Icelandic *Volsungasaga* and *Thidreksaga*.[7] In fashioning the *Ring* Wagner linked the death of Siegfried as he found it in these tales with the *Götterdämmerung* (or *Ragnarok*) of Germanic myth and created an ethical drama about the problem of evil, the corruption of innocence, and the possibility of redemption in a fallen world. Wagner's mythic plot has many parallels in the Biblical account of the fall of man and in the Christian concepts of sin and salvation. But there is an important variation: the fall from grace in Wagner's cosmology is attributed not to defiance of the Creator but to the corruptibility of an *allzumenschlich* god – Wotan, who, despite his weaknesses, attracted Wagner's strongest sympathies. The *Ring* and the *Wake* invite comparison. Both are mammoth four-part works, the *Ring* three dramas with a shorter prelude, the *Wake* three long books and a brief one; both, like the myths on which they draw, explain creation, dissolution, and the end of the world through tales of gods, heroes, and men; both express sympathy for a "human, erring and condonable" (*FW* 58.19) Allfather. The near-continuous presence of the *Ring* in Joyce's "great myth of everyday life"[8] and the near-perfect consonance of the Wagnerian theme of sin and redemption in Joyce's mythic score suggest that *Finnegans Wake* was shaped from its inception, both structurally and conceptually, by Joyce's lifelong experience of Wagner and the *Ring*. Wagner's *Ring* deserves a place among the "structural books" at *Finnegans Wake*.[9]

The *Ring* begins in a "golden age" of gods and nature, Wagner's analogy to the prelapsarian period of Adam and Eve in Paradise.[10] The first scene of *Das Rheingold*, set in the pre-dawn darkness of the riverbed, captures the age in the pristine beauty of the gold and in the purity of the Rhine itself. ("In the beginning," wrote Mann, "was the Rhine."[11]) Wagner's score opens with 136 measures of chords and arpeggios in E-flat major, the memorable music that "Sirens," which links Wagner's Rhinedaughters with their Homeric cousins, had borrowed.[12] In these measures, Wagner's almost exclusive use of the triad, the most basic of harmonic tools, reflects the elemental simplicity of this prelapsarian world. And just as the Rhine generates life in Wagner's cosmos, his straightforward music here will generate many of the most important leitmotifs in the entire cycle.[13] When dawn breaks and illuminates the gold, the Rhinedaughters rejoice in what they call "the golden radiance which sleeps and wakes in turn" (*R* 14). Thus, in praising the beauty of the gold, the Rhinedaughters are actually celebrating the reflected glory of the sun, the dawning of day, and the assurance of continued life. The natural innocence of the Rhine and the gold has an ethical counterpart both in the riverbed and in the heavens. The Rhinedaughters, though aware of the gold's material potential, are content simply to rejoice in its sunlit splendor; and in Wotan's world, we learn in scene 2, love reigns supreme.

The main symbol of innocence and fecundity in the *Wake* is a river as well, the Liffey, embodied in the maternal figure of Anna Livia Plurabelle. In the section of the *Wake* specially devoted to ALP, I.8, two women wash clothes in the river, an act that illustrates the restorative power that Wagner's Rhine and Joyce's Liffey share. One of the washerwomen, speaking of ALP's legendary fertility, exclaims, "They did well to rechristien her Pluhurabelle. O loreley! What a loddon lodes!" (201.35–6). The Lorelei are the mythic cousins of Wagner's Rhinedaughters, and the "loddon lodes" evoke Wagner's gold. Later in the *Wake* the Rhinegold appears in a reference to ALP's demotic role as a publican's wife: "Selling sunlit sopes to washtout winches and rhaincold draughts to the props of his pubs" (578.23–4). "Sunlit sopes" is a closer approximation to "rhaincold draughts" than at first meets the eye. "Soaps" (like "suds") is slang for beer, and, as we have seen, Wagner's gold is "sunlit" in a notable passage in scene 1 of *Rheingold*; the once-popular American "Rhinegold" beer knits the two phrases still more tightly.

ALP, the passage implies, is a descendant of the "bronze by gold" barmaids of "Sirens," where, as I have suggested, *Rheingold* is an important presence. "Sunlit," in fact, recalls the description of sun in Miss Kennedy's hair (*U* 11.81–2; 258), the "gold" color of which "Sirens" mentions repeatedly. The centrality of the river in Joyce's book is reinforced, as in the *Ring*, by its appearance at the beginning – in the first word, in fact. Moreover, the book's opening description of prelapsarian place – "riverrun, past Eve and Adam's, from swerve of shore to bend of bay" (3.1–2) and time – "passencore" (3.4–5) or "not yet" (3.10) – parallels the extended passage in E-flat major at the beginning of *Rheingold*. Joyce's two-paragraph introduction concludes, appropriately, with reference, albeit oblique, to the precedent in Wagner: "rory end to the regginbrow was to be seen ringsome on the aquaface" (3.13–14). "Regginbrow" may be an allusion to the rainbow bridge that appears at the end of *Rheingold* and "ringsome" a reference to the entire *Ring*. That Joyce associated the Liffey and the Rhine is made clear in his personal correspondence. On his way to Zurich in 1937, he wrote to C. P. Curran about his hotel accommodations in Rheinfelden: "Anna Rhenana runs under my window all night complaining in guttural Schwyz-Duitsch of being pressed into service by me … as train bearer to a drunken draggletail Dublin drab" (*L* 1:396).

The golden age of the *Ring* is short-lived. The Nibelung Alberich, who is fiercely attracted to these guardians of the gold, interrupts their play and attempts to impose himself on whichever is nearest his grasp. Alberich's insidious presence is marked not only by his voracious desire (and by Wagner's chromatic harmonies) but also by his Philistine deprecation of the Rhinedaughters' simple pleasure in the gold: "Is that all it's good for, to shine at your games? Why, then it is worthless!" (*R* 14). (In *Götterdämmerung* Alberich will say of Siegfried, "Laughter and love fill his heart, gaily he wastes all his life" [*R* 283].) In defense of the gold's latent powers, the Rhinedaughters point out that, fashioned into a ring, the gold will confer on its possessor the power to rule the world. The Rhinedaughters feel secure in imparting this information to Alberich because only he who forswears love can wield this power, and in the golden age no man – least of all, they assume, the lustful Alberich – will renounce the pleasures of love. When the Rhinedaughters make sport of the Nibelung's clumsy advances, the frustrated Alberich pronounces the unthinkable curse and wrests the gold from the riverbed. Alberich's actions in the first scene of *Rheingold* help define the nature of evil in the Wagnerian scheme: the exploitation of something or someone – a piece of gold, an ash tree, a woman – for selfish ends. The rape of the Rhinegold becomes the archetypal sin, a crime against nature and against love, throwing the cosmos out of joint and engendering new crimes. Only when the gold is restored to its original place in the riverbed can the fallen world of the *Ring* be redeemed. Alberich's ring will become Wagner's elemental symbol of power and ambition, always in opposition to "nature" and to "love." [14]

The corruption of innocence is a Wakean preoccupation as well. ALP's loss of virginity, the pollution of the Liffey, Patrick's conversion of Druidic Ireland: all reenact the fall of Adam and Eve. Joyce's precarious ("not yet") evocation of a prelapsarian world at the beginning of his book is soon interrupted by "the fall ... of a once wallstrait oldpaar" and a clap of thunder (3.15–17), the sound of which, in the book's cyclic orientation, is both cause and effect of the fall. The passage from grace to corruption is thus an easy one, as the following transformation implies: "O, foetal sleep! Ah, fatal slip!" (563.10). In the *Wake* innocence suggests corruptibility; perfection and imperfection are coincident contraries. "The Second Watch of Shaun" borrows the opening of *Das Rheingold*, as did "Sirens." Here Jaun, like Alberich, has renounced love, and in his lecture to his sisters on chastity, he borrows Wagner's connection between the innocence of the Rhinedaughters and the purity of the unspoiled gold, between sexual and natural innocence. The celibate Jaun speaks in what "Sirens" had called "the voice ... of unlove" (*U* 11.1007; 283):

Guard that gem, Sissy, rich and rare, ses he. In this cold old worold who'll feel it? Hum! The jewel you're all so cracked about there's flitty few of them gets it for there's nothing now but the sable stoles and a runabout to match it. Sing him a ring. Touch me low. And I'll lech ye so, my soandso. (441.18–22)

Jaun and Alberich move in opposite directions: the Nibelung from intense desire to "unlove," Jaun from renunciation to coarse lechery. Jaun's insistence that his sisters "guard that gem" is a reminder of the Rhinedaughters' task in *Rheingold*, a task they perform poorly, to say the least; and the reference to singing a "ring" reinforces the link to Wagner. The Rhinedaughters' famous song – "Weialala leia, / Wallala leialala" (*R* 312) – a reminder of the rape of the gold and the violation of nature, appears at several points in the *Ring*. The *Wake* borrows this song and its variations at least five times. Most notably, a passage in "Questions and Answers," while evoking the restrained hush of the Wagnerian audience, captures the light-heartedness, even in lamentation, of the life principle in both Joyce and Wagner: "But the river tripped on her by and by, lapping as though her heart was brook: *Why, why, why! Weh, O weh! I'se so silly to be flowing but I no canna stay!* No applause, please!" (159.16 – 19). Blending the Rhinedaughters' "Weia" with the more familiar "O Weh," ALP laments her loss of innocence and the passing of time, which, as the flowing Liffey, she also represents. ("Stream of life," reflects a melancholy Bloom, accepting Milly's inevitable sexual awakening [*U* 8.176; 155].) Significantly, Wagner's Rhine-daughters and their song had provided the same evocation of lost innocence for "The Fire Sermon" of *The Waste Land*.

If Alberich represents the demonic element in the cosmology of the *Ring*, Wotan is its Heavenly Father. But the moral distinction between "Licht-Alberich" and "Schwarz-Alberich" (*R* 171 – 2), between the ruler of gods and men and the enslaver of Nibelungs, is, in Wagner's scheme, only a matter of degree.[5] "Alberich and his ring," wrote Wagner, "would have been powerless to harm the gods had they not themselves been suscep-tible to evil."[6] Wotan's vanity and ambition are immediately apparent when he appears in *Rheingold*. In scene 2 we discover that he has commissioned the giants to build him a castle, Valhalla, that will extend and solidify his rule. The god who once pledged his single eye for the love of a woman (*R* 21) has promised the Germanic goddess of love, Freia, as payment for Valhalla. Pressed, when the reckoning comes, to find a substitute, Wotan steals Alberich's ring and hoard of gold and uses them to ransom

Freia; in Wakean parlance, he "has a tussle with the trulls and then does himself justice" (134.33). The decline of love and the ascendancy of power among Wotan's priorities are nowhere more apparent than in scene 4 of *Rheingold*, where the hoard, including the ring, is piled to the point where it obscures Freia from view. In failing to restore the ring to the Rhine, Wotan perpetuates Alberich's offense and brings the ring's curse on himself. But the consequences of Wotan's corruptibility, which undermines the moral stability of the world over which he presides, extend well beyond his own fate and that of his fellow gods. As Alberich points out in *Rheingold*, scene 4, "against all that was, is, and shall be, you are planning a crime by laying your hand on the ring!" (*R* 57). Sieglinde's enslavement in marriage, Fasolt's murder, the servitude of the Nibelungs, and Gunther's feckless rule all reflect the fallibility at the ethical center of the *Ring*. Wotan's ruthless pursuit of power and his subjugation of love will engender the postlapsarian world of *Die Walküre* and, eventually, the Twilight of the Gods.[17]

Throughout the *Wake* Wotan supports the character of HCE. Like Wotan, HCE in his various incarnations is a father figure, lawmaker, conquerer, Masterbuilder, and establisher of church and state. Like Wotan, HCE is guilty of an elemental crime, analogous to original sin, that visits mortality upon him and, by implication, upon the generation he represents. (Like Wotan, then, HCE combines elements of Adam and the Judeo-Christian God.) HCE's compromised authority is developed late in the *Wake* with the help of the "Entrance of the Gods into Valhalla" from *Das Rheingold*: "They know him, the covenanter, by rote at least, for a chameleon at last, in his true falseheaven colours from ultraviolet to subred tissues. That's his last tryon to march through the grand tryomphal arch. His reignbolt's shot" (590. 7–10). Here the use of the word "covenanter" in connection with the rainbow bridge from the final scene of *Rheingold* is a reminder of the position Wotan and HCE share as "staidy lavgiver[s]" (*FW* 545.32), "faulter[s]-in-law" (325.15), and makers of dishonest bargains in these two versions of Genesis. Through the disingenuous agreement he makes with the builders of Valhalla, Wotan becomes a moral "chameleon ... in his true falseheaven colours"; and despite the grandeur of the conclusion to *Rheingold*, Wagner's audience cannot help feeling that Wotan's "reignbolt's shot." HCE's gloomy demeanor as he contemplates his waning powers and awaits his demise, "hungerstriking all alone and holding doomsdag over hunselv" (199.4 – 5), evokes Wotan's weary acceptance of his own self-induced extinction, as Waltraute reports it in act 1.3 of *Götterdämmerung*. Like his Wagnerian counterpart, HCE presides over a fallen world of his own creation, a world whose nature is revealed most clearly in the squalid city of "Haveth Childers Everywhere." In a Wakean adaptation of Germanic myth, "odinburgh" (487.9 – 10) has supplanted the "garthen of Odin" (69.10). Both Wotan and HCE have subliminated the sexual impulse in personal ambition and in what they regard as social progress, and the poor domestic lives of Wotan and Fricka on the one hand and HCE and ALP on the other are virtual parodies of the sacred marriage as Frazer describes it in *The Golden Bough*.[18] Finally, both HCE and Wotan are related to the scapegoat of fertility myth and to the dying, impotent god who must be replaced if life is to continue.

Wotan first appears in the *Wake* as the Jute, a stranger who attempts, like the many invaders of Ireland compressed into HCE, to cheat an Irish native:

Jute. —One eyegonblack. Bisons is bisons. Let me fore all your hasitancy cross your qualm with trink gilt ...
Mutt. —Louee, louee! How wooden I not know it, the intellible greytcloak of Cedric Silkyshag! (16.29 – 34)

In his earthly manifestations, as both Wälse in *Die Walküre* and the Wanderer in *Siegfried*, Wotan (here "wooden") wears a long, dark cloak ("the intellible greytcloak") and a large hat, the brim of which conceals the missing eye ("One eyegonblack") that is his trademark. (Wotan's identifying mark is analogous to HCE's hump and to the large ears of two of HCE's avatars – Midas and King Mark.[19]) Wotan appears, again as the Wanderer, immediately after the "Butt and Taff" episode of II.3, in a description of postlapsarian man: "We all, for whole men is lepers, have been nobbut wonterers in that chill childerness which is our true name after the allfaulters" (355.33 – 5). "Wonterer" includes

"Wanderer" just as "allfaulter" does "Allfather," another of Wotan's names in Germanic mythology.[20] Joyce's modification of "Allfather" emphasizes the point that HCE and Wotan, like Adam, are not only archetypal fathers but archetypal sinners as well, "fafafather of all schemes for to bother us" (45.15). Indeed, as Atherton has suggested, one of the fundamental axioms of the *Wake*, and certainly the most significant departure from the Genesis parallel, is the attribution of original sin to God himself.[21] The implication of this passage in II.3 is that the consequences of the first sin are visited upon the children: "after the allfaulters we all have been nobbut wonterers." There may also be an oblique allusion to Wotan later in II.3, when HCE speaks of his wife as "calling ... upon all herwayferer gods" (364.36 – 365.1). Indeed, both HCE and Wotan are wayward husbands, their wives sufferers of inattention and infidelity. Elsewhere in the *Wake*, Wagner's Allfather appears as "the Wodin Man" (535.5 – 6), and he is suggested by frequent allusions to "Ygg" and "Odin" (two more of his Germanic names); his notorious crime by the Magazine Wall in Phoenix Park – the "wutan whaal" (325.31) – involves, at least in one version, "a woden affair in the shape of a webley" (82.16). HCE and ALP are "Yggely ogs Weib" (267.19 – 20), and, most interestingly, the tale of Earwicker's crime (on one level, the *Wake* itself) is "this Eyraw*ygg*la saga" (48.16 – 17, my emphasis). Wotan was ideally suited to help Joyce portray his idea of a limited, erring god.

In *Rheingold* Wotan is warned that by using the ring to pay for Valhalla rather than returning it to the Rhine he is arranging his own destruction. But in the Prelude of *Götterdämmerung*, the Norns ascribe the Dusk of the Gods to another cause, a crime much like the plucking of the golden bough in the sacred grove of Diana: Wotan's having broken a branch from the *Weltesche* ("World Ash"), or Yggdrasill, and fashioning a spear on which he would engrave the laws and treaties of his rule. The Norns' story of the *Weltesche*'s subsequent death helps explain why, despite the return of the ring in *Götterdämmerung* 3.3, the gods' decline should be inevitable. It also extends the ethical significance of Wotan's crime and further defines the nature of evil in the *Ring*. Wotan's crime against nature in this parable is closely linked to his position as a maker and enforcer of law, as a builder of civilization at nature's expense. These two versions of Wotan's crime, therefore, are conceptually the same: for the making and engraving of the spear, like the building of Valhalla, represent Wotan's desire to civilize and govern. In breaking the bow from the Tree of Life, in building Valhalla, and in subjecting men and gods to his rule, Wotan, like Alberich, exchanges life and love for worldly power. Without Freia and her golden apples, the gods quickly age; without the *Weltesche*, life cannot be sustained. Throughout the *Ring*, Valhalla, supported by its stately musical motif, functions as a splendid symbol of law, civilization, and the power that enslaves and ultimately destroys both its subjects and its wielder.

In the *Wake* Joyce numbers Valhalla among the phallic monuments of worldly ambition and institutional power that appear, like leitmotifs, throughout the book: Wellington's Memorial, Howth Castle, Wall Street, the house that Jack built, the Eiffel Tower, Halvard Solness' tower, the Tower of Babel. According to Adaline Glasheen, HCE "is damned because he is Masterbuilder of this our masculine civilization ... HCE builds, therefore he falls."[22] The first reference to Valhalla in the *Wake* is connected with the fall of "Bygmester Finnegan" (4.18) from the ladder on which he is constructing a wall in Dublin – indeed, on which he helps erect the congested modern city itself: "wallhall's horrors ["Valhalla's heroes"] of rollsrights, carhacks, stonengens, kisstvanes, tramtrees, fargobawlers, autokinotons, hippohobbilies, streetfleets, tournintaxes, megaphoggs, circuses and wardsmoats and basilikerks and aeropagods" (5.30–3). This hod carrier's fall, a version of HCE's crime in the park, is analogous to "Der Fall Adams" (70.5), itself an echo of Nietzsche's *Der Fall Wagner*. The site of the crime, Phoenix Park, is linked to Valhalla in the "Third Watch of Shaun":

—And what sigeth Woodin Warneung thereof?
—Trickspissers vill be pairsecluded.
—There used to be a tree stuck up? An overlisting eshtree?
(503.28–30)

Here is Wotan, with a decidedly German accent, as law-
("Woodin-Warneung") giver and proprietor of the heavenly
city that, as we have seen, he has established at the cost of the
Weltesche, here an "overlisting eshtree." (In some sources the
Weltesche stands in the middle of Valhalla, with its branches
spreading over the roof.) Like the elm at the end of the first book
of the *Wake*, the great ash represents the life principle in the *Ring*,
and Wotan, we learn in *Götterdämmerung* 1.3, has ordered that the
dying tree be cut down. Hence, before this postlapsarian age of
"wallhall's horrors," it "used to be ... stuck up":

—Woe! Woe! So that was how he became the foerst of our treefellers?
— *Yesche* and ... the fanest of our truefalluses.

(506.15–18, my emphasis)[23]

In the *Wake* Valhalla helps represent man's impulse to civilize
and govern and provides a tangible reminder of the sin committed
by "the first of our tree fellers." Indeed, if HCE is "the fanest
of our truefalluses," then man and his handiwork – Valhalla
is Wotan's "fane" – have become indistinguishable.

Valhalla is most important in the "Haveth Childers Everywhere" section of III.3, where Joyce's Allfather discourses proudly
on the cities of the world, the "Megalopolis" (128.3) that he
embodies. Just before HCE begins, a heckler challenges his
confident proprietorship in a derisive reference to Wotan's new
home: "Wallpurgies! And it's this's your deified city?" (530.31).
The sarcasm is well founded, for what follows is a description of
urban blight and squalor: "but never a blid had bledded or
bludded since long agore when the whole blighty acre was bladey
well pessovered" (553.6–8). HCE describes the founding of
Dublin, his "Urbs in Rure" (551.24) as follows: "and I fenced it
about with huge Chesterfield elms ... and pons for aguaducks ...
the hallow vall" (553.18–22). "Hallow vall" is simply "Valhalla" reversed, and a "pons" in this context recalls the rainbow bridge that Donner and the nearby "[F]roh, the frothy
freshener" (553.27) build as a path to Valhalla in the memorable
conclusion to *Rheingold*. The rainbow, stretching from earth to
sky, is rich in literary and theological meaning: it is a sign of
God's covenant with Noah, a pathway to heaven, and, in

Germanic mythology, a symbol of the gods' rule over men.[24]
"Haveth Childers Everywhere" borrows the rainbow bridge to
compare the first bridging of the Liffey to HCE's sexual conquest
of ALP. (The washerwomen of I.8, we recall, take up the case
of when ALP was first "bridged.") Civilization, according to the
Wake, is male resourcefulness acting upon receptive, female
nature; it is, to borrow one of the many copulative images in the
Wake, a "dom on dam" (625.20), a cathedral by a river, a priest
or gentleman and his mother:

> and I abridged with domfine norsemanship till I had done abate her
> maidan race, my baresark bride, and knew her fleshly when with all
> my bawdy did I her whorship, min bryllupswibe: Heaven, he hall-
> thundered; Heydays, he flung blissforhers. And I cast my tenspan
> joys on her ... from bank of call to echobank ... and to ringstresse I
> thumbed her with iern of Erin. (547.26 – 33)

"Norsemanship" helps establish the context, "Heydays" echoes
the thundergod's "Heda! Heda! Hedo!" (*R* 69), and "tenspan
joys ... from bank of call to echobank" is Wagner's bridge, the
"ringstresse" (with Ger. *Strasse*, "*Ring*-street") that arches from
the banks of the Rhine to the gate of Valhalla.[25] The presence of
Donner's thunder in this passage is important, for thunder in the
Wake is God's stuttering admission that he has sinned, and Finnegan's fall takes place on a "thundersday" (5.13). It must have
seemed perfectly appropriate to Joyce that the gods' entrance into
Valhalla, the symbol of Wotan's rule and of his capacity for evil,
should have been marked by thunder. In fact, thunder sounds a
dozen or more times in the score to the *Ring*, nearly always in
association with Wotan; similarly, thunder, heard ten times in the
Wake, is one of the book's most important leitmotifs, always appearing in connection with HCE and his crime. Finally, the song of the
Rhinedaughters makes two appearances in "Haveth Childers
Everywhere," in lamentation of ravished nature. The first places
the Rhinedaughters in uneasy but altogether Wakean combination
with Valhalla, their thematic antithesis: "Walhalloo, Walhalloo,
Walhalloo, mourn in plein!" (541.22); the second, occurring at
the end of "Haveth Childers Everywhere," gives nature the final
word, as Wagner did in *Rheingold* and in the *Ring* as a whole:
"Mattahah! Marahah! Luahah! Joahanahanahana!" (554.10).[26]

Wotan's wisdom in the *Ring* consists in his coming to understand that, for the good of the world, he must abdicate his ir-
revocably compromised rule in favor of a free-thinking, god-
disdaining humanity that can accomplish what he cannot – the
restoration of the ring to the Rhine and of the world to its original
condition. "The development of the whole poem," wrote Wagner
to August Roeckel,

sets forth the necessity of recognising and yielding to the change, the
many-sidedness, the multiplicity, the eternal renewing of reality and
of life. Wotan rises to the tragic height of *willing* his own destruction.
This is the lesson that we have to learn from the history of mankind:
to will what necessity imposes, and ourselves to bring it about. The creative
product of this supreme, self-destroying will, its victorious achievement,
is a fearless human being, one who never ceases to love: Siegfried.[7]

Siegfried is to some extent anticipated by his father Siegmund,
who proves his mettle by drawing Wotan's sword out of the ash
tree in Hunding's hut (as Arthur drew Excalibur out of the stone)
and, when he faces death in act 2.4 of *Die Walküre*, by choosing
Sieglinde over Valhalla's "loveless pleasures" (*R* 121). But Wotan's
role in raising and providing for Siegmund has compromised the
young hero's independence – "in him," Fricka tells Wotan,
"I find only you" (*R* 101) – and when Fricka demands Siegmund's death for his adultery and incest with Sieglinde, Wotan
must give his reluctant assent. Siegfried, however, raised in the
bosom of nature and in ignorance of his godly pedigree, represents
the fulfillment of Wotan's "great idea" – "a fearless human
being ... who never ceases to love." Siegfried's famous fearless-
ness applies to divinity as well as to man and beast, and when
he confronts his grandfather in the pivotal act 3.2 of *Siegfried*, he
joyfully shatters Wotan's spear, another symbol of godly rule,
with the newly forged Nothung. Wotan's equivocal position as
he faces his demise in this scene is outlined, as we saw in chapter
2, in Joyce's notes to *Exiles*: "If Robert really prepares the way
for Richard's advance and hopes for it while he tries at the same
time ... to combat this advance ... the position is like that of
Wotan who in willing the birth and growth of Siegfried longs for
his own destruction" (*E* 118–19). (Elsewhere, another represen-
tative of authority tells another revolutionary, "I like to break

a lance with you, old as I am" [*U* 2.424 – 5; 35].) In the *Ring* the healthy – and thoroughly natural – impulses of a liberated Humanity, "doing exactly what it likes, and producing order instead of confusion thereby because it likes to do what is necessary for the good of the race,"[28] replace law, coercion, and the rule of God. The progress from divine to heroic – and perhaps, with Siegfried's death, to human – follows the Vichian pattern very closely.[29]

In the *Wake*, as in the *Ring*, only through the ascendancy of the son is the new order established. Shem and Shaun, who represent new ages or ways of life, supplant their erring father, whose demise is the price he pays for his corruptibility. The murder of the would-be emperor Caesar and the preservation of the Roman republic provide one of the best variations on the book's generational theme – "The older sisars (Tyrants, regicide is too good for you!) become unbeurrable from age" (162.1 – 2) – but further analogies are available in Tristan's cuckolding of King Mark, Patrick's defeat of the Druid, and Buckley's shooting of the Russian General, to mention just a few. Siegfried's contribution to the struggle between generations in the *Wake* is most important in "Night Lessons" (II.2), where Shem and Shaun, as Dolph and Kev, acquire the knowledge that the overthrow of their father, in II.3, will require – "Art, literature, politics, economy, chemistry, humanity" (306.13 – 15); as the acrostic shows, they study their parents themselves. The boys' period of preparation parallels the heroic apprenticeship that Wagner's naive hero serves in the first two acts of *Siegfried* – learning to forge his father's sword, studying the voices of nature, and slaying the dragon Fafner – before he confronts Wotan in act 3. Again the parallel to Genesis, here in connection with the apple and tree of knowledge, is appropriate. According to Weston, Siegfried's coming to understand the voices of birds when he tastes the dragon's blood is analogous to the Irish story of Finn, who acquires "the gift of all wisdom" when he tastes the legendary Salmon.[30] In the *Wake* Joyce associates this acquisition of knowledge with original sin and with defiance of the father; so in challenging HCE's claim to knowledge, the boys are reenacting the archetypal crime in Phoenix Park.

The first allusion to Siegfried in "Night Lessons" occurs in an implied comparison between Issy's love for her brother and Brutus' love for Caesar in *Julius Caesar*: "What if she love Sieger less though she leave Ruhm moan?" (281.22 – 3). (The theme of incest, a love Wagner felt nature condoned if law did not, is of crucial importance in *Die Walküre*.) The allusion is reinforced on the same page in a Wakean spelling of Vercingetorix, the Gaul who, like Siegfried, revolted against the "older sisars" (162.1): 'Valsinggiddyrex' (281.F1). (Siegfried is a *Wälsung* or Volsung.) Siegfried's woodbird, whose motif Dixon whistled in *A Portrait* (237), may be evoked in the summary of subjects taken up in "Night Lessons": "Is the Pen Mightier than the Sword? ... The Voice of Nature in the Forest, Your Favorite Hero or Heroine" (306.18 – 21). Dolph mentions Siegfried's sword in the middle of the "geomater" (297.1) lesson he is giving Kev: "I bring town eau and curry nothung up my sleeve" (295.17 – 18). "Nothung," apparently, is one of the weapons the boys will use against their father, as Siegfried did against Wotan; that Shem-Dolph apparently carries the sword is a reminder of his kinship to Stephen Dedalus, who brandished his own *Nothung* in "Circe," shouting defiance to authority in all its forms: "*Non serviam!* ... Break my spirit, all of you, if you can! I'll bring you all to heel!" (*U* 15. 4228 – 36; 582). (Indeed, because Shem is a revolutionary figure and Shaun a god-fearing man, Siegfried is closer to Shem.) Siegfried's forging of the sword may be invoked in an apostrophe to Shem and to Joyce himself: "Forge away, Sunny Sim!" (305. 4 – 5). "Sunny Sim" is a reminder that Siegfried, Shem, and Shaun, heralding "new dawns," are related to the sun-god of fertility myth; "Sunny Jim" was Joyce's childhood nickname. In the conclusion of *Siegfried*, Brünnhilde greets her redeemer and awakener as follows:

> O Siegfried! Siegfried!
> Seliger Held!
> Du Wecker des Lebens,
> siegendes Licht! (*R* 236)[31]

Indeed, according to Weston, Brünnhilde's awakening by Siegfried is the "central incident" of the entire *Ring*, revealing the "originally mythic character of the hero" and "typifying the awakening of the earth from her winter sleep by the vivifying power of the sun."[32] In "The Mime of Mick, Nick and the Maggies," the Flowermaidens' admiration of Shaun, appropriately, is "heliolatry" (237.1).

Siegfried is an important revolutionary presence elsewhere in the *Wake* as well. In I.6 the Mookse, analogous to Shaun, "set off with his father's sword, his *lancia spezzata* [It. "broken spear"] ... every inch of an immortal" (152.31–4). Here the equivocation between spear and sword, the symbols, respectively, of Wotan's rule and of Siegfried's independence, may reflect Shaun's attachment to his father (as opposed to Shem's to his mother) even as he prepares to assume HCE's position of authority. In III.2 Shaun-Jaun, again taking Siegfried's part,

made out through his eroscope the apparition of his fond sister Izzy for he knowed his love ... nor could he forget her so tarnelly easy as all that since he was brotherbesides her benedict godfather. (431.14–18)

This passage draws on a series of events in *Götterdämmerung*. Gunther, Gutrune, and Hagen plot to give Siegfried a potion that will erase his memory of Brünnhilde and focus his affections on Gutrune. This accomplished, the three conspirators persuade Siegfried to use his magic helmet, the *Tarnhelm*, evoked here in "tarnelly easy," to assume Gunther's form and win his forgotten love Brünnhilde – technically Siegfried's aunt, if not his sister – for Gunther, his newly acquired blood-brother. Elsewhere, Hodgart finds "forge Nothung" buried in the "Mime": "he shall not *forget* that pucking Pugases ... Like *gnawthing* unheardth!" (231.20–2, my emphasis);[33] and the woodbird's song appears in III.1: "How mielodorous is thy bel chant, O songbird, and how exqueezit thine after draught!" (412.7–8). Elsewhere, Butt-Shaun and the demonic cad in the park, respectively, assume Siegfried's role in "sieger besieged" (352.25) and "Snakeeye!" (534.27), a reference to the identifying mark of the Volsungs.[34]

If, as Carl Dahlhaus has written, in composing the *Ring* Wagner has resurrected the gods of Germanic myth, "it is not to glorify them but to render them up to self-destruction."[35] Wagner's version of the *Ragnarok* – "yours," writes Shem, "till the rending of the rocks'' (170.23–4) – links the *Götterdämmerung* and *Weltenuntergang* of Germanic myth with the death of Siegfried. After Brünnhilde's immolation in Siegfried's pyre, the hall of the Gibichungs begins to burn,[36] and the conflagration is shown to include Valhalla, where, according to the stage directions, the gods have calmly assembled. The *Wake* borrows Wagner's ''guttergloomering'' (565.2) to help represent the ends of its cycles of day, individual human life, and civilization generally. The title of the conclusion to the *Ring* appears in two evocations of twilight: ''the hour of the twattering of bards in the twitterlitter'' (37.17) and ''Gwds with gurs are gttrdmmrng. Hlls Vlls'' (258.1–2), the latter of which occurs at the book's actual twilight hour, in II.1. Two further uses of the title are related to death. In I.1 the Jute, who, as we have seen, is linked to Wotan, curses the Mutt's garbled speech: ''I can beuraly forsstand a weird from sturk to finnic in such a patwhat as your rutterdamrotter ... See you doomed'' (17.13–16). A passage in II.3 discusses speculation that the Norwegian captain has gone down with his ship: ''fearsome where they were he had gone dump in the doomering [cf. *Dämmerung*] this tide where the peixies would pickle him down to the button of his seat'' (316.16–18). ''Peixies'' recalls the Rhinedaughters – in *Rheingold* Alberich calls them ''nixies'' (cf. Ger. *Nicker* [R 5]) – who drag Hagen into the Rhine at the end of the *Ring*. Indeed, Hagen's last words – ''Zurück vom Ring!'' (*R* 328) – may lurk in the play of the children in II.1: ''Oh backed von dem zug!'' (249.20).[37] Allusions to Siegfried's death appear at least twice in the *Wake*. The first, linking the funeral of Wagner's hero with that of Tim Finnegan, draws on the flooding Rhine at the conclusion of *Götterdämmerung*: ''And rivers burst out like weeming racesround joydrinks for the fewnrally'' (277.3–5). The second, in one of the densest Wagnerian passages in Joyce's book, underscores the writer's preoccupation with betrayal:

—Sold! I am sold! Brinabride! My ersther! My sidster! Brinabride, goodbye! Brinabride! I sold! ...
—Fort! Fort! Bayroyt! March!
—Me! I'm true. True! Isolde. Pipette. My precious!
—Zinzin.

—Brinabride, bet my price! Brinabride! ...
—Brinabride, my price! When you sell get my price!
                    SILENCE. (500.21–501.6)

In the penultimate scene of *Götterdämmerung*, Siegfried has been
betrayed ("sold") by Hagen, Gunther, and, as this passage
affirms, Brünnhilde. Immediately before he dies he regains his
memory of his first love (his "ersther"), and his last bit of music
begins, "Brünnhilde! Holiest bride!" (*R* 320), here "Brinabride!"
(These were the words that, in Italian, so deeply moved Joyce
in 1907.[38]) The allusions to Bayreuth and to the Wagnerian
"Silence" (compare 14.6 and 159.19) reinforce the composer's
presence in this passage. Tristan and Parnell, both betrayed by
erstwhile followers, are evoked, respectively, in "I sold ... Isolde"
and in Parnell's famous disdain for those he suspected of plotting
against him: "When you sell, get my price."[39]

The *Wake* draws most heavily on Wagner's apocalypse in its
final pages, as Joyce developed the *ricorso* phase to which Vico
had given comparatively little attention.[40] Book IV, with its
allusions to revolution, Mongolian hordes, and "Deemsday"
(602.20), portrays the darkest hour of the night, the death of HCE,
the crumbling of civilization. Wagner's doomed gods, gathered
in a burning Valhalla at the end of *Götterdämmerung*, appear early
in book IV as "Gaunt grey ghostly gossips growing grubber in
the glow" (594.25–6). Valhalla is mentioned at 597.14 and 609.18,
and Finn MacCool's birds, who begin their flight in ALP's final
monologue, may owe something to Wotan's ravens, whose appearance at Siegfried's murder signals Wotan that the death of
the gods is at hand: "Or the birds start their treestirm shindy.
Look, there are yours off, high on high! And cooshes, sweet good
luck they're cawing you, Coole! You see, they're as white as the
riven snae" (621.35–622.2). Returning to her father at the book's
end, ALP imagines herself carried by an Amazonian Valkyrie
to Valhalla and to Allfather Wotan:

I can seen meself among them, allaniuvia pulchrabelled. How she was
handsome, the wild Amazia, when she would seize to my other breast!
And what is she weird, haughty Niluna, that she will snatch from my
ownest hair! For 'tis they are the stormies. Ho hang! Hang ho! And
the clash of our cries till we spring to be free. (627.27–32)

Here "stormies" evokes the storm clouds on which Wotan's daughters ride, in act 3.1 of *Die Walküre*, as they bear slain warriors to Valhalla; "Ho Hang! Hang Ho!" is Wakean for the Valkyries' famous "Hoyotoho! Hoyotoho!" (*R* 126), which Brünnhilde echoes in her last bit of music in the cycle (*R* 328). As ALP's final monologue comes to a close, these Valkyries may be arranging what Wagner, in another context, had called an "Erlösung dem Erlöser" (*Pars* 126), or "redemption to the redeemer."[41] The Immolation scene, where Brünnhilde and Siegfried are reunited in death, may contribute to the reunion between the Liffey and the sea on the last page of the *Wake*: "the near sight of the mere size of him … makes me seasilt saltsick and I rush, my only, into your arms. I see them rising" (628.2 – 5). "Them" in this passage evokes the dual presence of fire and water – Siegfried's pyre and the flooding Rhine – at the end of the *Ring*.

But death and destruction are not final in either work. Brünnhilde's return of the ring to the Rhine, though too late to save Wotan, nonetheless dissolves Alberich's curse and assures that life will rise from the ruins that fire and water have purified. That the gods themselves are to "arise from the general wreck… purified from their sins, and restored to a condition of innocency," as they do in Wagner's mythic sources,[42] is highly doubtful, since this would run counter to the humanism and anti-authoritarianism of the work. In abdicating his power, however, and in submitting to the ebb and flow of life, Wotan leaves the world a better place, for humanity is now free of these gods and of the enslaving influence of religious belief. The *Ring* is Wotan's tragedy but the triumph of the liberated humanity that endures – "a race of men," as Shaw puts it, "in whom the life-giving impulses predominate."[43] Wagner's idealized race of godless, freely loving men is adumbrated throughout the *Ring* in the actions of the Volsungs and of Brünnhilde: Siegmund and Sieglinde's obedience to natural law and defiance of Fricka and Wotan in consummating their love; Siegfried's scorn for authority in rescuing Brünnhilde; Brünnhilde's willing acceptance of humanity and mortality when Wotan punishes her for exercising her free will. In the conclusion of *Siegfried*, Wagner's heroine sings,

> Farewell, Walhall's
> bright glittering world!
> Your glorious halls
> now may fall to dust!
> Farewell, proud, radiant,
> godly race!
> End in joy,
> you eternal clan! (*R* 243)

Significantly, the hall of the Gibichungs, who make religious sacrifices in act 2.3 of *Götterdämmerung*, goes up in the collective smoke at the end of the *Ring*. The gods are gone, but the world is better off without them. The optimism of the conclusion is affirmed musically in the cycle's final measures by the "rapturous love" or "redemption through love" motif, which first appeared in *Die Walküre* in connection with Siegfried's conception and which expresses the optimism associated with new life.[44] Indeed, the fact that the rising "Nature" and falling "Twilight of the Gods" motifs are melodic inversions emphasizes Wagner's principle of restoration: what goes down must come up.[45]

The *Wake* offers the same promise of new life. Book IV takes place immediately before dawn on Holy Saturday night, just before the Resurrection. In her monologue ALP bids her Christ-like husband rise, and we know that he does, since he is in position to fall once again, as Finn MacCool, on the book's first page. "Phall if you but will," we learn early in the *Wake*, "rise you must" (4.15–16). Water, which gives, destroys, and purifies life in the *Ring*, has important symbolic value for Joyce in both *Ulysses* and the *Wake*. The "hydrophobe" Stephen hates both "immersion" and "submersion" (*U* 17.237–8; 673) throughout *Ulysses*; the "waterlover" Bloom appreciates water's "universality ... constancy to its nature ... properties for cleansing, quenching thirst and fire, nourishing vegetation" (17.183–215; 671–2). Many allusions to Ariel's "Full Fathom Five" in *The Tempest* establish Joyce's interest in the destructive and regenerative properties of water. Baptism, the sacrament of new life or "the regeneration of all man by affusion of water" (*FW* 606.11–12), is a preoccupation in the *Wake*. In 1.8 the souls of sinful Dubliners are cleansed in the purifying waters of the Liffey:

"They've moist come off her ... Baptiste me, father, for she has
sinned!" (204.35–6); and the leitmotif "tauftauf" (Ger. *taufen*,
to baptize) is scattered throughout the book. True to the dictum
of Quinet, Nature, embodied in the Rhine and Liffey, gets the
last word over civilization in both works. Indeed, ALP's final
words are analogous to Molly's in *Ulysses*: "In conception and
technique," Joyce explained to Harriet Weaver, "I tried to
depict the earth which is prehuman and presumably posthuman"
(*L* 1:180). Harry Levin has written that in the *Wake*, "Joyce is
finally taking his leave of the monumental ruins of the city of
man, and attaching his hope to the matriarchal continuity of the
years, the seasons, and the months."[46] In *Finnegans Wake*, as in
the *Ring*, our end is at our beginning – with the river and the
song of the Rhinedaughters: "A way a lone a last a loved a long
the" (628.15–16). ALP has returned to her source – "For as
Anna was at the beginning lives yet and will return" (277.12–13)
– and the gold to the Rhine. The cycle is complete.[47]

Much of the influence of the *Ring* on the *Wake* may be found
not in specific allusions but in the many character types, situations,
and themes which contribute to the mythic tone and for which
Joyce may be at least partially indebted to Wagner. The dragon
guarding a treasure hoard – Fafner in the *Ring* – is a common
mythic figure. In the *Wake* he helps form the Jute: "Me seemeth
a dragon man ... Lets we overstep his fire defences and these kraals
of slitsucked marrogbones. (Cave!)" (15.34–16.3). Giants who
build walls or castles – like Fafner and Fasolt, who live in
"Riesenheim" – are represented by Finn MacCool, Joyce's
"Riesengebirger" (133.6). (Joyce told Budgen that Wagner's
"creative unreproductive" giants were "of the same breed" as
those whom Stephen mentions in "Proteus" [*U* 3.289–93;
44–5].[48]) Incest between brother and sister, frequent in myth,
appears in the love of Siegmund and Sieglinde. The *Wake*,
especially in II.1 and III.2, develops sexual relationships between
Issy and all the men in her family. Riddling contests, like that
of Mime and the Wanderer in *Siegfried*, occur in the tale of the
Prankquean in I.1 and in the children's games in "The Mime
of Mick, Nick and the Maggies," in which title Wagner's riddling
smith may himself appear. Finally, two kinds of struggle in the

Wake find precedent in many mythic sources, including the *Ring*. The first is a battle between brother figures who are polar opposites, Shem and Shaun. In the *Ring*, Wotan and Alberich share this relation, as the names they are given in *Siegfried* – Licht-Alberich and Schwarz-Alberich – suggest; Hagen and Siegfried, descendants, according to Weston,[49] of primeval antagonists, bear the same relation. Joyce expressed this duality throughout the *Wake* with the aid of Giordano Bruno and Nicholas of Cusa. As we have seen, he used another Wagnerian character to explain Bruno's theory of antithesis: "His philosophy is a kind of dualism – every power in nature must evolve an opposite in order to realise itself and opposition brings reunion etc etc. Tristan on his first visit to Ireland turned his name inside out" (*L* 1:226). The second kind of encounter, between fathers and sons, entrenched power and revolutionary action, has been of special importance in this chapter on the cyclic structure of the *Wake*. Wotan and Siegfried provide this sort of parallel for HCE and his sons, Mark and Tristan, the Druid and Patrick, the Russian General and Buckley.

Parsifal appears in the *Wake* as well, most frequently, as chapter 4 suggests, in connection with the hero's temptation by the Flowermaidens, who wear "the wieds of pansiful heathvens" (*FW* 426.21) in Wagner's second act. But as another mythic tale of sin, expiation, and redemption, Wagner's last opera contributes to the cyclic structure of the *Wake* much as the *Ring* does, though less pervasively, helping make Joyce's book "solid as a rock" (*CW* 43). In both operas, an erring ruler presides over a fallen world and longs openly for extinction; in each case, a youthful hero restores or helps restore a sacred object to its rightful place (the ring to the Rhine, the spear to Monsalvat), fulfills a prophecy, and replaces or redeems the declining ruler. The connection between the two works is perhaps most apparent in the identification of these two naive heroes, both posthumous children: Siegfried the boy "who knows no fear," Parsifal the "pure fool." Indeed, Weston has concluded that "there is a common mythic element at the root of both stories, and that, however differently the legends have developed, the two heroes were originally *one*."[50] In some ways Amfortas, in fact, makes a better parallel for HCE than does Wotan, for, like HCE, he has squandered his sexual energy, and his punishment is not only psychological but physical as well: Amfortas endures a wound that will not heal, HCE a hunchback and a stutter. Amfortas is a direct descendant of the mythic Fisher King, and his wound represents both his loss of procreative function and the death of vegetation in winter. All Joyce's mature male figures – Richard Rowan, Bloom, and HCE – suffer wounds to their masculinity in real or imagined cuckoldry or in sexual dysfunction. As we saw in chapter 4, the conclusion to *Exiles* invoked Amfortas in Richard's "deep wound of doubt which can never be healed" (*E* 112).

In the *Wake*, Parsifal, as the Grail King's successor, provides a strong parallel for the sons who replace their vulnerable father. We saw in chapter 4 how "The Mime" of II.1 compares its "month's bunch of pretty maidens" to Wagner's Flowermaidens and Mick-Shaun, by implication, to Wagner's chaste hero. In book IV Parsifal appears in ironic contrast to HCE: "Once you are balladproof you are unperceable to haily, icy and missilethroes" (616.31–3). Parsifal's purity and compassion make him impervious to Kundry's assault on his chastity; HCE's fallibility subjects him to temptation and, in demotic modern life, to gossip and slander, especially in the form of "The Ballad of Persse O'Reilly." He is neither "unperceable" nor "balladproof," nor would he make a suitable Grail King; "missilethroes" evokes both the spear that wounded Amfortas and the "mistletoe" that killed Amfortas' Norse cousin Balder, the god of light. A Wagner-intensive passage in I.6 includes the following reference to *Parsifal*: "and what het importunes our *Mitleid* for in accornish with the Mortadarthella taradition is the poorest commononguardiant waste of time ... Tyro a toray!" (151.19–24). "Mortadarthella taradition" and "accornish" are reminders of the British-Celtic origin of the legend and of Parsifal's association, in some sources, with Arthur's Round Table; "Mitleid" and "toray" evoke the Grail's oracle about Amfortas' redeemer: "Durch Mitleid wissend, / der reine Tor" (*Pars* 91). In I.2 the *Wake* compares Hosty, HCE's musical antagonist and composer of the "Ballad," to the priest who presides over the consecration of the Host, borrowing the Grail scene of act I, complete with orchestration:

The wararrow went round … and the ballad … soon fluttered its secret on white highway and brown byway … through the five pussyfours green of the united states of Scotia Picta … To the added strains (so peacifold) of his majesty the flute, that onecrooned king of inscrewments, Piggott's purest, *ciello alsoliuto*, which Mr Delaney … horn … piped out of his decentsoort hat, looking still more like his purseyful namesake as men of Gaul noted … "Ductor" Hitchcock hoisted his fezzy fuzz at bludgeon's height signum to his companions of the chalice for the Loud Fellow, boys' and *silentium in curia*! … and the canto was chantied there chorussed and christened where by the old tollgate, Saint Annona's Street and Church. (43.21–44.6)

Here Parsifal's name appears in three variations: "pussyfours," "peacifold," and "purseyful"; "Hitchcock," ironically, is the impotent Fisher King Amfortas, who, in this scene from act I, still performs his duties as priest of the Grail; the "companions of the chalice" are the Grail Knights gathered to receive the bread and wine; and the "boys' … canto … chantied there" is the choirboys' music that, during the Communion supper, emanates from the dome of Monsalvat. (These choirboys would reappear in Paul Verlaine's "Parsifal" and in Eliot's allusion to Verlaine's poem in *The Waste Land*: "Et O ces voix d'enfants, chantant dans la coupole!"[5]) The hint of "Parsifal" in the title of Hosty's "ballad" identifies Wagner's hero with the Wakean son who supplants a weakened father.

We have seen, then, how the *Ring* and, to some extent, *Parsifal* provided Joyce with characters, situations, themes, and especially a conceptual framework that would help support *Finnegans Wake*. More important, perhaps, is the extent to which Joyce's lifelong experience of all Wagner's prose writings and operas may have encouraged his general interest in myth and helped shape his own capacity for making myth. In "The Myth of Adonis" Frazer speculates about the origins of myth in the human imagination:

The spectacle of the great changes which annually pass over the face of the earth has powerfully impressed the minds of men in all ages, and stirred them to meditate on the causes of transformations so vast and wonderful. Their curiosity has not been purely disinterested; for even the savage cannot fail to perceive how intimately his own life is bound up with the life of nature, and how the same processes which freeze the stream and strip the earth of vegetation menace him with extinction. At a certain stage of development men ... pictured to themselves the growth and decay of vegetation, the birth and death of living creatures, as effects of the waxing or waning strengths of divine beings, of gods and goddesses, who were born and died, who married and begot children, on the pattern of human life.[52]

This anthropomorphism, including its association between human and natural fertility, is an increasingly important feature of Joyce's writing. Characters in his earlier work, especially women, are deepened by their association with natural forces: Bertha is "the earth, dark, formless, mother, made beautiful by the moonlit night" (*E* 118); Molly suggests "Gea-Tellus, fulfilled, recumbent, big with seed" (*U* 17.2313–14; 737). In the *Wake*, however, Joyce's characters *are*, on one level, natural phenomena – a river, the sea, the sky, a mountain – anthropomorphized into human figures. ALP, in fact, is not only the Liffey but, ultimately, nature itself, and her parents are "the old man of the sea and the old woman in the sky" (599.34–5). Mrs. Porter, the innkeeper's wife, is a human embodiment of that spirit of nature – analogous, in some ways, to Erda in the *Ring*. Joyce's analogies between human and natural fertility are probably most evident in the Blooms' marriage and in that of ALP and HCE. "Calypso," like *The Waste Land* after it, borrows natural imagery to describe passionless, infertile human relations, in this case the marriage of Molly and Bloom: "A barren land, bare waste. Vulcanic lake, the dead sea: no fish, weedless, sunk deep in the earth ... Desolation" (*U* 4.219–29; 61); and the birth of Mina Purefoy's child in "Oxen of the Sun" coincides with the end of a long drought. In the *Wake* HCE must die not only because he has sinned, but also because, like the priest-king of fertility myth, his potency has waned. In I.8 we learn of ALP's efforts to rouse her husband from "his winter's doze" (201.11), and in book IV her desire that he "rise" has sexual as well as spiritual implications.

Joyce, however, extends the mythic link between human and natural fertility to include his own idea of artistic fertility. In Germanic myth the demise of the gods parallels the death of the earth in winter, and the gods' regeneration in a condition of innocence is associated with springtime. In the 1902 essay on Mangan, Joyce used the concept of *Götterdämmerung* to express his notion of artistic fertility, arguing that just as "the ancient gods ... die and come to life many times ... the miracle of light is renewed eternally in the imaginative soul" (*CW* 82–3). "Light," we know, is associated with creation: in Genesis God brings light to the world. Joyce's interest in artistic fertility emerges once again in *A Portrait*, when he tells Lynch the requirements of his aesthetic philosophy: "When we come to the phenomena of artistic conception, artistic gestation and artistic reproduction I require a new terminology and a new personal experience" (209). In *Ulysses* the association between natural and artistic fertility is reinforced by the structure of "Oxen of the Sun," where the human embryo and English literature develop together; and in "Scylla and Charybdis" God is "the playwright who wrote the folio of this world" (9.1046–7; 213). After Him "Shakespeare has created most" (9.1029; 212). Indeed, "Scylla and Charybdis" associates Shakespeare's supposed cuckolding with the fate of many mythic heroes: "The tusk of the boar has wounded him there where love lies ableeding" (9.459–60; 196).[53] In "Circe" when the artist-hero brandishes Siegfried's phallic weapon and "shiver[s] the lamp image, shattering light over the world" (15.99–100; 432), he invokes not only the sun-god of the *Ring* but the God of Genesis as well. The *Wake* develops the analogy between God and the artist still further: "In the buginning is the woid" (*FW* 378.29). According to Atherton, the "fundamental assumption" of this book is that "the artist is God-like in his task of creation."[54] But creation is also associated with original sin, as we have seen in connection with Wotan's building of Valhalla. Thus HCE's notorious crime is really a reenactment of God's original sin: it is his public masturbation, defecation, or urination in Phoenix Park; it is Shem's spilling of ink; it is the writing of *Finnegans Wake*. The idea of a "creative drought," such as Stephen suffers in *Ulysses*, was not alien to Wagner, who endured some five years of artistic inactivity before the opening of *Rheingold* came to him as he "sank into a kind of somnambulistic state, in which I suddenly had the feeling of being immersed in rapidly flowing water."[55]

Another important quality of the mythopoeic imagination, one
which is closely related to its cyclical perception of existence, is
its participation in what Susanne Langer has called "the comic
rhythm." "What justifies the term 'Comedy,'" according to
Langer, "is ... that the Comus was a fertility rite, and the god
it celebrated a fertility god, a symbol of perpetual rebirth, eternal
life."[56] Harold Watts has written of the function that myth performed in ancient communities in offering a kind of imaginative
control over an environment that often seemed hostile and
undependable:

It was myth and rite that could assure men that what man could not
control was, in the long run, as much to be depended on as what he
could control ... Nature and society, myth testified, would always
come full circle, would offer apprehensive man familiarity and not
novelty.[57]

Comic drama, with its episodic plot based on restoration of a
disrupted order, has inherited this mythic function: "Comedy...
offers man the assurance that he can bank on the universe and
its laws and, more importantly, on society and its structure."[58]
Whereas tragic plots convey the sense that the world is alien and
uncontrollable, comic plots offer the illusion that humanity and
nature are in harmony. Comedy and tragedy therefore are defined
less by their tone or thematic material than by the use to which
the material is put. Tragedy, focusing on the career of an individual, makes a *linear* assertion about the nature of existence;
comedy, focusing on a general restoration of equilibrium, makes
a broader *cyclical* assertion.[59] In the mythic world-view, tragedy
and comedy are not antithetical; death is a part of life – a part,
in fact, on which life depends – not the end of it. Or as Bloom
would put it in "Hades," "In the midst of death we are in life"
(*U* 6.759; 108). "Society is continuous though its members, even
the strongest and fairest, live out their lives and die; and even
while each individual fulfills the tragic pattern it participates
also in the comic continuity."[60]

It is tempting to contrast the *Ring* and the *Wake* as "tragic"
and "comic" works.[61] Certainly in departing from the mythic
Ragnarok, with its implication that the gods will experience rebirth,

purified, Wagner detached some of the comic force that naturally adheres to his mythic material. But a powerful comic substructure remains.[62] Many scenes, especially in *Rheingold* and *Siegfried*, are "comic" in the popular sense, the sense that makes the comic nature of the *Wake* so much more apparent: Alberich's oafish pursuit of the Rhinedaughters, Wotan and Loge's capture of Alberich, Wotan and Mime's riddling contest. But in depicting the triumph of the natural order over the acquisitiveness and megalomania of men and gods, the triumph of maternal nature over phallocentric culture, the *Ring* is a comic work in a much deeper sense. In dying Wotan leaves a better world behind: the gold has been restored to its home, and humanity is now free of the gods who denied them free will. Thus while the *Ring* may portray the tragedies of Wotan and Siegfried, it also depicts the victory of life as a whole, as Wagner's cosmos recovers its health and achieves "redemption." The same is true of *Finnegans Wake*, which expresses its rhythm in its cyclical structure, in the presence of the river at both its end and its beginning, in the triumph of eternal Nature over ephemeral civilization, and in its assurance that after his death in book IV, a redeemed HCE will arise (if only, as erring male, to "phall" [4.15] once more) in book I.[63] Indeed, the importance of Wotan's submitting to the powerful rhythms of life, "what necessity imposes," is the lesson that the mourners at Joyce's *Wake* impress upon a stubborn Tim Finnegan: "Now be aisy, good Mr Finnimore, sir" (24.16). Like the *Ring*, the *Wake* portrays individual tragedy but asserts, in its comic rhythm, the omnipotence of life.

CHAPTER 6

The art of arts

> Fiction ... must strenuously aspire to the plasticity of sculpture, the colour of painting, and to the magic suggestiveness of music – which is the art of arts.
>
> Conrad, Preface to *The Nigger of the "Narcissus"*

> But, of course, the real villain is Wagner. He has done more than any man in the nineteenth century towards the muddling of arts.
>
> Forster, *Howards End*

In chapter 4 of *A Portrait*, Stephen Dedalus grapples with the question of his vocation, and he begins to test his capacities as an artist. A passage near the chapter's climax explains the attraction that Stephen feels for language, an attraction that, he now understands, is much stronger than his recent fascination with the mystical powers of the priesthood:

He drew forth a phrase from his treasure and spoke it softly to himself.
—A day of dappled seaborne clouds.
The phrase and the day and the scene harmonised in a chord. Words. Was it their colours? He allowed them to glow and fade, hue after hue: sunrise gold, the russet and green of apple orchards, azure of waves, the greyfringed fleece of clouds. No, it was not their colours: it was the poise and balance of the period itself. Did he then love the rhythmic rise and fall of words better than their associations of legend and colour? Or was it that, being as weak of sight as he was shy of mind, he drew less pleasure from the reflection of the glowing sensible world through the prism of a language manycoloured and richly storied than from the contemplation of an inner world of individual emotions mirrored perfectly in a lucid supple periodic prose? (166–7)

In this synesthetic passage Stephen creates a dichotomy between the "visual" and the "aural" in language, and he links these qualities, respectively, with the mimetic and expressive properties of art: in the "colour" of words, he sees a "reflection of the glowing sensible world"; in their "rhythmic rise and fall," he senses "an inner world of individual emotions." Here Stephen's rejection of color for rhythm amounts, according to his formulation, to a rejection of the objective and "sensible" for the subjective and "emotional." The suitability of his phrase for the day and scene is expressed in a harmless metaphor – they "harmonised in a chord" – but the use of the phrase reflects the hegemony of music over visual art in Stephen's aesthetic vocabulary. Like his future self in *Ulysses*, his descendant Shem in the *Wake*, and, indeed, his own creator, Stephen is "weak of sight" and thus finds more aesthetic pleasure in his ear than in his eye. "Shut your eyes and see," Joyce's young man reflects when we find him, once again on the strand, in "Proteus" (*U* 3.9; 37).[1]

It is tempting to regard Stephen's use of this musical idiom as symptomatic of his ninetyishness and as evidence, therefore, of his distance from the artistic standard that *A Portrait* itself represents. But an interest in the possibilities of "musical" expression persisted in Joyce's own career well after he had reached the artistic majority that Stephen only approaches. As a youth Joyce was content to invoke musical standards, however imprecisely, in his literary criticism: Shakespeare was to be praised for his "gift of seraphic music" (*CW* 39), Ibsen for his "orchestral harmony" (*L* 1:52), Defoe for a narrative style that is "masterly and ... orchestral."[2] In so doing Joyce may have been following the example of Arthur Symons, whose *Symbolist Movement*, where the idea of fusing music and literature is a persistent theme, he had read with great interest at University College (*JJ* 76). But as his career developed, music seemed to offer his own work a range of possibilities. In 1920 Joyce wrote to Frank Budgen that he was thinking of adding a "matutine," an "entr'acte," and a "nocturne" to *Ulysses* (*L* 1:149), and his contention that "Sirens" represented a *fuga per canonem* is well known. A conversation with Budgen on similarities between writing fiction and composing music elicited a characteristically wry discussion of musical analogies in literature:

Writing a novel, he said, was like composing music, with the same elements involved. But how can chords or motifs be incorporated into writing? Joyce answered his own question, "A man might eat kidneys in one chapter, suffer from a kidney disease in another, and one of his friends could be kicked in the kidney in another chapter." (*JJ* 436)

The aim of the modernists, Joyce asserted to Arthur Power, was "to enlarge our vocabulary of the subconscious," and the limitation of the "classical style" was as follows: "It can deal with facts very well, but when it has to deal with motives, the secret currents of life which govern everything, it has not the orchestra, for life is a complicated problem ... [I]t is an intellectual approach which no longer satisfies the modern mind." Here, in the early 1920s, we discover Joyce working with the same association between music and "internal" experience and with elements of the same musical vocabulary – "orchestra" and even "motive" – that Stephen had developed in *A Portrait*; only the earlier dichotomy between the "sensible" and the "inner" now expands to oppose the "intellect" and the "subconscious." When the *Wake* was in its beginnings, Joyce told Power,

To fault a writer because his work is not logically conceived seems to me poor criticism, for the object of a work of art is not to relate facts but to convey an emotion ... Indeed, judging from modern trends it seems that all the arts are tending towards the abstraction of music; and what I am writing at present is entirely governed by that purpose.[3]

In what amounts to a defense of more than his own work, Joyce links "abstract" musical expression with the increasing subjectivity of modern art.

The allusion in this last passage to Walter Pater, whose *Renaissance* had proclaimed famously that "all art constantly aspires towards the condition of music," reminds us that the attraction to music was a constant in modern art, beginning as early as the Romantic movement and extending well into the twentieth century. Eichendorff, Poe, Baudelaire, Verlaine, and Mallarmé had all written poems intended to be musical in an auditory sense;[4] the Symbolists were absorbed with the idea that poetry should be in some sense "musical."[5] Pater's "School of Giorgione" suggested that all art be judged by the extent to which it approaches "musical law,"[6] and Teodor de Wyzewa, in his series on "L'Art wagnérien" for the *Revue wagnérienne*, argued that "Literature only becomes art ... by grafting upon itself a musicality quite alien to its essential, intellectual, nature." [7] An example of criticism conducted according to this musical standard may be found in Symons' praise of "L'Après-midi d'un faune" and "Hérodiade" in *The Symbolist Movement*:

In these two poems I find Mallarmé at the moment when his own desire achieves itself; when he attains Wagner's ideal, that "the most complete work of the poet should be that which, in its final achievement, becomes a perfect music": every word is a jewel ... every image is a symbol, and the whole poem is visible music. [8]

Even after the turn of the century, Proust would call the first section of *Swann's Way* an "overture," and Gide would describe *The Counterfeiters* as "fugal." This impulse toward music developed, not coincidentally, during an era when music itself, particularly "programme" music, had begun to draw inspiration from literary works. Liszt would create "symphonic poems" on subjects like *Hamlet* and *Tasso*, Berlioz would write his *Harold in Italy* and *Romeo and Juliet* symphonies, Strauss his *Don Juan*, and Debussy his *Prelude à l'après-midi d'un faune*. [9] As Edmund Wilson has suggested, "at the time when Romantic music had come closest to literature, literature was attracted toward music." [10] The tendency was for all the arts, in fact, to mingle and draw inspiration from one another. [11]

For writers of fiction the affiliation with music was particularly strong. Music and narrative share temporality; the score and the book must be "enacted" or "performed" over time. Writers of fiction, therefore, as Wyzewa conceded in "La Littérature wagnérienne," might go beyond the experiments with rhythm and tone that lyric poets like Mallarmé and Verlaine had conducted; they could create analogies to musical structures as well: "The music of words can be expressed just as clearly, and even more completely, in prose: a wholly musical and emotional prose ... a harmonious union of tones and rhythms, varied indefinitely to follow the indefinite movement of the nuances of emotion." [12] A celebrated passage in Aldous Huxley's *Point Counter Point* on the "musicalization of fiction" considers the

idea of "contrapuntal plots" as well as a symphonic model of
theme, development, and recapitulation.[13] Thomas Mann, likewise, is supposed to have constructed *Tonio Kröger* according to the
principles of sonata form.[14] At a time when fiction had focused
on "internal" experience and was motivated less by plot than
by character, musical form seemed to offer a measure of structure
and unity. For D'Annunzio, modern writers were "psychologists"
calling upon the expressive resources of music; his preface to
Il trionfo della morte articulates a musical role in representing a
center of consciousness, what the Symbolists would have called
"l'âme":

> Here is just a single *dramatis persona*, and here is represented ... *his
> universe* ... [Y]ou will not find here the continuity of a well-laid plot,
> but rather the continuity of an individual existence manifesting itself ...
> over a limited period of time.
>
>   You will find, above all ... the resolve to make a work of beauty and
> poetry, a plastic and symphonic prose, rich in imagery and music.[15]

E. M. Forster was probably expressing a literary consensus when,
in *Aspects of the Novel*, he claimed that "in music fiction is likely
to find its nearest parallel."[16] In fact, music held the advantage
over language in expressing the "continuity" between one
moment in "la vie de l'âme" and the next, in managing the art
of transition without the abrupt and artificial divisions created
by words and sentences.[17]

   The attraction to music was sustained by two major factors,
both related to an erosion, beginning in the mid-eighteenth
century, of the mimetic theory of art as applied to music. At that
time music gradually came to be considered as inherently more
"pure" or "formal" than literature and the visual arts because
it seemed to represent nothing but itself; it imposed no ethical
values; the artist, as Flaubert, in another context, would eventually
put it, was "everywhere felt but nowhere seen." Schopenhauer,
who identified music as the unmediated expression of an ultimate
reality behind a world of appearances, made music exceptional,
more than "merely" mimetic. The influence of this view may be
seen in D'Annunzio's ambition, expressed in musical vocabulary,
to create "an ideal book of modern prose ... rich in its tones and
rhythms ... which might seem, not to imitate, but to *continue*

Nature."[18] According to this principle of autonomy, Stephen's method of composition in chapter 4 of *A Portrait* might be regarded as "musical." His "day of dappled seaborne clouds" exists in a "treasure" independent of the situation to which he will eventually apply it. It is for him primarily a phrase that is beautiful formally, as a phrase – he calls it a musical "period" – rather than as a "reflection of the glowing sensible world ... many-coloured and richly storied." In chapter 1 we saw that to pledge allegiance to Wagner was to declare war on Philistinism and prudery. Similarly, to claim the affiliation with music, where form and content, means and end were indistinguishable, was for literary artists a way to assert the autonomy and supremacy of art.[19]

The affiliation with music was supported by a second factor as well. As music became detached from a theory of imitation, it was associated more and more with a theory of expression – the idea that the primary function of music was to express or to arouse emotion. If writers of the eighteenth century had looked to the art of painting for inspiration, the Romantic movement in literature, with its emphasis on feeling, spontaneity, and the figure of the artist, and the Symbolist movement, with its emphasis on the expression of individual sensibility, began to turn to music.[20] "After the symphonies of Beethoven," Shaw would write, "it was certain that the poetry that lies too deep for words does not lie too deep for music."[21] Many artists, encouraged by Schopenhauer's distinction between will and reason, saw a dichotomy between emotional and intellectual life.[22] Pater worked with this distinction in his discussion of "ideal types of poetry":

the very perfection of such poetry often appears to depend, in part, on a certain suppression or vagueness of mere subject, so that the meaning reaches us through ways not distinctly traceable by the understanding, as in some of the most imaginative compositions of William Blake, and often in Shakespeare's songs, as pre-eminently in that song of Mariana's page in *Measure for Measure*, in which the kindling force and poetry of the whole play seems to pass for a moment into an actual strain of music.[23]

The emotions and the "understanding" were easily related to "interior" and "exterior" life, respectively, and when Symons described the Symbolists as working to escape "the old bondage of exteriority,"[24] he might have been speaking for the artist in *A Portrait* who draws his pleasure "from the contemplation of an inner world of individual emotions mirrored perfectly in a lucid supple periodic prose." If earlier literature – the literature that Joyce described to Power as "classical" – had focused too much on the intellectual and rational, the modernists would extend their focus into the emotional and irrational – into the domain, as they saw it, of music. They would both *portray* internal life and *address* their reader's emotions. ("[T]he object of a work of art," Joyce told Power, "is not to relate facts but to convey an emotion.") Music was thus the exceptional art not only for its formalism but also for its power to express pure feeling.

Wagner's position in this fertile intellectual climate, where music had become the "art of arts," was central. As a "total artist," responsible for all the elements in his work, Wagner satisfied the claim for the artistic integrity of opera and personified the Romantic ideal of individual genius. His achievement was magnified by his success in overcoming difficulties thought to be inherent in opera: its slavery to the vicissitudes of production and performance as well as the necessity of compromise in artistic collaboration, particularly between composer and librettist.[25] A successful "synthesis of arts" in "music drama" made the affiliation with music already current in nineteenth-century letters seem plausible: for if a composer had made music "literary," could not a writer make literature "musical"? In the *Revue* Wyzewa presented a series of four articles on "L'Art wagnérien," and Mallarmé argued that Wagner had supplanted the poet's rightful position in the theatre through "the theatrical miracle" of his synthesis of arts. "Oh strange defiance," wrote Mallarmé, "hurled at poets by him who has usurped their duty with the most open and splendid audacity: Richard Wagner!"[26] Mallarmé almost certainly envisioned his great "Oeuvre" in response to the challenge posed by Wagner's "total artwork," as Symons would point out in *The Symbolist Movement*:

Carry the theories of Mallarmé to a practical conclusion, multiply his powers in a direct ratio, and you have Wagner. It was his failure not to be Wagner ... It was "the work" that he dreamed of, the new art, more than a new religion, whose precise form in the world he was never quite able to settle.[27]

The arts, to be sure, had already been "muddled" by the time Wagner had achieved his position in nineteenth-century culture, but as Forster's Margaret Schlegel would suggest, Wagner's part in the enterprise was greater than any other. The image of his "total artwork" exerted two strains of influence in literary circles: first, it inspired writers to conceive of "great" or universal work (a subject to which I return in chapter 7); second, and more to our purposes here, it encouraged an attempt in literature to achieve a synthesis of arts on its own, more narrow, terms. In a fusion of musical and verbal expression, literature might approach the *Gesamtkunstwerk* ideal.[28]

It is not surprising that writers of fiction, especially those who concentrated on the internal lives of their characters, would turn to Wagner, for his works explore the realm of psychology to a far greater extent than anything attempted in opera before his time. In *Opera and Drama*, working with the common dichotomy between emotion and intellect, Wagner wrote that the operatic orchestra, "as pure organ of the Feeling ... speaks out the very thing which Word-speech in itself can *not* speak out ... [t]hat which, looked at from the standpoint of our human intellect, is *the Unspeakable*" (*PW* 2:317). "Continuous melody," with the irregular phrasing of its *arioso* style, enabled the vocal line to depict the subtlest nuances of text and permitted the orchestra to offer a sort of commentary, using motifs, on the dramatic situation of the focal character. The capacity of Wagnerian music for expressing the unexpressible was not lost on the literary Wagnerites: for Symons, Wagner provided "the whole expression of the subconscious life, saying more of himself than any person of the drama has ever found in his own soul"; for Mann, the Wagnerian orchestra expressed "the true repository of subliminal knowledge."[29]

As writers of fiction began to focus attention on the psychological side of experience and to deepen their analysis of character, Wagner's "pure organ of the Feeling" proved irresistible. George Moore's *Confessions of a Young Man* identified a "realistic school" in the late nineteenth century that had accomplished with

elements of fiction what Wagner had done with the traditional
distinction between operatic aria and recitative: "Description is
narrative, analysis of character is narrative, dialogue is narrative;
the form is ceaselessly changing, but the melody of narration is
never interrupted."[30] It was not a giant step from "continuous
melody" to "internal monologue" or even "stream of consciousness." Dujardin's book on *Le Monologue intérieur* discusses the aims
and methods of *Les Lauriers sont coupés*, the novel often described
as the first to be written completely in internal monologue:

I am going to reveal a secret: *Les Lauriers sont coupés* was undertaken
with the crazy ambition to transpose into the literary domain Wagnerian
methods that I defined to myself as follows: the life of the soul represented by the ceaseless urging of musical motifs that express, one
after another, indefinitely and successively, "states" of thought, sentiment, or sensation; which [i.e. the ambition] realized itself, or attempted
to realize itself, in the indefinite succession of short phrases, each
rendering one of these states of thought, without logical order, in the
manner of surges rising from the depths of self – one would say
nowadays from the unconscious or subconscious.[31]

In the aesthetic climate that produced the techniques of the
modern psychological novel, a dual Wagnerian influence is
apparent. First, as we have seen, the idea of a synthesis of arts,
especially as articulated in *Opera and Drama*, acted as *inspiration*
to writers attempting to fuse music and literature; second, as we
shall see, Wagnerian opera itself acted as a *source* of musical
material for literary use.

From Wagner's score writers of fiction drew most particularly
the leitmotif: the brief phrase that, repeated and varied, comes
to represent the character, object, idea, or emotion in connection
with which it sounds. For Wagner leitmotifs were closely linked
to feeling – he called them, awkwardly, "thought's *Emotional-
content brought to presence*" (*PW* 2:328) – and even leitmotifs clearly
attached to an object or character, like the "Sword" and "Siegfried" motifs, were meant to evoke the accumulation of feeling
associated with them during the course of the drama. Leitmotifs,
Wagner felt, should at some point be declaimed by a particular
character in connection with a particular gesture on stage; but
purely orchestral motifs made possible a highly sophisticated

presentation of character and manipulation of audience response, establishing the orchestra as a "guides-to-Feeling through the whole labyrinthine building of the drama" (*PW* 2:346).[32] Even when a character was unconscious of a particular emotion or idea, as *Opera and Drama* points out, the tell-tale orchestra might let the audience in on the secret (*PW* 2:328).[33] The function of the leitmotif was many-fold. First, as Wagner's musical syntax became freer and less "quadratic," his music required what Carl Dahlhaus has called "a compensatory formal basis." The increasingly sophisticated use of orchestral motifs in Wagner's works reflects the increasing relaxation of his "musical prose."[34] Second, if, as Joseph Kerman has suggested, unity in Wagner is to be sought dramatically rather than musically,[35] leitmotifs can be seen as offering thematic continuity, linking one context with another and underlining relationships between characters and ideas. In the *Ring*, for example, the use of the pentatonic scale for the motifs of the Woodbird and the Rhinedaughters emphasizes the conceptual proximity of both these figures to pristine nature. The extension of a network of these motifs over several hours or, indeed, several days of performance constituted Wagner's contribution to what Kerman has described as "the characteristic formal ideal of romantic music ... a grandiose organic unity according to the principles of the symphonic style."[36] The minutiae of the Wagnerian artwork are thus connected to its "totality."[37]

For writers of fiction, the leitmotif appeared to solve a problem that had troubled the Symbolists and other poets – the difficulty of making music accessible to language. For though, to Wagner, leitmotifs expressed feeling, his critics and admirers have seen them as essentially *representational* because, within the Wagnerian opera, they evoke particular characters, symbols, and themes. Writing from the point of view of the musician rather than the literary artist, Franz Liszt credited Wagner's leitmotifs with extending the range of musical expression from the emotions to the intellect: "he makes [music] capable of ... appealing to our minds, of stirring our reflections, and he endows it with a moral and intellectual meaning ... His melodies are, in a sense, *personification of ideas*."[38] Once, indeed, Wagner's leitmotifs had acquired more or less specific meaning, they could be used in a kind of narrative commentary, creating, in effect, the musical counterpart of a literary allusion.[39] Leitmotif practice, further-more, made Wagner's orchestra the counterpart of the epic poet, or even, Wagner suggested, that of the Greek Chorus, "sup-porting and elucidating on every hand" (*PW* 2:335–6): describing the feelings of characters and relating present events to past and future.[40] Mann, who noted the relationship between these musical phrases and Homeric epithets, extended their literary quality to all Wagner's music:

> The insatiable chromaticism of the *Liebestod* is a literary idea. Likewise the deep, elemental flow of the Rhine, the seven primitive blocks of chords on which Valhalla is built. A famous conductor once said to me, on his way home after conducting a performance of *Tristan*: "This is no longer music." ... It was too much to ask that [critics] should give the name of "music" to the E flat major triad that shapes the *Rheingold* Prelude. Nor indeed *was* it music. It was an acoustic idea: the idea of the beginning of all things.[41]

Wagner's manipulations of tonality, furthermore, helped him represent "ideas" like instability, imperfection, and unsatisfied desire,[42] and his key signatures can be interpreted to embody themes like godhood, manhood, and heroism.[43] It is ironic, perhaps, that in attempting to harness the resources of music writers would borrow the most literary – and most accessible – of musical techniques. But it may be that only the literary qualities of the leitmotif made its adoption possible. Only, apparently, when music had become "literary" – in the work of this most Romantic of composers – could literature become musical.[44]

Indeed, if one strain of "Wagnerian" novel might include works that, like *Evelyn Innes* and *Il fuoco*, explore Wagnerian themes and aesthetics, another might comprise novels that have consciously attempted to develop a literary leitmotif.[45] George Moore, as we have seen, considered the idea of imitating con-tinuous melody; D'Annunzio and Zola are both said to have at-tempted to use themes and phrases in the manner of leitmotifs.[46] Thomas Mann describes his lifelong attempt to do the same:

> To me the novel was always a symphony ... in which ideas play the role of musical motives. People have occasionally remarked – I have

done it myself – on the influence that the art of Richard Wagner has exercised on my work. I certainly do not deny this influence; and in particular I followed Wagner in the use of the leitmotif, which I brought into the narrative not, indeed, merely in a naturalistic, characterizing, "mechanical" way, but in the symbolic style of music.[47]

Dujardin's *Les Lauriers sont coupés* owes a great deal to the author's conscious attempt to develop a literary leitmotif that would help portray subconscious life or, as he put it, "la vie de l'âme." *Le Monologue intérieur* reveals the considerable extent to which the editor of the *Revue wagnérienne* understood Wagner's own intentions:

In its pure state, the Wagnerian motif is a detached phrase which always carries an emotional meaning, but which is not logically connected to those [phrases] that precede and follow it ... Just as a page of Wagner is often a succession of undeveloped motifs, each of which expresses a gesture of the soul, the interior monologue is a succession of short phrases, each of which likewise expresses a gesture of the soul ... following a purely emotional order, without any intellectualized method at all.[48]

In *Aspects of the Novel* Forster cites the recurrence of Vinteuil's musical phrase in *Remembrance of Things Past* as an example of what he means by "rhythm" in the novel,[49] the sort of "rhythm," in fact, that Wagner's leitmotifs offered many writers.

As a product of a culture in which literary Wagnerism played such an important role, Joyce encountered Wagner's theories and technical innovations at every turn, and as an artistic innovator he must have found the leitmotif irresistible.[50] At University College Joyce's invention of the phrase *idée-mère* as a French equivalent for the term (*JJ* 60) distinguished him from disparagers like Debussy and Saint-Saëns who saw leitmotifs as simple "banners" or "calling-cards."[51] In 1907 his ear was good enough to judge who in the audience of *Götterdämmerung* had accurately hummed one of the motives in Siegfried's funeral music (*L* 2:214). He was certainly aware of the attempts by Moore and D'Annunzio to borrow Wagnerian orchestral techniques; but another track of influence, albeit unconscious, may have been of greater importance. Joyce's account of the origin of the interior monologue in *Ulysses* wends its way back to Wagner and his leitmotifs.

Joyce always maintained that Dujardin's *Les Lauriers sont coupés*, which he had read during his first stay in Paris in 1902 and 1903, inspired this technique; as *Le Monologue intérieur* reveals, the internal monologue in *Les Lauriers* was inspired by Wagner. Perhaps the best evidence that Joyce consciously adapted the leitmotif to his own work is in Stuart Gilbert's description of recurring phrases and themes in *Ulysses* as musical motives and leitmotifs. Significantly, Gilbert submitted his work to Joyce's scrutiny before publication (*JJ* 616). Years later, Gilbert, whose professional collaboration and close friendship with Joyce give him special credibility, would write that "the recurrence of certain leitmotivs" helped to unify *Ulysses* (*L* 1:31).

Since the publication of Gilbert's book, Wagner's leitmotifs have been conceded an important place in Joyce's work, particularly *Ulysses* and *Finnegans Wake*. Joyce's critics have defined the term broadly, and Joyce himself, given his discussion with Budgen on "incorporating motifs" into writing, might have given them license to do so. Recurring literary and musical allusions (to *Hamlet, Don Giovanni*, the *Odyssey*); reappearing characters (Paddy Dignam, the blind piano tuner, the man in the mackintosh); phrases that become attached to particular characters ("bronze by gold" to the barmaids, "jingle" to Boylan); and major themes (parallax, the search for the father, metempsychosis): all have been likened to leitmotifs.[52] The broader the definition, however, the weaker its connection to music. Here I propose a more narrow, "Wagnerian" definition. Strictly speaking, literary themes or characters could not be leitmotifs, since they have no *musical* counterparts in Wagnerian opera. (For example, the musical phrase, or *signifier*, often called "Siegfried" is a leitmotif; obviously, Siegfried himself, the *signified*, is not.) On the analogy between the literary text and the musical score, I shall describe the literary leitmotif as a brief, distinctive phrase which, through repetition and variation in appropriate contexts, establishes its meaning, acquires intrinsic importance (that is, importance residing not simply in what it signifies or represents), accumulates in thematic and emotional significance, and draws together the contexts in which it appears.[53]

Ulysses and the *Wake*, in fact, would put the literary leitmotif to the most Wagnerian of uses. First, in books where the author, if not "refined out of existence" (*P* 215), is at least difficult to fix, Joyce's leitmotifs substitute, in part, for the kind of authorial commentary that earlier writers might have supplied more directly. As we have seen, Wagner developed his leitmotifs to give the orchestra its narrative role of "supporting and elucidating on every hand" (*PW* 2:335 – 6). Second, these brief phrases help constitute Joyce's stream of consciousness (as they did Dujardin's interior monologue), since they disrupt "logical" narration for structure by association; leitmotifs constitute Wagner's stream of melody, as the composer drew further away from conventional musical syntax, in an analogous way. Third, the leitmotifs link one context with another and offer an organic structure, a centripetal "intratextuality" (what Forster would call "rhythm") especially significant in sprawling and highly allusive or "intertextual" books like *Ulysses* and the *Wake*; as we have seen, leitmotifs gave Wagner's massive scores a similar unity. Finally, the leitmotif helped Joyce "to thicken the texture of the narrative," as Gilbert puts it in his discussion of "Sirens," [54] to emphasize the signifier as well as the signified in the "foregrounding" that is characteristic of much modern fiction. Joyce's later works shows the most thorough – and the most thoroughly Wagnerian – use of the literary leitmotif in the device's history. [55]

In *Ulysses* the leitmotif is closely connected with Joyce's depiction of internal life, working in the tradition of Dujardin, D'Annunzio, Proust, and, later, Mann. "Agenbite of inwit" – Middle English for "remorse of conscience" – makes an excellent leitmotif. Its lapidary quality gives it special weight as a signifier, almost the quality of a musical phrase; its relative obscurity enables the text to establish its meaning free of associations outside *Ulysses*. And like all leitmotifs, Joycean or Wagnerian, it will only establish the full range of its associations over time and in several contexts. The phrase first appears in "Telemachus," in Stephen's thoughts as he converses with Haines and Mulligan: "Speaking to me. They wash and tub and scrub. Agenbite of inwit. Conscience. Yet here's a spot" (1.481 – 2; 16). At this point, the emotion that "agenbite of inwit" invokes, as the allusion to *Macbeth* makes clear, is guilt, probably inspired by the milkwoman who has just left the tower. "They" are Irish women collectively, who "wash" and "scrub" for little reward, and a second appearance of the motif later in "Telemachus" reinforces the connection between Stephen's remorse and the Irish woman who makes clothes clean: Buck Mulligan's "hands plunged and rummaged in his trunk while he called for a clean handkerchief. Agenbite of inwit" (17).[56] Here the clean handkerchief, possibly because another Irish woman has made it so, evokes Stephen's guilt, and the leitmotif sounds again. The motif appears a third time in "Scylla and Charybdis," in connection with Stephen's favorite prostitute: "Go to! You spent most of it in Georgina Johnson's bed, clergyman's daughter. Agenbite of inwit" (9.195 – 6; 189). The fourth appearance of the phrase also invokes a woman; here Stephen projects his own guilt on the figure of Shakespeare's dying and repentant wife: "Venus has twisted her lips in prayer. Agenbite of inwit: remorse of conscience. It is an age of exhausted whoredom groping for its god" (9.809 – 10; 206). Why should all these women evoke the same response in Stephen's consciousness? The answer is implicit in the last and most important appearance of the leitmotif, when Stephen encounters his sister Dilly in "Wandering Rocks":

She is drowning. Agenbite. Save her. Agenbite. All against us. She will drown me with her, eyes and hair. Lank coils of seaweed hair around me, my heart, my soul. Salt green death.
    We.
    Agenbite of inwit. Inwit's agenbite.
    Misery! Misery! (10.875 – 80; 243)

In this passage, "she" is superficially Dilly, doomed by her father's – and to some extent her brother's – irresponsibility, but "she" is ultimately Stephen's mother, whose hold on his conscience this passage subtly evokes. In fact, Stephen's guilty recollection of his conduct at the time of his mother's death lurks behind all the passages in which "agenbite of inwit" appears, and it becomes apparent that Stephen cannot separate the women he encounters in his daily life from his mother. Joyce has not told us this directly; he has used the leitmotif to link one context with another and to make implicit that which, in a more traditional book, might have been revealed more directly by a less protean narrator.[57]

Another leitmotif, this one Bloom's rather than Stephen's, is "met him pike hoses," Molly's corruption of "metempsychosis," the jawbreaker she encounters in *Ruby: The Pride of the Ring*. The phrase appears some eight times, always in connection with the emotion Bloom feels when he thinks of Molly in a particular way, and it is dispersed fairly evenly throughout *Ulysses*, contributing to the book's "rhythmic" structure. "Met him pike hoses" is especially "musical" because, like a leitmotif in one of Wagner's scores, it conveys no real sense before the work begins to develop it. But it gradually comes to express, simultaneously, two qualities in Molly that mean a good deal to Bloom: as a corruption of a formal, abstruse term, the phrase reveals Molly's healthy scorn for pretension; its association with the salacious literature Molly enjoys emphasizes her sensuality. When either, or both, of these qualities occurs to Bloom, the phrase appears in the text, "interrupting" (but, in fact, helping to constitute) his internal monologue. The first reference is in "Lestrygonians": "There's a priest. Could ask him. Par it's Greek: parallel, parallax. Met him pike hoses she called it till I told her about the transmigration. O rocks! Mr Bloom smiled" (8.iii–14; 154). In "Sirens" the phrase appears, appropriately, just after Bloom has thought of Blazes Boylan, and it serves as a reminder that Molly's sensual nature will express itself most actively at four that afternoon: "Jingle jaunted down the quays. Blazes sprawled on bounding tyres ... Mrs Marion. Met him pike hoses. Smell of burn. Of Paul de Kock. Nice name he" (11.498–501; 269). A final example should suffice. Near the end of "Nausicaa," Bloom's recollection of the phrase in connection with Gerty MacDowell reveals the extent to which his latent desire for Molly may be a source of his attraction not only to Gerty but to all the women whom he encounters during the day: "O sweety all your little girlwhite up I saw dirty bracegirdle made me do love sticky we two naughty Grace darling she him half past the bed met him pike hoses frillies for Raoul de perfume your wife black hair" (13.1279–91; 382). Like Stephen, Bloom cannot effectively separate the women he meets from the most important woman in his life. Two other leitmotifs that function in like manner and whose appearances coincide with Bloom's thoughts about Molly are "O rocks," which expresses Molly's anti-intellectualism, and "Cuckoo. Cuckoo. Cuckoo," which expresses, perhaps, the pathos of the cuckold.

In his *Introduction to the* Ring, Deryck Cooke shows the extent to which harmonic and melodic relationships between Wagner's leitmotifs underscore thematic parallels and intensify the orchestra's epic commentary on the progress of the drama. For example, the fact that the "Servitude" motif, which expresses the misery of Alberich's enslaved Nibelungs, is simply a minor-key version of the Rhinedaughters' "Joy in the Gold" motif emphasizes the contrasting values of the gold in its pristine state and gold as an instrument of power. Also, the similarity between two of the cycle's most important leitmotifs – the "Ring" and "Valhalla" – emphasizes "the near-identity of the ultimate aims of Alberich and Wotan – absolute power in each case; and the harmonic contrast between them expresses the much nobler character of Wotan's conception of absolute power compared with Alberich's."[58] Because Joyce's prose emphasizes the value of the phrase itself as well as what it signifies (and this is perhaps the most "musical" quality of his work), his leitmotifs permit a similar development of thematic relationships. "Agenbuyer" ("Redeemer"), for example, is implicitly linked to "agenbite of inwit"; and the similarity of "agenbite of inwit" to "Agendath Netaim," the name of the Zionist colony that occurs to Bloom several times, suggests that the key to the Hellenic Stephen's "redemption" or escape from artistic lethargy is somehow the Jewish Bloom. Similarly, "met him pike hoses" is a variant of "metempsychosis," according to Gilbert one of the most important themes in *Ulysses*.[59]

These two examples by no means exhaust and, indeed, scarcely represent the leitmotifs of *Ulysses*. If phrases like "agenbite of inwit" and "met him pike hoses" embody characters' emotional preoccupations, others represent certain ideas – "ineluctable modality of the visible," "retrospective arrangement," and "the incertitude of the void," to name a few. Many leitmotifs, like the simplest of Wagner's, evoke or even introduce particular characters – the "u.p." attached to Denis Breen, the "tap" of the piano tuner, the "bronze by gold" of the Ormond barmaids, the "jingle" of Boylan. In all, much of *Ulysses* is composed of repeated words and phrases that function as leitmotifs – both literary and Wagnerian – do: helping form the stream of narration, providing "rhythmic" form, developing texture as well as structure.

"Neither before nor since *Finnegans Wake*," Clive Hart has written, "has the literary *leitmotiv* been used so consistently or to such brilliant effect."[60] Indeed, never before had a literary work so much to gain from the leitmotif's power to shape a text and guide its reader. In chapter 5 we saw how the cyclical perception of history embodied in myth provides a conceptual structure for the *Wake*. In fact, myth and leitmotif are intimately related in Joyce's last work, as they are in the work of Thomas Mann,[61] for a tenet of mythic art, that history repeats itself with a difference, is reflected in the repetition and variation of these hundreds of leitmotifs throughout the text. Indeed, Joyce's modification of his motifs in the *Wake* represents an even closer analogy to Wagnerian technique than does his practice in *Ulysses*, since Wagner's motifs are themselves generally altered in key or orchestrated differently when they reappear. In the *Wake* the leitmotif provides structure on the stylistic level that perfectly complements the mythic theme. "Structure" and "motif" come together in the literary leitmotifs of *Finnegans Wake*.

The most important leitmotifs in the *Wake* are connected with this central mythic theme, phrases like "the seim anew" and "ashes to ashes and dust to dust," the baptismal motif "*taufen*," the one-hundred letter "word" for thunder that, for Joyce and Vico, heralds a new age. One of the most interesting of these leitmotifs is "O felix culpa," the phrase from the liturgical "Exultet" that characterizes original sin, a sin that, according to the *Wake*, is repeated throughout history, initiating each time a "fall" and a new cycle. This motif appears at least twenty-three times in the *Wake*, in fifteen of the seventeen chapters.[62] The first reference is in I.1, immediately after the tale of Jarl van Hoother and the prankquean: "O foenix culprit!" (23.16). The "culprit" is probably van Hoother, but "foenix" links his sins to HCE's crime in Phoenix Park. The idea of the phrase in its original form is that great good ultimately resulted from Adam and Eve's fall;

here the reference to the mythic bird that rises from its own ashes underscores this point. In I.5 we learn that a title of Anna Livia's manifesto is "Ophelia's Culpreints" (105.18), and in I.8 the leitmotif (here in English) draws ALP's loss of virginity into its web of associations: "She thought she's sankh neathe the ground with nymphant shame when he gave her the tigris eye! O happy fault! Me wish it was he!" (202.32 – 4). The motif appears in "Night Lessons," when Dolph-Shem gives Kev-Shaun a lesson in anatomy, the implication being that the boys' pursuit of sexual knowledge is a reenactment of Adam's eating from the tree: "we carefully, if she pleats, lift by her seam hem ... (like thousands done before since fillies calpered. Ocone! Ocone!) the maidsapron of our A.L.P." (297.7 – 11). As tavernkeeper in II.3 HCE acknowledges his previous wrongdoings to his guests: "Guilty but fellows culpows!" (363.20); and, finally, in III.4 Mr. Porter gazes on his sleeping twins and reflects on the precariousness of childhood innocence: "O, foetal sleep! Ah, fatal slip!" (563.10). If, in *Ulysses*, the variants of a motif are minor and relatively unimportant, in the *Wake* the reader's ability to relate one set of circumstances to another depends upon them. Both history and the leitmotif repeat themselves with a difference in *Finnegans Wake*.

Like *Ulysses*, the *Wake* attaches many leitmotifs to particular characters in order to signal their entrance into the text. Indeed, the *Wake* depends upon this sort of leitmotif to a greater extent than does *Ulysses*, for in many cases characters are not recognizable without them. Hart lists thirty-eight leitmotifs associated with ALP. One of the most interesting appears in what might be called its "definitive" form at the end of the section that bears her name: "Beside the rivering waters of, hitherandthithering waters of. Night!" (216.4 – 5).[63] This leitmotif is especially musical in its clear rhythm, which serves as a formula into which various words can be inserted, as in "arride the winnerful wonders off, the winnerful wonnerful wanders off" (265.15 – 16) and in "the race is to the rashest of, the romping, jomping rushes of" (441.3 – 4). The main appearance of the motif in I.8 helps link ALP to the onset of darkness ("Night!"); it seems appropriate, therefore, that the romantic description of the evening at the end of II.1 should bring her into the text:

Darkpark's acoo with sucking loves. Rosimund's by her wishing well. Soon tempt-in-twos will stroll at venture and hunt-by-threes strut musketeering. Brace of girdles, brasse of beauys. With the width of the way for jogjoy. Hulker's cieclest elbownunsense. Hold hard! And his dithering dathering waltzers of. Stright! (245.17–22)

Another appearance of the motif in II.3 helps clarify ALP's relation to night and darkness, for she is the archetypal mother and therefore the source of rest and comfort. The narrator describes the end of the battle of Sevastopol as follows:

While the Hersy Hunt they harrow the hill for to rout them rollicking rogues from, rule those rackeeter romps from, rein their rockery rides from. Rambling.

Nightclothesed, arooned, the conquerods sway. After their battle thy fair bosom. (355.15–20)

The many contexts in which this motif appears (fourteen in ten chapters) help portray the full complexity of the mythic figure who is ALP, and her frequent incarnation is a reflection of the book's cyclic theory. Similarly, each of the four old Masters of Ireland has a characteristic sigh, and many literary and historical figures have a leitmotif as well (the "pipette" of Swift, for example). One special device which is not, according to my strict definition, a leitmotif, but which has the same identifying function, is the appearance of ALP's and HCE's initials in the text. The following sentence in II.3 employs this device to answer the question that it implicitly raises: "As to whom the major guilt-feather pertained it was *H*ercushiccups' *c*are to *e*duce" (355.11–12, my emphasis). Joyce's narration and Wagner's orchestration share this ability to provide authorial commentary with indirection and technical skill.

These few leitmotifs merely begin to describe *Finnegans Wake*, for Joyce makes use of every phrase that swims into his ken – proverbs, religious mottos, excerpts from popular songs, biblical quotations, even clichés. The linking of one leitmotif with another, made possible by *portmanteau* technique, is, of course, much more extensive than that of *Ulysses*. Indeed, the leitmotif system of the *Wake* seems to take on a life of its own – a "musical" life – and thus to lose the connection (except at the level on which the *Wake* is dream-vision) with emotion and subconscious thought.

In this sense, the *Wake*, with its increasing formalism, represents an extension of the literary leitmotif tradition, for previous practitioners, including the Joyce who wrote *Ulysses*, linked the leitmotif with emotion and used it to represent internal life. In the *Wake* the leitmotif has almost become an end in itself. We might say that whereas *Ulysses* borrows from music, *Finnegans Wake* aspires to *be* music.

Though it is the most "Wagnerian" analogy to music in Joyce's writing, the leitmotif does not fully represent the musical quality of his work. But the more general musicality that Joyce is acknowledged is in part Wagner's legacy as well, since much of the literary affinity for music may be traced, as we have seen, through important figures in nineteenth-century culture to Wagner's synthesis of arts in music drama. Part of the musicality of Joyce's work is provided by the huge number of musical references; these can evoke for some readers the sound of a certain musical phrase – from "La ci darem," for example, or "M'appari." To some extent, in fact, Joyce's unprecedented use of allusion, including literary allusion, reflects a "musical" orientation: allusions, like Stephen's "day of dappled seaborne clouds," exist independent of their eventual contexts. Stuart Gilbert and Valéry Larbaud, in fact, found Joyce's work habits very much like Stephen's: Joyce collected and stored words and phrases in notebooks before dispersing them through *Ulysses* and the *Wake*.[64] The sections of *Ulysses*, with their own styles, tones, and techniques, are like musical pieces or movements of a symphony in their relative autonomy and self-contained quality. With Henry James, for instance, and his consistent narrative style, we have chapter 2, with Joyce, chapters like "Nestor" to which individual names have stuck.[65] Joyce may also have attempted to adopt particular musical forms: sonata form for *Ulysses* as a whole, *fuga per canonem* as well as overture and opera for "Sirens."[66] "Sirens" may even "contain" a quintet, "as in *Die Meistersinger*, my favorite Wagnerian opera" (*JJ* 459), and the introduction of "Sirens" is, as Hodgart has suggested, analogous to the catalogue of leitmotifs that traditionally appears inside the front covers of Wagner's scores.[67] The multiple meanings or "polysemantics" of the *Wake* suggest another parallel. "O, foetal sleep" (563.10), for example, is both "O fatal slip" and an apostrophe to pre-natal innocence. Musical counterpoint works analogously, and Joyce's practice has led critics to describe the *Wake* as "polyphonic" or "chordal": the "hearer" of Joyce's prose must "listen *vertically* as well as horizontally."[68] Most pervasive, in Joyce's writing, finally, is the musicality reflected in the tonal and rhythmic qualities of his language, his "sound" as well as his "sense," to borrow Huxley's formulation in *Point Counter Point*. It is this aural quality that makes his prose as compelling when read aloud as that of any writer.

The study of interrelations between music and literature is subject to qualifications of many kinds. On one hand, much of what we commonly regard as "musical" is simply a matter of convention. There is probably nothing inherently musical about structures and techniques like sonata form or, indeed, the leit-motif, both of which depend on a principle of theme, repetition, and variation. Music and literature share acoustic features like tone and rhythm, though these are more apparent in oral than in written traditions. The evocation or expression of feeling, moreover, is not exclusively musical.[69] On the other hand, those qualities inherent in music do separate it, ultimately, from other arts. Symons, elsewhere an uncritical enthusiast, identified restraints on the impulse toward music; he realized, too, that outside the domain of grand opera the total artwork would prove an elusive quarry:

All art is a compromise, in which the choice of what is to be foregone must be left somewhat to the discretion of nature. When the sculptor foregoes colour, when the painter foregoes relief, when the poet foregoes the music which soars beyond words and the musician that precise meaning which lies in words alone, he follows a kind of necessity in things, and the compromise seems to be ready-made for him. But there will always be those who are discontented with no matter what fixed limits, who dream, like Wagner, of a possible, or, like Mallarmé, of an impossible, fusion of the arts.[70]

My goal in this discussion has not been to determine whether modern literature in general or Joyce's work in particular actually achieves a condition of music in any absolute sense: for it was precisely the inaccessibility of music that made it so attractive to writers "discontented" with the "limits" of literary expression. My aim has been, rather, to determine what these writers meant by "musical" and to assess how the impulse toward musical expression influenced their work. The status of music as an exceptional art helped these artists to define their own genres more precisely and to imagine how literature might be different. It encouraged them to pursue the subjective realm of experience, to make their writing self-reflexive and organically unified, to cultivate rhythm and sonority in their prose and poetry: to develop what students of psychoanalytic literary theory today would call the "genotext" of language as opposed to its "phenotext."[71] It also helped them assert the autonomous value of their craft. In his attempt to bring the resources of music to literature, Joyce's ability approached that of Shaw and his ambition surpassed even that of George Moore. When asked if the *Wake* were a combination of music and literature, the Irish writer, with characteristic hyperbole, replied, "No, it's pure music" (*JJ* 703). It is this quality to which Samuel Beckett was alluding when, in his contribution to the *Exagmination of James Joyce*, he described *Work in Progress* as follows: it "is not *about* something; *it is that something itself*."[72] Indeed, if Joyce's work is not in some sense "musical," it must be concluded that literature cannot be musical at all.

CHAPTER 7

Joyce and Wagner

Ah, what heights and what depths had he not touched,
that formidable Master of human souls! What effort could
ever equal his? What eagle could ever hope to soar
higher? His gigantic work was there, finished, amidst
men ...

    The young man saw his pathway blazed before him by
victory – the long art, the short life. "Forward, still
forward! Higher, ever higher!"   D'Annunzio, *Il fuoco*

Michael Robartes remembers forgotten beauty and,
when his arms wrap her round, he presses in his arms the
loveliness which has long faded from the world. Not this.
Not at all.   Joyce, *A Portrait*

In *Ulysses* Stephen Dedalus borrows a line from George Meredith
and telegraphs Buck Mulligan a subtle accusation of ingratitude:
"The sentimentalist is he who would enjoy without incurring
the immense debtorship for a thing done" (*U* 9.550–1; 199).
James Joyce, reluctant to acknowledge certain creditors of his
own, may be accused of a similar offense. The Joyce of letters
and conversation emerges as an artist whose imagination was
conditioned by medieval churchfathers like Thomas Aquinas,
classical figures like Homer and Aristotle, obscure philosophers
like Vico and Bruno, and insufficiently appreciated modernists
like Dujardin. An individualist and iconoclast by nature, Joyce
was not inclined to recognize the distinguished artists and
thinkers of his time. He would not concede "any special talent"
in Proust (*JJ* 488), and of Lawrence he said, "That man really
writes very badly ... [H]is friend Aldous Huxley ... at least
dresses decently" (*JJ* 615n). Freud's stature in contemporary

thought earned the Viennese psychoanalyst unflattering comparisons to Vico (*JJ* 340, 693).[1] Similarly, when Joyce encountered "the infatuation of people" for *Die Meistersinger*, he called it "pretentious stuff" (*L* 1:67); advised of Nora and Lucia's affection for *Tristan*, he found the opera oversexed;[2] confronted with a friend's preference for *Die Walküre* over "Sirens," he stalked out of the opera house (*JJ* 460). On the other hand, Joyce enjoyed pointing out the importance of more obscure figures, past and present, perhaps to give the impression that he had discovered them. Thus "The Day of the Rabblement" begins with a veiled reference to a mysterious authority of uncertain national origin: "No man, said the Nolan, can be a lover of the true or the good unless he abhors the multitude" (*CW* 69).[3] Years later, Joyce's resuscitation of Dujardin as the inspiration for the internal monologue of *Ulysses* may have been calculated to do the same. This cultivation of the role of contrarian is evident in a shifting attitude toward the movement for an Irish national theatre. When the first performance of Yeats's *The Countless Cathleen*, in 1899, was heckled by a hostile audience, Joyce "clapped vigorously" (*JJ* 67); as the movement began to win the "rabblement" over, he found less to admire.[4]

Joyce's frequent denigration of Wagner, however, implies much more than simple iconoclasm, for it represents a general antagonism toward the cultural authorities of his day. He found Goethe, for example, " '*un noioso funzionario*' (a boring civil servant)" (*JJ* 394), he called Shaw a "mountebank" (*JJ* 440), and he dismissed *Das Kapital* as "absurd" after reading the first sentence (*JJ* 142n). "In the last two hundred years," Joyce insisted in 1917, "we haven't had a great thinker."[5] Wagner, for Joyce, did not merely represent the modern; he epitomized it. "[M]odern man has an epidermis rather than a soul," Joyce wrote in 1912. "Place *Tristan und Isolde* next to the *Inferno* and you will notice how ... [o]ne is the art of circumstance, the other is ideational." In *Daniel Defoe*, composed in the same year, Wagner and *Tristan* are again the modern examples. "Contemporary composers," according to Joyce, "would find nothing at all" in the healthy realism of the English novelist, which "defies and transcends the magical beguilements of music ... Different from Tristan and Isolde!'' Both essays acknowledge Wagner's position as ''a great modern artist,'' but only in a context that disparages modern art.[6] Joyce's efforts to avoid artistic suffocation are among the most celebrated elements of his career: that he imposed a geographical exile on himself is an historical fact, and that he kept himself apart from the Irish literary movement is a critical commonplace. But that he may also have required a sense of isolation in time, a sense of independence, however illusory, from the historical ''modern,'' has been less often remarked. Certainly the ubiquitous Wagner, whose influence peaked at the end of the century and in the years before the Great War – Joyce's formative years – presented a significant challenge to so proud and independent an artist as Joyce.

Harold Bloom has warned students of literary history to be wary in evaluating an artist's assessments of his precursors. Such assessments, according to Bloom, inevitably tell us more about the needs of the artist than about the nature of those who came before him.[7] If Joyce's antagonism toward the work of his contemporaries and recent predecessors seems disproportionate, it may reflect the Irish writer's need to defend the integrity of a highly allusive body of work by asserting its independence: ''for what strong maker,'' Bloom writes, ''desires the realization that he has failed to create himself?''[8] If, on the one hand, a writer makes earlier works his ''own'' when he writes them into his work, he also, on the other hand, exposes his work to the centrifugal forces of ''intertextuality,'' risks its claim to originality, and suffers ''the immense anxieties of indebtedness.''[9] And the risk is increased when the allusiveness, as in Joyce's case, is so radical; the larger the empire, the more vulnerable its borders may feel. In *The Burden of the Past and the English Poet*, W.J. Bate identifies a phenomenon in literary history that helps illuminate Joyce's portraits of his predecesors, both distant and immediate. Distinguishing ''ancestral'' from ''parental'' forms of influence, Bate argues that poets of the Restoration, confronted by the vast, and relatively recent, achievements of the English Renaissance, turned to classical antiquity for guidance not only because its authority was more ''pure'' but also because they found it less threatening to the achievement of their own identity. Bate finds this "leap-frog" effect in the English Romantics and in twentieth-century poets as well, and Joyce's "Universal Literary Influence," with its juxtaposition of Dante and Wagner, illustrates it perfectly.[10] If Joyce felt the anxiety of influence, it was *proximity* – of place, of time, and of stature – that made him most anxious. Evidently, the discomfort created by proximity in artistic stature could be overcome when the rival was remote in time: among Joyce's many creditors the "ancestral" Homer, Aristotle, and Dante are paid their due, while the "parental" Wagner is turned away.

Even the quickest glance, however, shows the extent to which Joyce's work takes up the Wagnerian gauntlet. Both artists created epic, even monumental work; went to extreme limits to portray interior life; made sexual relations a thematic focus; extended the limits of musical and linguistic syntax; exploited the resources of myth. Dujardin may have felt some of these affinities in scale, shape, and tone when, after his first reading of *Ulysses*, he told Joyce that the book gave him the "sensation of swimming in an ocean of spirituality, the very one I experienced at twenty when I first heard ... the four days of *The Ring of the Nibelung*" (*L* 3:192).[11] It is more than coincidence that Joyce's critics, especially earlier ones still assessing his position in modern culture, have found Wagnerian vocabulary so congenial in describing their experience of Joyce. "Circe," wrote Stuart Gilbert, gives us "a *Götterdämmerung* of brimstone fires"; the *Wake*'s final monologue, according to Clive Hart, an "old crone's *Liebestod*."[12] It is impossible to take Joyce's disparagement of Wagner at face value when we set their work side by side.

Wagner's greatest legacy to Joyce may have been the simple fact of his existence, which challenged the ambitious young writer to aspire to a certain stature – that of "a great modern artist" who would create "great" works of art. Franz Liszt knew the value of an ideal of artistic greatness; and when Wagner told him, in 1851, of his plans for the work that would eventually become the *Ring*, Liszt encouraged him by quoting the mandate given the architect of the cathedral at Seville: "Build us a temple such that future generations will say the canons were mad ever to undertake such an extraordinary work."[13] The image of Wagner's "total artwork" helped shape the ambition in Joyce that the figure of Wagner had inspired. Its effect was to stoke Joyce's desire for the absolute in art, for the sort of "totality" that would be expressed in the schematic exposition of colors, arts, and bodily organs in *Ulysses*; in the languages, cultures, and religions of the *Wake*; in the inclusion of the world's rivers in "Anna Livia Plurabelle"; and in the universalizing mythic "stuff" with which Joyce's later work is infused. Together *Ulysses*, a book of the waking hours, and *Finnegans Wake*, the book of the night, comprise all experience. An anecdote from Joyce's Dublin days shows a youthful ambition to take on the great themes of art, even as it reminds us, parenthetically, that Wagner was not Joyce's sole inspiration. In 1904 Joyce promised John Eglinton that he would someday rewrite *Paradise Lost*,[14] notwithstanding George Russell's assertion two years before that the young man had "not enough chaos" in him "to make a world" (*JJ* 99). The fulfillment of that vow was the *Wake*, which is as much, however, a rewriting of the *Ring* as of *Paradise Lost*. A lesser genius than Joyce's might have found Wagner's image overwhelming – "What eagle," wrote D'Annunzio of Wagner in a passage that *A Portrait* would echo, "could ever hope to soar higher?"[15] – and in *The Symbolist Movement* the young Joyce read the cautionary tale of an artist defeated by his "absolute aim at the absolute" and "disdain for … compromise." "It was his failure," Symons wrote of Mallarmé, "not to be Wagner."[16] Indeed, to have established such lofty goals and to have achieved them is a distinction that Joyce and Wagner share with few others. It may be that the Irish writer, in *A Portrait* and *Ulysses*, required a Wagnerian hero like Siegfried to represent the grandeur of his ambition, even as his ironic temperament maintained a characteristic distance from it.[17]

Wordsworth believed that "every author, as far as he is great and at the same time *original*, has the task of *creating* the taste by which he is to be enjoyed."[18] The greatness that Joyce and Wagner share is nowhere more apparent than in their aggressive interpretation of this responsibility: it was not simply to mold the tastes of their audiences but to forge their audiences anew. Joyce and Wagner helped liberate opera and the novel, both traditionally regarded as entertainment rather than art, from their historical domination by the public, "that tyrant," the young Wagner complained, "whose favors we all seek." [19] They forced their audiences to take their work seriously and prepared them for the artwork of the future. Joyce's struggle with Grant Richards for the integrity of *Dubliners* was much like Wagner's battle for *Tannhäuser* a half century before. Joyce insisted that he could not "prostitute" his talents to accommodate Richards' fear of a censorious public. He invoked *Areopagitica* and underlined his point with reference to a "higher" form: "if the art were any other, if I were a painter and my book were a picture you would be less ready to condemn me ... if I refused to alter certain details" (*L* 2:177, 137, 135). Wagner brought the same moral fervor and intransigence to his battle for artistic integrity in opera: Italian opera had been a "wanton," German opera a "prude," French opera a "coquette" with a "chilling smile" (*PW* 2:112–13). [20] Joyce and Wagner would also insist that their audiences be prepared to find sexual themes treated with new candor. The sensuality of *Tristan* and *Parsifal* intoxicated some and scandalized others, and Joyce's work would evoke a similar dichotomy of responses. (Among the many scraps of nineteenth-century Wagneriana is Ernest Newman's story of a young clergyman overheard at a performance of *Götterdämmerung* in London, trying his best, apparently, to adjust to Wagner's world: "Was Siegfried," he asked his neighbor, "*engaged* to Brynhilda?" [21]) For his part, Joyce felt that in depicting what he called "the subterranean forces ... the ascending fumes of sex," his achievement had been "to liberate literature from its age-old shackles." [22] Both artists, finally, fashioned audiences that could meet the challenge of such innovative and technically complex works; they taxed their powers of intellect and imagination much as, in the personal realm, they had strained the patience of their loved ones. About the difficulty of *Ulysses* E. M. Forster would write, "And the citizen who does survive the ordeal and gets to the end is naturally filled with admiration of his own achievement, and is apt to say that here is a great book, the book of the age. He really means that he himself is a great reader."[23] If the critical term "modern" describes an artistic position more than it does an historical period, a position of uncompromising artistry, then Joyce and Wagner may be said to epitomize it.

Not only did these great "modern" artists test their audiences; they also challenged the forms in which they worked. As cultural Bolshevists,[24] working at first within but quite soon against tradition, Joyce and Wagner expanded the possibilities of expression within opera and the novel far beyond what their predecessors had imagined, much less achieved. What Wagner demanded of harmony, orchestration, and melodic line Joyce required of narrative, syntax, and language generally. Having exhausted one possibility, moreover, each – like fellow "moderns" Picasso and Stravinsky – moved on to something radically different; each work seems unique, unprecedented.[25] If asked to choose a single work that is "characteristically" Joycean or Wagnerian, we would be hard pressed. The same hand wrote *Tristan, Meistersinger*, and the *Ring* – another fashioned *A Portrait, Ulysses*, and the *Wake* – but each work is distinct and a *tour de force*. Joyce's extravagance or "provection" is nowhere more apparent than in the Irish writer's sense of genre, which developed geometrically, almost chapter by chapter. Compare "The Sisters" with "The Dead," the first chapter of *A Portrait* with the last, "Telemachus" with "Ithaca" or "Penelope." Joyce once said that each completed chapter of *Ulysses* left behind "a burnt up field" (*L* 1:129); and as early as the appearance of "Sirens" in the *Little Review*, one of Joyce's most faithful admirers would complain that "even the assing girouette of a postfuturo Gertrudo Steino protetopublic dont demand a new style per chapter."[26] Despite their epic dimensions, the *Ring* and *Ulysses* were scarcely able to contain the ambition of these supremely confident and demanding artists who had resolved to be "great."

Though they may have been attempted on the conceptual scale of Genesis or *Paradise Lost*, the works of Joyce and Wagner are not religious in any traditional sense. The *Ring*, as we saw in chapter 5, grants humankind a higher evolutionary position than it does the decaying gods; *Tristan*, though preoccupied with death, does not mention God; and even *Parsifal*, which Nietzsche thought revealed that Wagner, near the end, had "broken on his knees before the Christian cross," is more about the rebirth of nature in spring than about the Resurrection of Christ at Easter.[27] Joyce's own comparative mythology identifies Creation with original sin and conflates God with Adam; Christ simply takes a place among the countless sons who constitute Shem and Shaun. Like many of their contemporaries, however, both artists were drawn to the language and thematic patterns of Christianity. Joseph Kerman finds *Tristan*, with its emphasis on the idea of "conversion" and its "progress towards a state of illumination which transcends yearning and pain," essentially religious, if not Christian, and in *Parsifal* the story of Christ helps present a position of renunciation that Wagner had also found in Schopenhauer and in the teachings of the Buddha.[28] When Stephen in *A Portrait* encounters "the wild heart of life," his "soul" cries "Heavenly God! ... in an outburst of profane joy" (171); and when the "spirit" enters "the virgin womb of the imagination," Stephen's villanelle is conceived: "the word was made flesh" (217). A humble communion of Epps's cocoa marks the rapprochement of Stephen and Bloom in "Ithaca." Both Joyce and Wagner would sanctify their own work, as if it were qualitatively different from that of others. Wagner considered *Parsifal* simply the "most sacred" work in a corpus that would require its own temple: productions of *Parsifal* were forbidden outside Bayreuth until its copyright expired, and at Wagner's *Festspielhaus* applause after act I of *Parsifal* was thought sacrilegious. Stephen's artist is "a priest of eternal imagination, transmuting the daily bread of experience into the radiant body of everliving life" (*P* 221); the narrators of the *Wake* are, on one level, the four evangelists; and the *Wake* itself, as I.5 makes clear, is a sacred Book of Kells. At one point Wagner regarded *Lohengrin* as a watershed in his career: "With that work," he wrote, "the old world of opera comes to an end. The spirit moved over the waters and there was light."[29] Likewise, "Scylla and Charybdis" tells of a star that appeared at the birth of Shakespeare (*U* 9.928–9; 210). The artist's work, itself immortal, rivaled God's own Creation.[30]

Notwithstanding their post-Christian humanism, Joyce and Wagner were preoccupied with problems traditionally regarded as spiritual, with sin, evil, guilt, atonement, and redemption. The unhealing wound of Amfortas represents the spiritual condition of nearly all Wagner's heroes (excepting those of *Lohengrin* and *Die Meistersinger*), and the figure of the sinner-outcast, suffering the curse of exile, was a preoccupation of both artists. In *Tannhäuser* the flowering of the Pope's staff, signifying the hero's absolution through the intercession of Elisabeth in spite of his condemnation by the Church, is an excellent symbol of Wagnerian redemption, and nothing could be more congenial to the *Wake* than the implicit link between the rebirth of the Minnesinger's soul and the regeneration of the earth in spring. Both artists, as the example of *Tannhäuser* suggests, made woman, not Christ, the agent of redemption. In his *Letters to Roeckel* Wagner argues that "the transcendent act" of a man's life is the "consummation of his humanity" through sexual intercourse. Siegfried, he tells Roeckel, only becomes fully himself through his union with Brünnhilde.[31] Stephen, for his part, awaits a "holy encounter" with the ideal figure in whose embrace he will be "transfigured" (*P* 99, 65), and Bertha, we learn, has "made... a man" of Richard (*E* 100). Wagner, for whom traditional opera was "redeemed" in music drama, brought this idea to his notion of the artist's development. According to *A Communication to My Friends*, Lohengrin is an explicit type of the modern artist, seeking in Elsa "the Unconscious... into which [his] conscious, deliberate being yearns to be redeemed" (*PW* 1:346). A similar ideal is suggested by Stephen's notion of the archetypal artist Shakespeare as "an androgynous angel, being a wife unto himself" (*U* 9.1052; 213). Wagner's earliest ambition was to become a playwright, and he once wrote that he had been "saved" by Music, "the good angel which preserved me as an artist" (*PW* 1:305). Conversely, Beethoven's Ninth Symphony, with its use of Schiller's poem, was "the redemption of Music ... into the realm of *universal Art*" (*PW* 1:126) – an "Erlösung dem Erlöser" (*Pars* 126). Given the Irish writer's fascination with these quasi-religious themes, it is not surprising that *Meistersinger*, his consistent favorite as "opera," makes only cameo appearances in his work.

For both Joyce and Wagner, redemption is achieved not through pursuit but in submission. Heroic action is generally out of place; inaction and renunciation are the norm. Thus Tristan surrenders to Melot's sword, Hans Sachs resigns himself to a life without Eva, Wotan abdicates the throne of heaven, and the enervated Amfortas, as Wagner wrote Mathilde Wesendonck, is "the centre and the principal subject" of *Parsifal*. The heroic, unselfconscious Siegfried is anomalous in Wagner's canon. In *A Portrait* Stephen waits to be encountered by his redeemer (65), and he "swoons" passively in sin when he meets her stand-in, the prostitute of chapter 2 (101). Bloom turns the other cheek in "Hades" and "Cyclops," and in "Ithaca" he rules out immediate action against Molly and Boylan (*U* 17.2200–9; 733–4). Indeed, one of the most remarkable similarities between Joyce and Wagner is that, in the middle of writing their most celebrated works, their sympathies deserted the artist and revolutionary for the resigned victim of fate and circumstance. As the *Ring* evolved from the prose sketch of 1848 to the massive cycle Wagner completed in 1874, Wotan, carrying the philosophical burden of renunciation, became the work's main character and thematic focus. In mid-stream, that is, the *Ring* became the psychodrama of Wotan, who "watches, takes no action" (*R* 193), instead of the heroic tragedy of Siegfried. *Ulysses* displays a similar shift in interest, from the artist-hero of *A Portrait* and the Telemachiad to the victim of the vagaries of contemporary life who became the book's ethical center. As we saw in chapters 2 and 3, Joyce's decreasing interest in Siegfried and increasing attraction to the Dutchman reflect this development.[32] In fact, Joyce saw the emergence of the passive hero as characteristic of modern art generally: "Since the publication of the lost pages of *Madame Bovary*," he wrote in connection with *Exiles*, thinking ahead, perhaps, to *Ulysses*, "the centre of sympathy appears to have been esthetically shifted from the lover or fancyman to the husband or cuckold" (*E* 115). Ultimately, for both artists, renunciation meant submitting oneself to the ebb and flow of life and finally to death. To Roeckel Wagner wrote, in partial explanation of his intentions in the *Ring*,

to be at one with truth is to give oneself up as a sentient human being wholly and entirely to reality – to encounter birth, growth, bloom, blight and decay frankly, with joy and with sorrow, and to live to the full this life made up of happiness and suffering – so to live and so to die.[33]

Finnegan's mourners have the same advice for the stirring hod-carrier: "Now be aisy, good Mr Finnimore, sir" (*FW* 24.16). Both artists of renunciation, Joyce and Wagner abandoned the social criticism of their early careers for, in Wagner's case, rejection of the pallid satisfactions of ordinary experience, and, in Joyce's, calm acceptance of the nature of things. "Woman," Bloom thinks, as he weighs his last opportunity to intervene between Molly and Boylan. "As easy stop the sea" (ii.641; 273).

The real action in Joyce and Wagner lies not outside but within their characters. If, for Shaw, the crucial scene in the *Ring* was *Siegfried* 3.2, when the ruler of the gods confronts his heroic grandson, for Wagner himself it was *Walküre* 2.2, when Wotan directs a kind of exterior monologue at Brünnhilde.[34] Thomas Mann identified psychology, with myth, as the two elements in Wagner's work that raised it far above the "intellectual level" of earlier opera,[35] and Eliot, in his seminal review of *Ulysses*, found the same elements crucial to Joyce's achievement. Oedipal themes – the revolt against the father in the *Ring*, for example, mother-love in *Siegfried* and *Parsifal* – abound in his work, as they do in *Ulysses* and the *Wake*. *Tristan* has been described as "theatre of the psyche," where dramatic action is identified with the growth and expression of sexual passion.[36] As we saw in chapter 6, Wagner's increasingly sophisticated use of leitmotifs was instrumental in his complex psychology. Indeed, his orchestra helped him depict material that is scarcely accessible to the art of drama but fully available to the art of fiction. The *Dutchman* and especially *Tristan*, as we saw in chapter 4, distinguish "diurnal" experience, associated with the common concerns of everyday life, from "nocturnal" experience, associated with the innermost workings of their characters' psyches. The evidence provided by *Finnegans Wake*, to the extent that it represents the world of sleep and dream, suggests that Joyce was working with the same duality. Despite his usual reluctance to place himself in the context of his age, Joyce, when the *Wake* was in its earliest stages, told Arthur Power:

classical literature represents the daylight of human personality while
modern literature is concerned with the twilight, the passive rather than
the active mind. We feel that the classicists explored the physical world
to its limit, and we are now anxious to explore the hidden world, those
undercurrents which flow beneath the apparently firm surface ...
[A] writer must maintain a continual struggle against the objective: that
is his function. The eternal qualities are the imagination and the
sexual instinct, and the formal life tries to suppress both.[37]

Wagner and Joyce share the conviction that the "undercurrents"
of erotic feeling that "flow beneath the apparently firm surface"
are at the heart of human experience. The "modernness" of
Joyce and Wagner is as apparent in their depiction of the nature
and intensity of the sexual impulse as in their technical experiments or their ideas about total art.[38]

   Stephen Spender has written that artists of the modern period
believed the artistic imagination had been crippled by the
materialism and rationalism of contemporary society and that,
to compensate, they would allow "unconscious forces" antithetical
to culture to emerge and find expression in their work.[39] Yeats,
a good example, sought inspiration, as he attempted to define
and recreate a "Celtic element" in literature, in what he called
"the symbolical movement," which had reacted against "the
rationalism of the eighteenth century" and "the materialism of
the nineteenth century."[40] A powerful tendency throughout the
work of Joyce and Wagner, in fact, is to define a clear antithesis
between reason or intellect – the "daylight" of human personality
– and passion or instinct – its "twilight"; to ascribe the former
to man and the latter to woman; and to argue that man must
surrender to the twilight forces in order to "complete" his otherwise insufficient self. Thus Lohengrin and Siegfried, as we have
seen, become whole only in their unions with Elsa and Brünnhilde;
the "dark horse" Bloom earns our admiration – and the
animosity of conventional Dublin – for those qualities that justify
his elevation as the "new womanly man" (*U* 15.1798–9; 493).
The antithesis operates in the aesthetic realm for Joyce and
Wagner as well. According to *Opera and Drama*, the "eternal
Womanly" in music draws the "manly" intellect "out of its
egoism" (*PW* 2:236), and the poet-musician, who consummates

the marriage of poetry and music in music drama, is the artist-androgyne *par excellence*. In attempting to bring the expressive power of music to literature, Joyce, as we saw in chapter 6, felt that he was confronting the limitations of "an intellectual approach which no longer satisfies the modern mind." Earlier literature lacked the "orchestra" to deal with "the secret currents of life which govern everything."[41] The Joyce who had called *Ulysses* his "mistresspiece" (*L* 1:206) had also praised his archetypal artist Ibsen for his "womanliness."[42] The irrationalist impulse carried both artists into cultural criticism as well: not only must intellect be "feminized" by emotion, but, as we saw in our discussion of the *Ring* and the *Wake* in chapter 5, corrupt masculine culture must be "redeemed" by maternal nature. The affection for myth and the attachment to an idealized nature in both artists are entirely consistent with what Lionel Trilling has called "the disenchantment of our culture with culture itself."[43]

In his controversial lecture of 1933, "The Sorrows and Grandeur of Richard Wagner," Thomas Mann admitted that he could hardly separate his love for Wagner from his love for the century that he felt the composer "so perfectly epitomizes." In Wagner and his epoch Mann identified a paradox manifest in two apparently contradictory tendencies: an impulse, on one hand, toward "the monumental, the grand production on a massive scale"; and a love, on the other, for "the very small and painstaking, the psychologically detailed."[44] Joyce's work, as some of his most distinguished critics have shown, lends itself readily to discussion in similar terms. Harry Levin writes of "structure" and "texture," Edmund Wilson of "symbolism" and "naturalism," Clive Hart of "structure" and "motif."[45] For Nietzsche, Wagner's mixture of the grand and the particular was an uncomfortable one. *The Case of Wagner* labels the composer "our greatest musical *miniaturist*" and finds Wagnerian opera "decadent," the details always threatening to overwhelm or undermine the work's entirety: "Life, equal vitality, all the vibration and exuberance of life, driven back into the smallest structure ... The whole no longer lives at all." The *Gesamtkunstwerk*, Nietzsche asserted, was a good deal less than the sum of its parts, and Joyce's unsympathetic readers might cite the

heterogeneous prose styles, the punning, and the radical allusiveness in leveling the same charge.[46]

But there is much more of the nineteenth century in both Joyce
and Wagner, as this chapter has suggested, than a precarious
balance between the monumental and the minute. Total art, a
mythic method, a romantic mythology of women, a redemptive
philosophy, religious skepticism, irrationalism, a fascination
with sin, sexuality, the problem of exile: clearly the composer
who epitomized the nineteenth century and the writer who was
its child have much in common. One implication of *Joyce and
Wagner*, in fact, is that Joyce's work is much more a product of
nineteenth-century culture – a culture on which literary modernism is built and to which Wagner contributed in great measure –
than the proud Irishman cared to acknowledge, more even,
perhaps, than he knew. "There is no help for it," Nietzsche
had acknowledged, "we must first be Wagnerites."[47] But the
challenge of Wagner was one that Joyce, having exorcized the
Wagnerism of his University College days – the "memories of
my youth" (*L* 2:154) – would meet in his own way. Having
"first" been a Wagnerite, the mature Joyce was equipped to
draw on Wagner's achievement; being a "strong poet" himself,
he was able to escape domination. "Weaker talents idealize,"
Harold Bloom has written; "figures of capable imagination
appropriate for themselves."[48]

Perhaps the most significant differences between Joyce and
Wagner lie in their material. If Wagner composed in what Mann
would call a "language without tense,"[49] Joyce worked in the
mundane present. If Wagner's art explores the heroic sensibility
and turns on the grand gesture, Joyce's depicts the family man
and focuses on subtle changes in family relationships.[50] Early in
his career, Wagner identified Tannhäuser's desire for the "pure,
chaste, virginal, unseizable" Elisabeth with the composer's own
"longing for release from the Present" (*PW* 1:323), and in his
celebrated essay Baudelaire explained that Wagner could create
his "ideal drama" only by eliminating "technical, political or
even too specific historic details." The poet quoted the composer
on the efficacy of myth in the artwork of the future:

Myth ... strips human relations of their conventional form, intelligible
only to abstract reason; it reveals what is truly human in life, what is
eternally comprehensible, and reveals it in that concrete form, free of
all imitation, which gives to all true myths their individual character,
recognizable at the first glance.[51]

True art, for Wagner, thrives in opposition to bankrupt contemporary culture, and the artwork of the future must be sought in
the purity of a mythic past.[52] Wagner's rejection of "our
frivolous Present" (*PW* 1:339) produced the fairy-tale mood of
parts of *Siegfried*, the other-worldly love of Tristan and Isolde, the
sixteenth-century setting of *Die Meistersinger*, and the asceticism
of the knights of the Grail.

Joyce, in contrast, was immersed in contemporary life, and
his mature art attempts to locate the "truly human" and
"eternally comprehensible" in ordinary experience – to find,
in other words, the universal or mythic in the quotidian. Even
as early as "Drama and Life" Joyce had insisted,

Life we must accept as we see it before our eyes, men and women as
we meet them in the real world, not as we apprehend them in the world
of faery. The great human comedy in which each has share, gives
limitless scope to the true artist, to-day as yesterday and as in years gone.
(*CW* 45)

Meistersinger, among all Wagner's operas, earned Joyce's affection
as much for its *bürgerlich* characters and historical setting as for
the wit and beauty of its music. The mature Joyce saw the distance
between Wagner and the common citizen who would become his
chief concern in *Ulysses* and the *Wake*. He wondered after a
performance of *Götterdämmerung* "what relation music like this
can possibly have to the gentlemen I was with in the gallery" (*L*
2:218), and he underscored the point in "Eumaeus," where the
common man *par excellence* finds "Wagnerian music, though
confessedly grand in its way ... a bit too heavy ... and hard to
follow at the first go-off" (*U* 16.1735 – 7; 661). Significantly, the
Stephen Dedalus who longs to awake from "the nightmare of
history" is a figure from whom *Ulysses*, which plunges headlong
into history, establishes considerable distance. After his early
experiments with lyric poetry, Joyce's creative imagination settled

comfortably into the novel, the natural home of the ordinary and demotic. If he had been a mythic artist of the same stripe as Wagner, Joyce might, like the poet that *A Portrait* identifies as Michael Robartes (251), have devoted his career to mystical poetry and mythic drama. Instead, he fused the mythic and contemporary, producing (in *Ulysses*) "the epic of the mediocre" and (in the *Wake*) "the great myth of everyday life." [53] If Wagner seems to anticipate historical modernism in so many ways, and if the era is characterized, as Irving Howe has suggested, "by a repugnance for the commonplace materials of ordinary life," then Joyce, in his affection for common experience, may be said to transcend it. [54]

Indeed, it is this fusion that gives Joyce's art a dimension we do not find in his German predecessor. To his earliest readers, certainly, the Joyce who wrote *Ulysses* appeared to hold an idealized Odysseus against an ineffectual Bloom, much as Wagner had, for instance, held Hans Sachs against Meyerbeer and the critic Eduard Hanslick. Eliot, the classic example, thought Joyce's mythic parallel indicted "the immense panorama of futility and anarchy which is contemporary history," even as it gave this history "shape." [55] More recent Joyce criticism, however, less influenced by a nineteenth-century use of myth that questions the validity of contemporary experience, has recognized that Joyce's characters – Bloom is the best example – are ennobled by association with a mythic past. Thus one might say that, in his use of myth at least, Joyce once appeared more Wagnerian than he does now. Furthermore, if for Wagner myth was a constant against which the materialism and pallor of contemporary life are to be measured, for Joyce it is a variable that alters when it encounters ordinary experience. Just as some of Odysseus, in the intertextual friction between the *Odyssey* and *Ulysses*, rubs off on Bloom, so does a bit of Bloom rub off on Odysseus. (In this sense *Ulysses* may provide some justification for the notion in recent literary theory that a work may "influence" its historical predecessor.) Homer's hero, Joyce told Frank Budgen,

"was a war dodger who tried to evade military service by simulating madness. He might never have taken up arms and gone to Troy, but the Greek recruiting sergeant was too clever for him and, while he was

ploughing the sands, placed young Telemachus in front of his plough ...
And then'' – Joyce laughed – ''he was the first gentleman in Europe.
When he advanced, naked, to meet the young princess he hid from
her maidenly eyes the parts that mattered of his brine-soaked, barnacle-
encrusted body.''[56]

In the same ironic spirit Joyce imagined a gentlemanly Siegmund
''offering his girl a box of chocolates'' (*JJ* 460) and Isolde as a
''mudheeldy wheesindonk'' (*FW* 230.12). Seeking the mythic in
the quotidian, Joyce finds the quotidian in the mythic. When
Bloom inspects the statue of Venus in Dublin's National Museum
to determine whether it is anatomically correct, he is simply
performing, in microcosm, the work of his creator. ''Purely
human,'' for Joyce, would be an oxymoron.

It is tempting to describe this distinction between Wagner and
Joyce as the difference between the idealist and realist, or, to
borrow a formulation from *Stephen Hero*, between what Joyce
himself had defined as ''romantic'' and ''classical'' tempers:

The romantic temper ... is an ... unsatisfied, impatient temper which
sees no fit abode here for its ideals and chooses therefore to behold
them under insensible figures. As a result of this choice it comes to
disregard certain limitations ... The classical temper on the other hand,
ever mindful of limitations, chooses rather to bend upon these present
things and so to work upon them and fashion them that the quick
intelligence may go beyond them to their meaning which is still
unuttered.[57]

Wagner found his ''ideal'' subject matter – ''a life that is more
ample than our own,'' Baudelaire had put it[58] – in the world of
myth, his ''ideal'' art in ancient Greek drama, where the artist,
he felt, had secured a comfortable position. The ''heroic vitalism''
of his characters, who strain for superabundant life, for the sort
of life that Siegfried and Brünnhilde share within the circle of fire
in the Prelude of *Götterdämmerung*, expresses his idealism in
dramatic form. In *Tristan* the longing for oblivion in love and death
reflects, paradoxically, a desire for more intensity and passion
than ordinary existence can sustain. Wagner's disillusionment
with ''present things'' is reflected in the gradual disappearance
of the political arena from his work, in the distance, for example,
between the optimism of the 1848 prose sketch for the *Ring* and

the spirit of renunciation in *Meistersinger, Tristan,* and, finally, *Parsifal,* where political themes are entirely absent.[59] "Unsatisfied" and "impatient" with the "real," Wagner sought the "Real" in myth and legend.[60]

Certainly the young Joyce, still grappling with his nineteenth-century heritage and with his Wagnerism, among other influences, was an idealist in this sense. Nothing could be more Wagnerian than, in "Araby," the boy's bearing his young love in a chalice, protecting it from the squalor of his own worldly circumstances; and the romantic artist of *A Portrait,* welcoming at the height of his Daedalian flight an envoy from "the wild heart of life" (171) and leaving Ireland to seek "the reality of experience" (253), is much more Wagnerian than the writer of *Ulysses* and the *Wake* will turn out to be. Richard Rowan and the Stephen of *Ulysses* are transitional figures who have not yet turned their experience of disillusionment to account. Pointedly, Robert Hand tells his Icarian friend in act I of *Exiles,* "You have fallen from a higher world, Richard, and you are filled with fierce indignation, when you find that life is cowardly and ignoble" (43–4). By the time of his fully mature work, however, Joyce and his characters have recovered from their rapid descent. But instead of trying to reascend, they burrow into the "fallen world," as Ellmann puts it, that Joyce had found to be "his natural habitat."[61] The world above which the Daedalian Wagner attempts to soar is the sort of world that every page of *Ulysses* and *Finnegans Wake* affirms. *Ulysses* replaces the chalice of "Araby" with the Gold Cup at Ascot Heath. Nowhere is Joyce's reversal of the modernist's withdrawal from ordinary life – his "post-modernism," according to some definitions – more apparent than in his depiction of women. Adaline Glasheen has argued that "the great revelation of Joyce's life" was the conversion of disgust in and fear of woman's sexuality into affirmation of her vitality and sexual energy.[62] And as Joyce accepted the "natural" in woman he embraced the "world," in all its imperfections, that woman seemed to represent. "It was revealed to me," Stephen reflects as he turns over an idea from Augustine's *Confessions,* "that those things are good which yet are corrupted which neither if they were supremely good nor unless they were good could be corrupted'' (*U* 7.842–4; 142). The bird girl of *A Portrait*, distilled of sexuality and other natural impurities, is an inadequate source of inspiration for the mature Joycean artist, and the result is the feeble villanelle. As Joyce's faith in ordinary experience grew, he eventually abdicated the role of social critic that was of such importance in his youth. Social criticism, in fact, fades from Wagner's work as well, but the difference in motivation – between romantic disillusionment with the ephemeral pursuits of ordinary life and a "classicist" affirmation of the imperfect nature of things – is crucial. "The great human comedy" of Joyce's work is nowhere more evident than in the endless cycles of sin, death, and resurrection in the *Wake*. Whereas Wagner's *Ring* restores the world to its original innocence and leaves us with a vision of "perfectibility," the *Wake* brings its hero to his redemption only to teach us about "fallibility." The Romantic idealist stands behind Wagner's single cycle, the skeptic or realist behind Joyce's countless ones.

The distance between Stephen Dedalus and the artist that he fails to be is measured, simultaneously, by his aversion to water and by his dissociation from the demotic life of Dublin that, as *Ulysses* progresses, becomes his creator's true subject. To achieve the sort of regeneration that Wagner, after his own creative drought of some six years, claimed to have found in his dream-vision of the Prelude to *Das Rheingold*, Stephen requires immersion in the common experience that his antithesis, Bloom the "water-lover" (*U* 17.183; 671), represents. For both Joyce and Wagner, water came to represent the resources of the artist: it was artistic inspiration; it was life itself. A river – "life" in motion – turns out to be the most powerful symbol in the work of each: the surging, unspoiled Rhine, the humble, polluted Liffey. And to set "Anna Rhenana" beside the "drunken draggletail Dublin drab" (*L* 1:396) is to summarize the great contrast in the art of Joyce and Wagner. Wagner's artistic ideal flows abundantly in prelapsarian time and place, inaccessible to the modern world; Joyce's art flows into all the corners, even the meanest, of life. Wagner gives us the "purely," ideally human, Joyce the all-too-human but, perhaps, if we remember the epigraph to *Tess of the d'Urbervilles*, the no less pure. In "Lestrygonians" Bloom strolls by the Liffey and reflects, "How can you own water, really? It's always flowing in a stream, never the same ... Because life is a stream" (*U* 8.93 – 5; 153). But the artist, in recreating life, may capture the flood that in its "buoyancy ... variety ... potentiality ... ubiquity" (*U* 17.213 – 26; 672) slips through Bloom's fingers. Artists of affirmation both, Wagner and Joyce gave us "Life" and "life"; one, a distillation of human experience, the other, an adulterated draught of it. Wagner helped us imagine what life might be like; Joyce taught us to love what ineluctably comes our way.

APPENDIX

Allusions to Wagner in Joyce's work

For two almost entirely opposite reasons, both having to do with *Finnegans Wake*, no list of allusions in Joyce's work can claim to be definitive. In the first place, the *Wake* requires a more unrestrained search than would be conducted in a less obscure and less highly wrought text. At the risk of lengthening his list with false identifications, the compiler must consider many allusions that can only be called "possible." The second difficulty comes from the opposing need to define *some* limits to a search in the *Wake*. Glasheen puts an extreme case in her *Third Census*: "Every 'is' indicates Issy and it is out of [the] question to list them all."[1] And this problem is compounded by the book's principle of correspondences – "everybody is somebody else."[2] For example, if Issy "is" on some level Isolde, then is every "Issy" an allusion to *Tristan und Isolde*? Is every "is"? To follow out the implications of this principle in creating this appendix would trivialize the enterprise, producing a list of ridiculous length and dubious value.

Here the method of selection is to judge each case on its own merits – a reference to "Venus," for example, may be listed as an allusion to *Tannhäuser* if its context seems to draw on themes from the opera or if another reference to Wagner is present – but to err on the side of inclusion. Thus *Joyce and Wagner*, taken as a whole, splits the difference between narrow (or "minimalist") and broad (or "maximalist") approaches to identifying allusions in the *Wake*: whereas the arguments advanced in the seven main chapters of this book rest on identifications I take to be "mandatory," or nearly so, this appendix includes many "possible" listings and thus acquits the responsibility to make as thorough a case for Wagner as common sense allows. In erring on the side of inclusion, the appendix lays the individual case before its readers and permits them to reject it. I have not listed allusions to Bédier's *Tristan and Iseult* where they can be extricated from allusions to Wagner, though, as I said in chapter 4, they often cannot be. My aim in developing this list has been simply to gather and increase our store of information about Joyce and one of his most important "parental" sources and to show Wagner's pervasiveness in Joyce's work without pretending to close the subject.

The main method of organization, by Wagner's works (with the date of the first performance) rather than Joyce's, reflects my sense that the list will be used for reference, as, for example, the *Third Census* is, rather than as a companion, as O Hehir and Dillon's *Classical Lexicon* is used. A reader who consults the appendix to corroborate the impression that an allusion is present is more likely to have a particular opera in mind than something generally "Wagnerian." Moreover, the reader who is concentrating on one of the operas is spared the trouble of searching the entire list.

In the many passages where, within a few lines, Joyce has compounded references from more than one opera, I have made cross-references. Sometimes, in fact, the validity of my claim for an allusion is fully supported only by the proximity of a second or a third reference to Wagner. At *FW* 553.29 – 30, for example, the word "waggonways" may be counted as a reference to the composer himself because it appears in close company with relatively clear allusions to Froh in *Das Rheingold* and to Valhalla, both of which the appendix lists under the *Ring*. My reader is urged to check cross-references if at first the claim for an allusion seems suspect.

I have consulted Glasheen's *Third Census*, McHugh's *Annotations*, Hart's *Concordance*, Mink's *Gazetteer*, and Hodgart's *Student's Guide* in search of allusions that escaped my imperfect Wagnerism. Indeed, without the help of these scholars – and in particular without that of Hodgart, who apparently turned over his list of allusions to McHugh – I would have missed many of the best ones. Where previous identification of an allusion seems especially noteworthy, the appendix gives the source. Even with this assistance, however, I must offer this list certain that many references to Wagner remain to be discovered.

Richard Wagner (1813 – 1883)

CW 37: it is [,?] to pervert Wagner, the attitude of the town

40: Even the least part of Wagner – his music – is beyond Bellini.

43: The author of Parsifal has recognized this and hence his work is solid as a rock. (Also listed under *Parsifal*.)

179: The question that Wagner put into the mouth of the innocent Parsifal must come to mind when we read from time to time certain English criticism (See *Pars* 95. Also listed under *Parsifal*. Cf. *CW* 75 – 6.)

263: And how confederate of gay old Gioacchino [Rossini] to have composed this finale so that Kamerad Wagner might be

saved the annoyance of finding flauts for his *Feuerzauber*!
(Also listed under the *Ring*.)

Daniel Defoe 22: Different from Tristan and Isolde! Contemporary
composers... would find very little in the story of this woman
... The realism ... of this writer defies and transcends the
magical beguilements of music. (Also listed under *Tristan*.)

"Universal Literary Influence of the Renaissance," in Berrone 21–2:
A great modern artist wishing to put the sentiment of love
to music reproduces, as far as his art permits, each pulsation, each trembling, the lightest shivering, the lightest sigh;
the harmonies intertwine and oppose each other secretly:
one loves even as one grows more cruel, suffers when and
as much as one enjoys, hate and doubt flash in the lovers'
eyes, their bodies become one single flesh. Place *Tristan und
Isolde* next to the *Inferno* (Also listed under *Tristan*.)

E 58: See how artistic I have become ... I was just strumming out
Wagner when you came.

U 1.23; 3: Silence, all. (The Wagnerian "hush," associated with
the curtain of act I of *Parsifal*. Cf. *FW* 14.6, 159.19, 334.31,
501.7. Also listed under *Parsifal*.)

15.1368–9; 478: That's the music of the future. That's my programme.
(Wagner's "Music of the Future." Cf. *FW* 407.32–3,
518.28. See proximate reference to the *Dutchman*.)

16.1735–7; 661: Wagnerian music, though confessedly grand in its
way, was a bit too heavy for Bloom and hard to follow at
the first go-off

FW 012.25: Make strake for minnas! (Possibly Wagner's wife Minna
Planer.)

014.6: (Silent.) (The Wagnerian "hush." Cf. *U* 1.23; 3, *FW* 159.19,
334.31, 501.7. Also listed under *Parsifal*.)

070.4–5: and swobbing broguen eeriesh myth brockendootsch,
making his reporterage on Der Fall Adams for the Franko-
furto Siding (Nietzsche's *Der Fall Wagner*.)

126.10–11: secondtonone myther rector and maximost bridgesmaker
(Possibly, in this context, Wagner as mythmaker. Also listed
under the *Ring*.)

149.13: a wag on my ears ("Wagner.")

150.15–159.19: (A major Wagnerian passage. See listings under
"Wagner," *Tannhäuser*, *Tristan*, *Meistersinger*, the *Ring*, and
Parsifal.)

150.15: Professor Loewy-Brueller (Hermann Levi and Hans von
Bülow, conductors of Wagnerian opera. Cf. *FW* 151.11,
151.32–3. See Hodgart, *Student's Guide*, 147.)

151.1: cosm (Wagner's second wife Cosima Liszt von Bülow.)

   .11: Professor Levi-Brullo (Cf. *FW* 150.15, 151.32 – 3.)

   .32 – 3: Professor Llewellys ap Bryllars (Cf. *FW* 150.15, 151.11.)

159.19: No applause, please! (The Wagnerian "hush." Cf. *U* 1.23; 3, *FW* 14.6, 334.31, 501.7. Also listed under *Parsifal*. See proximate reference to the *Ring*.)

189.12: as many as the minneful (Possibly, in this context, "Minna": see proximate reference to *Tristan*.)

206.15 – 16: Minneha, minnehi minaaehe, minneho! (Possibly "Minna.")

229.33 – 5: a hadtobe heldin, thoroughly enjoyed by many so meny on block at Boyrut season and for their account ottorly admired by her husband ("Bayreuth," "Otto" Wesendonck.)

230.12 – 13: as a wagoner would his mudheeldy wheesindonk at their trist in Parisise after tourments of tosend years ("Wagner," "Mathilde Wesendonck." Also listed under *Tristan*.)

241.26: berberutters ("Bayreuthers." See proximate reference to *Parsifal*.)

243.17: ladwigs out of his lugwags ("Ludwig" II, Wagner's patron. See proximate reference to the *Ring*.)

301.14 – 15: And how are you, waggy? (Possibly, in this context, "Wagner": see proximate reference to *Tristan*.)

318.17 – 18: Listeneath to me, veils of Mina! (Possibly, in this context, "Minna": see proximate references to the *Dutchman* and the *Ring*.)

334.31: (Silents) (Cf. *U* 1.23; 3, *FW* 14.6, 159.19, 501.7. Also listed under *Parsifal*.)

360.8 – 9: you wheckfoolthenairyans with all your badchthumpered peanas ("Wagnerians." Cf. *FW* 42.1: "whackfolthediddlers.")

407.32 – 3: embelliching the musics of the futures (Cf. *U* 15.1368 – 9; 478, *FW* 518.28.)

431.11: the most purely human being that ever was called man (Wagner's *Reinmenschliche*. See proximate reference to the *Ring*.)

434.21 – 3: ribbons of lace, limenick's disgrace … to make Languid Lola's lingery longer ("Lola" Montez, Limerick-born mistress of Ludwig I, "Limerick's disgrace." Cf. 525.14. See proximate reference to the *Dutchman*.)

500.24 – 501.7: Fort! Fort! Bayroyt! March! … SILENCE. ("Bayreuth"; the Wagnerian "hush." Cf. *U* 1.23; 3, *FW* 14.6, 159.19, 334.31. See proximate references to *Tristan*, the *Ring*, and *Parsifal*.)

508.22: music minnestirring (Possibly, in this context, "Minna."
Also listed under *Meistersinger*.)

518.28: The mujic of the footure (Cf. *U* 15.1368–9; 478, *FW* 407.
32–3.)

525.14: Lalia Lelia Lilia Lulia and lively lovely Lola Montez. (Cf.
FW 434.23. Also listed under the *Ring*.)

540.24–5: dudder wagoners, pullars off societies ("Wagner,"
often linked with Ibsen. See, for example, *CW* 45.)

543.27: wageearner

553.29–30: my stony battered waggonways ("Wagner": see
proximate references to the *Ring*.)

562.32: O, I adore the profeen music! (Possibly, in this context,
Wagner's *Die Feen* or his music in general.)

565.2–5: It is often quite guttergloomering in our duol and gives
wankyrious thoughts to the head but the banders of the
pentapolitan poleetsfurcers bassoons into it on windy
woodensdays their wellbooming wolvertones. (A description
of Wagnerian music. Also listed under the *Ring*.)

577.13: voguener

The Flying Dutchman (1843)

E 35: To end it all – death. To fall from a great high cliff, down, right
down into the sea … Listening to music and in the arms
of the woman I love – the sea, music and death. (The
opera's final scene. Also listed under *Tristan*.)

U 3.397–8; 48: He comes, pale vampire, through storm his eyes, his
bat sails bloodying the sea, mouth to her mouth's kiss.
(Cf. *U* 7.522–5; 132. Details from Senta's Ballad, the Steersman's Song, the Spinning Song. See discussion in chapter
3. Also listed under *Tristan*.)

7.522–5; 132: On swift sail flaming / From storm and south / He
comes, pale vampire, / Mouth to my mouth. (Cf. *U*
3.397–8; 48. See discussion in chapter 3. See also listing
under *Tristan*.)

13.1077–8; 376: Were those nightclouds there all the time? Looks
like a phantom ship. (By tradition the Dutchman's is a
"phantom ship." Cf. *U* 15.1369–70; 478, 16.863; 636, *FW*
327.25–6. See proximate reference to *Tannhäuser*.)

15.1369–70; 478: our bucaneering Vanderdeckens in their phantom
ship of finance (Cf. *U* 13.1077–8; 376, 16.863; 636, *FW* 323.1,
327.25–6. See proximate reference to "Wagner.")

15.1390–1; 479: These flying Dutchmen or lying Dutchmen as they recline in their upholstered poop

16.859–64; 636: who reminded him a bit of Ludwig, *alias* Ledwidge, when he occupied the boards ... in the *Flying Dutchman* ... everyone simply flocking to hear him though ships of any sort, phantom or the reverse, on the stage usually fell a bit flat (Cf. *U* 13.1077–8; 376, 15.1369–70; 478, *FW* 327.25–6.)

FW 126.16: his hullender's epulence (The "Holländer's opulence" the subject of a long discussion in act 1. See *FD* 53–6.)

202.19: Nieman from Nirgends found the Nihil (*FD* 52: "Nirgends ein Grab! Niemals der Tod!" See McHugh, *Annotations*.)

220.25–6: King Ericus of Schweden and ... his magical helmet (Possibly, in this context, "Erik": see listing under the *Ring*.)

229.14: A Wondering Wreck ("Vanderdecken.")

232.36–233.2: He's a pigtail tarr and ... he'd a telltale tall of his pitcher on a wall (The Dutchman's portrait in act 2.)

268.3: conchitas with sentas stray ("Senta." Cf. *FW* 327.24–5.)

277.23: Eric aboy! ("Erik.")

311.5–332.9: (The "Norwegian Captain" episode. See discussion in chapter 3.)

311.5: once there was a lealand in the luffing (McHugh, *Annotations*: Charles "Leland" wrote a poem about the Dutchman legend. Possibly also "Daland," Senta's father.)

312.5–8: And aweigh he yankered on the Norgean run so that seven sailend sonnenrounders was he breastbare to the brinabath, where bottoms out has fatthoms full ... evenstarde and risingsoon. (The Dutchman's seven-year term; the opera's setting in Norway. Also listed under *Tannhäuser*.)

.19–20: off his Cape of Good Howthe (The "Cape of Good Hope," where the Dutchman incurred his doom.)

314.22: their dutchuncler mynhosts

316.8: swore his eric ("Erik.")

.15–16: hiberniating after seven oak ages (The Dutchman's seven-year term. See proximate reference to the *Ring*.)

318.3–10: Take thee live will save thee wive? ... Her youngfree yoke stilling his wandercursus (Senta as the Dutchman's redeemer. See proximate references to "Wagner" and the *Ring*.)

319.16–17: Ampsterdampster that had rheumaniscences in his netherlumbs (An "ancient" mariner, the Dutchman suffers the maladies of old age.)

323.1–8: the bugganeering wanderducken, he sazd ... the bloedaxe
bloodooth baltxebec ... voyaging after maidens, belly jonah
hunting the polly joans, and the hurss of all portnoysers
befaddle him (Cf. *U* 15.1369; 478. Also listed under the *Ring*.)

327.22–6: titting out through her droemer window for the flyend
of a touchman over the wishtas of English Strand ... where
our dollimonde sees the phantom shape of Mr Fortunatus
Wright (Senta, especially as act 2 opens.)

336.13–14: keen and able and a spindlesong (The "Spinning Song"
of act 2.)

359.26: Eeric Whigs ("Erik.")

362.8–9: the manyfathom bringeroom

416.30–2: Had he twicycled the sees of the deed ...? Was he come
to hevre with his engiles or gone to hull with the poop?
(Possibly the *Dutchman*'s conclusion. Also listed under
Tannhäuser.)

423.22–3: barnacled up to the eyes when he repented after seven
(The Dutchman's seven-year term.)

434.23–4: Scenta Clauthes stiffstuffs your hose and heartsies full of
temptiness. ("Senta." See proximate reference to "Wagner.")

456.22: erics

469.19–20: The brine's my bride to be. ("Euch, des Weltmeer's
Fluthen, / bleib' ich getreu"; "To you, the ocean tide, I
remain faithful" [*FD* 51, my translation].)

487.15: ericulous imagining ("Erik.")

530.20–1: Roof Seckesign van der Deckel ... Seckersen, magnon
of Errick. ("Vanderdecken," "Erik.")

620.6–8: You make me think of a wonderdecker I once. Or somebalt thet sailder, the man megallant, with the bangled ears.
("Vanderdecken.")

Tannhäuser (1845)

CP 12: (Poem 4 borrows the situation and setting of the beginning of
act 3. See discussion in chapter 4.)

33: the hour of evenstar (*Tann* 87: "O du, mein holder Abendstern."
Cf. *FW* 312.8.)

CW 263–4: Saving is believing but can thus be? Is this our model
vicar of Saint Wartburgh's, the reverend Mr Townhouser,
Mus. Bac., discovered flagrant in a *montagne de passe*? She
is obvious and is on her threelegged sofa in a half yard of
casheselks, Madame de la Pierreuse. How deutonically she
hands him his harp that once, bitting him, whom caught is

willing: do blease to, fickar! She's as only roman as any *puttana maddonna* but the trouble is that the reverend T is reformed. She, *simplicissima*, wants her little present from the reverend since she was wirk worklike never so nice with him. But he harps along about Salve Regina Terrace and Liza, mine Liza, and sweet Marie. Till she cries: bilk! And he calls: blak! O. u. t. spells out! (A synopsis of *Tannhäuser* 1.2: Venus and Tannhäuser, he late of the "Wartburg," discovered together; they sing together ["duetonically"]; Venus bids him tell the praise of love: "Mein Sänger, auf! ... ergreife die Harfe"; the Minnesinger, now "reformed," sings of his desire to return to earth and of his love of Mary: "Mein Heil liegt in Maria!"; Venus calls him a "traitor" ["bilk!"] and bids him depart: "Zieh hin!" ["o.u.t. spells out!"] [*Tann* 61–7]. "Liza, mine Liza" is Elisabeth, not mentioned in *Tannhäuser* 1.2. See proximate reference to *Tristan*.)

264–5: was that really in faith the reverend Townhouser for he seemed so verdamnably like? ... Nor used he to deny his Mary neither.

E 57–8: He plays softly in the bass the first bars of Wolfram's song in the last act of "Tannhäuser." (The song is "O du, mein holder Abendstern.")

U 13.1076; 376: A star I see. Venus? Can't tell yet. ("Venus": see proximate reference to the *Dutchman*.)

14.356; 393: better were they named Beau Mount and Lecher (Possibly, in "Beau Mount," the Venusberg.)

FW 079.18: Venuses were gigglibly temptatrix

113.21: any Genoaman against any Venis (See proximate reference to *Tristan*.)

152.15–159.19: (The story of "The Mookse and the Gripes" parallels that of the penitent Tannhäuser and the unforgiving Pope.)

154.20: urban (In this context, possibly Urban IV, the Pope who would not absolve Tannhäuser.)

156.33–4: Mee are relying entirely, see the fortethurd of Elissabed, on the weightiness of mear's breath. ("Elisabeth" as Tannhäuser's intercessor. Does Elisabeth sing a "forte third" at some point?)

203.19–20: one venersderg in junojuly (The "Venusberg.")

232.11: call her venicey names (Possibly "Venus": see proximate reference to *Tristan*.)

289.26: the pretty Lady Elisabbess, Hotel des Ruines ("Elisabeth": the Venus de Milo appears at 291.14–15.)

312.8: evenstarde (*Tann* 87: "O du, mein holder Abendstern." Cf. *CP* 33. See proximate reference to the *Dutchman*.)

315.16 – 18: his stickup in his hand ... had a mushroom on it (Possibly the pope's staff, which, in flowering, signifies Tannhäuser's absolution.)

328.36: with Elizabeliza blessing the bedpain

403.18 – 22: Methought as I was dropping asleep somepart in non-land of where's please ... I heard at zero hour as 'twere the peal of vixen's laughter among midnight's chimes from out the belfry of the cute old speckled church tolling so faint (*Tann* 62: In act 1.2 Tannhäuser dreams of churchbells. See Hodgart, *Student's Guide*, 172.)

416.31 – 2: Was he come to hevre with his engiles or gone to hull with the poop? (Possibly the question of Tannhäuser's fate. Also listed under the *Dutchman*.)

486.7: Tantris, hattrick, tryst and parting, by vowelglide! (Walther von der "Vogelweide," one of the opera's Minnesingers. Also listed under *Tristan*.)

495.25: Elsebett (Also listed under *Lohengrin*.)

542.23: elisaboth

561.8: Halosobuth, sov us! ("Elisabeth." See proximate reference to *Parsifal*.)

562.9 – 11: that she spin blue to scarlad till her temple's veil, that the Mount of Whoam it open it her to shelterer (Possibly a hint of "Venusberg" in "temple" and "Mount of Whoam." See also listing under *Tristan*.)

569.10 – 11: S. Mary Stillamaries with Bride-and-Audeons-behind-Wardborg (The "Wartburg.")

Lohengrin (1850)

CW 45: Lohengrin, the drama of which unfolds itself in a scene of seclusion, amid half-lights, is not an Antwerp legend but a world drama.

58: He recalls to her the time when they made a boat of leaves, and yoked a white swan to it, in imitation of the boat of Lohengrin.

58: "You said I was the swan that drew your boat." (In this review of *When We Dead Awaken*, Joyce quotes from a French version of the play, supplying his own translation.)

FW 139.32 – 3: a riverpaard was spotted, which is not Whichcroft Whorort (Act 1, act 3.3: possibly the swan, approaching in the distance; also, a hint of "Ortrud" and her "witchcraft.")

197.17–18: Don Dom Dombdomb (The Wedding March.)
444.31: Annybettyelsas ("Elsa.")
495.25: Elsebett ("Elsa." Also listed under *Tannhäuser*.)
548.33: I wound around my swanchen's neckplace a school of shells (Act 3.3: Ortrud admits having placed a magic chain around the neck of Gottfried, who now takes the form of a swan.)

Tristan und Isolde (1865)

Daniel Defoe 21–2: The scene of the meeting between Christian and her faithless husband ... presents the eternal feminine in an unexpected light ... Different from Tristan and Isolde! Contemporary composers ... would find very little in the story of this woman ... The realism ... of this writer defies and transcends the magical beguilements of music. (Also listed under "Wagner.")

"Universal Literary Influence of the Renaissance," in *Berrone* 21–2: A great modern artist wishing to put the sentiment of love to music reproduces, as far as his art permits, each pulsation, each trembling, the lightest shivering, the lightest sigh; the harmonies intertwine and oppose each other secretly: one loves even as one grows more cruel, suffers when and as much as one enjoys, hate and doubt flash in the lovers' eyes, their bodies become one single flesh. Place *Tristan und Isolde* next to the *Inferno* (Also listed under "Wagner.")

CW 264: But he harps along about ... Liza, mine Liza ("Mild und leise," the first words of Isolde's *Liebestod* [*TI* 91]. Tristan a harpist in some sources. See proximate references to *Tannhäuser*.)

E 35: To end it all – death ... Listening to music and in the arms of the woman I love – the sea, music and death. (The opera's conclusion. Also listed under the *Dutchman*.)

106: Where you mine in that sacred night of love? Or have I dreamed it? (*TI* 74: the "*Liebesnacht*" of act 2.2.)

112: I have a deep, deep wound of doubt in my soul ... I have wounded my soul for you – a deep wound of doubt which can never be healed. (Possibly the wound that Isolde heals or the wound that, eventually, kills Tristan. Also listed under *Parsifal*.)

U 3.397–400; 48: He comes, pale vampire ... mouth to her mouth's kiss ... Mouth to her kiss ... Mouth to her mouth's kiss. (*TI* 71: "Herz an Herz dir, / Mund an Mund." Cf. *U* 7.524–5; 132. Also listed under the *Dutchman*.)

7.524–5; 132: He comes, pale vampire, / Mouth to my mouth. (*TI*
71: "Herz an Herz dir, / Mund an Mund." Cf. *U* 3.397–
400; 48. Also listed under the *Dutchman*.)

11.21; 256: A sail! A veil awave upon the waves. (Possibly a conflation
of the veil of act 2.1 with the flag of act 3.1, both of which
Isolde employs as signals to Tristan. See Gilbert, *Joyce's
Ulysses*, 146n.)

12.176–92; 296–7: Irish heroes and heroines of antiquity ... Tristan
and Isolde

12.1455; 332: Isolde's tower (Cf. *FW* 87.29.)

FW 003.4–6: Sir Tristram, violer d'amores ... his pen*isol*ate war
("Tristan," "Isolde." My emphasis.)

004.14: But was iz? Iseut? (Tristan's first words in the opera: "Was
ist? Isolde?" [*TI* 50]. Cf. *FW* 75.10–11, 203.8–9. See
Hodgart, *Student's Guide*, 138.)

005.31: tramtrees (*TI* 52: "Tantris," Tristan's alter ego. See
proximate reference to the *Ring*.)

007.28–9: Seeple Isout ("Isolde," "Chapelizod.")

017.1: Monomark
    .35–6: this sound seemetery which iz leebez luv (*"Liebestod."*)

018.2: Meldundleize! (*TI* 91: "Mild und leise," the first words of
Isolde's *Liebestod*.)

021.5–23.15: (In the story of Jarl van Hoother and the Prankquean,
the mixing up of the two "jiminies" parallels Brangäne's
substitution, in act 1, of the love potion for the poison.)

021.12: Tristopher ("Tristan.")
    .18: Mark the Wans (Cf. *FW* 372.4.)
    .21: jiminy Tristopher ("Tristan.")
    .24–8: And there was a brannewail that same sabboath night ...
    And the prankquean ... washed the blessings of the lovespots
    off the jiminy (Brangäne, possibly in lamentation over
    having substituted the love potion ["lovespots"] for the
    poison in act 1: "Wehe! Wehe!" [*TI* 61]. See Hodgart,
    Student's Guide, 139.)

022.5: Mark the Twy
    .17: and he became a tristian
    .29: Mark the Tris ("Mark," "Tristan." See proximate
    reference to the *Ring*.)

023.23: Murk

025.30–1: elmstree ... stone ("Tree-stone" or "Tristan.")

026.17: chempel of Isid ("Chapelizod," "Isolde.")

031.31–2: roadside tree ... cladstone ("Tree-stone" or "Tristan.")

040.16–17: O'Mara ... locally known as Mildew Lisa (*TI* 91: "Mild und leise.'' See McHugh, *Annotations*: O'Mara a tenor who sang in *Tristan*.)

050.19: treu and troster

057.27–8: his mild dewed cheek (*TI* 91: "Mild und leise.'')

066.21: twist stern ("Tristan.'')

.29: handharp ... tristinguish ("Tristan'' a harpist in some sources.)

075.10–11: where corngold Ysit ("Isolde''; possibly Tristan's first words in the opera: "Was ist? Isolde?'' [*TI* 50]. Cf. *FW* 4.14, 203.8–9.)

080.36: Issy-la-Chapelle! ("Chapelizod,'' "Isolde.'')

087.29: Isod's towertop (Cf. *U* 12.1455; 332.)

091.13: Markarthy (Cf. *FW* 519.24.)

092.7: tristitone

095.24: putting out her netherlights (Isolde extinguishes the torch in act 2.1.)

096.5–6: old markiss ... marcus

.15: triss

100.28–9: tristurned initials (*TI* 52: Tristan's reversal of his name.)

101.9: mark oom for yor ounckel ("Mark'' is Tristan's "uncle.'')

104.10: Amoury Treestam and Icy Siseule

113.18–19: the tale of a Treestone with one Ysold, of a Mons held by tentpegs ("Tristan,'' "Isolde,'' possibly "Mark.'' See proximate reference to *Tannhäuser*.)

117.2: Here, Ohere, insult the fair! Traitor, bad hearer, brave! (Cf. *FW* 398.29.)

119.30–1: a tea anyway for a tryst someday

126.23–4: allmarken ... Cornish ("Mark of Cornwall.'')

128.1–2: isst and herit and though he's mildewstaned he's mouldy-stoned ("Isolde''; *TI* 91: "Mild und leise.'')

133.8–9: Liebsterpet ("*Liebestod*.'' See proximate reference to the *Ring*.)

134.27–8: husband your aunt and endow your nepos (Tristan "husbands'' Isolde, his "aunt'' through her marriage to Mark.)

.31–2: marked three in the shade

.36–135.2: the king was in his cornerwall melking mark so murry, the queen was steep in armbour feeling fain and furry ("Mark of Cornwall,'' Isolde.)

136.34: trees down

143.29–148.32: (A major Wagnerian passage in which Isolde addresses her alter ego in the mirror; many details drawn from Bédier.)

144.10–11: My Eilish assent he seed makes his admiracion. (Tristan admires the "Irish" Isolde.)

145.14–15: hug me, damn it all, and I'll kiss you back to life, my peachest (Act 3.2.)

.36–146.1: when I'd run my burning torchlight through (to adore me there and then cease to be? Whatever for, blossoms?) (Possibly Isolde's torch in act 2.1; also, the *Liebestod* theme.)

146.7: my trysting of the tulipies

.17: isabeaubel

.34: bigtree ... gravstone ("Tree-stone" or "Tristan.")

148.11: I sold

157.33–4: Mrs Cornwallis-West

.35–6: the daughter of the queen of the Emperour of Irelande

158.1: Tristis Tristior Tristissimus

159.4: an only elmtree and but a stone ("Tree-stone" or "Tristan.")

.18: I'se so silly to be flowing ("Isolde." See proximate reference to the *Ring*.)

.32: charge of the night brigade on Tristan da Cunha

161.13: soldthere ("Isolde.")

169.19–20: a bladder tristended

175.23: His Murkesty

185.20: tristitiae

189.5–6: a philtred love, trysting by tantrums, small peace in ppenmark (The love potion, "Tristan," "Tantris" [*Tristan* 52]; "Penmark," in Brittany, the site, in some sources, of Tristan's death.)

.17–19: consumed by amorous passion ... one son of Sorge for all daughters of Anguish (The *Liebestod* theme. In some sources, Sorge is son of Tristan and Isolde, Anguish is father of Isolde. See proximate reference under "Wagner.")

196.17–18: the mouldaw stains (*TI* 91: "Mild und leise.")

201.8: my life in death companion ("*Liebestod.*")

203.8–9: Wasut? Izod? (Tristan's first words in the opera: "Was ist? Isolde?" [*TI* 50]. Cf. *FW* 4.14, 75.10–11.)

209.24–5: Isolabella

220.7: IZOD

221.11: under the influence of the milldieuw (*TI* 91: "Mild und leise.")

222.27: eyesoult

223.11: Isot given yoe?

.31: mark

226.4–14: Isa ... Hey, lass! Woefear gleam she so glooming, this

pooripathete I solde? Her beauman's gone of a cool ... If
he's at anywhere she's therefor to join him. If it's to nowhere
she's going to too. Buf if he'll go to be a son to France's
she'll stay daughter of Clare ... And among the shades that
Eve's now wearing she'll meet anew fiancy, tryst and trow.
("Isolde," "Tristan," the reunion in Brittany in act 3.
If Isolde joins Tristan in death, "it's to nowhere she's going
to too." See proximate reference to the *Ring*.)

228.19: banishment care of Pencylmania, Bretish Armerica (Possibly
Tristan's exile in Brittany.)

230.13: their trist in Parisise after tourments of tosend years
("Tristan," the *Liebestod* theme. See proximate references
to "Wagner.")

   .26: treetrene ... stone ("Tree-stone" or "Tristan.")

   .32: patriss

   .35–36: treed ... stohong ("Tree-stone" or "Tristan.")

232.13: Isle wail for yews ("Isolde.")

234.3: his tristiest cabaleer

237.8–9: all alisten to his elixir. Lovelyt! (The love potion in act 1;
possibly also Isolde's torch ["love light"] in 2.1. Cf. *FW*
615.24.)

245.29: how matt your mark

247.4: Elmstree to Stene ("Tree-stone" or "Tristan.")

   .22–3: how slight becomes a hidden wound? Soldwoter he
wash him (*TI* 52: Isolde heals, with "Isoldewater," Tristan's
wound during his first journey to Ireland.)

249.3: my first viewmarc

251.15–16: murkery viceheid

   .17: wishmarks

259.1–2: tree over tree become stone to stone ("Tree-stone" or
"Tristan.")

261.F2: Izalond ("Isolde" of "Ireland.")

265.13–14: Izolde, her chaplet gardens ("Isolde,"
"Chapelizod.")

266.9–10: murk of the mythelated

267.19: Issossianusheen

270.F3: trust in (Possibly, in this context, "Tristan.")

278.25–6: wounded our way on foe tris prince ("Tristan"; possibly
also his wounds.)

279.1–2: treebark ... rainstones ("Tree-stone" or "Tristan.")

   .F1: Trestrine

280.22–3: prints chumming, can be when desires Soldi

282.L1: Tricks stunts.

288.13–14: when he landed in ourland's leinster ... for the twicedhe-
     came time (Tristan makes two voyages to Ireland.)
     .22: tristar
289.28–290.2: Isolade ... where in the rose world trysting, that
     was the belle of La Chapelle, shapely Liselle ("Isolde,"
     "Tristan," "Chapelizod." See proximate reference to
     Tannhäuser.)
290.12–13: gave him then that vantage of a Blinkensope's cuddle-
     bath at her proper mitts (*TI* 52: Isolde heals Tristan.)
     .15–17: such a coolcold douche as him ... doubling back (*TI*
     53: Tristan's coolness towards Isolde on his second journey
     to Ireland, here "Dublin.")
     .19: Multalusi (*TI* 91: "Mild und leise.")
291.1–2: Unic bar None, of Saint Yves by Landsend cornwer (Mark
     of "Cornwall," "Uncle" of Tristan.)
     .5: inseuladed
299.1–2: trist sigheds to everysing ("Tristan" and his notorious
     gloominess.)
301.8: moultylousy (*TI* 91: "Mild und leise.")
     .15–18: My animal his sorrafool! And trieste, ah trieste ate I
     my liver! ... He was sadfellow ("Tristan" means "sad-
     fellow.")
302.6–9: bis*tris*pissing ... a capital Tea for Thirst ("Tristan,"
     emphasis mine.)
304.1–3: And his countinghands rose. Formalisa. Loves deathhow
     simple! (*TI* 91: "Mild und leise"; the "*Liebestod*" con-
     ducted. See proximate reference to the *Ring*.)
     .20–2: With her listeningin coiffure, her dream of Endsland's
     daylast and the glorifires of being presainted maid to
     majesty. (Act 1.3: Brangäne tries to persuade Isolde of the
     "glory" of being Mark's wife [*TI* 54]. Cf. *FW* 434.17.)
314.34: in sola
317.36: trystfully
325.14: Capel Ysnod ("Isolde," "Chapelizod.")
332.29: ysendt
334.36: Izd-la-Chapelle ("Isolde," "Chapelizod.")
348.23–4: old Djadja Uncken who was a great mark ("Mark,"
     Tristan's "uncle.")
349.22: Izodella
353.2: Trisseme
363.15: He's their mark
     .24: trust ... in
     .26: trisspass through minxmingled hair

.28: theactrisscalls

367.8–14: Mask one. Mask two. Mask three. Mask four ... Our
four avunculusts. ("Mark," Tristan's "uncle.")

372.4: Moke the Wanst (Cf. *FW* 21.18.)

.28: till Dew Mild Well (*TI* 91: "Mild und leise.")

378.14: Magtmorken, Kovenhow. ("Mark of Cornwall.")

380.4–5: Mocked Majesty

383.1–399.36: (Book II.4 was composed in 1938, when Joyce inter-
laced his early sketch "Tristan and Isolde," based on
Wagner, with the slightly later "Mamalujo," based on
Bédier. The two sources inform the entire chapter passim
and are virtually inextricable.)

383.1: Three quarks for Muster Mark!

.3: beside the mark

.8: Hohohoho, moulty Mark!

.11: Fowls, up! Tristy's the spry young spark

.14: his money and mark

.15–18: Overhoved, shrillgleescreaming. That song sang sea-
swans. The winging ones. Seahawk, seagull, curlew and
plover, kestrel and capercallzie. All the birds of the sea they
trolled out rightbold when they smacked the big kuss of
Trustan with Usolde. (Act 1 is set on board a ship.)

384.8–11: old Marcus Lyons ... old Marcus

.31–2: Isolamisola ... whisping and lisping her about Triso-
lanisans

385.19: Marcus

386.8–9: a cup of kindness yet (Possibly, in this context, the love
potion.)

387.14: poor Marcus of Lyons

.28: Merkin Cornyngwham ("Mark" of "Cornwall.")

388.1–6: Exeunc throw a darras Kram of Llawnroc, ye gink guy,
kirked into yord. Enterest attawonder Wehpen, luftcat
revol, fairescapading in his natsirt. Tuesy tumbles. And
mild aunt Liza is as loose as her neese ... Ne hath his
thrysting. Fin. (Reversed names: "Mark of Cornwall,"
"Tristan," "Yseut"; *TI* 91: "Mild und leise"; "Tristan.")

.10: Marcus

.34: Marcus

389.24: thirstuns

391.14: poor Mark or Marcus Bowandcoat

394.20: issle issle

.23–5: till he was instant and he was trustin, sister soul in
brother hand, the subjects being their passion grand

.30: eysolt

395.1–2: murky whey ... theemeeng Narsty meetheeng Idoless ("Mark," "Tristan," "Isolde.")

.29: deaf with love ("*Liebestod.*")

396.7–8: a strapping modern old ancient Irish prisscess (Isolde of Ireland.)

.31: her knight of the truths thong ("Tristan.")

397.18–19: a potion a peace, a piece aportion, a lepel alip, alup a lap, for a cup of kindest yet (The "love potion.")

.21: Marcus

398.2: Marcus

.10: down to death and the love embrace ("*Liebestod.*")

.18: here's Tricks and Doelsy

.29: Hear, O hear, Iseult la belle! Tristan, sad hero, hear! (Cf. *FW* 117.2.)

399.31: Markeehew

403.1–3: Hark! ... Hork! (Cf. Isolde's "Hörst du sie noch?" at the beginning of act 2. See Hodgart, *Student's Guide*, 172. Also listed under *Meistersinger*.)

.6: Mark as capsules. ("Mark of Cornwall.")

416.9–10: a jungle of love and debts and ... a jumble of life in doubts ("*Liebestod.*")

419.16–17: treacling tumtim with its tingtingtaggle. The blarneyest blather in all Corneywall! (A hint of "Tristan"; also, "Tintagel," in some sources, is Mark's castle in "Cornwall.")

423.3: markshaire parawag and his loyal divorces

424.5–6: For onced I squeaked by twyst I'll squelch him. ("Tristan.")

.28: his treestem sucker cane. Mildbut likesome! ("Tristan"; also, *TI* 91: "Mild und leise.")

.34: threestar ("Tristan.")

425.29–30: mark my words and append to my mark twang

434.17: lead her to the halter? Sold in her heyday ("Isolde," wooed by Tristan to be Mark's bride [*TI* 54]. Cf. 304.20–2.)

442.1: ministriss for affairs ("Tristan.")

.18: a markt man

444.34–5: isod? ... Mark mean then! ("Isolde," "Mark.")

446.6–7: I'm a man of Armor ... let me see your isabellis

449.7: any tristys

450.30–2: Lethals lurk heimlocked ... Dash the gaudy deathcup! (Act 1.5: Isolde casts away the cup that the lovers believe contains poison.)

455.28-9: SPQueaRking Mark

459.31-2: trust ... that though I change thy name though not the letter (*TI* 52; also, see *L* 1:226: "Tristan on his first visit to Ireland turned his name inside out.")

465.1-3: This is me aunt Julia Bride, your honour, dying to have you languish to scandal in her bosky old delltangle. (Possibly a mock introduction of Isolde to Mark by Tristan: Isolde is Tristan's legal "aunt"; "Anguish," in some sources, is Isolde's father.)

466.6: love potients for Leos, the next beast king (Act 1.3: Isolde's mother has prepared a "love potion" for the aging King Mark [*TI* 54-5].)

467.7-8: Triss! ... A full octavium below me!

478.26: Trinathan (A hint of "Tristan," combined with "Jonathan" Swift.)

.30: I am sohohold! ("Isolde." Cf. *FW* 500.21.)

480.3-4: that girl with the tan tress awn (*TI* 52: "Tantris.")

481.10: your tristich

483.16-17: blarneying Marcantonio

.34: patristic motives ("Tristan" combined with "Patrick.")

484.5: eyesalt

486.4-7: *Triple my tryst. Tandem my sire.* —History as her is harped ... Tantris, hattrick, tryst and parting, by vowel-glide! ("Tris-tan," "Tantris" [*TI* 52], Tristan a harpist in some sources. Also listed under *Tannhäuser*.)

.20-1: What sound of tistress isoles my ear? ("Tristan," "Isolde.")

.23-4: I feel a fine lady ... floating on a stillstream of isisglass ... with gold hair to the bed ("Isolde" the Fair. Cf. *FW* 84.29, 460.21.)

487.23: Mr Trickpat (Cf. *TI* 52: "Tantris.")

.26: God save the monk! ("Mark.")

.32: Capalisoot ("Isolde," "Chapelizod.")

490.24: his tantrums (*TI* 52: "Tantris.")

491.12-13: You told of a tryst too

.17: Marak! Marak! Marak!

499.30: *Tris tris a ni ma mea!* Prisoner of Love!

500.21-5: Sold! I am sold! ... I sold! ... I'm true. True! Isolde. (Cf. 478.30. See proximate references to "Wagner," the *Ring*, and *Parsifal*.)

501.4: Am I thru' Iss? Miss? True?

502.9: Icecold. Brr na brr, ny prr! ("Isolde." Also listed under the *Ring*.)

505.11: twisty hands

    .16–21: trees ... steyne ("Tree-stone.")

506.24: Now you are mehrer the murk

512.3: father of Izod

513.5: Marcus of Corrig ("Mark of Cornwall.")

    .25–6: Lillabil Issabil maideve ... Trists and thranes and trinies and traines. ("Isolde," "Tristan.")

519.24: your Corth examiner, Markwalther ("Mark of Cornwall." Cf. *FW* 91.13.)

521.22: my tristy minstrel ("Tristan," a harpist in some sources.)

527.1–528.13: (A mirror-image passage in which details from Wagner and Bédier are intermingled.)

    .1: Iscappellas ("Isolde," "Chapelizod.")

    .23–4: My veil will save it undyeing from his ethernal fire! (Act 2.1: Isolde signals Tristan with her veil. See Gilbert, *Joyce's Ulysses*, 146n.)

    .29–30: How me adores eatsother simply (Mon ishebeau! Ma reinebelle!)

533.9: an always sadfaced man, in his lutestring pewcape (The "sad" Tristan, a harpist in some sources.)

    .20: First Murkiss

538.8: resolde

550.1: bissed and trissed

551.7: you merk well ("Mark of Cornwall.")

556.1–16: night by silentsailing night ... infantina Isobel ... when she took the veil ... sister Isobel ... nurse Saintette Isabelle ... Madame Isa Veuve La Belle, so sad but lucksome ... with orange blossoming weeper's veil ... Isobel (The setting of act 1, aboard ship; Isolde "La Belle"; the veil of act 2.1: see Gilbert, *Joyce's Ulysses*, 146n.)

560.26–7: leading lady, a poopahead, gaffneysaffron nightdress, iszoppy chepelure ("Isolde," "Chapelizod.")

561.12–16: Buttercup ... now that I come to drink of it filtred, a gracecup fulled of bitterness. She is dadad's lottiest daughterpearl and brooder's cissiest auntybride. (The lovepotion or "philtre"; Isolde technically Tristan's "aunt.")

562.9–10: that she spin blue to scarlad till her temple's veil (Possibly Isolde's veil in act 2.1. See Gilbert, *Joyce's Ulysses*, 146n. See proximate reference to *Tannhäuser*.)

563.17–18: a gold of my bridest hair betied. Donatus his mark, address as follows. ("Mark"; also, the story, in Bédier, of Mark's discovering one of Isolde's hairs.)

564.2: Mark!

565.8: mark well ("Mark of Cornwall.")

571.6–7: Do you can their tantrist spellings? (*TI* 52: Tristan reverses his name. See *L* 1:226: "Tristan on his first visit to Ireland turned his name inside out.")

.8: take a message, tawny runes ilex sallow (Acrostic for "Tamtris," a version of the reversed name. [See McHugh, *Annotations*.] See *TI* 52.)

.9–10: to the water trysting

.12–15: Yes, sad one of Ziod? Sell me, my soul dear! Ah, my sorrowful ... how it is triste to death, all his dark ivytod! Where cold in dearth. ("Isolde," the "sad" Tristan, the "*Liebestod*.")

580.18: gentle Isad Ysut

581.8–9: never was worth a cornerwall fark ("Mark of Cornwall.")

588.29–32: Triss! ... trees ... Trem! (See proximate reference to the *Ring*.)

594.18: tanderest (*TI* 52: "Tantris.")

598.22: Mildew, murk, leak and yarn (*TI* 91: "Mild und leise"; also, "Mark.")

606.26–7: anticidingly inked with penmark ... kuvertly falted ("Penmark," in Brittany, the site of Tristan's death in some sources; possibly also "Kurvenal.")

607.30–1: Boergemester "Dyk" ffogg of Isoles, now Eisold ("Isolde." See also listing under *Meistersinger*.)

608.1: mark you

615.24: but he daydreamsed we had a lovelyt face for a pulltomine (Possibly Isolde's torch – "love light" – in act 2.1. Cf. *FW* 237.9.)

621.18–20: Market Norwall ... Mrknrk? ("Mark of Cornwall.")

.35–6: their treestirm shindy ("Tristan." See proximate reference to the *Ring*.)

628.6–8: leaves ... Lff! ... taddy (Possibly "*Liebestod*." See Hodgart, *Student's Guide*, 187.)

.10–11: I sink I'd die down over his feet, humbly dumbly, only to washup (*TI* 71: "O sink' hernieder"; *TI* 92: "In dem wogenden Schwall ... versinken." See Hodgart, *Student's Guide*, 187.)

Die Meistersinger von Nürnberg (1868)

U 14.1457; 424: Silentium! (Act 3.5: "Silentium! Silentium! / Macht kein Reden und kein Gesumm'!" [*MS* 118]. Cf. *FW* 44.4, 427.33.)

FW 004.18: Bygmester ("Beckmesser.")

    044.4–5: *silentium in curia!* ... and the canto was chantied there chorussed and christened (Act 3.5: Apprentices call for silence before Walther sings the *Preislied* [*MS* 118]; theme of baptism in *Meistersinger*. Cf. *U* 14.1457; 424, *FW* 427.33. See proximate reference to *Parsifal*.)

    151.13: Nuremberg (See proximate references to "Wagner" and *Parsifal*.)

    191.35: bourgeoismeister

    403.1–3: Hark! Tolv two elf kater ten (it can't be) sax. Hork! (The end of act 2, when the Nightwatchman announces the tenth and eleventh hours [here "ten" and "elf"]: "Hört ihr Leut', und lasst euch sagen, / die Glock' hat Zehn [later "Eilfe"] geschlagen" [*MS* 82, 97]; also, Hans "Sachs." Also listed under *Tristan*. See Hodgart, *A Student's Guide*, 172.)

    427.32–3: our specturesque silentiousness (Act 3.5: "Silentium! Silentium! / Macht kein Reden und kein Gesumm'!" [*MS* 118]. Cf. *U* 14.1457; 424, *FW* 44.4.)

    473.3–4: only Walker himself is like Waltzer, whimsicalissimo they go murmurand (Possibly "Walther" von Stolzing.)

    508.21–2: the semidemihemispheres and, from the female angle, music minnestirring ("*Meistersinger*." See also listing under "Wagner.")

    513.34–5: mastersinging always with that consecutive fifth of theirs

    530.31–2: Wallpurgies! ... And it's we's to pray for Bigmesser's conversions? (Possibly Beckmesser's cribbing ["conversion"] of Walther's *Preislied* in act 3. See proximate reference to the *Ring*.)

    586.8–9: and what do you think my Madeleine saw (Possibly "Magdalene.")

    607.30–31: Boergemester (See proximate references to *Tristan* and the *Ring*.)

Der Ring des Nibelungen (1876)

Early poem on the "Valkyrie," lost. (See *My Brother's Keeper*, 86.)

CW 82–3: for when this feeble-bodied figure departs dusk begins to veil the train of the gods, and he who listens may hear their footsteps leaving the world. But the ancient gods ... die and come to life many times, and, though there is dusk about their feet and darkness in their indifferent eyes, the miracle of light is renewed eternally in the imaginative soul. (*The "Dusk" of the Gods*. See discussion in chapter 5.)

263: And how confederate of gay old Gioacchino to have composed this finale so that Kamerad Wagner might be saved the annoyance of finding flauts for his *Feuerzauber!* (Also listed under "Wagner.")

P 237: The birdcall from *Siegfried* whistled softly followed them from the steps of the porch. (In act 2, scenes 2 and 3.)

252–3: Welcome, O life! I go to encounter for the millionth time the reality of experience and to forge in the smithy of my soul the uncreated conscience of my race. (Siegfried as "forger." Discussed in chapter 2.)

E 83: *A gust of wind enters through the porch, with a sound of moving leaves. The lamp flickers quickly.* (Cf. *Walküre* 1.3. See Stoddard Martin, 147–8. Cf. *E* 88.)

88: *A gust of wind blows in through the porch, with a sound of shaken leaves. The flame of the lamp leaps.* (Cf. *Walküre* 1.3. See Stoddard Martin, 147–8. Cf. *E* 83.)

U 2.424–5; 35: I like to break a lance with you, old as I am. (Siegfried breaks the Wanderer's spear in *Siegfried* 3.2.)

3.16; 37: My ash sword hangs at my side. (Among some thirty references to Stephen's ashplant in *A Portrait* and *Ulysses*, this list includes only those that make it a "sword.")

3.289–93; 44–5: And these, the stoneheaps of dead builders ... Hide gold there ... Sir Lout's toys ... I'm the bloody well gigant rolls all them bloody well boulders, bones for my steppingstones. (*Das Rheingold*'s giants, builders of Valhalla. About this passage see Joyce's remark in Budgen, 52: "They were giants right enough, but weak reproductively. Fasolt and Fafnir in Das Rheingold are of the same breed, sexually weak as the music tells us. My Sir Lout has rocks in his mouth instead of teeth." See also Budgen, 183.)

3.304–5; 45: Then from the starving cagework city a horde of jerkined dwarfs (In this context, the Nibelungs.)

3.489; 50: He took the hilt of his ashplant, lunging with it softly

9.295–6; 192: Stephen looked down on ... his ashplanthandle over his knee. My ... sword.

9.946–7; 210: Stephen looked on his hat, his stick, his boots. *Stephanos*, my crown. My sword.

10.813–14; 242: Grandfather ape gloating on a stolen hoard. (Alberich and the stolen Rhinegold.)

11.1–1294; 256–91: (The "Sirens" episode is informed, passim, by *Rheingold* 1. See pp. 245–6 n.12.)

11.42–9; 257: Low in dark middle earth. Embedded ore … Tiny, her tremulous fernfoils of maidenhair. Amen! He gnashed in fury. Fro. To, fro. A baton cool protruding. Bronzelydia by Minagold. By bronze, by gold, in oceangreen of shadow. (*Rheingold* 1: the gold, the Rhinedaughters, Alberich.)

11.1005–8; 283: But wait. But hear. Chords dark. Lugugugubrious. Low. In a cave of the dark middle earth. Embedded ore. Lumpmusic. The voice of dark age, of unlove, earth's fatigue made grave approach and painful, come from afar (Description of music in *Rheingold* 1; also, Alberich's entrance. Discussed in chapter 5.)

12.569; 307: Kriegfried Ueberallgemein ("Siegfried.")

15.99; 432: *He flourishes his ashplant, shivering the lamp image* (Cf. *P* 197: "Do you think you impress me, Stephen asked, when you flourish your wooden sword?")

15.3648–53; 560: STEPHEN (*extends his hand to her smiling and chants to the air of the bloodoath in* The Dusk of the Gods) Hangende Hunger, / Fragende Frau, / Macht uns alle kaputt. (See *Walküre* 1.2, where Sieglinde is a "fragende Frau" [*R* 84]; see *Götterdämmerung* 1.2 for the bloodoath [*R* 267–8]. Cf. *FW* 323.4, 325.25–6.)

15.3660; 561: Sheet lightning courage. The youth who could not shiver and shake. (Siegfried's ignorance of fear.)

15.4242–4; 583: *Nothung! (He lifts his ashplant high with both hands and smashes the chandelier.)* (Cf. *Siegfried* 1.3.)

15.4244–5; 583: *Time's livid final flame leaps and, in the following darkness, ruin of all space, shattered glass and toppling masonry.* (In this context, the *Götterdämmerung*.)

FW 003.1: riverrun (Cf. the flowing Rhine at the beginning of the *Ring*.)

.13–14: rory end to the regginbrow was to be seen ringsome on the aquaface (The rainbow bridge in *Rheingold* 4; also, the "*Ring*.")

004.35–6: a waalworth of a skyerscape (A hint of "Valhalla.")

005.6: Riesengeborg (*R* 172: "Riesenheim" the home of the *Ring*'s giants. Cf. *FW* 133.6.)

.9–12: Hohohoho, Mister Finn … Hahahaha, Mister Funn (Possibly, in this context, the forging song in *Siegfried* 1.3.)

.30: wallhall's horrors ("Valhalla's heroes." See proximate reference to *Tristan*.)

013.26 – 7: o'brine a'bride (*R* 320: "Brünnhilde! Holiest bride!"
    See *L* 2:214: "O sposa sacra." Cf. *FW* 399.4, 500.21 – 30,
    502.9.)

014.30 – 1: all dimmering dunes and gloamering glades ("*Götter-
    dämmerung*"; also "*Godsgloaming*," a standard translation of
    the opera's title.)

015.34 – 16.3: Me seemeth a dragon man ... Lets we overstep his
    fire defences and these kraals of slitsucked marrogbones.
    (Cave!) (Possibly, in this context, Siegfried and the dragon
    Fafner in *Siegfried* 2.2.)

016.29: One eyegonblack. (In this context, Wotan's missing eye.)
   .33 – 4: How wooden I not know it, the intellible greytcloak of
    Cedric Silkyshag! (*Walküre* 1.3 and *Siegfried* 1.2: "Wotan,"
    as the Wanderer, with his cloak.)

017.15 – 16: rutterdamrotter ... Gut aftermeal! See you doomed.
    ("*Götterdämmerung*.")
   .30: erde from erde ("Erda." See proximate reference to
    Tristan.)

019.25: allhorrors ("Valhalla.")

022.28: the arkway of trihump (Possibly the rainbow bridge in
    Rheingold 4. See proximate reference to *Tristan*.)

037.17: the hour of the twattering of bards in the twitterlitter
    ("*Götterdämmerung*"; also, "Twilight" of the Gods.)

055.8 – 9: the establisher of the world by law (Wotan as maker of
    laws and covenants.)
   .27 – 30: the gigantig's lifetree ... whose roots they be asches
    (*Götterdämmerung* 1.3: the "*Weltesche*" [*R* 274].)

056.5 – 8: the doomed but always ventriloquent Agitator, (nonot
    more plangorpound the billows o'er Thounawahallya Reef!)
    silkhouatted, a whallrhosmightiadd, aginsst the dusk of
    skumring ("Valhalla"; also, hints of "*Dusk*" *of the Gods* and
    of Wotan in the "doomed ... Agitator ... silkhouatted.")

063.12 – 13: Myramy Huey or Colores Archer, under Flaggy Bridge
    (The rainbow bridge.)

068.13 – 16: true dotter of a dearmud ... with so valkirry a licence
    as sent many a poor pucker packing to perdition (A hint
    of "*Götterdämmerung*" in "dotter ... dearmud"; also, the
    "Valkyrie." Cf. *FW* 220.5 – 6.)

069.7 – 8: and such a wallhole did exist. Ere ore or ire in Aaarlund.
    ("Valhalla"; also, a hint of the Rhinegold in "ore.")
   .10 – 11: a garthen of Odin and the lost paladays when all the
    eddams ended with aves (Valhalla as "garden of Wotan."
    Cf. *FW* 487.9 – 10.)

074.2 – 4: earthsleep ... and o'er dun and dale the Wulverulver-
lord ... his mighty horn (Possibly Brünnhilde's, or Erda's,
sleep; *Walküre* 1.2: Wotan is "Wolfe," Siegmund "Wölfing"; Siegfried's horn. See Hodgart, *Student's Guide*, 142.)

082.16: a woden affair ("Wotan.")

084.28: leaving clashing ash, brawn and muscle (Possibly the "clash"
between Siegfried and the Wanderer in *Siegfried* 3.2, when
the "ash" spear is shattered by the "ashplanted" sword.)

091.29 – 30: heroes in Warhorror

099.16: Valkir lockt (The "Valkyrie.")

105.11 – 12: Intimier Minnelisp of an Extorreor Monolothe (Cf. *FW*
254.13 – 14. *Siegfried* 2.3: Mime inadvertently gives himself
away. Hodgart calls this passage Joyce's tribute to Mime
as an anticipator of the interior monologue. See *Student's
Guide*, 143.)

107.36: who in hallhagal ("Valhalla.")

117.5 – 6: a good clap, a fore marriage, a bad wake, tell hell's well
(The four-part *Ring*. Discussed in chapter 5.)

126.10 – 11: secondtonone myther rector and maximost bridgesmaker
(Possibly Donner and Froh's building of the rainbow bridge
in *Rheingold* 4. Also listed under "Wagner.")

130.4 – 5: drinks tharr and wodhar for his asama and eats the un-
parishable sow to styve off reglar rack ("Wotan"; also, the
"*Ragnarok*" or *Götterdämmerung*.)

131.13 – 14: put a matchhead on an aspenstalk and set the living a
fire (Possibly the burning of Valhalla, fueled by the "World
Ash-tree." See *R* 273 – 4.)

133.6: Riesengebirger (*R* 172: "Riesenheim" is the giants' home.
Cf. *FW* 5.6. See proximate reference to *Tristan*.)

134.33: has a tussle with the trulls and then does himself justice
(Wotan and the Nibelungs in *Rheingold*.)

152.31 – 4: As he set off with his father's sword, his *lancia spezzata* ...
he clanked ... every inch of an immortal. (Siegfried and
Nothung, Siegmund's [Siegfried's father's] "broken sword.")

156.24 – 5: Us shall be chosen as the first of the last by the electress
of Vale Hollow (The Valkyrie, "Valhalla.")

.31 – 3: Wee ... shall not even be the last of the first ... when
oust are visitated by the Veiled Horror. (The Valkyrie,
"Valhalla." See proximate reference to *Tannhäuser*.)

158.25 – 8: there came down to the thither bank a woman of no
appearance ... and she gathered up ... the Mookse ... and
carried him away to her invisible dwelling (The Valkyrie,
carrying the slain hero to Valhalla.)

.31 – 159.1: And there came down to the hither bank a woman
to all important ... and ... she plucked down the Gripes ...
and cariad away its beotitubes with her to her unseen
shieling, it is, *De Rore Coeli.* (The Valkyrie, carrying the
slain hero to Valhalla.)

159.16 – 17: But the river tripped on her by and by, lapping as
though her heart was brook: *Why, why, why! Weh, O weh!*
(The Rhinedaughters' song in *Rheingold* 1: "Weia! Waga!
... Wallala weiala weia!" [*R* 4]. See proximate references
to "Wagner," *Tristan,* and *Parsifal.*)

177.18: gunnard (Possibly "Gunther." Cf. *FW* 257.34, 510.13,
596.15.)

178.24: the sevenspan ponte *dei colori* (*Rheingold*'s rainbow bridge.)

199.4 – 5: hungerstriking all alone and holding doomsdag over
hunselv (Wotan as Waltraute reports him in *Götterdämmerung*
1.3.)

201.3 – 4: Tarn your ore ouse! (Possibly the *Tarnhelm,* the Rhinegold.)

.35 – 6: O loreley! What a loddon lodes! Heigh ho! (The Rhinegold; possibly also Hagen's call in *Götterdämmerung* 2.3 and
3.2. Cf. *U* 4.546 – 8; 70, 11.858; 279, 15.1186; 471, 15.4086; 577,
17.1233 – 4; 704. See proximate reference to *Parsifal.*)

202.19 – 20: Worry you sighin foh, Albern, O Anser? Untie the
gemman's fistiknots (The "gemman" "Alberich" is
captured and bound in *Rheingold* 3 and 4.)

211.3 – 4: a way in his frey (Possibly "Freia," character in *Rheingold.*)

213.6: Hoangho (The Cry of the Valkyries: "Hoyotoho! Hoyotoho!"
[*R* 126ff.]. Cf. *FW* 627.31.)

219.18: The Mime (Possibly the Nibelung "Mime.")

220.5 – 6: with valkyrienne licence (The "Valkyrie." Cf. *FW* 68.15.
See proximate references to *Tristan* and *Parsifal.*)

.26: his magical helmet (Possibly, in this context, the *Tarnhelm.*
See proximate reference to the *Dutchman.*)

221.36: a smoker from the gods (Possibly the *Götterdämmerung.*)

225.2 – 3: the wordchary is atvoiced ringsoundinly by their toots
ensembled (The "*Ring.*" Also listed under *Parsifal.*)

226.4 – 15: Poor Isa sits a glooming so gleaming in the gloaming ...
Hey, lass! Woefear gleam she so glooming, this pooripathete
I solde? ... And among the shades that Eve's now wearing
she'll meet anew fiancy, tryst and trow. Mammy was,
Mimmy is, Minuscoline's to be. (Possibly "*Godsgloaming,*"
"Mime." See also listing under *Tristan.*)

231.12–13: regally freytherem ("Freia." See Hodgart, "The Mime," in Begnal and Senn, 89.)

.20–2: forget ... gnawthing (Possibly "forge *Nothung*." See Hodgart, "The Mime," in Begnal and Senn, 89.)

.23–5: after at he had bate his breastplates for, forforget, forforgetting his birdsplace, it was soon that, that he, that he rehad himself (*Götterdämmerung* 3.2: Siegfried recovers his lost memory as he recounts, among other events, the forging and Woodbird episodes of *Siegfried*.)

235.7–8: allahlah lahlah lah (The Rhinedaughters' song: *via The Waste Land?*)

243.16–17: Signur's tinner roumanschy to fishle the ladwigs out of his lugwags (Possibly a hint of Siegfried, Sieglinde, Siegmund: see also listing under "Wagner.")

245.1: Rhinohorn (Possibly Siegfried's Rhine Journey in *Götterdämmerung*; also, his horn.)

.24: wenderer (Wotan as "Wanderer.")

246.32: healing and Brune ("Brünnhilde.")

249.20: Oh backed von dem zug! (Possibly the last words of the cycle, spoken by Hagen: "Zurück vom Ring!" [*R* 328]. See Hodgart, "The Mime," in Begnal and Senn, 89.)

254.13–14: with her minnelisp extorreor to his moanolothe inturned (Mime gives himself away in *Siegfried* 2.3. Cf. *FW* 105.11–12.)

257.34–258.2: Gonn the gawds, Gunnar's gustspells ... Rendningrocks roguesreckning reigns. Gwds with gurs are gttrdmmrng. Hlls vlls. ("Gunther," "*Ragnarok*," "*Götterdämmerung*," "Valhalla." Cf. 177.18, 510.13, 596.15.)

262.15: Erdnacrusha, requiestress, wake em! ("Erda," who wakes in *Rheingold* 4 and in *Siegfried* 3.1. See proximate reference to *Parsifal*.)

273.4–5: Heil, heptarched span of peace! (Possibly the rainbow bridge in *Rheingold* 4.)

277.3–5: And rivers burst out like weeming racesround joydrinks for the fewnrally (Possibly conclusion to *Götterdämmerung*.)

279.2: rainstones ringing (Possibly the Rhinegold, the "*Ring*.")

281.22–3: What if she love Sieger less though she leave Ruhm moan? (Possibly "Siegmund," "Siegfried.")

.F1: Valsinggiddyrex and his grand arks day triump (The "Wälsungs" or "Volsungs"; possibly also *Rheingold* 4: the Gods' Entrance into Valhalla, *via* the rainbow bridge.)

295.18: nothung up my sleeve

303.21: woodint ("Wotan.")

304.8 – 9: I'm seeing rayingbogeys rings round me (Possibly the rainbow bridge, the "*Ring*." See proximate reference to *Tristan*.)

305.4 – 5: Forge away, Sunny Sim! (Siegfried as smith.)

306.20 – 1: The Voice of Nature in the Forest, Your Favorite Hero or Heroine (The Woodbird's song in *Siegfried* 2.2 and 2.3.)

313.23: if you guess mimic miening ("Mime," especially in *Siegfried* 2.3.)

316.16 – 18: he had gone dump in the doomering this tide where the peixies would pickle him down to the button of his seat (Hagen's death; also, a hint of "*Götterdämmerung*" in "doomering." See also listing under the *Dutchman*.)

318.13 – 14: While this glowworld's lump is gloaming off (A hint of "*Godsgloaming*": see proximate references to "Wagner" and to the *Dutchman*.)

.32 – 319.1: wooving nihilnulls from Memoland and wolving the ulvertones of the voice ... Hillyhollow, valleylow! (In *Walküre* 1.2 Siegmund calls himself "Wölfing" and identifies his father as "Wolfe"; also, "Valhalla.")

319.27: The kersse of Wolafs (Possibly "Wotan.")

323.4 – 5: the bloedaxe bloodooth baltxebec (The bloodoath in *Götterdämmerung* 1.2. Cf. *U* 15.3648 – 53; 560, *FW* 325.25 – 6. See also listing under the *Dutchman*.)

325.25 – 6: Brothers Boathes ... ye have swallen blooders' oathes. (The bloodoath in *Götterdämmerung* 1.2. Cf. *U* 15.3648 – 53; 560, *FW* 323.4 – 5.)

.31: you wutan whaal ("Wotan.")

335.4 – 23: Au! Au! Aue! Ha! Heish! ... Let us propel us for the frey of the fray! ... A lala! ... Ala lala! ... The sound of maormaoring ... Au! Au! Aue! Ha! Heish! A lala! (The Rhinedaughters' song, possibly *via The Waste Land*; possibly also "Freia.")

348.10 – 11: all them old boyars that's now boomaringing in waulholler, me alma marthyrs ("Valhalla" and its heroes.)

.29 – 30: heavinscent houroines that entertrained him (The Valkyries.)

352.25: seiger besieged (Possibly Siegmund, "besieged" by Hunding in *Walküre* 2.5, or Siegfried, "besieged" by Hagen in *Götterdämmerung* 3.2.)

355.33 – 5: We all, for whole men is lepers, have been nobbut wonterers in that chill childerness which is our true name after the allfaulters (Wotan as "Wanderer" and, in some sources, "Allfather." Cf. *U* 14.1409; 423: "the Allfather's air.")

356.17: a frishfrey (Possibly "Freia.")

359.34-5: on the heather side of waldalure ... whither our allies winged by duskfoil ("Valhalla"; a hint of *"Dusk" of the Gods.)*

360.13-16: Carmen Sylvae, my quest, my queen. Lou must wail to cool me airly! Coil me curly, warbler dear! May song it flourish (in the underwood), in chorush, long make it flourish (in the Nut, in the Nutsky) till thorush! (*Siegfried* 2.2: possibly the Woodbird's song.)

365.1: all herwayferer gods (Possibly Wotan as the Wanderer.)

.16: wholenosing at a whallhoarding ("Valhalla.")

379.12: volleyholleydoodlem ("Valhalla.")

.33-5: There goes the blackwatchwomen, all in white, flaxed up, purgad! ... We're been carried away. Beyond bournes and bowers. (The Valkyries.)

399.4: Brinabride (*R* 320: "Brünnhilde! Holiest bride!" See *L* 2:214: "O sposa sacra." Cf. *FW* 13.26-7, 500.21-30, 502.9.)

403.6: White fogbow spans. The arch embattled. (Possibly the rainbow bridge.)

412.7-8: How mielodorous is thy bel chant, O songbird, and how exqueezit thine after draught! (The Woodbird's song in *Siegfried* 2.2 and 2.3; possibly also the tasting of the dragon's blood.)

414.1: some rhino, rhine, O joyoust rhine (The Rhine; possibly also the Rhinedaughters' song in *Rheingold* 1.)

417.27-8: boundlessly blissfilled in an allallahbath of houris ("Valhalla," the Valkyries.)

431.3-4: frickyfrockies (In this context, "Fricka.")

.17-18: nor could he forget her so tarnelly easy as all that since he was brotherbesides her benedict godfather (The "*Tarnhelm*"; Siegfried forgets, then remembers Brünnhilde in *Götterdämmerung*. Discussed in chapter 5. See proximate reference to "Wagner.")

436.14-16: Love through the usual channels, cisternbrothelly ... taken neat in the generable way upon retiring to roost in the company of a husband-in-law (Possibly *Walküre* 1.3: the twins Siegmund and Sieglinde make love while her husband "in law" Hunding sleeps in the next room.)

441.18-22: Guard that gem, Sissy, rich and rare, ses he. In this cold old worold who'll feel it? Hum! ... Sing him a ring. Touch me low. And I'll lech ye so, my soandso. (*Rheingold*

1: Alberich, the Rhinedaughters, the Rhinegold; also, the "*Ring.*")

460.32: till Thingavalla ("Valhalla.")

473.18–19: Eftsoon so too will our own sphoenix spark spirt his spyre and sunward stride the rampante flambe. (Possibly Siegfried's funeral pyre. See Hodgart, *Student's Guide*, 178.)

487.9–10: odinburgh (Possibly Valhalla. Cf. *FW* 69.10.)

493.29–30: a pont of perfect, peace? On the vignetto is a ragin-goos. ("ragingoos ... pont": rainbow bridge.)

494.1–4: Yes, there was that skew arch of chrome sweet home, floodlit up above the flabberghosted farmament and bump where the camel got the needle. Talk about iridecencies! (*Rheingold* 4: the rainbow bridge, the Gods' Entrance into Valhalla.)

499.8: O Smertz! Woh Hillill! Woe Hallall! ("Valhalla"; also, the Rhinedaughters' lament.)

500.21–30: —Sold! I am sold! Brinabride! My ersther! My sidster! Brinabride, goodbye! Brinabride! I sold! ... —Brinabride, bet my price! Brinabride! ... —Brinabride, my price! When you sell get my price! (Siegfried's betrayal. *R* 320: "Brünnhilde! Holiest bride!" See *L* 2:214: "O sposa sacra." Cf. *FW* 13.26–7, 399.4, 502.9. See proximate references to "Wagner," *Tristan*, and *Parsifal*.)

502.9: Icecold. Brr na brr, ny prr! (*R* 320: "Brünnhilde! Holiest bride!" See *L* 2:214: "O sposa sacra." Cf. *FW* 13.26–7, 399.4, 500.21–30. See proximate reference to *Tristan*.)

503.7: An evernasty ashtray. (The "*Weltesche*," or Yggdrasill. Cf. *FW* 503.28–32.)

.28–32: —And what sigeth Woodin Warneung thereof? —Trickspissers vill be pairsecluded. —There used to be a tree stuck up? An overlisting eshtree? ... Oakley Ashe's elm. ("Wotan," the "*Weltesche*." Cf. *FW* 503.7.)

505.25: The form masculine. The gender feminine. (In *Siegfried* 3.3 Siegfried wakes Brünnhilde and exclaims, "Das ist kein Mann!" [*R* 233].)

506.15–18: —Woe! Woe! So that was how he became the foerst of our treefellers? —Yesche and, in the absence of any soberiquiet, the fanest of our truefalluses. (*Götterdämmerung* 1.3: Wotan cuts down the "*Weltesche*.")

510.9–10: With a hoh frohim and heh fraher. (Possibly "Froh," "Freia.")

.13: Gunner (Possibly "Gunther." Cf. *FW* 177.18, 257.34, 596.15.)

516.21: wolfling ("Wölfing" is Siegmund's name in *Walküre* 1.2.)

518.25–8: Farcing gutterish ... The mujic of the footure ("*Götterdämmerung*." Also listed under "Wagner.")

525.14: Lalia Lelia Lilia Lulia and lively lovely Lola Montez. (The Rhinedaughters' song. Also listed under "Wagner.")

530.31: Wallpurgies! And it's this's your deified city? ("Valhalla." See proximate reference to *Meistersinger*.)

532.6–554.10: ("Haveth Childers Everywhere" is informed passim by *Das Rheingold*, especially by Wotan's building of Valhalla. Discussed in chapter 5.)

532.6: Eternest cittas, heil! (Hodgart cites Brünnhilde's awakening in *Siegfried* 3.3: "Heil dir, Sonne!" [*R* 235]. See *Student's Guide*, 181.)

.27: duskguise (Possibly, with *"Dusk" of the Gods* in mind, Wotan's "disguise" as Wanderer in *Siegfried*.)

534.27: Snakeeye! (The image of a snake or dragon in the eyes of the Volsungs. Hunding mentions it in *Walküre* 1.2 [*R* 80]. The word "snake" is underscored in Joyce's copy of *The Perfect Wagnerite*. See Gillespie and Stocker, no. 448.)

535.5–6: whenby Gate of Hal, before his hostel of the Wodin Man (A hint of "Valhalla"; also, "Wotan.")

.15: First liar in Londsend! Wulv! (Wotan, who reneges on his bargains in *Rheingold*, is called "Wolfe" in *Walküre* 1.2.)

537.30: Frick's Flame, Uden Sulfer ("Fricka"; "Odin," or Wotan.)

539.13–14: stolemines ... Hohohoho! (The stolen Rhinegold; possibly also Siegfried's forging song in *Siegfried* 1.3.)

.27: upon martiell siegewin ("Siegfried," "Sieglinde," "Siegmund.")

.29–31: the soord on Whencehislaws was mine and mine the prusshing stock of Allbrecht the Bearn (Possibly *Nothung*, the sword that Wotan – "Whence-his-laws" – provided for Siegmund; possibly "Alberich.")

.36–540.1: two-toothed dragon worms with allsort serpents (Possibly, in this context, Fafner as dragon [German *Wurm*].)

541.22: Walhalloo, Walhalloo, Walhalloo, mourn in plein! ("Valhalla"; also, the Rhinedaughters' song.)

.24–5: I made praharfeast upon acorpolous and fastbroke down in Neederthorpe. (*Rheingold* 2 and 3: Wotan departs heaven for the subterranean home of the Nibelungs, "Nibelheim.")

545.28: on my siege of my mighty I was parciful of my subject ("Siegfried." Also listed under *Parsifal*.)

547.26–33: and I abridged with domfine norsemanship ... Heaven, he hallthundered; Heydays, he flung blissforhers. And I cast my tenspan joys on her, arsched overtupped, from bank of call to echobank ... and to ringstresse I thumbed her (*Rheingold* 4: Donner conjures a thunderstorm and creates, with Froh, the rainbow bridge, a "*Ring*-street" to Valhalla. He sings, "Heda! Heda! Hedo!" [*R* 69]. See Hodgart, *Student's Guide*, 181. Discussed in chapter 5.)

552.10–11: all truanttrulls made I comepull, all rubbeling gnomes I pushed, gowgow (Wotan "compels" the Nibelung Alberich in *Rheingold* 3 and 4; Alberich does the same to Mime in *Rheingold* 3.)

    .16: arcane celestials to Sweatenburgs Welhell ("Valhalla.")

553.22–30: the hallaw vall ... and ... froh, the frothy freshener ... my stony battered waggonways ("Valhalla," "Froh." See also listing under "Wagner.")

554.10: Mattahah! Marahah! Luahah! Joahanahanahana! (The Rhinedaughters' song.)

564.34: with one snaked's eyes (*Walküre* 1.2: the Volsungs' eyes.)

565.1–5: do not fail to point to yourself a depression called Holl Hollow. It is often quite guttergloomering in our duol and gives wankyrious thoughts to the head but the banders of the pentapolitan poleetsfurcers bassoons into it on windy woodensdays their wellbooming wolvertones. ("Valhalla," "*Götterdämmerung*," "Valkyrie," "Wotan," and possibly "Wolfe" or "Wölfing." See also listing under "Wagner.")

569.25: jollygame fellhellows (Heroes in "Valhalla.")

571.35–6: For our netherworld's bosomfoes are working tooth and nail overtime (Alberich's horde of industrious Nibelungs.)

578.23–4: Selling sunlit sopes to washtout winches and rhaincold draughts to the props of his pubs. (The "Rhinegold" is suddenly "sunlit" in *Rheingold* 1.)

588.28: Esch so eschess (The "*Weltesche*," or Yggdrasill. See proximate reference to *Tristan*.)

590.7–10: They know him, the covenanter, by rote at least, for a chameleon at last, in his true falseheaven colours from ultraviolent to subred tissues. That's his last tryon to march through the grand tryomphal arch. His reignbolt's shot. (*Rheingold* 4: Wotan, the "falseheaven ... covenanter," enters Valhalla *via* the rainbow bridge.)

    .17: Nephilim (*Siegfried* 1.2: "Nibelheim" is the home of the Nibelungs.)

594.25: floran frohn (Possibly "Froh.")

.25 – 6: Gaunt grey ghostly gossips growing grubber in the glow. (*Götterdämmerung* 3.3: flames engulf the assembled gods.)

596.13: Woodenhenge ("Wotan.")

.15: Gunnar, of The Gunnings, Gund ("Gunther." Cf. *FW* 177.18, 257.34, 510.13.)

597.14: allahallahallah ("Valhalla.")

607.27: to the hothehill from the hollow ("Valhalla." See proximate references to *Tristan* and *Meistersinger*.)

609.18: Hillewille and Wallhall ("Valhalla.")

.30 – 4: An I could peecieve amonkst the gatherings who ever they wolk in process? ... the ghariwallahs, moveyovering the cabrattlefield of slaine (The Valkyries, who select heroes ["gatherings"] from the slain in battle; also, a hint of "Valhalla" in "ghariwallahs.")

612.31 – 2: That was thing, bygotter, the thing, bogcotton, the very thing, begad! (Possibly "*Götterdämmerung*.")

613.1: Goldselforelump! (Possibly the Rhinegold.)

.12: With a hottyhammyum all round. Gudstruce! ("*Götterdämmerung*.")

.20: skullhullows ("Valhalla.")

621.34 – 622.2: they ring the earthly bells ... Or the birds start their treestirm shindy. Look, there are yours off, high on high! And cooshes, sweet good luck they're cawing you, Coole! You see, they're as white as the riven snae. (Possibly the "*Ring*"; also, Wotan's "ravens" appear in *Götterdämmerung* 3.2. See proximate reference to *Tristan*.)

625.35: gooder (In this context, a hint of "*Götterdämmerung*.")

627.30 – 2: For 'tis they are the stormies. Ho Hang! Hang ho! And the clash of our cries till we spring to be free. (*Walküre* 3.1: The Cry of the Valkyries: "Hoyotoho! Hoyotoho!" [*R* 126ff.]. Cf. *FW* 213.6.)

628.2 – 5: till the near sight of the mere size of him ... makes me seasilt saltsick and I rush, my only, into your arms. I see them rising! (Possibly Brünnhilde's self-immolation in the "rising" flames of the pyre; Hodgart finds "Siegfried! Sieh!" [*R* 328] in "seasilt ... see" [*Student's Guide*, 186]. See proximate reference to *Tristan*.)

.15 – 16: A way a lone a last a loved a long the (The Rhine-daughters' song.)

Parsifal (1882)

CW 43: The author of Parsifal has recognized this and hence his work is solid as a rock. (Also listed under "Wagner.")

75–6: That was a strange question which the innocent Parsifal asked – "Who is good?" (See *Pars* 95. Cf. *CW* 179.)

179: The question that Wagner put into the mouth of the innocent Parsifal must come to mind when we read from time to time certain English criticism (See *Pars* 95. Also listed under "Wagner." Cf. *CW* 75–6.)

E 112: I have a deep, deep wound of doubt in my soul ... I have wounded my soul for you – a deep wound of doubt which can never be healed ... And now I am tired for a while, Bertha. My wound tires me. (Cf. Amfortas in act 1. Also listed under *Tristan*.)

U 1.20–3; 3: He added in a preacher's tone: —For this, O dearly beloved, is the genuine christine: body and soul and blood and ouns. Slow music, please. Shut your eyes, gents. One moment. A little trouble about those white corpuscles. Silence, all. (Possibly the Grail scene in act 1; also, the Wagnerian "hush," associated with the curtain of act 1. Cf. *FW* 14.6, 159.19, 334.31, 501.7.)

15.1–4967; 429–609: (The setting and general situation of "Circe" may owe a good deal to act 2 of *Parsifal*.)

15.1269–76; 474–5: *The kisses, winging from their bowers fly about him, twittering, warbling, cooing ... They rustle, flutter upon his garments, alight, bright giddy flecks, silvery sequins.* (The Flower-maidens of act 2.)

15.1324–30; 477: *Gazelles are leaping, feeding on the mountains. Near are lakes. Round their shores file shadows black of cedargroves. Aroma rises, a strong hairgrowth of resin. It burns, the orient, a sky of sapphire, cleft by the bronze flight of eagles. Under it lies the woman-city, nude, white, still, cool, in luxury. A fountain murmurs among damask roses. Mammoth roses murmur of scarlet winegrapes. A wine of shame, lust, blood exudes, strangely murmuring.* (Klingsor's Magic Garden in act 2. See *Pars* 104.)

15.3340–2; 549: (*Whispered kisses are heard in all the wood. Faces of hamadryads peep out from the boles and among the leaves and break, blossoming into bloom.*) Who profaned our silent shade? (The Flowermaidens. See *Pars* 104.)

15.4712; 600: THE VOICE OF ALL THE BLESSED (Possibly, in the Grail scene of act 1, the choirboys singing from the castle's dome. See Blissett, "Joyce in the Smithy," 123.)

FW 003.20–1: the humptyhillhead of humself prumptly sends an unquiring one well to the west in quest of his tumptytumtoes (Parsifal, in the Grail legend, as quester and questioner; also, Jessie Weston, student of the Grail myth.)

008.4: so gigglesomes minxt the follyages (The Flowermaidens.)

014.6: (Silent.) (The Wagnerian "hush," associated with the curtain of act I. Also listed under "Wagner." Cf. *U* 1.23; 3, *FW* 159.19, 334.31, 501.7.)

015.20: floras

043.29: pussyfours

  .31–2: To the added strains (so peacifold) of his majesty the flute ("Parsifal.")

  .35–6: purseyful namesake

044.2–3: "Ductor" Hitchcock hoisted his fezzy fuzz at bludgeon's height signum to his companions of the chalice for the Loud Fellow (The Grail scene of act I. Cf. *U* 1.21–3; 3. See McHugh, *Annotations*.)

  .9: piersified ("Parsifal." See proximate reference to *Meistersinger*.)

072.35: purse, purse, pursyfurse

092.12–18: the maidies of the bar … fluttered and flattered around the willingly pressed … complimenting him, the captivating youth … stincking thyacinths through his curls … and bringing busses to his cheeks (Parsifal and the Flowermaidens in act 2.)

107.18: persequestellates his vanessas from flore to flore ("Parsifal," the "Flowermaidens.")

114.4–20: while the others go west-east in search … Sleep, where in the waste is the wisdom? (Jessie Weston ["west … in"], student of Wagner's mythic sources; also, a hint of "durch Mitleid wissend" [*Pars* 87].)

143.3–4: the panaroma of all flores (The "Flowermaidens.")

151.10: parcequeue

  .13: watches cunldron (Possibly the "witch Kundry." See Hodgart, *Student's Guide*, 147.)

  .17: cupolar (The Grail scene. See Verlaine's sonnet "Parsifal," quoted in *The Waste Land*: "Et O ces voix d'enfants, chantant dans la coupole!")

  .19–24: *Mitleid* … in accornish with the Mortadarthella taradition … Tyro a toray! (*Pars* 87: "durch Mitleid wissend … Der reine Tor.")

152.1–2: where me arts soar … I cling (Possibly "Klingsor." See Hodgart, *Student's Guide*, 147.)

158.9 – 10: the waste of all peacable worlds ("Parsifal.")

159.19: No applause, please! (The Wagnerian "hush," associated with the curtain of act 1. Also listed under "Wagner." Cf. *U* 1.23; 3, *FW* 14.6, 334.31, 501.7. See proximate reference to the *Ring*.)

201.33: the cane for Kund (Possibly, in this context, "Kundry." See proximate reference to the *Ring*.)

219.1–259.10: (In the "Mime of Mick, Nick and the Maggies" the girls are parallel to the Flowermaidens of act 2, Shaun to Parsifal.)

220.3–4: THE FLORAS ... a month's bunch of pretty maidens (See proximate references to *Tristan* and to the *Ring*.)

222.32–6: Aminxt that nombre of evelings, but how pierceful in their sojestiveness were those first girly stirs, with zitterings of flight released and twinglings of twitchbells in rondel after, with waverings that made shimmershake rather naightily all the duskcended airs and shylit beaconings from shehind hims back. (Flowermaidens, "Parsifal.")

224.22–3: The youngly delightsome frilles-in-pleyurs are now showen drawen, if bud one, or, if in florileague (The Flowermaidens.)

225.2–3: the wordchary is atvoiced ringsoundinly by their toots ensembled (In this context, possibly the "witch" Kundry. Also listed under the *Ring*.)

226.1–2: knew whitchly whether to weep or laugh (*Pars* 114: the "witch" Kundry's punishment is to laugh for all eternity.)

.30–33: R is Rubretta and A is Arancia, Y is for Yilla and N for greeneriN. B is Boyblue with odalisque O while W waters the fleurettes of novembrance. (The Flowermaidens – "fleurettes" – in their colorful "RAINBOW" garb.)

227.14–15: Here they come back, all the gay pack, for they are the florals

241.25: purely simply (Cf. *FW* 561.9. In French, "Der reine Tor" is "le pur simple." See *Pars* 87. See proximate reference to "Wagner.")

245.10: simwhat toran (*Pars* 87: "Der reine Tor," the "simple" or "pure" fool.)

250.33: a floral's school

262.8–9: pearse ... be dumbed (Act 1.2: Parsifal and his inability to speak.)

.18: wise fool (*Pars* 87: "durch Mitleid wissend ... Der reine Tor." See proximate reference to the *Ring*.)

271.20: brood our pansies (Possibly the Flowermaidens.)

334.31: (Silents) (The Wagnerian "hush," associated with the curtain of act 1. Also listed under "Wagner." Cf. *U* 1.23; 3, *FW* 14.6, 159.19, 501.7.)

353.24–6: Parsuralia ... perceivable

358.20: Perseoroyal

360.1–2: to pour their peace in partial (floflo floreflorence) (Possibly "Parsifal," the "Flowermaidens.")

407.14–15: and cert no purer puer palestrine e'er chanted pan-angelical mid the clouds of Tu es Petrus (The chanting choirboys in the Grail scene.)

411.18–19: Hek domov muy, there thou beest on the hummock, ghee up, ye dog, for your daggily broth (Act 1.2: Amfortas, on his couch, unable to partake of the communion supper, "our daily bread.")

426.21: the wieds of pansiful heathvens (The Flowermaidens' colorful garb, or "weeds," in act 2.)

446.3: purseproud in sending uym loveliest pansiful thoughts ("Parsifal.")

468.34–469.1: And, remember this, a chorines, there's the witch on the heath, sistra! 'Bansheeba peeling hourihaared while her Orcotron is hoaring ho. (Possibly the witch Kundry.)

493.3: Pearcey

498.7–499.1: the halle of the vacant fhroneroom ... his pani's annagolorum ... salvage ... with his arthurious clayroses ... on the table round ... and a dozen and one by one ... round in ringcampf, circumassembled by his daughters in the foregiftness of his sons, lying high as he lay in all dimensions ... healed cured and embalsemate (The Grail scene in act 1: "Monsalvat," the Communion supper, the Knights of the Grail, Amfortas, Titurel. This sequence identified by Hodgart, *Student's Guide*, 179.)

501.7–9: SILENCE. Act drop. Stand by! Blinders! Curtain up. Juice, please! Foots! (The Wagnerian "hush," associated with the curtain of act 1. See proximate references to "Wagner," *Tristan*, and the *Ring*. Cf. *U* 1.23; 3, *FW* 14.6, 159.19, 334.31.)

545.28: parciful of my subject ("Parsifal." See proximate reference to the *Ring*.)

561.9: A pussy, purr esimple. (Cf. *FW* 241.25. In French, "Der reine Tor" is "le pur simple." See *Pars* 87. See proximate reference to *Tannhäuser*.)

603.34: Tyro a tora. (*Pars* 87: "Der reine Tor.")

616.32–3: unperceable to haily, icy and missilethroes ("Parsifal.")

Notes

PREFACE

1 Bloom, *Anxiety of Influence*; Eliot, "Tradition and the Individual Talent," in *Selected Prose*, 40. This dichotomy is suggested by Litz, in "*Ulysses* and Its Audience," 222.
2 Fritz Senn has developed this term to describe the constant tendency in Joyce's writing toward "exaggeration and change" (7). Provection is "an excessive bias, a tendency to overdo, to break out of norms, to go beyond" (1).
3 "Tradition and the Individual Talent," in *Selected Prose*, 38.
4 Mann, "The Sorrows and Grandeur of Richard Wagner," in *Pro and contra Wagner*, 91.

1 JOYCE AND LITERARY WAGNERISM

1 My discussion of Wagner's contributions to opera in relation to an autonomous theory of art is indebted to two sources in particular: *New Grove Dictionary*, s.v. "Wagner, Richard"; and William Weber, "Wagner, Wagnerism, and Musical Idealism," in Large and Weber, 28–71. Wagner's position in the history of opera as a polemicist insisting on the seriousness of his craft might be likened to that of Henry James in the history of fiction. *Opera and Drama* was Wagner's "Art of Fiction."
2 The *New Grove Dictionary* describes "the replacement of the number by the scene" as "the breakthrough" in Wagner's manner of composition (20:127). Hans Mayer and Hans Gals ascribe the same importance to this development, though both think the real breakthrough happens later, in *Lohengrin* (Mayer, 55; Gals, 152–3).
3 On Wagner's "musical prose," see Dahlhaus, 17–20, 44–8, 104–9. See also Shaw, *Perfect Wagnerite*, 111–15.
4 *Perfect Wagnerite*, 2. Having abandoned four-bar phrasing as the basis of his musical syntax, however, Wagner was free to revert to

it on occasion for parodic or deliberately archaic effects, as, for example, in Mime's *Starenlied* in act 1 of *Siegfried* or in Beckmesser's Serenade in act 2 of *Meistersinger*. See Dahlhaus, 128–9.

5 The term "music drama," which once enjoyed wide currency among Wagner's critics, especially partisans, is generally avoided in this study. It is a term that Wagner himself rejected, though his own preference – simply "drama" – begs an important question, that of Wagner's actual relation to operatic tradition.

In fact, the extent to which Wagner's works represent a clear departure from the forms and methods of nineteenth-century opera is very much open to discussion. Elements of romantic melodrama common in the operas of Weber, Donizetti, and Verdi – the duel, the curse, the magic potion, the figure of the intriguer – and set operatic pieces like the prayer, the storm, the conspiratorial oath, and even the ballet may be found throughout Wagner's work (Gals, 172–8; Lindenberger, 31–41). Robin Holloway cites Wagner's affection for operatic spectacle – Valkyries on horseback and rainbow bridges, for example – worthy of the Meyerbeer whom *Opera and Drama* had charged with creating "effect" without "cause" (*PW* 2:95–6). (See Holloway, pt. 4, 34.) There are conventional formal elements as well. Choruses reappear in the last four operas, and in *Siegfried* the aria makes, as Robert Gutman puts it, "a swaggering re-entry" (289). It may be that only *Das Rheingold* and *Die Walküre* approach the concept of "music drama" for which the composer had become famous through the influential prose writings of 1849 to 1851 (*Art and Revolution, The Art-Work of the Future, A Communication to My Friends*, and *Opera and Drama*).

Indeed, the power of these widely disseminated essays to crystallize Wagner's theories created difficulties for early critics who either ignored the "operatic" elements that remain in Wagner's works or – Shaw is the most famous example – held Wagner's theories against his works. With *Götterdämmerung, The Perfect Wagnerite* complains, it is "back to opera again" (54–6). A more contemporary view is to recognize, as Holloway suggests, that Wagner's achievement was to transform opera "from within" the genre, "infusing its ludicrous conventions with tragic magnificence, using its folly as the vehicle for sublimity that still remains to a certain extent absurd" (pt. 3, 36). In this sense, Wagner's answer to Meyerbeer was not to eliminate the spectacular or "extravagant" in grand opera but to imbue the effects that are its essence with causal significance. Gals finds, in fact, that Wagner succeeds because of, not despite, the "operatic" elements in his work (196).

The temptation is simply to discard the theories of 1849 to 1851 as inapplicable to most of Wagner's operas, as, in Martin Gregor-Dellin's words, "an empty chrysalis... tossed to [Wagner's] devotees and detractors to squabble over" (459). Jack Stein explains the apparent return to operatic convention in *Siegfried* by arguing that, after 1854, when Wagner read of the special position of music in Schopenhauer's philosophy, the "absolute music" against which the composer had railed in *Opera and Drama* began to occupy an increasingly dominant position in his synthesis of arts, and Stein's position has been widely accepted. But Dahlhaus shows that this argument is vitiated by a false equation of "drama" and "text." He argues persuasively that "drama," of which music, poetry, and stage action are all constituent parts, was always the "end" of Wagner's efforts and that most of the composer's reversions to traditional forms and conventions can be explained dramatically or thematically (Dahlhaus, especially 4–6; see also Garten, 9–10). At any rate, because for many years actual performances of Wagner's operas were much less readily available than were his prose writings, his admirers were scarcely aware of these apparent contradictions, much less troubled by them. The prolific theorizing, of course, only added to Wagner's stature as a "total artist."

These questions – whether Wagner's practice contradicts his theories or whether, in the first place, Wagner is theoretically consistent – remain subjects of fascination, though, strictly speaking, they are outside the boundaries of this study.

6 Nietzsche, *Case of Wagner*, 22–5.
7 See especially Zdenko von Kraft, "Wahnfried and the Festival Theatre," in Burbidge and Sutton, 425–6.
8 A summary of Wagner's contributions to stagecraft and to theatre decorum is available in Dent, *Opera*, 76, 83, 128–31.
9 Quoted in Percy Scholes 1:253. My attention was drawn to this passage by Sessa, *Wagner and the English*, 30.
10 *Perfect Wagnerite*, 130. The nineteenth-century perception of Wagner as a reformer and iconoclast has gradually been tempered by an understanding of the composer's considerable debt to innovative predecessors like Liszt and Berlioz. Many critics, in fact, assess Wagner's role in the development of opera more as a matter of extension and execution of principles first articulated by others than as one of complete revolution. (See, for example, Barzun, 242–56.) This developing sense of Wagner's place in cultural history as the culmination of an era rather than the beginning of one inspired the poet in admirers and detractors alike. Nietzsche wrote of Wagner's "Music without a Future," parodying the epithet that had become attached to the composer during the 1861 production of *Tannhäuser*

in Paris. For Debussy Wagner was "a beautiful sunset mistaken for a dawn"; for Max Nordau he was "the last mushroom on the dunghill of romanticism" (*Nietzsche contra Wagner*, 63 – 5; Debussy, quoted in Zuckerman, 120; Nordau, 194).

Whether, in fact, Wagner was the revolutionary he at first seemed to be; whether, on the other hand, he represented the culmination of an era; whether he stands, because of his unique combination of talents, to some extent outside the continuity of the history of music and of the theatre; or whether, as is doubtless the case, all these are partly true: these questions are better pursued by the musicologist than by the literary critic.

11   This figure appears in two of my sources: Blissett, "Bernard Shaw," 187; and Magee, 51.

12   Barzun, 285.

13   In Paris years later Blanche's distinguished subject was James Joyce, who remarked, "I was fond of pictures, but now the nails on the walls are quite enough" (*JJ* 627n).

14   Rolland, 253, quoted in Zuckerman, 108.

15   For my general information on Wagner's second period in Paris, I am especially indebted to the following sources: Baudelaire; Newman, *Life of Wagner* 3:3 – 128; Zuckerman, 83 – 122; Gutman, 190 – 202; Westernhagen, 267 – 93; Gregor-Dellin, 293 – 303; and Gerald D. Turbow, "Art and Politics: Wagnerism in France," in Large and Weber, 134 – 66. The first chapter in Newman's third volume is called "The Second Assault on Paris," a phrase my own prose echoes.

16   The term "music of the future," derived from Wagner's *Art-Work of the Future*, had been coined around 1850 and picked up quickly by both admirers and detractors. During the controversial period in Paris, Wagner gave the phrase even wider currency when he finally used it himself, as a title for the preface to his newly published librettos, though he kept his distance from it by enclosing it in quotation marks. See Zuckerman, 5.

17   Baudelaire, 226.

18   Newman, *Life of Wagner* 3:67.

19   Quoted in Zuckerman, 94.

20   Zuckerman, 95. The importance of the 1861 *Tannhäuser* to literary Wagnerism is indicated by the fact that many of the earliest borrowings from Wagner came from this opera, including Robert Bulwer-Lytton and Julian Fane's "Tannhäuser; or, The Battle of the Bards" (1861), Swinburne's "Laus Veneris" (1864), William Morris' "Hill of Venus" (1869), and Cézanne's painting *Overture to Tannhäuser* (mid to late 1860s).

21 For previous work on the relationship between Joyce and Wagner, see Hayman, "Tristan and Isolde in the *Wake*"; Zuckerman, 186–8; Blissett, "Joyce in the Smithy"; Hodgart, "Music and the Mime of Mick, Nick, and the Maggies," in Begnal and Senn, 83–92; MacNicholas, "Joyce contra Wagner"; DiGaetani, *Wagner and the Novel*, 130–57; Hodgart, *Student's Guide*, especially 130–88; Kestner; Furness, 123–6; Stoddard Martin, 135–67; Gillespie, "Wagner in the Ormond"; Mahaffey, "Wagner, Joyce and Revolution"; and Dasenbrock. See the list of works consulted for my own publications on the subject.

22 See O'Connor, 41.

23 John Joyce "took James for a walk into the country, and stopped with him at a village inn for a drink. There was a piano in the corner; John Joyce sat down at it and without comment began to sing. 'Did you recognize that?' he asked James, who replied, 'Yes, of course, it's the aria sung by Alfredo's father in *Traviata*.' John Joyce said nothing more, but his son knew that peace had been made" (*JJ* 276–7).

24 Beach, 44.

25 See Robert Scholes, *Cornell Joyce Collection*, nos. 60 and 61.

26 Antheil, 151–4.

27 Newman's position as a leading Wagner scholar would not have been lost on Joyce: Newman had published the first of many books on Wagner in 1899, and his four-volume biography would begin to appear in 1933.

28 In this chapter and elsewhere in this book, my account of Wagner's presence in late nineteenth and early twentieth-century letters must, for want of space, omit many figures who shared rather than influenced Joyce's own interest in the composer. These figures would include, among many others, contemporary writers of fiction like Woolf, Ford, Forster, and above all D. H. Lawrence. See Blissett, "Wagnerian Fiction in English."

29 Interestingly, Baudelaire may have encouraged, if not inspired, the beginnings of literary Wagnerism in England. In gratitude for a favorable review of *Fleurs du mal*, the French poet sent Swinburne a copy of his essay on Wagner. Soon afterward, Swinburne published "Laus Veneris," which uses the *Tannhäuser* motif, in his *Poems and Ballads*. Sessa argues, however, that Swinburne probably wrote the poem before he had received Baudelaire's gift (*Wagner and the English*, 93–4).

30 In his *Books at the Wake*, Atherton argues that Symons' *Symbolist Movement* was Joyce's primary source of information about Mallarmé, Mallarmé himself included (48–52).

31 Loewenberg, cols. 822, 886, 1014, 850.

32 As Wagnerism began to gather its own momentum, it would gradually detach itself from the actual composer and his work and enter the realm of myth and hagiography. Mythologized and distorted, in many cases, by literary Wagnerites who, however musical, may have had little actual experience of his operas in performance, the "Wagner" who eventually came to Joyce in the late nineties – this "mediated" Wagner – would have to be corrected by the Wagner Joyce would encounter more directly – in his own library and at the opera.

33 See Blissett, "Lawrence, D'Annunzio, Wagner."

34 Stanislaus Joyce, *My Brother's Keeper*, 147. See also *CW* 71.

35 During the 1970s the collection now known as Joyce's Trieste library was assembled by Richard Ellmann from the shelves of Nelly Joyce, the widow of Stanislaus, and their son James in England. Ellmann published a list of these books, together with titles of other works that Joyce can be shown to have owned or read before he left Trieste for Paris, as "Joyce's Library in 1920." (See Ellmann, *Consciousness*, 97–134.) After the Humanities Research Center at the University of Texas acquired the Trieste library, Michael Patrick Gillespie, with the assistance of Erik Bradford Stocker, undertook a more thorough examination of the collection and published *Joyce's Trieste Library*. In *Joyce and Wagner* I rely on Gillespie and Stocker for detailed information about books in the Trieste collection. Ellmann's list continues to be useful for general information about Joyce's reading up to 1920. In addition to consulting these lists, I have examined the collection at the Humanities Research Center for markings and other evidence of use. The books by Nietzsche mentioned here are Gillespie and Stocker, nos. 350 and 351.

See also Connolly's *Personal Library of James Joyce*, a catalogue of 468 books, periodicals, and pamphlets, now at the University of Buffalo, that Joyce owned at the end of the 1930s, shortly after he had reduced the size of his library in anticipation of moving. The collection includes a number of books on music, but nothing by Wagner or about him primarily. References to books in the Buffalo collection are always cited in separate notes; any uncited references to Joyce's books may be assumed to be those on Ellmann's list or in the Texas collection.

36 See Dujardin, *Les Lauriers*, 214, 226–9, 254–8. The link, through Dujardin, between Joyce's interior monologue and Wagner's continuous melody has been known for some time. Blissett discusses it in "Joyce in the Smithy," 113–15.

In 1929, on first looking into a French translation of *Ulysses*,

Dujardin would write to Joyce, comparing Joyce's book to the *Ring* (*L* 3:191–2).

37 For my general information on Wagner and his reception in England I am especially indebted to the following: Hueffer, *Music in England*; Davison; Newman, *Life of Wagner*, especially 1:250–5, 2:446–80, 4:553–64; Moser; Blissett, "Ernest Newman"; Sessa, *Wagner and the English*; Gregor-Dellin, 259–63; and Sessa, "At Wagner's Shrine: British and American Wagnerians," in Large and Weber, 246–77.

38 About Wagner's visit to London in 1855, J. W. Davison, the distinguished music critic of the *Times*, noted the following impressions: "The iconoclast, the revolutionist bent on demolishing the classical temples in order on their site to build up his own fane, the abuser of Jews, the detractor of Mendelssohn, was received with a mingled curiosity and excitement which further acquaintance increased" (Davison, 167).

39 Because European copyright law forbade productions of *Parsifal* outside Bayreuth, London settled, in 1884, for a concert version of the opera. For the dates of English premieres of Wagner's operas, see Loewenberg, cols. 823, 825, 850, 885, 974, 1001, 1056, 1097, and 1098.

40 See Gregor-Dellin, 262.

41 Victoria's apparent affection for the controversial German's music would later earn her the title of "the first Englishwoman to recognise the genius of Wagner." See Hueffer, *Music in England*, v.

42 For my knowledge of Hueffer's role in English Wagnerism, I am especially indebted to Moser, 29–32.

43 Wagner's influence on these Pre-Raphaelite painters and writers is beyond the scope of this study, but see Moser's discussion of similarities between Wagner and these nineteenth-century "decadents" who saw contemporary life as inimical to art and believed in the mission of art to change the world (28–9).

44 Sessa, *Wagner and the English*, 36.

45 My translation of quotation in Moser, 11.

46 Weston's reputation as a student of the Grail legend was not lost on Joyce, who brought her into *Finnegans Wake* at least twice. The following reference is on the book's first page: "the humptyhillhead of himself promptly sends an unquiring one well to the *west in* quest of his tumptytumtoes" (3.20–1, my emphasis). See Glasheen, *Third Census*, 303.

47 Years earlier, Joyce would have found several of Beardsley's Wagnerian drawings reproduced in his copy of Wolfgang Golther's *Richard Wagner as Poet*. (See Gillespie and Stocker, no. 194.) In the

Wake II.3, HCE has been reading a book by "Aubeyron Birdslay" with "expurgative plates" (356.30–357.3). Hayman, in "Tristan and Isolde in the *Wake*," thinks *Under the Hill* is this book's "prototype" (106).

48 Quoted in Blissett, "Bernard Shaw," 193. In 1900 Joyce would encounter the same William Archer in connection with his review of *When We Dead Awaken*, which Archer had translated. Over the next several years Archer would read Joyce's work and give the aspiring writer a good deal of encouragement (*CW* 47; *JJ* 78–80, 83).

49 Quoted in Sessa, *Wagner and the English*, 156 n. 2.

50 Shaw's Wagnerism seems to have had less influence on his own dramas than one might expect. See Blissett, "Bernard Shaw."

51 Stanislaus' son James has speculated that some of Joyce's books may have been used in this way. See Jane Ford, "James Joyce's Trieste Library: Some Notes on Its Use," in Oliphant and Zigal, 148 n. 25. Erik Stocker made the same conjecture to me in Austin in 1985. Also, see Gillespie and Stocker, 16–17.

52 Connolly, no. 267.

53 See Stoddard Martin, 56.

54 Symons, *Symbolist Movement*, 62.

55 Symons, *Studies in Seven Arts*, 247.

56 See Yeats, *Letters*, 458–60.

57 See Worth, 35–7.

58 See Zuckerman, 109.

59 I owe this anecdote to Blissett, "George Moore," 69.

60 On Moore and continuous melody, see *Confessions of a Young Man*, 158; on Moore and Siegfried, see *Hail and Farewell* 3:305–6.

61 See Blissett, "George Moore," 52–6; and Stoddard Martin, 104–10.

62 My knowledge of Moore's Wagnerism is much indebted to Blissett's article on the subject.

63 The count of fourteen volumes is based on Ellmann's list in *Consciousness*, 120. Markings in *Evelyn Innes* are noted in Gillespie and Stocker, no. 330.

64 In fact, among Wagner's operas Loewenberg lists only *The Flying Dutchman* and *Lohengrin* as having been produced in Ireland even as late as 1940 (cols. 826, 885).

65 For Ibsen's influence on the Irish literary theatre, see Smidt, 337–41.

66 Yeats, *Letters*, 459–60.

67 Yeats, *Essays and Introductions*, 186.

68 See Howarth, *Irish Writers*, 26.

69 *My Brother's Keeper*, 98.

70 See Worth, 19–23, 122–5; Blissett, "George Moore," 64–5.

71 Yeats, *Letters*, 371.

72 *My Brother's Keeper*, 86.

73 In Potts, 71.

74 In Berrone, 21.

75 Antheil, 153.

76 Among these books, four are pocket librettos now at Texas (Gillespie and Stocker, nos. 527, 528, 532, and 534). The fifth, *Die Meistersinger*, is not extant, but Joyce probably owned a vocal score, as Ellmann conjectures, when he was preparing a performance of the quintet from *Meistersinger* in 1909. (See *Consciousness*, 132; see also *L* 1:67.) In addition to these books, Joyce at one time owned a collection of Wagner's librettos (*L* 2:25), as I argue below.

77 The Italian Joyce quotes here comes from Siegfried's last bit of singing, which begins, in German, "Brünnhilde, heilige Braut!" (*R* 320). The phrase would eventually contribute to the "Brinabride" motif that appears some eight times in the *Wake*, six clustered around 500.21–30, one at 399.3, another at 502.9.

78 By "funeral motive" Joyce probably meant the nine-note motive in E-flat major, usually known as the "Helden" motive, which occurs twice in the funeral music. Based on Siegfried's sprightly F-major horn call, this grand motive is surely one of the most memorable (and therefore hummable) snippets from the entire *Ring*.

79 Gillet, 93.

80 In Potts, 168. Joyce's affection for *Meistersinger* is confirmed by two other sources: Jacques Mercanton, in Potts, 248; and Frank Budgen, 182–3. Herbert Gorman reports that Joyce "never missed a performance of *Die Meistersinger*" (239). But, interestingly, this in many ways un-Wagnerian opera makes only cameo appearances in Joyce's work.

81 This number is derived from Ellmann's list of "Joyce's Library in 1920," in *Consciousness*, 104, 110, 121, 125, 128, and 132. My contention that "only Shakespeare occupied more space on Joyce's shelves" is based on a count of both secondary and primary material. Among other favorites, for example, Ellmann records thirteen books by Ibsen but only one book on Ibsen, thirteen books by Balzac but no books on Balzac.

82 A more detailed discussion of Joyce's use of Byron's *Day with Richard Wagner* is available in my note, "Wagner's *Tannhäuser* in *Exiles*." Ellmann has shown how Byron's *Day with Shakespeare*, written under the name of "Maurice Clare," made a similar contribution to "Scylla and Charybdis" and "Sirens" (*Consciousness*, 59–61).

83 See Gillespie and Stocker, nos. 93, 194, 351, 405, 448, 529, 530, 531, and 533 for more complete information on the books discussed in this paragraph.

84 See Zuckerman, 32; and Gregor-Dellin, 349.
85 Beach, 162.
86 Doubtless Joyce got this idea from Isolde herself, who interprets the "Einsam wachend" of act 2, in which Brangäne warns the lovers of approaching dawn, as an intrusion by an "Envious watcher," or "Neid'sche Wache" (*TI* 72).
87 Colum and Colum, 119–20.
88 Hueffer, *Music in England*, 83.
89 See Introduction to Large and Weber, 15, 22.
90 See Baudelaire, 192, 196–201.
91 Wilde, *Dorian Gray*, 135.
92 See Marion S. Miller, "Wagnerism, Wagnerians, and Italian Identity," in Large and Weber, 174–6. Thomas Mann witnessed a similar altercation in Rome in the 1890s. See *Pro and contra Wagner*, 56–7.
93 See Introduction to Large and Weber, 16–19.
94 Yeats, *Essays and Introductions*, 187.
95 Nordau, 213. See also Sessa, "At Wagner's Shrine: British and American Wagnerians," in Large and Weber, 264.
96 Symons, *Plays, Acting, and Music*, 314.
97 Moore, Introduction to *The Heather Field and Maeve*, by Martyn, ix.
98 Shaw, *Perfect Wagnerite*, 65; Nordau, 181.
99 Both quotations from the Anglican rector are taken from Moser, 19.
100 Nordau, 181, 182, 171.
101 Weston, *Legends of the Wagner Drama*, 72–8.
102 Gautier, 2. Zuckerman first drew my attention to this passage (103).
103 In fact, over one hundred books on Wagner, many of them books for children and illustrated guides, were published in England in the nineties. (See Blissett, "Ernest Newman," 312.) In 1895, a writer for the *Saturday Review* would aver, "we are all Wagnerites now" (quoted in Moser, 18).
104 *Perfect Wagnerite*, 2.
105 In Davison, 517.
106 Quoted in Moser, 19.
107 Wilde, *Dorian Gray*, 45.
108 Baudelaire, 225–6.
109 Quoted in Zuckerman, 96.
110 This point is made in Conclusion to Large and Weber, 281. See also Lindenberger, 218–27. Lindenberger writes that "the avant-gardist mentality" in music was "largely created by Wagner" (227).
111 In associating Bach and Wagner in this context, Joyce may have remembered something that had struck him in Moore's *Evelyn Innes* years before. The following passage, linking Bach and Wagner

in connection with "tempered" and "untempered" tuning, is marked with two vertical pencil lines in Joyce's copy: "According to Mr Innes, Bach was the last composer who had distinguished between A sharp and B flat. The very principle of Wagner's music is the identification of the two notes" (220). See Gillespie and Stocker, no. 330.

112 Joyce was hardly unique in linking Ibsen and Wagner as examples of progressive artists. Moore, as we have seen, did the same in his introduction to Edward Martyn's plays; so did Yeats in "The Celtic Element in Literature" and, as late as 1928, Thomas Mann, in his essay "Ibsen and Wagner." (See Introduction to *The Heather Field and Maeve*, by Martyn, ix; Yeats, *Essays and Introductions*, 186; and *Pro and contra Wagner*, 84–6.) Indeed, it may have been this widespread association with his beloved Ibsen that drew Joyce to Wagner in the first place.

113 Eglinton et al., *Literary Ideals in Ireland*, 17, 25, 32, 46, 57.

114 Joyce had made a similar stand the year before, publicly applauding Yeats's *Countess Cathleen* in defiance of Dublin's disapproval of the play (*JJ* 66–7).

115 Shaw, *Perfect Wagnerite*, 1–3.

116 Stoddard Martin also links Bloom and the gentleman in the gallery at *Götterdämmerung* (136).

117 Shaw, *London Music in 1888–89*, 189.

118 In Berrone, 21–2.

119 See Power, 53–4. Richard Brown, in fact, argues in *James Joyce and Sexuality* that "writing about sexuality represented for [Joyce] a kind of modernity that … was as important to Joyce's own stated concept of literature as was formal experimentation" (10–11).

120 In Potts, 64.

121 Wagner, *Letters to Roeckel*, 44–5.

122 Byron, 6. Joyce would have found the same general description in H. S. Chamberlain's preface to the *Letters to Roeckel* (5–6).

123 The fragment is reprinted in MacNicholas, *Joyce's* Exiles, 167.

124 Colum and Colum, 16.

125 Beach, 162.

126 See, for example, Hayman, "Tristan and Isolde in the *Wake*," III n. 18. Hayman concedes, however, that Joyce might have separated Wagner from his decadent surroundings: "the Wagnerian parody constituted not so much a commentary upon the composer or the opera as an interpretation of a particular historical instant: decadence" (100).

127 *My Brother's Keeper*, 197.

128 I have borrowed the phrase "comic rhythm" from Langer, 326–50.

2 THE ARTIST-HERO

1 On the artist as protagonist, see Beebe, *Ivory Towers and Sacred Founts*; on artistic values replacing shared cultural values, see Daiches, 1–11.

2 D'Annunzio, 175–6; Nietzsche, *Case of Wagner*, 40.

3 Mayer suggests that Wagner intended this lusty and energetic figure "to point the way out of the isolation that was at the heart of the dramas centered around the artist" (145).

4 Indeed, there are hints in *The Art-Work of the Future*, written shortly after Wagner had begun work on the *Ring*, that Siegfried may have held the same appeal, however subliminally, for Wagner himself. According to that essay, Beethoven, in creating the Ninth Symphony, liberated the symphony from the hackneyed formulas of "absolute music" (*PW* 1:126) and "forged for us the key" to the "universal Drama" of the future. Beethoven "took the basic essence of the Christian's Harmony" and, as Siegfried does in his confrontation with the Wanderer, "clove in twain the fetters of its freedom" (*PW* 1:121).

Around 1850, while the *Ring* was still in its earliest stages, Wagner made an artist-smith his protagonist in a plan for an opera called "Wieland the Smith." In this sketch Wieland is captured, lamed, and imprisoned by a king who recognizes his ability to make weapons and finery. "He," writes Wagner, "the free artist-smith who, of very joy in his art, had forged the most wondrous of smithery ... – here must he, spurned and spat upon, smite out the chains for his own body, and swords and trappings to adorn the man who cast him into shame" (*PW* 1:238). The sketch concludes when Wieland, as Daedalus did before him, forges himself a pair of wings and flies to freedom.

Mahaffey links Stephen's bird girl in chapter 4 of *A Portrait* with the swan girl of "Wieland" ("Wagner, Joyce and Revolution," 243).

5 *Letters to Roeckel*, 102.

6 The idea of "heroic vitalism" was suggested to me by Michael Tanner, "The Total Work of Art," in Burbidge and Sutton, especially 159–78.

7 See Howarth, *Irish Writers*, 271; Sultan, *Argument of* Ulysses, 338–9; Zuckerman, 186; Blissett, "Joyce in the Smithy," 96–102, 123–7; Magee, 73–4; Thornton, *Allusions in* Ulysses, 560.26n, 583.2n; Epstein, *Ordeal of Stephen Dedalus*, 102, 111–12, 145, 163–7; Bowen, *Musical Allusions*, 45, 81–2, 291; Hodgart, "Music and the Mime of Mick, Nick, and the Maggies," in Begnal and Senn, 88–9; Sultan, *Modernism*, 36, 40; DiGaetani, *Wagner and the Novel*, 136–44; Hodgart, *Student's Guide*, 5, 63, 150, 160, 174, 179–80; Furness, 124–5;

Stoddard Martin, 143–6; Gifford, *Notes for* Dubliners *and* Portrait, 275; Gifford and Seidman, Ulysses *Annotated*, 15.3649–50n, 15.4242n; and Dasenbrock, 520–8. An earlier version of this chapter was published as "Joyce, Wagner, and the Artist-Hero."

8 Nietzsche, *Birth of Tragedy*, 20, 185, 140.

9 See D'Annunzio, 125, 175–6.

10 D'Annunzio, 9, 116, 118–21. The influence of *Il fuoco* on *A Portrait* has been the subject of a good deal of critical attention. (See Scholes and Kain, *Workshop of Daedalus*, 269–79; Curran, 105–15; Zingrone; and Lucente.) D'Annunzio's position as one of the important sources of Joyce's early Wagnerism is less well known, though Adams hints at the connection in "Operatic Novel," 281.

11 Shaw, *Perfect Wagnerite*, 48.

12 Howarth, *Irish Writers*, 26–9, 67.

13 For the quoted passage, see *Essays and Introductions*, 249. For other examples, see 156, 164, 252, 254.

14 See Howarth, *Irish Writers*, 10–16. Yeats used the phrase "dusk of the nations" in an 1895 letter to actress Florence Farr (*Letters*, 259).

15 Moore, *Hail and Farewell* 1:170, 3:277–8, 3:306. Blissett, in "Joyce in the Smithy" (101–2), first drew my attention to the long passage quoted from *Hail and Farewell*.

16 See Howarth, *Irish Writers*, especially 1–31. Joyce's "Aeolus," in fact, casts the writer in the role of Moses, leading his people out of political and cultural exile.

17 D'Annunzio, 118.

18 Stanislaus Joyce, *My Brother's Keeper*, 147.

19 It is likely that Joyce read the popular *Perfect Wagnerite* shortly after it was first published in 1898, since his interest in opera developed very early in his life. His eventual acquisition of a 1913 Leipzig edition, possibly for his own artistic purposes, probably reflects a rekindling of this earlier interest. See also *Letters to Roeckel*, 74–116.

20 My discussion of the books in this paragraph draws, once again, on Ellmann's list of "Joyce's Library in 1920" (*Consciousness*, 97–134). I have consulted Gillespie and Stocker in the case of books that are extant.

21 Power, 36.

22 See Blissett's careful tracing of these parallels in "Joyce in the Smithy," 96–100.

23 According to Weston, Siegfried's tasting of the dragon's blood is analogous to the tale, in Celtic myth, of Finn's eating the Salmon of Wisdom. See *Legends of the Wagner Drama*, 103.

24 See Epstein, 145; and Bowen, *Musical Allusions*, 45.

25 Hanley's *Word Index* and Steppe and Gabler's *Handlist* have helped me identify the ashplant references in *Ulysses*.

26 Blissett discusses Stephen's manipulation of the ashplant in "Joyce in the Smithy," 124–6. "Do you think you impress me," Stephen asks MacCann, evidently Wotan's stand-in for *Siegfried* 3.2, "when you flourish your wooden sword?" (*P* 197).

27 Holloway calls the first two acts of *Siegfried* the "scherzo" of the *Ring* (pt. 4, 32).

28 Joyce's libretto to *Götterdämmerung* bears the "JJ" stamp with which he marked his books at the time of his return to Trieste from Zurich in 1919. (See Gillespie and Stocker, 13.) He therefore had the libretto with him when he began "Circe" in Trieste in 1920. My examination of this book shows that the bloodoath page has been stained by some food or liquid. See Gillespie and Stocker, no. 528.

29 This source may also reinforce a joint allusion to Odysseus and Adonis in the following passage from "Scylla and Charybdis," made in the context of Shakespeare's betrayal, according to Stephen's theory, by his wife and his brother: "The tusk of the boar has wounded him there where love lies ableeding" (9.459–60; 196).

30 Linking Zoe and Sieglinde, Ellmann identifies Stephen's use of the ashplant in "Circe" with Siegmund's withdrawal of the sword from the tree trunk in *Walküre* 1.3, rather than with Siegfried's smashing of the anvil in *Siegfried* 1.3 (*JJ* 460). This identification is tempting to the extent that it draws on Siegmund's status as a hero who is insufficiently free of his father's influence and emphasizes, in so doing, Stephen's artistic inadequacy. Siegmund's gloomy personality is certainly more like Stephen's than is that of the energetic Siegfried, and the discussion of act 1 of *Die Walküre* in Joyce's copy of *The Perfect Wagnerite* is extensively marked. (See Gillespie and Stocker, no. 448.) But there is much more cultural weight behind Siegfried, and the many supporting references – the birdcall in *A Portrait*, the bloodoath and discussion of fear in "Circe," for example – point toward the younger hero. Siegmund's contribution to Stephen's character is significant but secondary.

31 See Weston, *Legends of the Wagner Drama*, 78–9. In Joyce's copy of *The Perfect Wagnerite*, "snake," used in connection with the eyes of the Volsung twins, is among the many words underlined in pencil in Shaw's discussion of *Die Walküre*. (See Gillespie and Stocker, no. 448.) In the *Wake* "Snakeeye" will describe HCE's antagonist the cad (534.27).

32 Shaw, *Perfect Wagnerite*, 23.

33 "Who are Sir Lout and his family?" Budgen asked Joyce concerning the passage in "Proteus." Joyce replied, "They were giants right

enough, but weak reproductively. Fasolt and Fafnir in Das Rhein-gold are of the same breed, sexually weak as the music tells us'' (Budgen, 52).

34 See Gregor-Dellin's discussion of the figure of the orphan and of the recurrent themes of paternity and maternity throughout Wagner's works (20–4).

35 Nietzsche, *Birth of Tragedy*, 155.

36 Wagner joins a tradition of operatic reformers who had invoked the Greeks to justify attacks on current operatic practice, even though little was known about the music and its actual role in Greek drama. See Gals, 159; and Lindenberger, 97–100.

37 See Magee, 12–13.

38 Nietzsche, *Birth of Tragedy*, 152.

39 *Nietzsche contra Wagner*, 58.

40 Wilde, "Soul of Man under Socialism," in *Intentions*, 293.

41 In Joyce's copy of the *Prose Works* this passage is marked in blue pencil. (See Gillespie and Stocker, no. 531.)

42 See especially Shaw, *Perfect Wagnerite*, 28–31.

43 See Gillespie and Stocker, no. 531. An alternative, or perhaps com-plementary, reading of the end of *A Portrait* would suggest that Stephen, rather than creating a "public" conscience, intends to make *himself* the conscience of his race. It was in this sense that Wagner had called Heine "the conscience of Judaism" (*Judaism in Music*, 48).

44 D'Annunzio, 115–16.

45 *Perfect Wagnerite*, 57.

46 *Letters to Roeckel*, 97.

47 *Perfect Wagnerite*, 52. The quoted passage is not marked in Joyce's copy of *The Perfect Wagnerite*, but two others that bear on the issue of renunciation are marked. In his discussion of *Rheingold*, scene 1, Shaw writes that Godhead "finally begins secretly to long for the advent of some power higher than itself which will destroy its artificial empire of law, and establish a true republic of free thought." This passage shows a clear pencil marking in the left-hand margin. Later, in his introduction to *Die Walküre*, Shaw writes, somewhat inconsistently, that "in his longing for a rescuer, it does not occur to [Wotan] that when the Hero comes, his first exploit must be to sweep the gods and their ordinances from the path of the heroic will." In this sentence, "sweep" is underlined. (See Gillespie and Stocker, no. 448: markings at pp. 38 and 76.) These passages are found on pp. 12 and 34 of the 1923 edition.

48 Wagner's contribution to Robert and Richard's "blood brother-hood" is discussed by Kestner, 58. A possible allusion to *Die*

Walküre may deepen the presence of the *Ring* in *Exiles*. Robert and Bertha's tryst in act 2, as Stoddard Martin has suggested (147–8), may owe several motifs to the love scene in act 1. See the appendix.

49 Wilde identifies these three "despots" in "Soul of Man under Socialism," in *Intentions*, 323.

50 On the Joycean artist as forger, see Levin, *James Joyce*, 178–9; and Atherton, 69–71.

51 The quotation is Ellmann's paraphrase, drawn from a letter from Russell to Lady Gregory. See *Eminent Domain*, 36.

3 THE WANDERING JEW

1 Quoted in Kruse, 4. This libretto for the *Dutchman* was in Joyce's Trieste library. See Gillespie and Stocker, no. 527.

   Joyce's use of Wagner's *Dutchman* is touched on in the following articles, book chapters, and handbooks: Blissett, "Joyce in the Smithy," 123; Thornton, 478.24n, 636.34n; Bowen, *Musical Allusions*, 266, 308–9; MacNicholas, "Joyce contra Wagner," 37; DiGaetani, *Wagner and the Novel*, 139, 148–50, 153–4; Hodgart, *Student's Guide*, 167; Kestner, 57–8; Stoddard Martin, 149–50; Gillespie, "Wagner in the Ormond"; Gifford and Seidman, Ulysses *Annotated*, 15.1369–70n, 16.859n; and Mahaffey, *Reauthorizing Joyce*, 182–6. An independent version of this chapter was published as "Joyce, Wagner, and the Wandering Jew."

2 The widely accepted story of Wagner's imprisonment in Paris has recently been debunked by Gregor-Dellin, who argues that Wagner accomplished too much in October and November of 1840 to have spent time in prison. Gregor-Dellin suggests that Wagner may have primed Minna to inflate his problems in order to make appeals for money more compelling (102–3).

3 Heine, 349. In fact, it is this addition that Nietzsche, in *The Case of Wagner*, found so worthy of ridicule: "Someone always wants to be saved in his operas ... If it were not for Wagner, who would teach us ... that even the eternal Jew gets saved and *settled down* when he marries?" (6).

4 See, for example, Nietzsche, *Case of Wagner*, 6; Nordau, 184; and George Anderson, 8–9, 352. Joyce would have found the story of the Wandering Jew conveniently summarized in Mark Twain's *New Pilgrim's Progress* (197–9), which was among his books in Trieste. See Gillespie and Stocker, no. 517.

5 In "Wagner in the Ormond" (170–1), Gillespie quotes this passage, which he and I came across independently. Joyce would have encountered this striking juxtaposition of the Dutchman, the

Wandering Jew, and Odysseus not only in his copy of *A Communication to My Friends* but also in the introduction to his Reclam edition of the *Dutchman*, where it was quoted (12–13). See note 1 above.

6 Nietzsche, *Case of Wagner*, 7.

7 Wagner, *Letters to Roeckel*, 60.

8 Shaw, *London Music in 1888–89*, 418.

9 D'Annunzio, 176.

10 In 1902 Thomas Mann would write his friend Kurt Martens to thank him and his wife for their recent hospitality: "I wonder if *this* Flying Dutchman will ever be granted a 'redemption' anything like yours?" Mann emphasized his point by copying out a bar of music from Senta's Ballad in act 2, along with the accompanying phrase "fänd er ein Weib" ("if he could find a woman"). See *Pro and contra Wagner*, 23.

11 See William Vaughan, "Loneliness, Love and Death" (*FD* 27–32).

12 Wagner, *Judaism in Music*, 25, 19, 33.

13 Quoted in Gutman, 424.

14 L.J. Rather places Wagner's anti-Semitism in another context. According to Rather, Wagner participated in a fairly widespread metaphorical use of "Jewishness" to describe worldliness and materialism. The "anti-Semitism" in Wagner, Rather suggests, derives in part from Wagner's struggle against the "Jewishness" in himself (89–100).

15 In Potts, 168.

16 Golther, 31–7; Runcimann, *Wagner*, 12ff.

17 See Kruse.

18 See Gillespie and Stocker, nos. 527, 194, 405, 529, 478, and 531, for information about books discussed in this paragraph that are extant in the Trieste collection.

19 This passage, taken from the second of the essays on Mangan, closely follows the analogous passage in the first (*CW* 76).

20 See George Anderson, 128–31, 290; and Gifford and Seidman, Ulysses *Annotated*, 9.1209n.

21 My translation: "As I imagined it [the image of this maiden] for long eternities, I see it here before my eyes."

22 In the early stages of composition, the opera's heroine was called "Minna."

23 Dahlhaus writes, "The redemption the Dutchman seeks does not consist in being allowed, through Senta, to re-enter the world of day from which the curse has banished him; on the contrary, it is Senta's decision to descend into his nocturnal world that brings about his redemption" (12).

24 John MacNicholas identifies this allusion to the *Dutchman* in "Joyce contra Wagner," 37. In *Dublin's Joyce* Kenner describes this death wish as "the Liebestod of Robert Hand" (70–1).

25 Adams, *Surface and Symbol*, 120.

26 In *Joyce's* Ulysses, Gilbert describes the figure of Death in the proto-poem as "a Flying Dutchman in a phantom ship" (133).

27 Joyce, *Scribbledehobble*, 88.

28 Hyde, 31. Compare also the following lines from the *Liebesnacht* duet in act 2 of *Tristan und Isolde*; "Herz an Herz dir, / Mund an Mund" ("heart on your heart, mouth on [your] mouth") (*TI* 71, my translation). Did a bit of *Tristan* slip into Hyde's translation from the Irish?

29 See Gutman, 44, 73; and *New Grove Dictionary* 20:104–5.

30 Joyce's use of *The Flying Dutchman* in Stephen's vampire poem is the subject of my note, "Joyce and Wagner's Pale Vampire." The Spinning Song will appear as "spindlesong" in the *Wake* (336.14).

31 According to Thornton, William Ludwig appeared at the Gaiety with the Carl Rosa Company in an 1877 production of the *Dutchman* (636.34n). This is almost certainly the production that Loewenberg lists as the premiere of the *Dutchman* in Ireland (col. 826).

32 I found this marking during my examination of the Trieste library at Texas in January of 1985. Gillespie and Stocker do not list the marking in *Joyce's Trieste Library*.

33 Padraic Colum, reminiscing about his friendship with Joyce around 1923, shortly after the publication of *Ulysses*, wrote, "The Hellene and the Semite! Perhaps it was in Trieste that Victor Bérard's discoveries came home to Joyce: that the Semites were first in the Mediterranean, that they named the islands, and that it was their language that the poet of the Odyssey knew as the language of the gods. Odysseus and the Wandering Jew were different versions of the same character" (Colum and Colum, 75).

34 Wagner, *Judaism in Music*, 3n.

35 Campbell and Robinson long ago identified the Norwegian captain as "the Flying Dutchman aspect of HCE" (52 n. 27).

36 McHugh, *Annotations*, 311.

37 The term "bloodooth" in this passage refers to the oath of blood brotherhood, another "gentlemeants agreement," which Gunther and Siegfried swear in *Götterdämmerung* and to the rhythm of which Stephen chants in "Circe" (*U* 15.3649–53; 560).

38 See George Anderson, 8.

39 McHugh, *Annotations*, 620.

40 See McHugh, *Annotations*, 202.

41 See also Nordau, 187; Golther, 90; and George Anderson, 393.

42 Hodgart identifies this allusion in *Student's Guide*, 147.

4 REDEMPTION

1 *Case of Wagner*, 5.
2 In Potts, 71. Wagner, it turns out, realized that he was *not* "treating something entirely new" in *Parsifal*: Amfortas, he confessed to Mathilde Wesendonck, is "my Tristan in the third act, but inconceivably intensified" (quoted in Dahlhaus, 145). In pointing to this consistency in Wagner's themes, Joyce may have remembered Nietzsche's complaint that "Wagner takes us as if ... he repeats a thing so often that we become desperate, – that we ultimately believe it" (*Case of Wagner*, 2).
3 Shechner, 70–1, 249.
4 See Peckham, 245; also Rieff, 179–80.
5 See Brivic, 141–2.
6 This chapter focuses on three operas from which Joyce seems to have drawn a redemptive woman – the *Dutchman, Tannhäuser*, and *Tristan* – as well as *Parsifal*, which works with a similar character. Though the idea of redemption through a woman's love is also important in *Lohengrin*, an argument for the influence of *Lohengrin* on Joyce does not, as the appendix shows, have a strong textual basis. This theme is not present in *Meistersinger*, and its complex variation in the four-part *Ring* receives separate discussion in chapter 5.
7 My translation: "The dark desire that I feel burning here, / Should I, poor wretch, call it love? / Ah, no! It is the longing for salvation: / Would that this angel could make it mine!"
8 Nietzsche's gibe against *weibliche* redemption: "The 'Flying Dutchman' preaches the sublime doctrine that woman can moor the most erratic soul, or to put it into Wagnerian terms 'save' him ... Supposing that this were actually true, would it therefore be desirable?" (*Case of Wagner*, 7).
9 See Raphael on the idea of "Treue" in Wagner's operas, which means "utter dedication through empathy" (22).
10 Oddly, Joyce actually wrote, "Ich bin *der* Fleisch *der* stets bejaht," as if the German word for "flesh" were masculine rather than neuter (*L* 1:170, emphasis mine).
11 McHugh, *Annotations*, 268.
12 *Case of Wagner*, 4.
13 In contrast to Senta and Elisabeth, the doubting Elsa of *Lohengrin* is unable to maintain an unquestioning faith in her lover and to accept the near-impossible conditions of their union: that she should love him without fully knowing him. The opera ends with the separation of the lovers and the return of the unredeemed Lohengrin to his ascetic life.

14 This passage in "Nausicaa" provides another illustration of Joyce's predilection for combining references to Wagner: the Dutchman's "phantom ship" appears among the next few phrases (*U* 13.1078; 376).

15 See Mayer, 39–40; Dahlhaus, 24.

16 Wagner's appraisal of a madonna in a church at Aussig: "His opinion of this Mengs copy of a Carlo Dolci original was that 'had Tannhäuser seen it, I could well understand how he came to turn from Venus to Mary without being too much carried away by piety' " (Gregor-Dellin, 117–18).

17 For previous work on the presence of *Tannhäuser* in *Exiles*, see Bowen, *Musical Allusions*, 10; MacNicholas, "Joyce contra Wagner," 31–42; Kestner; and Stoddard Martin, 146–7. The two paragraphs here on *Tannhäuser* and *Exiles* borrow material from my essay "Wagner's *Tannhäuser* in *Exiles*."

18 Weston, *Legends of the Wagner Drama*, 332.

19 Quoted in Stewart Spencer, "Tanhusaere, Danheüser and Tannhäuser" (*Tann* 24).

20 My translation: "O sink down, night of love; let me forget that I live; take me up in your womb; release me from the world."

21 In *Beyond the Tragic Vision*, Peckham points out that "when you are dead you can scarcely enjoy the loss of identity." But his contention that *Tristan* "strips the mask" from the idea of a *Liebestod* and "reveals it as an illusion" is the rationalist's denial of the claim that *Tristan* so irrationally makes. See Peckham, 256–7.

22 See Berrone, 21–2; and Joyce, *Daniel Defoe*, 21–2.

23 See Hayman, "Tristan and Isolde in the *Wake*."

24 A note in *Scribbledehobble* suggests that Joyce took an idea from Ezra Pound: "Tantris is shadow of Tristan (E.P.)" (81). I owe this inference to Hayman, "Tristan and Isolde in the *Wake*," 95.

25 This according to Jacques Mercanton, in Potts, 248.

26 See Zuckerman, 30.

27 Moore, *Memoirs of My Dead Life*, 135. In *Hail and Farewell* Moore wondered, with the example of Wagner and Mathilde Wesendonck in mind, how Yeats's art might have been affected if the poet had consummated his love for Maud Gonne (3:176–82). Stoddard Martin (131) drew my attention to this passage. These two books are listed in Gillespie and Stocker, nos. 332–4, 336.

28 Hayman mentions several of these themes in "Tristan and Isolde in the *Wake*," 96.

29 In Berrone, 21–2. In describing the sensuality of *Tristan*, Joyce may have recalled his heavily marked copy of *Evelyn Innes*, where George Moore writes that Wagner was "full of sex – mysterious,

subconscious sex'' (192). The effect of *Tristan* on Moore's heroine is as follows: "The gnawing, creeping sensuality of the phrase brought little shudders into her flesh; all life seemed dissolved into a dim tremor and rustling of blood'' (73). (See Blissett, "George Moore,'' 55.) Markings in *Evelyn Innes* are noted in Gillespie and Stocker, no. 330.

30 *Daniel Defoe*, 21. David Hayman suggests that Joyce may have seen Isolde in his daughter and that Lucia's strong taste for *Tristan* may have encouraged Joyce to make use of the legend in the *Wake*. See "Shadow of His Mind: The Papers of Lucia Joyce,'' in Oliphant and Zigal, 76–7.

31 DiGaetani has written that ''A Painful Case'' makes "a pattern of references'' to *Tristan*, though he draws this conclusion on the slim evidence provided by the setting of the story in Chapelizod ("Chapel of Isolde,'' Isolde's legendary Irish home) and by the presence of the theme of adultery (*Wagner and the Novel*, 135–6). MacNicholas, in "Joyce contra Wagner'' (34–9), and Stoddard Martin (148–9) discuss the presence of *Tristan* in *Exiles*.

32 Joyce, who mulled the possibility of quasi-homosexual attraction between Richard and Robert (*E* 123), may have seen a similar relation between Tristan and Melot. See Gutman's discussion of sexual jealousy as the motivation for Melot's betrayal and killing of Tristan (247–53).

33 The allusion is even clearer in the German translation: "Gehörten Sie mir in dieser heiligen Liebesnacht?'' (Joyce, *Verbannte*, 143). Interestingly, a similar ambiguity – about whether the adulterous love has been consummated – attends Wagner's opera.

34 "Tristan and Isolde in the *Wake*,'' 97, III n. 22.

35 Hayman calls the ending of *Exiles* "a (symbolic) death-in-love'' ("Tristan and Isolde in the *Wake*,'' 98). That Richard is both Mark and Tristan may be explained, as Hayman suggests, by Joyce's notes in *Scribbledehobble* that "Mark & Trist change characters'' and that "Rich & Rob change'' (79). See Hayman, "Tristan and Isolde in the *Wake*,'' 97.

This paragraph on *Exiles* echoes a few points made in my "Wagner's *Tannhäuser* in *Exiles*.''

36 The following touch on the presence of *Tristan* in the *Wake*: Zuckerman, 187–8; Blissett, "Joyce in the Smithy,'' 129–31; DiGaetani, *Wagner and the Novel*, 151–3; and Stoddard Martin, 151–2. Two articles by Hayman have had considerable influence on my discussion of the subject: "Tristan and Isolde in the *Wake*''; and "Nodality.''

37 Shari Benstock discusses the older man – younger woman motif in

"The Genuine Christine: Psychodynamics of Issy," in Henke and
Unkeless, 179–82.

38 In 1926, offering Harriet Shaw Weaver assistance with *Work in
Progress*, Joyce wrote, "I shall send you Bédier's *Tristan et Iseult*
as this too you ought to read" (*L* 1:241). Combining this information
with textual evidence, Adaline Glasheen has concluded that Bédier,
not Wagner, is the important source for Tristan and Isolde in the
Wake (*Third Census*, lvi–lvii, 289). Joyce's intimacy with the opera,
however, antedates his knowledge of Bédier, and compared to one
of the most resonant achievements in nineteenth-century culture,
Bédier's book is minor. It seems fairer to say that after Wagner had
sparked Joyce's interest, Bédier provided minutiae that were un-
available in the more concentrated and thematically richer operatic
version of the legend. Bédier's book, in fact, written shortly after
the peak of French Wagnerism in the nineties, was itself at least
partially the product of Wagner's influence. Indeed, Bédier once
confessed that he had been unsuccessful in keeping Wagnerian
impurities out of a reconstruction intended to be authentically
medieval (Lot, 10). Hayman's analysis of Joyce's notes on Tristan
and Isolde in *Scribbledehobble* suggests that Joyce's prior knowledge
of Wagner conditioned his reading and use of Bédier: "in spite of
the wealth of detail available to him [in Bédier], [Joyce] drew
upon Bédier mainly for those aspects which fit his preconception
of the tale; that is, the outline traced by Wagner and applied by
Joyce to *Exiles*" ("Tristan and Isolde in the *Wake*," 101). Significantly, the references to the legend in *Exiles* (123) and *Ulysses* (12.192,
12.1455; 297, 332) use the German rather than the French spellings,
and Tristan's adoption of the pseudonym "Tantris," which Wagner
took from Gottfried and which, as we have seen, Joyce associated
with Bruno's "coincidence of contraries," is not mentioned in
Bédier. There can be no doubt that Wagner's *Tristan* was of seminal
importance to the *Wake*. It might be argued, in fact, that Wagner
is a more important *source* for the *Wake* than is Bédier partly
because *Tristan* is a more important *work* than is Bédier's book.

39 See Hayman, *First Draft*, 208–19; also *JJ* 794.

40 See Hayman, "Nodality," 143.

41 Wagner originally used the term *Liebestod* as a name for the opera's
prelude. Isolde's final aria, now generally known as "the *Liebestod*,"
he called *Verklärung*, or "transfiguration." "*Liebestod*" now describes
the opera's general theme of "love–death" as well as Isolde's aria.
See Zuckerman, 34.

42 It may be, as Hayman has suggested, that Joyce placed this material
in the last chapter of book II as "an interpretation of a particular

historical instant: decadence'' ("Tristan and Isolde in the *Wake*," 100).

43 See Glasheen, "Girls from Boston."

44 *Joyce's* Ulysses, 146. Quoting from the *Liebesnacht* of act 2 (*TI* 74), Gilbert writes of *Tristan* as follows: "in the fluttering of the veil there is a presage of the *sehnend verlangter Liebestod*" (146n).

45 On the source for this passage in Bédier, see Hayman, "Nodality," 145–6. For the identification of the acrostic, see McHugh, *Annotations*, 571. On Issy as writer and critic, see Scott, 192–5.

46 I owe this inference to Tindall, *Reader's Guide to the* Wake, 181.

47 See Hodgart, *Student's Guide*, 187.

48 *Student's Guide*, 187.

49 Quoted in Dahlhaus, 145.

50 In Hans Jürgen Syberberg's 1983 film *Parsifal*, the title role is divided between a young man and a young woman.

51 In his 1907 lecture on Mangan in Trieste, Joyce retained this allusion to Parsifal's question, altering it slightly (*CW* 179).

52 Blissett associates the "Kisses" with the Flowermaidens in "Joyce in the Smithy," 123.

53 Nietzsche, who thought in *Nietzsche contra Wagner* that the "preaching of chastity" in *Parsifal* "remains an incitement to unnaturalness" (73), wondered about an inconsistency in Wagner's oeuvre: "And now here is a fact which leaves us speechless: Parsifal is Lohengrin's father! How ever did he do it? Ought one at this juncture to remember that 'chastity works miracles'?" (*Case of Wagner*, 29).

54 Apparently Wagner at one point considered writing Parsifal into act 3 of *Tristan* and creating a Shem and Shaun-like encounter between his "renouncing one" and his "longing one." See Zuckerman, 25; and Dahlhaus, 145.

55 Rieff, 184, 182–3.

56 Rieff, 184.

5 THE COMIC RHYTHM

1 Mann, "Joseph Novels," 93.

2 Vickery, *Literary Impact*, 326–423; Atherton, 191–200, 218–23.

3 Hart, *Structure and Motif*, 47–77.

4 See Levin, *James Joyce*, 204–5; and Hart, *Structure and Motif*, 49.

5 Joyce encountered Ibsen's poem "To the Poet H.O. Blom" in a translation by C.H. Herford for Yeats's short-lived magazine *Beltaine*. (See Curran, 116–19.) Because Ibsen's original, containing many allusions to Norse mythology, was written in 1859, the Wagnerian tone and diction that Joyce preserved in his discussion of Mangan must have been originally Herford's.

6 The translation is McHugh's, in *Annotations*, 281.

7 Weston, *Legends of the Wagner Drama*, 9–151.

8 Joyce's phrase, quoted in Atherton, 51.

9 Atherton's discussion of these "structural books" comprises pages 25–55.

10 My understanding of the *Ring* is indebted to the following sources in particular: Shaw, *Perfect Wagnerite*; Gutman, 155–60, 287–300; Cooke, *Introduction*; Raphael, 37–54; Dahlhaus, 80–141; and Michael Tanner, "The Total Work of Art," in Burbidge and Sutton, 153–78. The term "golden age" is borrowed from Shaw.

11 *Pro and contra Wagner*, 185. Beardsley's *Under the Hill*, which Joyce gave Lucia to read in 1932, may have helped call Joyce's attention to the beginning of *Rheingold*. Beardsley's protagonist Fanfreluche, turning the opera's pages "with a loving hand," is "ravished with the beauty and wit of the opening scene," and one of Beardsley's illustrations depicts it. See *Under the Hill*, 32–3.

12 In characterizing the Misses Douce and Kennedy, whom Simon Dedalus chastises gallantly for "tempting poor simple males" (*U* 11.202; 261), Joyce borrows the Sirens' Wagnerian descendants to develop the link between woman, water, and music that he found so attractive in the *Dutchman*. The first hint of *Rheingold* in "Sirens" occurs in its "overture": "Low in dark middle earth. Embedded ore" (11.42; 257). Later in the chapter, the allusive pattern becomes clearer in an evocation of the opera's first bars of music:

But wait. But hear. Chords dark. Lugugugubrious. Low. In a cave of the dark middle earth. Embedded ore. Lumpmusic.

The voice of dark age, of unlove, earth's fatigue made grave approach. (11.1005–7; 283)

The "dark," "lugubrious" chords in the first scene of *Rheingold* anticipate the appearance of Alberich, "the voice ... of unlove," who, after he is spurned by the Rhinedaughters, pronounces the unthinkable curse against love and wrests the "embedded ore" from the riverbed. Lest these Wagnerian sirens be overshadowed by those of the *Odyssey*, Joyce frequently describes his barmaids as if they were submerged, as in "By bronze, by gold, in oceangreen of shadow" (11.49; 257), to cite just one example. At one point Misses Douce and Kennedy ridicule an unattractive suitor in the person of a lecherous druggist: "O greasy eyes! Imagine being married to a man like that ... With his bit of beard!" (11.169–70; 260). Flosshilde's mocking description of Alberich's charms is strikingly similar: "Deinen stechenden Blick, / deinen struppigen Bart" ("Your piercing look, your bristly beard") (*R* 10, my translation). (In their brief discussions of "Sirens" and *Das Rheingold*, DiGaetani [*Wagner and the Novel*, 146–7] and Furness [125] cite this allusion to the libretto of *Rheingold*, taking it, I think incorrectly, as referring to Bloom rather than to the druggist in Boyd's. But Alberich, as a man who has renounced love, does make a good parallel for the sexually frustrated Bloom.) In the chapter of *Ulysses* intended to bring "musical" expression to literature, it is not surprising that Joyce should have turned to the composer of the *Gesamtkunstwerk*.

13 Cooke, *Introduction*, 7–10 (record insert).

14 Cooke, *Introduction*, 19.

15 Cooke argues persuasively that the similarity between two of the opera's most important leitmotifs, those associated, respectively, with Alberich and Wotan (the "Ring" and "Valhalla" motifs), emphasizes "the near-identity of the ultimate aims of Alberich and Wotan – absolute power in each case" (*Introduction*, 15).

16 Wagner, *Letters to Roeckel*, 96.

17 Many of the *Ring*'s commentators have wondered why, with Brünnhilde returning the ring to the Rhine in act 3 of *Götterdämmerung*, the Twilight of the Gods nonetheless follows. Wagner's explanation to August Roeckel in 1854 was that Wotan "deliberately makes his own destruction part of the conditions on which must depend the annulling of the original mischief." The gods die because Wotan, who recognizes his corruptibility and sees the possibility of redemption in submitting to the "multiplicity, the eternal renewing of reality and of life," has *willed* that they should (*Letters to Roeckel*, 97–8). Later, Wagner thought the work's contradictions reflected his developing philosophy over the many years of its composition: the *Ring* had first taken shape when "I had built up an optimistic world, on Hellenic principles ... [But] I was scarcely aware that ... I was being unconsciously guided by a wholly different, infinitely more profound intuition, and that instead of conceiving a phase in the development of the world, I had ... realized its nothingness" (*Letters to Roeckel*, 149–50).

Nietzsche wrote that the optimistic, revolutionary spirit of the *Ring* in its earliest stages had "run aground" in 1854 on Schopenhauer's philosophy of pessimism and renunciation, and that Wagner's "escape" was to claim "the reef on which he had been wrecked ... as the actual purpose of his journey" (*Case of Wagner*, 10–11).

18 See Frazer 5:46–8.

19 See Roland McHugh, *Sigla*, 16–17. Shaw's description of Wotan in *The Perfect Wagnerite* is as follows: "In the blue cloak of the wanderer, wearing the broad hat that flaps over the socket of his forfeited eye, he appears in Hunding's house, the middle pillar of

which is a mighty tree'' (35). In Joyce's copy, evidently used for English lessons, the word "forfeited" is underscored, as are many words elsewhere in Shaw's discussion. See Gillespie and Stocker, no. 448.

20 Wotan is called "Allfather" in Golther (65), a copy of which Joyce owned. See Gillespie and Stocker, no. 194.

21 Atherton, 30–1, 53.

22 Glasheen, *Third Census*, lxv.

23 Joyce links Yggdrasill and Wagner in "Drama and Life" (*CW* 45).

24 See McHugh, *Sigla*, 54; and Weston, *Legends of the Wagner Drama*, 67. Elsewhere in the *Wake*, the Masterbuilder HCE is a "maximost bridgesmaker" (126.10–11) and "pontiff" (198.12), and rainbow bridges appear frequently in connection with his seven rainbow girls. HCE's crime, for example, is "supposedly in connection with a girls, Myramy Huey or Colores Archer, under Flaggy Bridge" (63.12–13).

25 Hodgart identifies this allusion in *Student's Guide*, 181.

26 Other allusions to Valhalla in the *Wake* are less closely connected with the idea of original sin. They simply evoke the abode to which, in Germanic mythology, the Valkyries deliver Wotan's chosen heroes after they fall in battle. These references include, among many others, "heroes in Warhorror" (91.29–30), "waulholler, me alma marthyrs" (348.10–11), and "Sweatenburgs Welhell" (552.16). The appendix offers a more extensive listing.

27 *Letters to Roeckel*, 97.

28 Shaw, *Perfect Wagnerite*, 60.

29 Blissett makes this point in "Joyce in the Smithy," 131–2.

30 Weston, *Legends of the Wagner Drama*, 103. See also *From Ritual to Romance*, 130.

31 "O Siegfried! Siegfried! Blessed hero! You waker of life, conquering light!" (my translation).

32 Weston, *Legends of the Wagner Drama*, 106–7. Thomas Mann brought the same reading to the end of the *Ring*: "it is the sun-hero himself who lies upon the bier, slain by the pallid forces of darkness" (*Pro and contra Wagner*, 100).

33 In *Student's Guide*, 160.

34 Siegfried and Gunther's bloodoath, which appears in "Circe" (*U* 15.3649–53; 560), crops up twice, as we saw in chapter 3, in the "Norwegian Captain" section of II.3: at 323.4 and 325.25–6.

35 Dahlhaus, 114.

36 "[A]s most halls would," wrote Shaw, "were a cremation attempted in the middle of the floor" (*Perfect Wagnerite*, 82). Actually, Wagner's stage directions call for the erection of the funeral pyre "before the hall, near the bank of the Rhine" (*R* 325).

37 I owe the identification of this allusion to Hodgart, *Student's Guide*, 160.
38 "Only when Siegfried dies I responded from the crown of my head to his cry 'O sposa sacra'" (*L* 2:214).
39 On Parnell, see McHugh, *Sigla*, 90.
40 See Hart, *Structure and Motif*, 51–2.
41 Throughout the *Wake* the Valkyries act as harbingers or agents of death and correspond, in their multiplicity, to the twenty-eight leap-year girls, the "valkyrienne" (220.5–6) form of Issy. (Weston writes that in Northern mythology the Valkyries "seem to be simply a multiplication of the goddess Freyja" [*Legends of the Wagner Drama*, 85].) In book II.3, which, at one point, reenacts the Napoleonic and Crimean Wars, the guests at HCE's inn compare their departure at closing time to the removal of dead heroes from the fields of Waterloo and Sevastopol: "There goes the blackwatchwomen, all in white, flaxed up, purgad! ... We're been carried away. Beyond bournes and bowers" (379.33–5). In I.3 the narrator describes the prankquean, who is said to have kidnapped the Earl of Howth's son, as "true dotter of a dearmud" (a hint of "*Götterdämmerung*"?) "with so valkirry a licence as sent many a poor pucker packing to perdition" (68.13–16). In the well-known "Mookse and the Gripes" section of I.6, the sanctimonious Mookse and the humble Gripes compare their chances for salvation in a passage that, as we saw in chapter 4, also draws on Elisabeth of *Tannhäuser*:

—Us shall be chosen as the first of the last by the electress of Vale Hollow, obselved the Mookse nobily ...
—Wee, comfused the Gripes limply, shall not even be the last of the first, wee hope, when oust are visitated by the Veiled Horror. (156.24–33)

The phrase "electress of Vale Hollow," with its allusion to Valhalla, makes the mythic Valkyrie an allegorical figure of Death, a "Veiled Horror."
42 Weston, *Legends of the Wagner Drama*, 106.
43 Shaw, *Perfect Wagnerite*, 60.
44 Michael Tanner, "The Total Work of Art," in Burbidge and Sutton, 172–3; Dahlhaus, 140–1; and Cooke, *Introduction*, 37.
45 See *New Grove Dictionary* 20:131–2.
46 Levin, *James Joyce*, 200. Stephen's attack on the chandelier in "Circe," whether or not it marks a *ricorso* in his personal sphere, produces the "ruin of all *space* [not *time*], shattered glass and toppling masonry" (*U* 15.4245; 583, my emphasis). See Epstein, 166–7; and Sultan, *Modernism*, 36–7.
47 A similar example of cyclic form may be found in *Lohengrin*, the first and last scenes of which take place on the banks of the Scheldt, near Antwerp.

48 Budgen, 183, 52.
49 Weston, *Legends of the Wagner Drama*, 141–2.
50 Weston, *Legends of the Wagner Drama*, 196.
51 Eliot, *Collected Poems*, 61.
52 Frazer 5:3.
53 After he has murdered Siegfried, Hagen reports to Gutrune in *Götterdämmerung* 3.3 that Siegfried has been killed by a wild boar (*R* 322).
54 Atherton, 27.
55 Wagner, *My Life*, 499. This account of the Prelude's inspiration, however, was almost certainly romanticized. See Gregor-Dellin, 248–9.
56 Langer, 331.
57 Harold H. Watts, "Myth and Drama," in Vickery, *Myth and Literature*, 79.
58 Watts, "Myth and Drama," in Vickery, *Myth and Literature*, 81.
59 Watts, "Myth and Drama," in Vickery, *Myth and Literature*, 77.
60 Langer, 363. See also Sypher, 220.
61 See, for example, Blissett, "Joyce in the Smithy," 121.
62 DiGaetani, in *Penetrating Wagner's Ring*, sees the comic substructure in the *Ring* as well: "The sun god is dead, but the radiant sun endures, implying that finally the Ring is a comedy about the power of light" (35).
63 A crucial distinction between Wagner and Joyce – that the four operas depict just one full "cycle," whereas the four books of the *Wake* give us endless cycles – is taken up in chapter 7.

6 THE ART OF ARTS

1 Sometime after this paragraph was substantially written, I came across Denis Donoghue's essay "The European Joyce," which focuses on the same passage from *A Portrait* and draws one or two similar points from it.
2 Joyce, *Daniel Defoe*, 17.
3 Power, 74, 73–4, 106.
4 See Scher, "Literature and Music," 230.
5 On music as a Symbolist ideal, see Balakian, 101; Dujardin, *Le Monologue intérieur*, 225; Lehmann, 149–75; Lockspeiser, 161; and Wilson, *Axel's Castle*, 19–21.
6 Pater, 139.
7 This quotation is a summary of Wyzewa by Lehmann, 200.
8 Symons, *Symbolist Movement*, 69.
9 See Scher, "Literature and Music," 227–8.

10 *Axel's Castle*, 19.

11 In *Howards End* Margaret Schlegel has some fun with this subject at the expense of her ninetyish sister Helen: "Now, doesn't it seem absurd to you? What *is* the good of the arts if they're interchangeable? What *is* the good of the ear if it tells you the same as the eye? Helen's one aim is to translate tunes into the language of painting, and pictures into the language of music... Now, this very symphony [Beethoven's Fifth] we've just been having – she won't let it alone. She labels it with meaning from start to finish; turns it into literature. I wonder if the day will ever return when music will be treated as music" (39).

12 *Revue wagnérienne* 2:164 (my translation).

13 See Huxley, 349–50:

> The musicalization of fiction. Not in the symbolist way, by subordinating sense to sound ... But on a large scale, in the construction. Meditate on Beethoven. The changes of moods, the abrupt transitions ... A theme is stated, then developed, pushed out of shape, imperceptibly deformed, until, though still recognizably the same, it has become quite different ... The whole range of thought and feeling ... Get this into a novel. How? The abrupt transitions are easy enough. All you need is a sufficiency of characters and parallel, contrapuntal plots.

14 On *Tonio Kröger*, see Calvin Brown, *Music and Literature*, 212–17.

15 D'Annunzio, trans. Adams, in "Operatic Novel," 263–4.

16 *Aspects of the Novel*, 168.

17 See Donoghue, 95.

18 From Preface to *Il trionfo della morte*, trans. Adams, in "Operatic Novel," 263.

19 Just as Symons argued that the ideal poem should be "visible music," Henry James would invoke another art form – by some standards a non-representational art in its own right – to assert the artistic integrity of *The Portrait of a Lady*: "a structure reared with an 'architectural' competence" (*Art of the Novel*, 52).

Ironically, to the novelist and the composer of opera, both conscious of the historical "inferiority" of genres regarded as entertainment rather than art, the formalism of music would have contrasting value. In his preface to *The Nigger of the "Narcissus,"* Conrad would argue that fiction "must strenuously aspire to the plasticity of sculpture, the colour of painting, and to the magic suggestiveness of music – which is the art of arts" (20). Wagner, on the other hand, taking the formal or "exceptional" quality of music as a starting point, worked in exactly the opposite direction. According to Dahlhaus, "The central maxim of Wagner's aesthetic theory is that music, musical form, if it is to communicate something, needs ... a reason for its existence. (The idea of 'absolute' music, conveying nothing beyond itself, was something he could not countenance)'' (115). For Wagner, drama, not music, was queen of the arts.

20 See Abrams, 50–1.

21 Shaw, *Perfect Wagnerite*, 117.

22 Shaw regarded this distinction as the philosopher's "great contribution to modern thought." (See *Perfect Wagnerite*, 97.) A discussion of Schopenhauer in Wagner's *Letters to Roeckel* takes up the same duality (146–53).

23 Pater, 137–8.

24 Symons, *Symbolist Movement*, 5.

25 Lindenberger writes that Wagner's "extensive participation in all aspects of the production of his own works, an activity unprecedented among composers, served to destroy the traditional hegemony of the singer in favor of an integrated dramatic whole" (61).

26 Mallarmé, "Revery of a French Poet," 74, 73.

27 Symons, *Symbolist Movement*, 62.

28 There is nothing exclusively Wagnerian about the idea of a *Gesamtkunstwerk*, as the composer freely acknowledged in identifying the combination of arts in Greek drama as his "standard" – a standard, in fact, that composers of opera before and since Wagner's time have often invoked. (See Lindenberger, 97–100.) Nor, indeed, is the term itself Wagner's own. It was characteristic of the Wagnerites, however, to fix upon "Wagnerian" terminology as a substitute, in some cases, for musical understanding, even when, in the case of "*Gesamtkunstwerk*," Wagner had used the phrase just once or twice, and then only in passing and unselfconsciously. (See Gregor-Dellin, 214–15.) Three further examples of "Wagnerian" terminology with which the composer had quite little to do may be discovered in "music drama," "music of the future," and even "leitmotif." Possibly the idea of a *Gesamtkunstwerk* became attached so strongly to Wagner because of his historically unique position as a "*Gesamtkünstler*," responsible for all the elements in his work.

To appreciate the influence that Wagner's "total art" exercized upon his literary admirers, we need not accept the composer's contention that the arts are incomplete and "degenerate" in isolation, nor must we credit, as many of his followers did, his "total art" with amounting to more than individual arts as practiced, for example, by Beethoven, Goethe, or Renoir. Mann's "Sorrows and Grandeur of Richard Wagner," in fact, asserting that art is "entire and perfect in all of its manifestations," identified "a wild, illegitimate quality about the constituent parts [of Wagner's operas], even about the music itself ... that disappears only when the parts are united in the sublime whole.'' Wagner's greatness, according to Mann, resides only in the totality that the parts create; and the case of Wagner represents – in a formulation that would earn Mann a good deal of enmity among more orthodox Wagnerites – ''dilettantism raised to the level of genius'' (*Pro and contra Wagner*, 100 – 8).

29 Symons, *Plays, Acting, Music*, 311; Mann, *Pro and contra Wagner*, 190 – 1.

30 Moore, *Confessions of a Young Man*, 158. Blissett's ''George Moore'' drew my attention to this passage (59).

31 Dujardin, *Les Lauriers*, 258 (my translation).

32 Dahlhaus, discussing Kundry's paradoxical desire for absolution in Parsifal's arms, credits Wagner's music with special expressivity: ''Once leitmotive[s] have been ... clearly expounded they are musical metaphors, and by their blending, mingling or allusion to each other they make it possible to express divided feelings or ambiguities which are otherwise beyond the scope of music'' (153).

33 An oft-cited example occurs in *Siegfried* 1.3, where Mime, in an attempt to save his neck, tries vainly to teach the young hero the meaning of fear. During Mime's narration, the orchestra sounds the motif of the sleeping Brünnhilde, from whom Siegfried eventually *will* learn the meaning of fear in the opera's final scene. See Mann, *Pro and contra Wagner*, 190 – 1; and, for a more critical discussion, see Ernest Newman, ''The Ring of the Nibelung,'' in DiGaetani, *Penetrating Wagner's Ring*, 179. On the rhetoric of leitmotifs, see the *New Grove Dictionary* 20:131 – 2.

34 Dahlhaus, 47 – 8.

35 Kerman, 206 – 7.

36 Kerman, 205. Kerman writes, ''As purely musical forms, Wagner's operas succeed as well as any romantic symphonic poems of their length might be expected to succeed; which is to say, not too well'' (207).

37 Wagner did not invent this particular use of musical motives, as he acknowledged in *A Communication to My Friends* (*PW* 1:370 – 1); neither, in fact, did he use the term ''leitmotif.'' Precedents for the allusive use of musical phrases may be found in Mozart, Gluck, Schumann, Weber, and Berlioz, among many others. (See Gutman, 362 – 3.) It is generally conceded, however, that such an extensive, varied, and systematic use of these motives was unprecedented in opera – ''a qualitative leap in the history of leitmotif technique'' (*New Grove Dictionary* 20:132). Certainly whatever impact the leitmotif has had upon literature is directly attributable to Wagner's influence.

38 Quoted in Baudelaire, 217–18.

39 On the allusive character of Wagner's leitmotifs, see Friedman, 130. Generally, of course, the allusions would be "intra-textual," but Wagner's canon shows at least one example of an allusion carried from one opera to another: the famous "Sehnsucht" motif from *Tristan*, which the orchestra of *Meistersinger* quotes in act 3.

40 "[I]n the music dramas Wagner is an epic writer: he does not allow the *dramatis personae* to become independent, but continually interrupts them with his own comments and asides ... The choice of subject, the musical technique, and the Romantic principle of expression act together to create ... a musical epic, in which the narrator, commenting on the events and reflecting the emotions, is really the principal character" (*New Grove Dictionary* 20:118). In 1871 Wagner told Cosima that Siegfried's funeral music was "a Greek chorus ... a chorus that will be sung, as it were, by the orchestra after Siegfried's death and during the scene change; the Siegmund theme will ring out, as if the chorus were saying, 'He was his father'; then the sword motif, and finally his own theme ... How could words ever convey the impression these solemn themes will evoke in their new form?" (quoted in Gregor-Dellin, 403).

41 Mann, *Pro and contra Wagner*, 25–6, 108.

42 See Gals, 183; and Katz, 194–247.

43 Holloway, pt. 3, 33–4.

44 Calvin Brown, in fact, describes the leitmotif as originally a literary device adopted by music (*Music and Literature*, 93–9). In *Degeneration* the grumpy Max Nordau attacked Wagner's leitmotifs on precisely their "literary" nature: "To express ideas is not the function of music; language provides for that as completely as could be desired" (199). The leitmotif, he complained, conceding, apparently, Wagner's achievement, "transforms music into dry speech" (197). Scher describes the leitmotif as "a rare instance of genuinely reciprocal impact of music and literature" ("Literature and Music," 233).

45 For my knowledge of the literary leitmotif and its tradition I am indebted to Calvin Brown, *Music and Literature*, 208–18; Friedman, 14–16, 128–31; and Hart, *Structure and Motif*, 161–81.

46 See Calvin Brown, *Music and Literature*, 211–12.

47 Quoted in Egri, 77 (my translation).

48 Dujardin, *Les Lauriers*, 227 (my translation).

49 Forster, *Aspects of the Novel*, 164–9.

50 Joyce's copy of *The Art-Work of the Future*, in fact, shows underlinings in ink and blue pencil in passages where Wagner discusses a synthesis of arts in works of the past and future. Italics in the

following excerpts represent these markings: "man has *not only one Sense* but separate Senses"; "Only *the Art* which answers *to this 'all-faculty'* of man is, therefore, free"; "This is the genuine Egoism, in which each isolated art-variety would give *itself the airs of universal Art*"; "The Grecian Lyric art-work shows us ... how, in *lively joy of fecund interaction*, the individuality of each several art was able thus to lift itself to its most perfect fill" (*PW* 1:97, 97, 99, 108). (To avoid confusion I have not indicated Wagner's own italics in these quotations.) See Gillespie and Stocker, no. 531.

51 See Zuckerman, 12, 192 n. 37.

52 Among critics who have described Joyce's prose in terms of the leitmotif are Blissett, "Joyce in the Smithy," 115–21; Bowen, *Musical Allusions*, 51–3; DiGaetani, *Wagner and the Novel*, 134; Gilbert, *L* 1:31, and *Joyce's* Ulysses, 242–3; Gross, 76; Levin, *James Joyce*, 89, 97, 191; Hodgart, "Shakespeare and 'Finnegans Wake,'" 738, and *Student's Guide*, 4–5, 99; Howarth, *Irish Writers*, 283; Atherton, 50; Litz, *Art of Joyce*, 64–70, and *James Joyce*, 108–9; Hart, *Structure and Motif*, 161–81; Egri, 37, 76–7; and Zuckerman, 186–7.

53 My definition of the literary leitmotif is closest to those of Calvin Brown (*Music and Literature*, 211) and Hart (*Structure and Motif*, 164–7).

54 *Joyce's* Ulysses, 253.

55 Though Joyce's conscious adaptation of the leitmotif probably begins with *Ulysses, A Portrait* shows a use of words, phrases, and images that anticipates the use of the leitmotif in his later work. Lee Lemon has suggested that Joyce's use of certain repeated motifs in *A Portrait*, like hands and eyes, is historically unique. Lemon finds *A Portrait* "the first novel in which motifs *per se* are of primary importance, the first novel in which both theme and structure depend upon such minor elements." Lemon distinguishes between a "symbol," the meaning of which is established by literary convention, and a "motif," the meaning of which depends upon its contexts within a particular work. Wagner's leitmotifs operate exactly as Lemon's "motifs" do: indefinite in meaning when first heard, they gradually define themselves as the drama progresses, developing in accordance with the contexts in which they appear. Certainly the idea that the work of art could create its own language would have been attractive to formalist writers in the late nineteenth and early twentieth centuries arguing for the "autonomy" of their work. See Lemon, especially 42.

56 This second "agenbite of inwit" is a casualty of the 1984 *Ulysses*. Editor Hans Gabler, Fritz Senn explains, determined that a compositor had inserted the phrase in the wrong place and that Joyce did not notice the error in subsequent proofreadings. (See "*Ulysses*

between Corruption and Correction,'' in Sandulescu and Hart, 191–2.) David Hayman, however, arguing that ''there are reasons to think that Joyce found the error a fortunate one,'' suggests that Gabler should have let the ''intrusion'' stand. (See ''Balancing the Book, or Pro and contra the Gabler *Ulysses*,'' in Sandulescu and Hart, 79–80.)

57 Friedman cites ''agenbite of inwit'' as an example of a leitmotif but does not discuss it in detail (231–2). Steppe and Gabler's *Handlist* and Hanley's *Word Index* have helped me locate repetitions of leitmotifs in *Ulysses*.

58 Cooke, *Introduction*, 12, 15.

59 Gilbert, *Joyce's* Ulysses, 33–41, 138.

60 Hart, *Structure and Motif*, 161. Hart's chapter on ''Leitmotif'' (161–81) and his ''Index of Motifs in *Finnegans Wake*'' (211–47) have been of immense help to my discussion of the leitmotif in the *Wake*.

61 See Heller, 126.

62 Hart, *Structure and Motif*, 236.

63 Hart, *Structure and Motif*, 174–5, 213–15.

64 Gilbert, in *L* 1:29; Larbaud, quoted in Dujardin, *Les Lauriers*, 229.

65 Friedman finds an analogy to changes in musical orchestration ''when each chapter appears to make a fresh start and may be distinguished, technically, from each of the others'' (125–6).

66 On sonata form, see Boyle; regarding *fuga per canonem*, see Gilbert, *Joyce's* Ulysses, 252–3; on ''Sirens'' as corresponding to an overture and opera (Flotow's *Martha*), see Sultan, *Argument of* Ulysses, 220–2.

67 Hodgart, *Student's Guide*, 99. Joyce, as we have seen, is reported to have asked Ottocaro Weiss during a performance of *Die Walküre*, ''Don't you find the musical effects of my *Sirens* better than Wagner's?'' (*JJ* 460), implying that he felt the works were comparable. This association between Wagner and ''Sirens,'' Joyce's most celebrated effort to blend music and literature, suggests that Joyce had Wagner's synthesis of arts in mind when he wrote this section of *Ulysses*.

68 The quotation is from Gilbert, *Joyce's* Ulysses, 253. On the contrapuntal qualities of Joyce's prose, see also Levin, *James Joyce*, 189–90; Friedman, 131–3; and Litz, *Art of Joyce*, 62–75, and *James Joyce*, 108–9.

69 For a skeptical view of the potential role of music in literature, see Wellek and Warren, 126–7.

70 Symons, *Plays, Acting, Music*, 277.

71 See especially Julia Kristeva's influential *Revolution in Poetic Language*.

72 Beckett, ''Dante, Bruno, Vico, Joyce,'' in *Our Exagmination*, 14.

7 JOYCE AND WAGNER

1 See Bishop's discussion of Joyce's reaction to Freud (15–18, 393 n. 34).

2 In Potts, 64.

3 Stanislaus writes that his brother "had kept the reference to 'the Nolan' advisedly," intending "that the readers of his article should have at first a false impression that he was quoting some little-known Irish writer … so that when they discovered their error, the name of Giordano Bruno might perhaps awaken some interest in his life and work. Laymen, he repeated, should be encouraged to think" (*My Brother's Keeper*, 146).

4 See *My Brother's Keeper*, 94.

5 In Potts, 71.

6 "Universal Literary Influence of the Renaissance," in Berrone, 21–2; *Daniel Defoe*, 22.

7 Bloom, *Yeats*, 3.

8 Bloom, *Anxiety of Influence*, 5.

9 *Anxiety of Influence*, 5.

10 Bate, 21–2.

11 I have amended Ellmann's slight mistranslation of the full title of the *Ring*.

12 Gilbert, *Joyce's* Ulysses, 346; Hart, *Structure and Motif*, 68. Not coincidentally, Mary Ellen Bute's film *Passages from* Finnegans Wake borrows music from *Tristan* for its sound track. Zack Bowen, one of the film's music consultants, told me in Milwaukee in 1987 that the continuous melody of *Tristan* seemed to provide ideal "accompaniment" for Joyce's flowing text.

13 Quoted in Mann, *Pro and contra Wagner*, 92–3.

14 This anecdote is reported by Howarth, in *Irish Writers*, 274.

15 D'Annunzio, 120.

16 *Symbolist Movement*, 62.

17 In "Scylla and Charybdis" Eglinton and Russell enjoy a smile at Stephen's expense: "Have you found those six brave medicals, John Eglinton asked with elder's gall, to write *Paradise Lost* at your dictation?" Stephen reflects, "He holds my follies hostage" (*U* 9.18–35; 184).

18 Wordsworth, 345. Litz directed my attention to this passage. See "*Ulysses* and Its Audience," 221.

19 Quoted in Large and Weber, 41.

20 The *New Grove Dictionary*, which discusses Wagner's "rigorous artistic morality," first drew my attention to this passage (20:115).

21 Reported in Percy Scholes (1:273).

22 Power, 54.

23 Quoted in Blissett, "Joyce in the Smithy," 134.

24 Mann's epithet for Wagner, in *Pro and contra Wagner*, 197. Litz applies the same term to Joyce, in *James Joyce*, 112.

25 On the compulsion of some modern artists to outstrip even themselves, see Levin, "What was Modernism?", 274–6.

26 Ezra Pound, in *Pound/Joyce*, 157.

27 See Michael Tanner, "The Total Work of Art," in Burbidge and Sutton, 214–16. Nietzsche's remark appears in *Nietzsche contra Wagner*, 73.

28 On *Tristan* see Kerman, 194–7; on *Parsifal* see Dahlhaus, 143.

29 Quoted in Barzun, 273.

30 This, according to Atherton (15–16), might be the point of Beckett's remark that the *Wake* is not "about something" but "is that something itself." (See chapter 6, n. 72.) For an excellent discussion of the secular use of religious ideas and terminology at the turn of the century, see Ellmann, "Two Faces of Edward," in *Edwardians and Late Victorians*, 188–210.

31 *Letters to Roeckel*, 85, 98–9.

32 Vicki Mahaffey has suggested in a similar context that in Joyce's later works " 'revolution' takes on a primary meaning of 'return.' A revolutionary, then, becomes a returning wanderer." See "Wagner, Joyce and Revolution," 245.

33 *Letters to Roeckel*, 82.

34 See Dahlhaus, 122.

35 *Pro and contra Wagner*, 96.

36 The phrase is Schorske's (225). See also Fergusson, 94.

37 Power, 74.

38 See Richard Brown, *Joyce and Sexuality*, 10–11; and Michael Tanner, "The Total Work of Art," in Burbidge and Sutton, 223.

39 See Spender, "Moderns and Contemporaries," in Howe, 43–9.

40 In *Essays and Introductions*, 187.

41 Power, 74.

42 See Ellmann, *Consciousness*, 69.

43 Trilling, "On the Modern Element in Modern Literature," in Howe, 60.

44 *Pro and contra Wagner*, 91–3. Zuckerman makes similar use of this passage from Mann (145). Mann's point is echoed in the *New Grove Dictionary* 20:117–18.

45 Levin, *James Joyce*, 184–5; Wilson, *Axel's Castle*, 202–8; Hart, *Structure and Motif*.

46 *Case of Wagner*, 19–22. In *Joyce and Prose*, John Porter Houston places Joyce's varied prose in the context of a "nineteenth-century French

technical definition of decadent style as one whose elements are excessively heterogeneous'' (169).

47 *Case of Wagner*, xxxi.
48 *Anxiety of Influence*, 5.
49 *Pro and contra Wagner*, 100.
50 See Wilson, *Wound and the Bow*, 220.
51 In Baudelaire, 206–7.
52 This point is made by Schorske, 216–17, 224; and by Dahlhaus, 81.
53 The phrases, respectively, are Howarth's, in *Irish Writers*, 286; and Joyce's, quoted in Atherton, 51. Bloom's views on the subject notwithstanding, Wagner's mythic art would prove much more accessible to the average citizen than would Joyce's testimonial to the common man. See Mann on Wagner's ''music for the layman'' (*Pro and contra Wagner*, 108–9).
54 Howe, Introduction to *Idea of the Modern*, 25.
55 Eliot, ''*Ulysses*, Order, and Myth,'' in *Selected Prose*, 177.
56 Budgen, 16–17. See also Epstein's revisionist discussion of Nestor as a ''Bronze-Age Polonius,'' in Hart and Hayman, 18.
57 *Stephen Hero*, 78. See Goldberg, *Classical Temper*.
58 Baudelaire, 192.
59 See Schorske, 230.
60 ''[T]he craze for myth,'' writes Philip Rahv, ''is the fear of history.'' See ''The Myth and the Powerhouse,'' in Vickery, *Myth and Literature*, 114.
61 Ellmann, *Eminent Domain*, 54.
62 Glasheen, ''Girls from Boston,'' 96. Howarth echoes this point in *Irish Writers*, 269.

APPENDIX

1 Glasheen, *Third Census*, 138.
2 *Third Census*, lxxii.

Works consulted

Abrams, M. H. *The Mirror and the Lamp: Romantic Theory and the Critical Tradition.* New York: Oxford University Press, 1953.

Adams, Robert Martin. "The Bent Knife Blade: Joyce in the 1960's." *Joyce: A Collection of Critical Essays.* Ed. William M. Chace. Twentieth Century Views. Englewood Cliffs, N.J.: Prentice, Spectrum, 1974, 166–75.

"The Operatic Novel: Joyce and D'Annunzio." *New Looks at Italian Opera: Essays in Honor of Donald J. Grout.* Ed. William W. Austin. Ithaca, N.Y.: Cornell University Press, 1968, 260–81.

Surface and Symbol: The Consistency of James Joyce's Ulysses. New York: Oxford University Press, 1962.

Anderson, Chester G., assisted by Carole Anderson. *Word Index to James Joyce's* Stephen Hero. Ridgefield, Conn.: Ridgebury Press, 1958.

Anderson, George K. *The Legend of the Wandering Jew.* Providence, R.I.: Brown University Press, 1965.

Anderson, Robert. *Wagner.* The Concertgoer's Companions. Hamden, Conn.: Shoe String, Linnet, 1980.

Antheil, George. *Bad Boy of Music.* 1945. Rpt New York: DaCapo, 1981.

Atherton, James S. *The Books at the Wake: A Study of Literary Allusions in James Joyce's* Finnegans Wake. New York: Viking, 1960.

Attridge, Derek, and Daniel Ferrer, eds. *Post-Structuralist Joyce: Essays from the French.* Cambridge University Press, 1984.

Auden, W. H. "James Joyce and Richard Wagner." *Common Sense* 10 (1941), 89–90.

Bakunin, Michael. *God and the State.* 1916. Rpt New York: Dover, 1970.

Balakian, Anna. *The Symbolist Movement: A Critical Appraisal.* Studies in Language and Literature. New York: Random, 1967.

Barish, Jonas. "The Nietzschean Apostasy." *The Antitheatrical Prejudice.* Berkeley and Los Angeles: University of California Press, 1981, 400–17.

Barzun, Jacques. *Darwin, Marx, Wagner: Critique of a Heritage.* 2nd edn. Garden City, N.Y.: Doubleday, Anchor, 1958.

Bate, W. Jackson. *The Burden of the Past and the English Poet.* Cambridge, Mass.: Harvard University Press, Belknap, 1970.

Baudelaire, Charles. "Richard Wagner and Tannhäuser in Paris." *Baudelaire as a Literary Critic: Selected Essays.* Ed. and trans. Lois Boe Hyslop and Francis E. Hyslop, Jr. University Park: Penn State University Press, 1964, 188–231.

Beach, Sylvia. *Shakespeare and Company.* New York: Harcourt, 1959.

Beardsley, Aubrey. *The Collected Drawings of Aubrey Beardsley.* Ed. Bruce S. Harris. New York: Crescent, 1967.

Under the Hill and Other Essays in Prose and Verse. New York: Dodd, 1903.

Beckett, Samuel, et al. *Our Exagmination round His Factification for Incamination of Work in Progress.* 2nd edn. New York: New Directions, [1962].

Bédier, Joseph. *The Romance of Tristan and Iseult.* Trans. Hilaire Belloc and Paul Rosenfeld. New York: Random, Vintage, 1945.

Beebe, Maurice. *Ivory Towers and Sacred Founts: The Artist as Hero in Fiction from Goethe to Joyce.* New York University Press, 1964.

"*Ulysses* and the Age of Modernism." *James Joyce Quarterly* 10 (1972), 172–88.

Beebe, Maurice, Phillip F. Herring, and Walton Litz. "Criticism of James Joyce: A Selected Checklist." *Modern Fiction Studies* 15 (1969), 105–82.

Begnal, Michael H., and Fritz Senn, eds. *A Conceptual Guide to* Finnegans Wake. University Park: Penn State University Press, 1974.

Benstock, Bernard. *Joyce-Again's Wake: An Analysis of* Finnegans Wake. Seattle: University of Washington Press, 1965.

Bérard, Victor. *Did Homer Live?* Trans. Brian Rhys. New York: Dutton, 1931.

Berrone, Louis, ed. *James Joyce in Padua.* New York: Random, 1977.

Bishop, John. *Joyce's Book of the Dark:* Finnegans Wake. Madison: University of Wisconsin Press, 1986.

Blanche, Jacques Emile. *Portraits of a Lifetime: The Late Victorian Era, the Edwardian Pageant, 1870–1914.* Trans. and ed. Walter Clement. New York: Coward-McCann, 1938.

Blissett, William. "Bernard Shaw: Imperfect Wagnerite." *University of Toronto Quarterly* 27 (1958), 185–99.

"D. H. Lawrence, D'Annunzio, Wagner." *Wisconsin Studies in Contemporary Literature* 7 (1966), 21–46.

"Ernest Newman and English Wagnerism." *Music and Letters* 40 (1959), 311–23.

"George Moore and Literary Wagnerism." *Comparative Literature* 13 (1961), 52–71.

"James Joyce in the Smithy of His Soul." *James Joyce Today: Essays on the Major Works.* Ed. Thomas F. Staley. Bloomington: Indiana University Press, 1966, 96–134.

"The Liturgy of *Parsifal.*" *University of Toronto Quarterly* 49 (1979–80), 117–38.

"Thomas Mann: The Last Wagnerite." *Germanic Review* 35 (1960), 50–76.

"Wagnerian Fiction in English." *Criticism* 5 (1963), 239–60.

Block, Haskell M. "Theory of Language in Gustave Flaubert and James Joyce." *Revue de littérature comparée* 35 (1961), 197–206.

Bloom, Harold. *The Anxiety of Influence: A Theory of Poetry.* New York: Oxford University Press, 1973.

Yeats. New York: Oxford University Press, 1970.

Bowen, Zack. "Goldenhair: Joyce's Archetypal Female." *Literature and Psychology* 17 (1967), 219–28.

"Libretto for Bloomusalem in Song: The Music of Joyce's *Ulysses.*" *New Light on Joyce from the Dublin Symposium.* Ed. Fritz Senn. Bloomington: Indiana University Press, 1972, 149–66.

Musical Allusions in the Works of James Joyce: Early Poetry through Ulysses. Albany: State University of New York Press, 1974.

Boyle, Robert. "*Ulysses* as Frustrated Sonata Form." *James Joyce Quarterly* 2 (1965), 247–54.

Brivic, Sheldon R. "James Joyce: From Stephen to Bloom." *Psychoanalysis and Literary Process.* Ed. Frederick Crews. Cambridge, Mass.: Winthrop, 1970, 118–62.

Brown, Calvin S. *Music and Literature: A Comparison of the Arts.* Athens: University of Georgia Press, 1948.

"Musico-Literary Research in the Last Two Decades." *Yearbook of Comparative and General Literature* 19 (1970), 5–27.

"The Relations between Music and Literature as a Field of Study." *Comparative Literature* 22 (1970), 97–107.

Brown, Richard. "Addenda and Corrigenda to Ellmann's *The Consciousness of Joyce.*" *James Joyce Quarterly* 17 (1980), 313–17.

James Joyce and Sexuality. Cambridge University Press, 1985.

Budgen, Frank. *James Joyce and the Making of* Ulysses. Bloomington: Indiana University Press, Midland, 1960.

Burbidge, Peter, and Richard Sutton, eds. *The Wagner Companion.* New York: Cambridge University Press, 1979.

Byrne, J. F. *Silent Years: An Autobiography with Memoirs of James Joyce and Our Ireland.* New York: Farrar, 1953.

Byron, May. *A Day with Richard Wagner.* Days with the Great Composers. New York: Hodder, [1911?].

Campbell, Joseph, and Henry Morton Robinson. *A Skeleton Key to Finnegans Wake.* New York: Viking, Compass, 1961.

Colum, Mary and Padraic. *Our Friend James Joyce.* Garden City, N.Y.: Doubleday, Dolphin, 1958.

Connolly, Thomas E. *The Personal Library of James Joyce: A Descriptive Bibliography.* University of Buffalo Studies, vol. 22, no. 1. Buffalo, N.Y.: University of Buffalo, 1955.

Conrad, Joseph. Preface. *The Nigger of the "Narcissus." Typhoon and Other Tales.* New York: NAL, Signet, 1963, 19–22.

Cooke, Deryck. *An Introduction to* Der Ring des Nibelungen. [Sound recording with insert.] London RDN S-1, 1969.

The Language of Music. Oxford University Press, 1959.

Courtney, Marie-Thérèse. *Edward Martyn and the Irish Theatre.* New York: Vantage, 1956.

Crews, Frederick. *Out of My System: Psychoanalysis, Ideology, and Critical Method.* New York: Oxford University Press, 1975.

Cross, Richard K. *Flaubert and Joyce: The Rite of Fiction.* Princeton University Press, 1971.

Culler, Jonathan. *The Pursuit of Signs: Semiotics, Literature, Deconstruction.* Ithaca, N.Y.: Cornell University Press, 1981.

Curran, C.P. *James Joyce Remembered.* New York: Oxford University Press, 1968.

Dahlhaus, Carl. *Richard Wagner's Music Dramas.* Trans. Mary Whittall. Cambridge University Press, 1979.

Daiches, David. *The Novel and the Modern World.* Rev. edn. University of Chicago Press, 1960.

D'Annunzio, Gabriele. *The Flame.* Trans. Dora Knowlton Ranous. Literature of Italy: 1265–1907. [New York]: National Alumni, 1907.

Dasenbrock, Reed Way. "Mozart contra Wagner: The Operatic Roots of the Mythic Method." *James Joyce Quarterly* 27 (1990), 517–31.

Davison, Henry, comp. *Music during the Victorian Era, from Mendelssohn to Wagner* ... London: Reeves, 1912.

Dent, Edward J. *Opera.* Rev. edn. Baltimore: Penguin, Pelican, 1949.

The Rise of Romantic Opera. Ed. Winton Dean. Cambridge University Press, 1976.

DiGaetani, John Louis, ed. *Penetrating Wagner's Ring: An Anthology.* Rutherford, N.J.: Fairleigh Dickinson University Press, 1978.

Richard Wagner and the Modern British Novel. Rutherford, N.J.: Fairleigh Dickinson University Press, 1978.

Donington, Robert. *Wagner's Ring and Its Symbols: The Music and the Myth.* London: Faber, 1963.

Donoghue, Denis. "The European Joyce." *We Irish: Essays on Irish Literature and Society.* New York: Knopf, 1986, 89–99.

Dujardin, Edouard. *Les Lauriers sont coupés suivi de Le Monologue intérieur.* Rome: Bulzoni, 1977.

We'll to the Woods No More: A Novel of Paris. Trans. Stuart Gilbert. [Norfolk, Conn.]: New Directions, 1938.

Eglinton, John. *Anglo-Irish Essays.* Dublin: Talbot, 1917.

Pebbles from a Brook. Kilkenny: O'Grady, 1901.

Eglinton, John, et al. *Literary Ideals in Ireland.* 1899. Rpt New York: Lemma, 1973.

Egri, Peter. *Avantgardism and Modernity: A Comparison of James Joyce's Ulysses with Thomas Mann's* Der Zauberberg *and* Lotte in Weimar. Trans. Paul Aston. Ed. H. Frew Waidner III. University of Tulsa Monograph Series, [no. 14]. Tulsa, Okla., [1972?].

Einstein, Alfred. *Music in the Romantic Era.* New York: Norton, 1947.

Eliot, T. S. *Collected Poems: 1909–1962.* New York: Harcourt, 1963.

Selected Prose of T. S. Eliot. Ed. Frank Kermode. London: Faber, 1975.

Ellmann, Richard. *The Consciousness of Joyce.* Toronto: Oxford University Press, 1977.

ed. *Edwardians and Late Victorians.* English Institute Essays, 1959. New York: Columbia University Press, 1960.

Eminent Domain: Yeats among Wilde, Joyce, Pound, Eliot, and Auden. New York: Oxford University Press, 1967.

James Joyce. Rev. edn. New York: Oxford University Press, 1982.

Ulysses on the Liffey. New York: Oxford University Press, 1972.

Eltzbacher, Paul. *Anarchism: Exponents of the Anarchist Philosophy.* Trans. Steven T. Byington. Ed. James J. Martin. New York: Chips, [1970?].

Engel, Monroe. "Contrived Lives: Joyce and Lawrence." *Modernism Reconsidered.* Harvard English Studies, no. 11. Cambridge, Mass.: Harvard University Press, 1983, 65–80.

Epstein, Edmund L. *The Ordeal of Stephen Dedalus: The Conflict of the Generations in James Joyce's* A Portrait of the Artist as a Young Man. Carbondale: Southern Illinois University Press, 1971.

Fay, Gerard. *The Abbey Theatre: Cradle of Genius.* Dublin: Clonmore, 1958.

Feldman, Burton, and Robert D. Richardson. *The Rise of Modern Mythology: 1680–1860.* Bloomington: Indiana University Press, 1972.

Fergusson, Francis. *The Idea of a Theatre, a Study of Ten Plays: The Art of Drama in Changing Perspective.* Garden City, N.Y.: Doubleday, Anchor, 1953.

Forster, E. M. *Aspects of the Novel*. New York: Harcourt, Harvest, 1927.
Howards End. New York: Random, Vintage, 1921.

Fox, C. Jay. "James Joyce's Literary Debt to Arthur Symons."
Encyclia 58 (1981), 69–78.

Frazer, James George. *Adonis, Attis, Osiris: Studies in the History of Oriental Religion*. Vols. 5 and 6 of *The Golden Bough: A Study in Magic and Religion*. 3rd edn. New York: Macmillan, 1935.

Freedman, William. *Laurence Sterne and the Origins of the Musical Novel*. Athens: University of Georgia Press, 1978.

Friedman, Melvin. *Stream of Consciousness: A Study in Literary Method*. New Haven: Yale University Press, 1955.

Furness, Raymond. *Wagner and Literature*. Manchester University Press, 1982.

Gabler, Hans Walter. "The Seven Lost Years of *A Portrait of the Artist as a Young Man*." *Approaches to Joyce's* Portrait: *Ten Essays*. Ed. Thomas F. Staley and Bernard Benstock. University of Pittsburgh Press, 1976, 25–60.

Gals, Hans. *Richard Wagner*. Trans. Hans-Hubert Schönzeler. New York: Stein, 1976.

Garten, H. F. *Wagner the Dramatist*. London: Calder, 1977.

Gautier, Judith. *Wagner at Home*. Trans. Effie Dunreith Massie. New York: Lane, 1911.

Gifford, Don. *Joyce Annotated: Notes for* Dubliners *and* A Portrait of the Artist as a Young Man. 2nd edn. Berkeley and Los Angeles: University of California Press, 1982.

Gifford, Don, with Robert J. Seidman. Ulysses *Annotated: Notes for James Joyce's* Ulysses. 2nd edn. Berkeley and Los Angeles: University of California Press, 1988.

Gilbert, Stuart. *James Joyce's* Ulysses: *A Study*. New York: Random, Vintage, 1955.

Gillespie, Michael Patrick. *Inverted Volumes Improperly Arranged: James Joyce and His Trieste Library*. Studies in Modern Literature, no. 10. Ann Arbor, Mich.: UMI Research Press, 1983.

"Wagner in the Ormond Bar: Operatic Elements in the 'Sirens' Episode of *Ulysses*." Irish Renaissance Annual, no. 4. Newark: University of Delaware Press, 1983, 157–73.

Gillespie, Michael Patrick, with the assistance of Erik Bradford Stocker. *James Joyce's Trieste Library: A Catalogue of Materials at the Harry Ransom Humanities Research Center*. Austin, Tex.: HRC, 1986.

Gillet, Louis. *Claybook for James Joyce*. Trans. Georges Markow-Totevy. London: Abelard-Schuman, 1958.

Glasheen, Adaline. "*Finnegans Wake* and the Girls from Boston, Mass." *Hudson Review* 7 (1954), 89–96.

Third Census of Finnegans Wake: *An Index of the Characters and Their Roles.* Berkeley and Los Angeles: University of California Press, 1977.

Goethe, J. Wolfgang von. *Faust: Parts One and Two.* Trans. George Madison Priest. New York: Covici-Friede, 1932.

Goldberg, S. L. *The Classical Temper: A Study of James Joyce's* Ulysses. New York: Barnes, 1961.

Joyce. Writers and Critics. New York: Barnes, 1966.

Goldman, Arnold. *James Joyce.* Profiles in Literature Series. London: Routledge, 1968.

Golther, Wolfgang. *Richard Wagner as Poet.* Trans. Jessie Haynes. Illustrated Cameos of Literature. [New York]: McClure, 1907.

Gorman, Herbert. *James Joyce.* New York: Rinehart, 1948.

Gottfried von Strassburg. *The Story of Tristan and Iseult.* Trans. Jessie L. Weston. 2 vols. Arthurian Romances Unrepresented in Malory's "Morte d'Arthur," no. II. London: Nutt, 1910.

Greenberg, Clement. "Necessity of 'Formalism.'" *New Literary History* 3 (1971), 171–5.

Gregor-Dellin, Martin. *Richard Wagner: His Life, His Work, His Century.* Trans. J. Maxwell Brownjohn. San Diego, Calif.: Harcourt, 1983.

Gross, John. *James Joyce.* Modern Masters. New York: Viking, 1970.

Grout, Donald Jay. *A History of Western Music.* New York: Norton, 1960.

Gutman, Robert W. *Richard Wagner: The Man, His Mind, and His Music.* New York: Harcourt, 1968.

Hall, Vernon, Jr. "Joyce's Use of Da Ponte and Mozart's *Don Giovanni.*" *PMLA* 66.2 (1951), 78–84.

Halper, Nathan. "James Joyce and the Russian General." *Partisan Review* 18 (1951), 424–31.

Hamilton, Walter. *The Aesthetic Movement in England.* 1882. Rpt New York: AMS, 1971.

Hancock, Leslie. *Word Index to James Joyce's* Portrait of the Artist. Carbondale: Southern Illinois University Press, 1967.

Hanley, Miles L. *Word Index to James Joyce's* Ulysses. Madison: University of Wisconsin Press, 1951.

Hart, Clive. *A Concordance to* Finnegans Wake. Minneapolis: University of Minnesota Press, 1963.

"*Finnegans Wake* in Perspective." *James Joyce Today: Essays on the Major Works.* Ed. Thomas F. Staley. Bloomington: Indiana University Press, 1966, 135–65.

Structure and Motif in Finnegans Wake. [Evanston, Ill.]: Northwestern University Press, 1962.

Hart, Clive, and David Hayman, eds. *James Joyce's* Ulysses: *Critical Essays*. Berkeley and Los Angeles: University of California Press, 1974.

Hassan, Ihab H. "The Problem of Influence in Literary History: Notes towards a Definition." *Journal of Aesthetics and Art Criticism* 14 (1955), 66–76.

Hayman, David, ed. *A First-Draft Version of* Finnegans Wake. Austin: University of Texas Press, 1963.

"Nodality and the Infra-Structure of *Finnegans Wake*." *James Joyce Quarterly* 16 (1978–79), 135–49.

"*A Portrait of the Artist as a Young Man* and *L'Education sentimentale:* The Structural Affinities." *Orbis Litterarum* 19 (1964), 161–75.

"Tristan and Isolde in *Finnegans Wake*: A Study of the Sources and Evolution of a Theme." *Comparative Literature Studies* 1 (1964), 93–112.

Heine, Heinrich. *Aus den Memoiren des Herren von Schnabelewopski. Sämtliche Werke.* 10 vols. Leipzig: Insel, 1910–15, 6:317–82.

Heller, Peter. "Some Functions of the Leitmotiv in Thomas Mann's Joseph Tetralogy." *Germanic Review* 22 (1947), 126–41.

Hendry, J. F. "James Joyce." *James Joyce: Two Decades of Criticism.* Ed. Seon Givens. New York: Vanguard, 1963, 436–49.

Henke, Suzette, and Elaine Unkeless, eds. *Women in Joyce.* Urbana: University of Illinois Press, 1982.

Herring, Phillip F. "The Bedsteadfastness of Molly Bloom." *Modern Fiction Studies* 15 (1969), 49–61.

Hodgart, Matthew. *James Joyce: A Student's Guide.* London: Routledge, 1978.

"Shakespeare and 'Finnegans Wake.'" *Cambridge Journal* 6 (1953), 735–52.

Hodgart, Matthew J. C., and Mabel P. Worthington. *Song in the Works of James Joyce.* Philadelphia: Temple University Publications, 1959.

Holloway, Robin. "The Problems of Music Drama." Parts 1–4. *Music and Musicians* 21.8–11 (1973), 22–30, 26–34, 32–40, 32–9.

Horton, W. T., and W. B. Yeats. *A Book of Images.* London, 1898.

Houston, John Porter. *Joyce and Prose: An Exploration of the Language of* Ulysses. Lewisburg, Pa.: Bucknell University Press, 1989.

Howarth, Herbert. *The Irish Writers, 1880–1940: Literature under Parnell's Star.* London: Rockcliff, 1958.

Notes on Some Figures behind T. S. Eliot. Boston: Houghton, Riverside, 1964.

Howe, Irving, ed. *The Idea of the Modern in Literature and the Arts.* New York: Horizon, 1967.

Hueffer, Francis. *Half a Century of Music in England, 1837–1887: Essays towards a History.* Philadelphia, 1889.

Richard Wagner and the Music of the Future: History and Aesthetics. London, 1874.

Huxley, Aldous. *Point Counter Point.* New York: Random, Modern Library, 1928.

Hyde, Douglas. *Love Songs of Connacht.* London: Unwin, 1905.

Ibsen, Henrik. *When We Dead Awaken.* Trans. William Archer. Green Tree Library. Chicago: Stone, 1900.

Jäckel, Kurt. *Richard Wagner in der französischen Literatur.* 2 vols. Breslau: Priebatsch, 1932.

Jacobs, Robert L. *Wagner.* Master Musicians Series. London: Dent, 1974.

James, Henry. *The Art of the Novel: Critical Prefaces.* New York: Scribner's, 1934.

   Theory of Fiction: Henry James. Ed. James E. Miller, Jr. Lincoln: University of Nebraska Press, 1972.

Jenny, Laurent. "The Strategy of Form." *French Literary Theory Today: A Reader.* Trans. R. Carter. Ed. Tzvetan Todorov. Cambridge University Press, 1982, 34–63.

Joyce, James. *Chamber Music.* Ed. William York Tindall. New York: Columbia University Press, 1954.

   Collected Poems. New York: Viking, Compass, 1957.

   The Critical Writings of James Joyce. Ed. Ellsworth Mason and Richard Ellmann. New York: Viking, 1959.

   Daniel Defoe. Ed. and trans. Joseph Prescott. Buffalo Studies, vol. 1, no. 1. State University of New York at Buffalo, 1964.

   Dubliners. New York: Viking, Compass, 1968.

   Exiles: A Play in Three Acts. New York: Viking, Compass, 1961.

   Finnegans Wake. New York: Viking, 1958.

   Giacomo Joyce. New York: Viking, 1968.

   Letters of James Joyce. 3 vols. Vol. 1, ed. Stuart Gilbert. Vols. 2 and 3, ed. Richard Ellmann. New York: Viking, 1966.

   A Portrait of the Artist as a Young Man. New York: Viking, Compass, 1964.

   Scribbledehobble: The Ur-Workbook for Finnegans Wake. Ed. Thomas E. Connolly. [Evanston, Ill.]: Northwestern University Press, 1961.

   Selected Letters of James Joyce. Ed. Richard Ellmann. New York: Viking, 1975.

   Stephen Hero. Ed. John J. Slocum and Herbert Cahoon. New York: New Directions, 1963.

   Ulysses. New York: Random, 1961.

   Ulysses: The Corrected Text. Ed. Hans Walter Gabler with Wolfhard Steppe and Claus Melchior. New York: Random, 1986.

Verbannte: Schauspiel in drei Akten. Trans. Hannah von Mettal. Zurich: Rascher, 1919.

Joyce, Stanislaus. *The Dublin Diary of Stanislaus Joyce.* Ed. George Harris Healey. London: Faber, 1962.

My Brother's Keeper: James Joyce's Early Years. Ed. Richard Ellmann. New York: Viking, Compass, 1969.

Katz, Adele T. *Challenge to Musical Tradition: A New Concept of Tonality.* London: Putnam, 1947.

Kellett, E. E. *The Northern Saga.* London: L. and Virginia Woolf, 1929.

Kenner, Hugh. *Dublin's Joyce.* Bloomington: Indiana University Press, 1956.

Kerman, Joseph. *Opera as Drama.* New York: Random, Vintage, 1956.

Kestner, Joseph. "Joyce, Wagner, and Bizet: *Exiles, Tannhäuser,* and *Carmen.*" *James Joyce: New Glances.* Modern British Literature Monograph Series, no. 2. Butler, Pa.: Kopper, 1980, 53–62.

King, C. D. "Edouard Dujardin, Inner Monologue and the Stream of Consciousness." *French Studies* 7 (1953), 116–28.

Kissane, James. "Victorian Mythology." *Victorian Studies* 6 (1962), 5–28.

Kristeva, Julia. *Revolution in Poetic Language.* Trans. Margaret Waller. New York: Columbia University Press, 1984.

Kruse, Georg Richard. Introduction. *Der fliegende Holländer: Romantische Oper in drei Aufzügen.* By Richard Wagner. Reclams Universal Bibliothek, no. 5635. Leipzig, [1914].

Langer, Susanne K. *Feeling and Form: A Theory of Art Developed from Philosophy in a New Key.* New York: Scribner's, 1953.

Large, David C., and William Weber, eds., in coll. with Anne Dzamba Sessa. *Wagnerism in European Culture and Politics.* Ithaca, N.Y.: Cornell University Press, 1984.

Lehmann, A. G. *The Symbolist Aesthetic in France: 1885–1895.* 2nd edn. 1968. Rpt Folcroft, Pa.: Folcroft Library, 1974.

Lemon, Lee T. "*A Portrait of the Artist as a Young Man:* Motif as Motivation and Structure." *Twentieth Century Interpretations of* A Portrait of the Artist as a Young Man: *A Collection of Critical Essays.* Ed. William M. Schutte. Englewood Cliffs, N.J.: Prentice, Spectrum, 1968, 41–52.

Lernout, Geert. "George Moore: Wagnerian and Symbolist." *Cahiers Irlandais* 5 (1980), 55–69.

Lesser, Simon O. *Fiction and the Unconscious.* Boston: Beacon, 1957.

Levin, Harry. "What Was Modernism?" *Refractions: Essays in Comparative Literature.* New York: Oxford University Press, 1966, 271–95.

James Joyce: A Critical Introduction. Rev. edn. New York: New Directions, 1960.

Lindenberger, Herbert. *Opera: The Extravagant Art*. Ithaca, N.Y.: Cornell University Press, 1984.

Litz, A. Walton. *The Art of James Joyce: Method and Design in* Ulysses *and* Finnegans Wake. New York: Oxford University Press, Galaxy, 1964.

James Joyce. Rev. edn. New York: Twayne, 1972.

"Pound and Eliot on *Ulysses*: The Critical Tradition." Ulysses: *Fifty Years*. Ed. Thomas F. Staley. Bloomington: Indiana University Press, 1974, 5–18.

"*Ulysses* and Its Audience." James Joyce: *The Centennial Symposium*. Ed. Morris Beja et al. Urbana: University of Illinois Press, 1986, 220–30.

Lockspeiser, Edward. *Music and Painting: A Study in Comparative Ideas from Turner to Schoenberg*. London: Cassell, 1973.

Loewenberg, Alfred, comp. *Annals of Opera: 1597–1940*. 3rd edn. Totowa, N.J.: Rowman, 1978.

Lorch, Thomas M. "The Relationship between *Ulysses* and *The Waste Land*." *Texas Studies in Literature and Language* 6 (1964), 123–33.

Lot, Ferdinand. *Joseph Bédier: 1864–1938*. Paris: Librairie Droz, 1939.

Lucente, Gregory L. "D'Annunzio's *Il fuoco* and Joyce's *Portrait of the Artist*: From Allegory to Irony." *Italica* 57 (1980), 19–33.

McGrath, F. C. *The Sensible Spirit: Walter Pater and the Modernist Paradigm*. Tampa: University of South Florida Press, 1986.

McHugh, Roland. *Annotations to* Finnegans Wake. Baltimore: Johns Hopkins University Press, 1980.

The Sigla of Finnegans Wake. Austin: University of Texas Press, 1976.

McLaughlin, Terence. *Music and Communication*. London: Faber, 1970.

MacNicholas, John. *James Joyce's* Exiles: *A Textual Companion*. New York: Garland, 1979.

"Joyce contra Wagner." *Comparative Drama* 9 (1975), 29–43.

Magalaner, Marvin, and Richard M. Kain. *Joyce: The Man, the Work, the Reputation*. New York University Press, 1956.

Magee, Bryan. *Aspects of Wagner*. London: Ross, 1968.

Mahaffey, Vicki. *Reauthorizing Joyce*. Cambridge University Press, 1988.

"Wagner, Joyce and Revolution." *James Joyce Quarterly* 25 (1988), 237–47.

Mallarmé, [Stéphane]. "Richard Wagner, Revery of a French Poet." *Mallarmé: Selected Prose Poems, Essays, and Letters*. Trans. Bradford Cook. Baltimore: Johns Hopkins Press, 1956, 72–8.

Selected Poetry and Prose. Ed. Mary Ann Caws. New York: New Directions, 1982.

Mann, Thomas. "The Joseph Novels." *The Atlantic Monthly* Feb. 1943, 92–100.

Pro and contra Wagner. Trans. Allan Blunden. University of Chicago Press, 1985.

Martin, Stoddard. *Wagner to* The Waste Land: *A Study of the Relationship of Wagner to English Literature.* Totowa, N.J.: Barnes, 1982.

Martin, Timothy P. "Joyce and Wagner's Pale Vampire." *James Joyce Quarterly* 23 (1986), 491–6.

"Joyce, Wagner, and the Artist-Hero." *Journal of Modern Literature* 11 (1984), 66–88.

"Joyce, Wagner, and the Wandering Jew." *Comparative Literature* 42 (1990), 49–72.

"Wagner's *Tannhäuser* in *Exiles*: A Further Source." *James Joyce Quarterly* 19 (1981), 73–6.

Martyn, Edward. *The Heather Field and Maeve.* London, 1899.

Mayer, Hans. *Portrait of Wagner: An Illustrated Biography.* Trans. Robert Nowell. New York: Herder, 1972.

Mercier, Vivian H. S. "James Joyce and an Irish Tradition." *Society and Self in the Novel.* English Institute Essays, 1955. New York: Columbia University Press, 1956, 78–116.

Mink, Louis O. *A Finnegans Wake Gazetteer.* Bloomington: Indiana University Press, 1978.

Moore, George. *Confessions of a Young Man.* Ed. Susan Dick. Montreal: McGill-Queen's University Press, 1972.

Evelyn Innes. London, 1898.

Hail and Farewell. 3 vols. New York: Appleton, 1917–19.

The Lake. New York: Appleton, 1906.

Letters from George Moore to Ed[ouard] Dujardin: 1886–1922. New York: Gaige, 1929.

Memoirs of My Dead Life. London: Heinemann, 1906.

Parnell and His Island. London, 1887.

Vain Fortune. Rev. edn. London, 1895.

Moser, Max. *Richard Wagner in der englischen Literatur des XIX. Jahrhunderts.* Bern: Francke, 1938.

Newman, Ernest. *The Life of Richard Wagner.* 4 vols. New York: Knopf, 1933–46.

The Wagner Operas. New York: Knopf, 1949.

Nietzsche, Friedrich. *The Birth of Tragedy, or Hellenism and Pessimism.* Trans. Wm. A. Haussmann. Vol. 1 of *The Complete Works of Friedrich Nietzsche.* Ed. Oscar Levy. 18 vols. 1909–11. Rpt New York: Russell, 1964.

The Case of Wagner, Nietzsche contra Wagner, Selected Aphorisms. Trans. Anthony M. Ludovici. *The Complete Works of Friedrich Nietzsche.*

Ed. Oscar Levy. 18 vols. 1909–11. Rpt New York: Russell, 1964, 8:xxvii–102.

Ecce Homo. Trans. Anthony M. Ludovici. Vol. 17 of *The Complete Works of Friedrich Nietzsche.* Ed. Oscar Levy. 18 vols. 1909–11. Rpt New York: Russell, 1964.

The Joyful Wisdom. Trans. Thomas Common. Vol. 9 of *The Complete Works of Friedrich Nietzsche.* Ed. Oscar Levy. 18 vols. 1909–11. Rpt New York: Russell, 1964.

Nordau, Max. *Degeneration.* 1895. Rpt New York: Fertig, 1968.

Norris, Margot. "Darwin, Nietzsche, Kafka, and the Problem of Mimesis." *MLN* 95 (1980), 1232–53.

O'Brien, Darcy. "Some Psychological Determinants of Joyce's View of Love and Sex." *New Light on Joyce from the Dublin Symposium.* Ed. Fritz Senn. Bloomington: Indiana University Press, 1972, 15–27.

O'Connor, Ulick, ed. *The Joyce We Knew.* Cork: Mercier, 1967.

Oliphant, Dave, and Thomas Zigal, eds. *Joyce at Texas: Essays on the James Joyce Materials at the Humanities Research Center.* Austin, Tex.: HRC, 1983.

Parsifal. [Motion picture.] Dir. Hans Jürgen Syberberg. Artificial Eye, 1983.

Passages from Finnegans Wake. [Motion picture.] Dir. Mary Ellen Bute. Grove, 1965.

Pater, Walter. *The Renaissance: Studies in Art and Poetry.* 1910. Rpt New York: Johnson Reprint Corp., 1967.

Peckham, Morse. *Beyond the Tragic Vision: The Quest for Identity in the Nineteenth Century.* New York: Braziller, 1962.

Peyre, Henri. "Poets against Music in the Age of Symbolism." *Symbolism and Modern Literature: Studies in Honor of Wallace Fowlie.* Ed. Marcel Tetel. Durham, N.C.: Duke University Press, 1978, 179–92.

Pickard, P.M. "Thomas Mann's *Dr. Faustus:* A Psychological Approach." *German Life and Letters,* n.s. 4 (1951), 90–100.

Potts, Willard, ed. *Portraits of the Artist in Exile: Recollections of James Joyce by Europeans.* Seattle: University of Washington Press, 1979.

Pound, Ezra. *Instigations of Ezra Pound, together with an Essay on the Chinese Written Character by Ernest Fenollosa.* 1920. Rpt Freeport, N.Y.: Ayer, Books for Libraries, 1967.

Pound/Joyce: The Letters of Ezra Pound to James Joyce, with Pound's Essays on Joyce. Ed. Forrest Read. New York: New Directions, 1967.

Power, Arthur. *Conversations with James Joyce.* Ed. Clive Hart. University of Chicago Press, 1974.

Raphael, Robert. *Richard Wagner.* Twayne's World Authors Series. New York, 1969.

Rather, L. J. *The Dream of Self-Destruction: Wagner's* Ring *and the Modern World.* Baton Rouge: Louisiana State University Press, 1979.

Redlich, Hans F. "Wagnerian Elements in Pre-Wagnerian Opera." *Essays Presented to Egon Wellesz.* Ed. Jack Westrup. Oxford: Clarendon, 1966, 145–56.

Revue wagnérienne. 3 vols. Paris, 1885–88. Rpt Geneva: Slatkine Reprints, 1968.

Reynolds, Mary T. *Joyce and Dante: The Shaping Imagination.* Princeton University Press, 1981.

——— "Joyce's Villanelle and D'Annunzio's Sonnet Sequence." *Journal of Modern Literature* 5 (1976), 19–45.

Rieff, Philip. *Freud: The Mind of the Moralist.* New York: Viking, 1959.

Rolland, Romain. *Musicians of Today.* 2nd edn. Trans. Mary Blaiklock. Musician's Bookshelf. New York: Holt, 1915.

Ross, Martin. *Music and James Joyce.* 1936. Rpt Norwood, Pa.: Norwood Editions, 1978.

Runciman, John F. "Neo-Ruskinism: A Protest." *The Dome,* n.s. 2 (1899), 118–24.

——— *Wagner.* Bell's Miniature Series of Musicians. London, 1905.

——— "Wanted: An English Bayreuth." *The Dome,* no. 4 (1898), 92–101.

[Russell, George W.]. *Letters from AE.* Ed. Alan Denson. London: Abelard-Schuman, 1961.

Sandulescu, C. George, and Clive Hart, eds. *Assessing the 1984* Ulysses. Totowa, N. J.: Barnes, 1986.

Scher, Steven Paul. "How Meaningful is 'Musical' in Literary Criticism?" *Yearbook of Comparative and General Literature* 21 (1972), 52–6.

——— "Literature and Music." *Interrelations of Literature.* Ed. Jean-Pierre Barricelli and Joseph Gibaldi. New York: MLA, 1982, 225–50.

Scholes, Percy A. *The Mirror of Music, 1844–1944: A Century of Musical Life in Britain …* 2 vols. London: Novello, 1947.

Scholes, Robert E. *The Cornell Joyce Collection: A Catalogue.* Ithaca, N. Y.: Cornell University Press, 1961.

Scholes, Robert, and Richard M. Kain, eds. *The Workshop of Daedalus: James Joyce and the Raw Materials for* A Portrait of the Artist as a Young Man. Evanston, Ill.: Northwestern University Press, 1965.

Schopenhauer, [Arthur]. *Essays.* Trans. Mrs. Rudolph Dircks. London: Scott, n.d.

Schorer, Mark. "Technique as Discovery." *Forms of Modern Fiction: Essays Collected in Honor of Joseph Warren Beach.* Ed. William Van O'Connor. Minneapolis: University of Minnesota Press, 1948, 9–29.

Schorske, Carl E. "The Quest for the Grail: Wagner and Morris." *The Critical Spirit: Essays in Honor of Herbert Marcuse.* Ed. Kurt H. Wolff and Barrington Moore, Jr. Boston: Beacon, 1967, 216–32.

Scott, Bonnie Kime. *Joyce and Feminism.* Bloomington: Indiana University Press, 1984.

Senn, Fritz. "Joycean Provections." [Photocopy.] 1987 James Joyce Conference, Milwaukee, 13 June.

Sessa, Anne Dzamba. *Richard Wagner and the English.* Rutherford, N.J.: Fairleigh Dickinson University Press, 1979.

Shattuck, Roger. *The Banquet Years: The Arts in France, 1885–1918* ... New York: Harcourt, 1958.

Shaw, Bernard. *London Music in 1888–89 as Heard by Corno di Bassetto* ... New York: Dodd, 1937.

Music in London: 1890–94. 3 vols. London: Constable, 1932.

The Perfect Wagnerite: A Commentary on The Niblung's Ring. 4th edn. 1923. Rpt New York: Dover, 1967.

The Sanity of Art: An Exposure of the Current Nonsense about Artists Being Degenerate. London: New Age, 1908.

Shechner, Mark. *Joyce in Nighttown: A Psychoanalytic Inquiry into* Ulysses. Berkeley and Los Angeles: University of California Press, 1974.

Smidt, Kristian. "'I'm Not Half Norawain for Nothing': Joyce and Norway." *James Joyce Quarterly* 26 (1989), 333–50.

Smith, Don Noel. "Musical Form and Principles in the Scheme of *Ulysses*." *Twentieth Century Literature* 18 (1972), 79–92.

Smith, James. "James Joyce and Music." *Dekalb Literary Arts Journal* 10.4 (1977), 27–36.

Staley, Thomas F. "James Joyce." *Anglo-Irish Literature: A Review of Research.* Ed. Richard J. Finneran. New York: MLA, 1976, 366–435.

"James Joyce and One of His Ghosts: Edouard Dujardin." *Renascence* 35 (1983), 85–95.

Stein, Jack M. "The Influence of Schopenhauer on Wagner's Concept of the *Gesamtkunstwerk*." *Germanic Review* 22 (1947), 92–105.

Steinberg, Erwin R. "Leopold Bloom and the Nineteenth-Century Fictional Stereotype of the Jew." *Cithara* 22.2 (1983), 48–61.

The Stream of Consciousness and Beyond in Ulysses. University of Pittsburgh Press, 1973.

Steppe, Wolfhard, with Hans Walter Gabler. *A Handlist to James Joyce's* Ulysses: *A Complete Alphabetical Index to the Critical Reading Text.* Garland Reference Library of the Humanities, vol. 582. New York, 1986.

Sultan, Stanley. *The Argument of* Ulysses. [Columbus]: Ohio State University Press, 1964.

Ulysses, The Waste Land, *and Modernism: A Jubilee Study.* Port Washington, N. Y.: Kennikat, National University Publications, 1977.

Symonds, John Addington. "Nature Myths and Allegories." *Essays Speculative and Suggestive.* 2 vols. 1890. Rpt New York: AMS, 1970, 2:126–49.

Symons, Arthur. *Plays, Acting, and Music: A Book of Theory.* New York: Dutton, 1909.

Studies in Seven Arts. New York: Dutton, 1925.

The Symbolist Movement in Literature. Rev. edn. 1919. Rpt New York: Dutton, 1958.

"Two Symbolists." *Figures of Several Centuries.* London: Constable, 1916, 300–9.

Sypher, Wylie. "The Meanings of Comedy." *Comedy.* Garden City, N. Y.: Doubleday, Anchor, 1956, 191–260.

Temple, Ruth Zabriskie. *The Critic's Alchemy: A Study of the Introduction of French Symbolism into England.* New York: Twayne, 1953.

Thornton, Weldon. *Allusions in* Ulysses: *An Annotated List.* Chapel Hill: University of North Carolina Press, 1968.

Tindall, William York. *A Reader's Guide to* Finnegans Wake. New York: Farrar, 1969.

A Reader's Guide to James Joyce. New York: Farrar, Noonday, 1959.

Twain, Mark. *The New Pilgrim's Progress, a Book of Travel in Pursuit of Pleasure: The Journey Home.* London, [1870?].

Verlaine, Paul. *Les Poètes maudits.* Testi di letteratura francese. Milan: Cisalpino-Goliardica, 1977.

Vickery, John B. *The Literary Impact of* The Golden Bough. Princeton University Press, 1973.

ed. *Myth and Literature: Contemporary Theory and Practice.* Lincoln: University of Nebraska Press, 1966.

Vico, Giambattista. *The New Science of Giambattista Vico.* 3rd edn. 1744. Trans. Thomas Goddard Bergin and Max Harold Fisch. Ithaca, N. Y.: Cornell University Press, 1968.

Wagner, Richard. *The Authentic Librettos of the Wagner Operas.* [English and German.] New York: Crown, 1938.

Der fliegende Holländer. With Gwyneth Jones, Sieglinde Wagner, Thomas Stewart, Karl Ridderbusch, Hermin Esser, and Harald Ek. Cond. Karl Böhm. Chorus and Orchestra of the Bayreuth Festival (1971). DGG 2709 040.

The Flying Dutchman. [Libretto, English and German, with commentaries.] Trans. David Pountney. English National Opera Guide no. 12. New York: Riverrun, 1982.

The Flying Dutchman. [Vocal score, English and German.] Arr. Otto Singer. Trans. Ernest Newman. Leipzig: Breitkopf, 1914.

Götterdämmerung. [Vocal score, English and German.] Arr. Karl Klindworth. Trans. Frederick Jameson. New York: Schirmer, n. d.

Götterdämmerung. With Birgit Nilsson, Claire Watson, Christa Ludwig, Wolfgang Windgassen, Dietrich Fischer-Dieskau, and Gottlob Frick. Cond. Georg Solti. Vienna Philharmonic Orchestra and Vienna State Opera Chorus. London OSA 1604.

Judaism in Music. Trans. Edwin Evans. New York: Scribner's, 1910.

Die Kunst und die Revolution. Leipzig, 1849.

Das Kunstwerk der Zukunft. Leipzig, 1850.

Letters to August Roeckel. Trans. Eleanor C. Sellar. Bristol, Eng., [1897].

Lohengrin. [Vocal score, English and German.] New York: Kalmus, n. d.

Lohengrin. With Jess Thomas, Elisabeth Grümmer, Dietrich Fischer-Dieskau, Christa Ludwig, Gottlob Frick, and Otto Wiener. Cond. Rudolf Kempe. Vienna Philharmonic Orchestra and Chorus of the Vienna State Opera. Angel 3641 E/L.

The Mastersingers of Nuremberg. [Libretto, English and German, with commentaries.] Trans. Frederick Jameson, rev. Norman Feasey and Gordon Kember. English National Opera Guide no. 19. New York: Riverrun, 1983.

The Mastersingers of Nuremberg. [Vocal score, English and German.] Arr. Karl Klindworth. Trans. Frederick Jameson. New York: Schirmer, 1904.

Die Meistersinger von Nürnberg. With Theo Adam, Karl Ridderbusch, Geraint Evans, René Kollo, Peter Schreier, Helen Donath, and Ruth Hesse. Cond. Herbert von Karajan. Dresden State Orchestra, Leipzig Radio Chorus, and Dresden State Opera Chorus. Angel SEL 3776.

My Life. Trans. Andrew Gray. Ed. Mary Whittall. Cambridge University Press, 1983.

Parsifal. [Libretto, English and German, with commentaries.] Trans. Andrew Porter. English National Opera Guide no. 34. New York: Riverrun, 1986.

Parsifal. [Vocal score, English and German.] Arr. R. Kleinmichel. Trans. H. and F. Corder. London: Schott, n. d.

Parsifal. With James King, Gwyneth Jones, Franz Crass, Thomas Stewart, Donald McIntyre, and Karl Ridderbusch. Cond. Pierre Boulez. Chorus and Orchestra of the Bayreuth Festival (1970). DGG 2713 004.

Prose Works. Trans. William Ashton Ellis. 8 vols. 1892–99. Rpt New York: Broude, 1966.

Das Rheingold. With Theo Adam, Wolfgang Windgassen, Gustav Neidlinger, Martti Talvela, Kurt Böhme, and Annelies Burmeister. Cond. Karl Böhm. Orchestra of the Bayreuth Festival. Philips 6747 046.

The Rhinegold. [Vocal score, English and German.] Arr. Karl Klindworth. Trans. Frederick Jameson. New York: Schirmer, n.d.

The Ring of the Nibelung. [Libretto, English and German.] Trans. Andrew Porter. New York: Norton, 1977.

Siegfried. [Vocal score, English and German.] Arr. Karl Klindworth. Trans. Frederick Jameson. New York: Schirmer, n.d.

Siegfried. With Birgit Nilsson, Wolfgang Windgassen, Hans Hotter, Gerhard Stolze, and Gustav Neidlinger. Cond. Georg Solti. Vienna Philharmonic Orchestra. London OSA 1508.

Tannhäuser. [Libretto, English and German, with commentaries.] Trans. Rodney Blumer. English National Opera Guide no. 39. New York: Riverrun, 1988.

Tannhäuser and the Song Contest at the Wartburg. With Wolfgang Windgassen, Eberhard Wächter, Gerhard Stolze, Josef Greindl, Anja Silja, and Grace Bumbry. Cond. Wolfgang Sawallisch. Chorus and Orchestra of the Bayreuth Festival (1962). Philips PHM 3-560.

Tannhäuser and the Tournament of Song at Wartburg. [Vocal score, English and German.] Ed. and trans. Natalia MacFarren. New York: Schirmer, n.d.

Tristan und Isolde. [Libretto, English and German, with commentaries.] Trans. Andrew Porter. English National Opera Guide no. 6. New York: Riverrun, 1981.

Tristan and Isold[e]. [Vocal score, English and German.] Arr. Richard Kleinmichel. Trans. Henry Grafton Chapman. New York: Schirmer, 1906.

Tristan und Isolde. With Birgit Nilsson, Fritz Uhl, Regina Resnik, Tom Krause, and Arnold van Mill. Cond. Georg Solti. Vienna Philharmonic Orchestra and Singverein der Gesellschaft der Musikfreunde. London OSA 1502.

Die Walküre. [Vocal score, English and German.] Arr. Karl Klindworth. Trans. Frederick Jameson. New York: Schirmer, n.d.

Die Walküre. With Birgit Nilsson, Régine Crespin, Christa Ludwig, James King, Hans Hotter, and Gottlob Frick. Cond. Georg Solti. Vienna Philharmonic Orchestra. London OSA 1509.

"Wagner, Richard." *The New Grove Dictionary of Music and Musicians.* Ed. Stanley Sadie. London: Macmillan, 1980.

Wellek, René. "The Parallelism between Literature and the Arts." *English Institute Annual, 1941.* New York: Columbia University Press, 1942, 29–63.

Wellek, René, and Austin Warren. *Theory of Literature.* 3rd edn. New York: Harcourt, Harvest, 1956.

Westernhagen, Curt von. *Wagner: A Biography.* Trans. Mary Whittall. 2 vols. Cambridge University Press, 1978.

Weston, Jessie L. *From Ritual to Romance.* Garden City, N. Y.: Doubleday, Anchor, 1957.

    The Legends of the Wagner Drama: Studies in Mythology and Romance. New York, 1896.

White, Terence. "James Joyce and Music." *Chesterian* July–Aug. 1936, 163–7.

Wilde, Oscar. *Intentions.* Vol. 7 of *The Complete Works of Oscar Wilde.* 10 vols. New York: National Library, 1907–9.

    The Picture of Dorian Gray. Ed. Isobel Murray. Oxford English Novels. Oxford University Press, 1974.

Wilson, Edmund. *Axel's Castle: A Study in the Imaginative Literature of 1870–1930.* New York: Scribner's, 1931.

    The Wound and the Bow: Seven Studies in Literature: New York: Oxford University Press, Galaxy, 1965.

Woolley, Grange. *Richard Wagner et le symbolisme francais: Les rapports principaux entre le wagnérisme et l'évolution de l'idée symboliste.* Paris: Presses Universitaires de France, 1931.

Wordsworth, William. "Essay Supplementary to the Preface of 1815." *English Romantic Writers.* Ed. David Perkins. New York: Harcourt, 1967, 335–47.

Worth, Katharine. *The Irish Drama of Europe from Yeats to Beckett.* London: Athlone, 1978.

Yeats, W. B. *Autobiographies: Reveries over Childhood and Youth and The Trembling of the Veil.* New York: Macmillan, 1927.

    Essays and Introductions. New York: Macmillan, Collier, 1968.

    The Letters of W. B. Yeats. Ed. Allan Wade. 1955. Rpt New York: Octagon, 1980.

    The Tables of the Law and The Adoration of the Magi. London: Mathews, 1904.

Zingrone, Frank. "Joyce and D'Annunzio: The Marriage of Fire and Water." *James Joyce Quarterly* 16 (1979), 253–65.

Zuckerman, Elliott. *The First Hundred Years of Wagner's* Tristan. New York: Columbia University Press, 1964.

Index

Abbey Theatre (Dublin), 14, 50
Adams, Robert Martin, 64
Adrian IV (pope), 92
AE, *see* Russell, George
Ahasuerus, *see* Wandering Jew,
  legend of
Albert (prince of England), 9
Antheil, George, 7, 16
Archer, William, 11, 229 n. 48
Aristotle, 47, 165, 168
Art and Revolution, 19, 47–50
The Art-Work of the Future, 19, 47,
  57–8, 225 n. 16, 233 n. 4, 253–4
  n. 50
Atherton, James, 113, 122, 139, 226
  n. 30
Augustine, Saint, 182–3

Bach, J.S., 26, 231–2 n. 111
Bakunin, Michael, 38, 41
Ballets russes, 4
Balzac, Honoré de, 230 n. 81
Barnacle, Nora, *see* Joyce, Nora
Bassi (Italian tenor), 18
Bate, W.J., 167–8
Baudelaire, Charles, 5, 7–8, 12, 22,
  25, 144, 178, 181, 226 n. 29
Bayreuth Festival, 3, 4, 11, 12, 13, 14,
  15, 20, 31, 37, 38, 40, 131, 172, 228
  n. 39
Bayreuther Blätter, 4
Beach, Sylvia, 21, 30
Beardsley, Aubrey, 10, 86, 228–9
  n. 47, 245 n. 11
Beckett, Samuel, 164, 257 n. 30

Bédier, Joseph, 94, 97–8, 101, 102,
  243 n. 38
Beethoven, Ludwig van, 1, 11, 35,
  48, 57–8, 79, 147, 173, 223 n. 4,
  250 n. 11, 251–2 n. 28
Bellini, Vincenzo, 15, 17, 32, 104
Bérard, Victor, 70, 239 n. 33
Berlioz, Hector, 1, 144, 224–5 n. 10,
  252 n. 37
Bishop, John, 103–4
Bizet, Georges, 32, 104
Blake, William, 113, 147
Blanche, Jacques Emile, 4, 225 n. 13
Blavatsky, Helena Petrovna, 113
Blissett, William, xi
Bloom, Harold, xiii, 167–8, 178
Book of the Dead, 113
Book of Kells, 172
Bowen, Zack, 256 n. 12
Brown, Ford Madox, 10
Browning, Robert, 10
Bruno, Giordano, 94, 100, 135, 165,
  166, 243 n. 38, 256 n. 3
Buddhism, 172
Budgen, Frank, 18
Bülow, Hans von, 20
Bulwer-Lytton, Robert, 225 n. 20
Burne-Jones, Edward, 10
Bute, Mary Ellen, 256 n. 12
Byron, May, 19, 29, 230 n. 82

Carl Rosa Company, 239 n. 31
Carroll, Lewis (Charles Dodgson),
  97
Cézanne, Paul, 4, 225 n. 20

278